International Relations and Non-Western Thought

International relations, as a discipline, tends to focus upon European and Western canons of modern social and political thought. Alternatively, this book explores the global imperial and colonial context within which knowledge of modernity has been developed.

The chapters sketch out the historical depth and contemporary significance of non-Western thought on modernity, as well as the rich diversity of its individuals, groups, movements and traditions. The contributors theoretically and substantively engage with non-Western thought in ways that refuse to render it exotic to, superfluous to or derivative of the orthodox Western canon of social and political thought. Taken as a whole, the book provides deep insights into the contested nature of a global modernity shaped so fundamentally by Western colonialism and imperialism. Now, as ever, these insights are desperately needed for a discipline that is so closely implicated in Western foreign policy-making and yet retains such a myopic horizon of inquiry.

This work provides a significant contribution to the field and will be of great interest to all scholars of politics, political theory and international relations theory.

Robbie Shilliam is a Senior Lecturer in International Relations at Victoria University of Wellington. He is currently working on the interface between the anti-colonial struggles of the indigenous Pacific and those of the Black Americas. He is author of *German Thought and International Relations* (Palgrave, 2009) and co-editor of *Silencing Human Rights* (Palgrave, 2008).

Interventions
Edited by Jenny Edkins, Aberystwyth University,
and Nick Vaughan-Williams, University of Warwick

"As Michel Foucault has famously stated, 'knowledge is not made for understanding; it is made for cutting'. In this spirit The Edkins–Vaughan-Williams
Interventions series solicits cutting edge, critical works that challenge
mainstream understandings in international relations. It is the best place to
contribute post disciplinary works that think rather than merely recognize
and affirm the world recycled in IR's traditional geopolitical imaginary."
Michael J. Shapiro, University of Hawai'i at Mãnoa, USA

The series aims to advance understanding of the key areas in which scholars
working within broad critical post-structural and post-colonial traditions have
chosen to make their interventions, and to present innovative analyses of important topics.

Titles in the series engage with critical thinkers in philosophy, sociology,
politics and other disciplines and provide situated historical, empirical and textual
studies in international politics.

Critical Theorists and International Relations
Edited by Jenny Edkins and Nick Vaughan-Williams

Ethics as Foreign Policy
Britain, the EU and the Other
Dan Bulley

Universality, Ethics and International Relations
A grammatical reading
Véronique Pin-Fat

The Time of the City
Politics, philosophy, and genre
Michael J. Shapiro

Governing Sustainable Development
Partnership, protest and power at the World Summit
Carl Death

Insuring Security
Biopolitics, security and risk
Luis Lobo-Guerrero

Foucault and International Relations
New critical engagements
Edited by Nicholas J. Kiersey and Doug Stokes

International Relations and Non-Western Thought
Imperialism, colonialism and investigations of global modernity
Edited by Robbie Shilliam

International Relations and Non-Western Thought

Imperialism, colonialism and investigations of global modernity

Edited by Robbie Shilliam

Routledge
Taylor & Francis Group

LONDON AND NEW YORK

First published 2011
by Routledge
2 Park Square, Milton Park, Abingdon, Oxon, OX14 4RN

Simultaneously published in the USA and Canada
by Routledge
711 Third Avenue, New York, NY 10017

Routledge is an imprint of the Taylor & Francis Group, an informa business

First issued in paperback 2011

Typeset in Times New Roman by Prepress Projects Ltd, Perth, UK

British Library Cataloguing in Publication Data
A catalogue record for this book is available from the British Library

Library of Congress Cataloging in Publication Data
International relations and non-western thought : imperialism, colonialism, and investigations of global modernity / [edited by] Robbie Shilliam.
p. cm. — (Interventions)
Includes bibliographical references.
1. International relations—Study and teaching—Developing countries. 2. Developing countries—Colonial influence. 3. Developing countries—Intellectual life. I. Shilliam, Robbie
JZ1238.D44I58 2010
327.101—dc22
2010013055

ISBN: 978-0-415-57772-4 (hbk)
ISBN: 978-0-415-52284-7 (pbk)

Contents

Acknowledgements

I would like to acknowledge the generosity of Wadham College, University of Oxford, in funding and hosting a workshop in 2007 in which some of the contributors to this volume participated. I would like to thank my old colleagues at Wadham, Paul Martin, Jane Garnett, Ankhi Mukherjee and Alexander Sedlmaier, for their enthusiasm, support and input into the workshop. A grant from the Faculty of Humanities and Social Sciences at Victoria University of Wellington helped to further the project. I would like to thank one reviewer for his or her critical, insightful and supportive comments. And I would like to thank the *Interventions* series editors for taking on this project with such enthusiasm and professionalism. Above all, I deeply thank the contributors for giving so generously of their time and intellect to this project. As always, the support of my friends, family and wife, Cynthia Mathonsi, is the unseen foundation.

Finally, I would like to thank Abby Wendy (Ngai Tahu) for her generosity in allowing her painting, *Te Hau*, to grace the front cover. *Te Hau* is fitting imagery for the aims and purposes of this volume in that it invokes the freedom and power of the wind that blows from many and sometimes opposite or conflicting directions. Abby drew her inspiration for the painting from the well-known Māori *karakia* (prayer, chant):

Whakataka te hau ki te uru
Whakataka te hau ki te tonga
Kia mākinakina ki uta
Kia mātaratara ki tai
Kia hi ake ana te atakura
He tio, he huka, he hauhū

Cease now the wind from the West
Cease also the wind from the South
Let the murmuring breeze sigh over the land
Let the stormy seas subside
And let the red dawn come
With a sharpened air, a touch of frost, and the promise of a glorious day.

Abby reads the *karakia* as a release from confronting forces and an opening up and acceptance of more gentle dialogues or relationships that view the future with optimism.

Contributors

Gerard Aching is Professor of Spanish Literature in the Department of Romance Studies at Cornell University. He is the author of *The Politics of Spanish American* Modernismo: *By Exquisite Design* (Cambridge University Press, 1997) and *Masking and Power: Carnival and Popular Culture in the Caribbean* (University of Minnesota Press, 2003). His research areas are nineteenth- and twentieth-century Caribbean literatures and intellectual histories, Latin American theories of modernism and modernity, and slavery and philosophy. He is currently completing a book project titled *Freedom From Liberation: Slavery and Literary Sensibility in Cuba.*

Anthony Bogues is Harmon Family Professor of Africana Studies at Brown University and an affiliated faculty of the departments of Political Science and Modern Culture and Media. He is an Honorary Professor at the Center for African Studies, University of Cape Town. His latest books are *Empire of Liberty: Power, Desire and Freedom* (University Press of New England, 2010); and *George Lamming: The Aesthetics of Decolonization* (IRP, 2010).

Priya Chacko is Lecturer in International Relations at the University of Witwatersrand. Her current research interests include Indian political thought on international relations and Indian foreign policy and identity. She has published on these topics in *Review of International Studies* and *International Studies Quarterly* and is completing a book on Indian foreign policy and the politics of post-colonial identity.

Arif Dirlik is Knight Professor of Social Science (History and Anthropology), University of Oregon (retired). He has served as Professor of History and Anthropology at Duke University (1971–2001), Knight Professor of Social Science and Director of the Center for Critical Theory and Transnational Studies at the University of Oregon (2001–2006), and Chair Professor of Chinese Studies at the Chinese University of Hong Kong (2007–2009). He has also served as visiting professor at the University of California–Los Angeles, the Universities of Victoria and British Columbia in Canada and Soka University of America. His most recent book-length publications are *Global Modernity:*

Modernity in the Age of Global Capitalism (Paradigm Publishers, 2007), two edited volumes, *Pedagogies of the Global: Knowledge in the Human Interest* (Paradigm Publishers, 2006) and *Snapshots of Intellectual Life in Contemporary PR China* (2008, a special issue of *boundary 2*), and a collection in Turkish of his essays under the title *Crisis, Identity, Politics: Writings on Globalization* (Iletisim Publishers, 2009). He serves on the editorial boards of a dozen journals. He lives in Eugene, OR, USA.

Willi Goetschel is Professor of German and Philosophy at the University of Toronto. His research interests include the relationship between literature and philosophy, the Enlightenment, German-Jewish culture and critical theory. His current projects include *Heine and Critical Theory, and Concepts of Alterity: the Philosophy of the Other in its Historical Context*. He is author of *Spinoza's Modernity: Mendelssohn, Lessing, and Heine* (University of Wisconsin Press, 2004), *Constituting Critique: Kant's Writing as Critical Praxis* (Duke University Press, 1994) and *Kant als Schriftsteller* (Passagen Verlag, 1990) as well as numerous articles in scholarly journals. He is also president of foundation Stiftung Dialogik and executive editor of *The Germanic Review* and is on the editorial board of *Weimarer Beiträge*.

Branwen Gruffydd Jones is Lecturer in International Political Economy at Goldsmiths, University of London. Her teaching and research interests encompass Africa's position in the global political economy; theories and histories of colonialism, imperialism and post-colonialism; African political thought; and theories of global political economy. She is currently conducting research into neoliberal governmentality and the post-colonial city in Africa, funded by the British Academy. She is author of *Explaining Global Poverty: A Critical Realist Approach* (Routledge, 2006) and editor *of Decolonising International Relations* (Rowman & Littlefield, 2006).

Sayed Khatab is a Senior Research Fellow at the School of Political and Social Inquiry and Global Terrorism Research Centre, Monash University. His research interests include the Middle East, Islamic political thought, fundamentalism, theory of government, Islamic law and politics, democracy in Islam, human rights and counter-terrorism related issues. His recent publications include, in addition to many papers published in leading peer-reviewed journals, *The Political Thought of Sayyid Qutb: The Theory of Jahiliyyah* (London: Routledge, 2006); *The Power of Sovereignty: The Political and Ideological Philosophy of Sayyid Qutb* (New York: Routledge, 2006); and with Gary D. Bouma *Democracy in Islam* (New York: Routledge, 2007). This last book has been selected for translation into other languages. His latest book, *Al-Qa'ida: The Theological and Ideological Basis of al-Qa'ida's Political Tactics*, is forthcoming with Routledge.

Christopher LaMonica is currently Assistant Professor at the US Coast Guard Academy, where he is teaching comparative politics, with a specialization in African politics and the politics of development. Prior to entering academia, Dr

LaMonica worked at the Organization for Economic Development (OECD), the Harvard Institute for International Development (HIID) and the US Agency for International Development (USAID) in Zambia. A graduate of the University of Massachusetts/Amherst, Harvard University and Boston University, he is especially interested in the prospects for improving cross-cultural dialogue in both international theory and international practice.

Kamran Matinis Lecturer in International Relations at the University of Sussex, UK. His current research revolves around the theorization of the mutually constitutive interaction between international relations and domestic processes of socio-political transformation in the Middle East with special reference to Iran. His research interests also include: international theory, historical sociology, Marxism, (trans)formation of 'political Islams', political history of the Iranian modernity and Kurdish nationalism. He has published in *European Journal of International Relations* (*EJIR*) and also contributed to *Capital & Class* and the online journal *Counterpunch*.

Martin Munro is Associate Professor of French at Florida State University. He has previously worked in Aberdeen, Cork, and Trinidad. He is the author of *Shaping and Reshaping the Caribbean: The Work of Aime Césaire and Rene Depestre* (Maney Publishing, 2000) and *Exile and Post-1946 Haitian Literature* (Liverpool University Press, 2007). He has published two co-edited volumes on the Haitian Revolution, and has another forthcoming on the author Edwidge Danticat. He edits the annual Francophone issue of the journal *Small Axe*. His new book, entitled *Different Drummers: Rhythm and Race in the New World*, is forthcoming from the University of California Press.

Ryoko Nakano is an Assistant Professor in the Department of Japanese Studies at the National University of Singapore. Her research interests include history of ideas and international relations theory with a particular emphasis on Japanese perspectives. Currently she is working on a book manuscript entitled *Empire as Society: The Work and Contribution of Yanaihara Tadao, 1893–1958*. She has published in *Millennium: Journal of International Studies* and *Social Science Japan Journal*.

Mustapha Kamal Pasha is Professor of International Relations at the University of Aberdeen. His research interests cover international relations theory, global political economy, critical theory, Islamic studies and South Asian politics. He is author of *Colonial Political Economy* (Oxford University Press, 1998) and co-author of *Out From Underdevelopment Revisited: Changing Global Structures and the Remaking of the Third World* (Macmillan, 1997), as well as having published numerous articles in journals such as *Civilization, Alternatives, Millennium, Journal of Developing Societies* and *Annals of the American Academy of Political and Social Science.*

Robbie Shilliam is Senior Lecturer in International Relations at Victoria University of Wellington and was formerly the Hedley Bull Junior Research Fellow at the University of Oxford. He has published on the history of political thought in international relations in journals such as *Millennium, European Journal of International Relations* and *History of Political Thought* as well as on slavery in modern world development in *Comparative Studies in Society and History, Review of International Studies* and *Cambridge Review of International Affairs.* He is author of *German Thought and International Relations* (Palgrave, 2009) and co-editor with Gurminder Bhambra of *Silencing Human Rights* (Palgrave, 2008).

1 Non-Western thought and international relations

Robbie Shilliam

The challenge

In one of those strange yet telling silences, explorations of the post-9/11 world within the international relations (IR) discipline have predominantly examined the effect that the 'war on terror' has had on one 'civilization': the West. Debates on the ethical significance of the contemporary conjuncture, for example, have focused, primarily, upon the ambivalent relationship between liberalism, security and freedom within Europe and the USA (see, for example, Behnke 2004; Buzan 2006; and the collection of essays in Walker 2006). In general, debates in IR exhibit a serious lack of sustained consideration of non-Western discussions on the so-called clash of civilizations[1] even though there has existed for some time now a sustained debate in Islamic jurisprudence regarding the 'law of minorities' whereby Muslims living in the non-Muslim world are no longer treated as transients, but as permanent residents (see, for example, Sulayman 1987; Soroush 2000; Euben 2002). Few IR scholars have engaged seriously with this sophisticated and long-running debate (exceptions include Hashmi 1998; Mandaville 2002; Piscatori 2003). The current debates in IR over Islam and the war on terror form merely the latest episode of sidelining the significance and value of what might be termed non-Western thought.

Paradoxically, regular attention has been paid to non-Western actors and the shape of non-Western political and cultural structures. For example, following the Second World War one can find Western philosophers and political scientists engaging with the problem of cultural difference in international relations (see, for example, Northrop 1949; Iyer 1965). And even the so-called 'godfather' of American realpolitik, Hans Morgenthau, believed that, rather than Russian communism, East Asian independence movements presented the deepest ethical challenge to US foreign policy-making (Morgenthau 1960, pp. 134–7). Moreover, if the 'English School' can be criticized as having built a Eurocentric narrative of the historical rise of international society (expanding outward from its post-Catholic European milieu to encompass, after decolonization, the world), it cannot be criticized for having ignored the practical and ethical challenges to this expansion emanating from extra-European political forces (for example, Vincent 1982; Bull 1984; Gong 1984).

Why is it that the non-Western world has been a defining presence for IR scholarship and yet said scholarship has consistently balked at placing non-Western thought at the heart of its debates? To answer this question we must dig deep into the bedrock of the Western Academy itself. After all, the content of the modern social sciences and humanities was at least in part cultivated by reference to non-European bodies of knowledge and culture. As has been increasingly documented, the encounter with Amerindians provided the impetus for the intensive development within Europe of natural law, enlightenment humanism, social contract theory and modern categorization of the social and natural world (Jahn 2000; Wynter 2003; Blaney and Inayatullah 2004). Travelogues of Europeans in strange lands helped to define what should be considered philosophical, economically, culturally and politically unique to 'civilized' Europeans.[2] And the successful pursuit of colonial missions required sovereignty and exceptions to sovereignty to be formulated in international law (Anghie 2005).

Even the influential comparative tradition of knowledge production, developed in the later eighteenth century, owed a great deal to the study of non-European thought and practice. Comparative studies arose out of the philological tradition (Panikkar 1988, p. 117), and both shared a special affinity to Indian studies. For example, artefacts brought back by officials of the East India Company awoke Johann Gottfried von Herder and Friedrich Schlegel to Sanskrit, an empirical linguistic and religious touchstone for future romanticism in German thought (Davies 1998, pp. 62–74). One might even say in this respect that non-European culture was a crucial resource deployed within that most enduring battle amongst European thinkers over the form and content of modernity, namely rationalism versus romanticism. Over time the field of comparative inquiry shifted from philology to philosophy, and it is this shift that is significant for understanding why the figure of a doing *and thinking* non-Western subject haunts the Western Academy.

The attribution of who can 'think' and produce valid knowledge of human existence has always been political; but it was made all the more so in the nineteenth century when Georg Hegel gave the philosopher a central role in the development and cultivation of the *modern self*. Hegel narrated the trajectory of this development through a comparative analysis wherein the spirit of modernity had moved from the East to the West (see Shilliam 2009, Chapter 4). Hegel's grand narrative of world development was, in part, informed by a deep pre-existing current in Enlightenment thought that had already started to draw a temporal division between a modern Western Europe and a premodern rest (Fabian 1983). Indeed, this is the broader context in which Hegel privileged European being as the teleological truth of human existence able to be legitimately uttered only by Europeans. And this context was defined by the rise to dominance of certain European powers over existing circuits of world commerce, the accumulation by these powers of overseas colonies, as well as their consolidation of control over the slave trade including the concomitant construction of plantation systems in the Americas. It is within this context that European scholars of the comparative tradition could assume a universal standard of civilization modelled upon an idealized Western Europe to define modernity *tout court*, and thus relegate all other peoples and cultures in the world to an object of inquiry rather than as thinking subjects of and on modernity (see, in general, Krishna 1988; Panikkar 1988).

Over the last twenty years a project has emerged that seeks to critically reinvent the comparative tradition of the Western Academy. Scholars associated with this project have sought to 'provincialize' thought on the Western experience of modernity, heretofore taken as a universal reference point, in order to provide anti-imperialistic resources through which to engage with the irreducible yet inter-related plurality of modern world development. Primarily, the project seeks to give legitimate standing to the traditions and figures of non-Western thought. This endeavour, it is claimed, has acquired urgency now that globalization has made it increasingly difficult for Western civilization to masquerade as the geo-cultural retainer of a universal experience of modernity.[3] As a discipline, IR is far overdue an explicit and sustained engagement with the philosophical, historical and ethical challenges grappled with by this new project (see especially Dallmayr 2001). The most important challenge for IR, in this respect, is to find a way of engaging with – rather than ignoring – non-Western political thought in a manner that is not beholden to colonial ideologies that drain the non-Western world of all significant content for the study of a modernity that is now, and perhaps was always, integrally global.

There are precedents to this project, broadly conceived, within the history of IR. Individual scholars have always challenged the discipline with non-Western perspectives (for example, Mazrui 1964). Programmatically, there was the 1960s' World Order Models Project (WOMP) that sought to interrogate global problems of war and poverty through a cross-cultural perspective (Mendlovitz 1975). The project eventually settled upon a comparative investigation of different national IR traditions that, although worthy in itself, has attended less to the global historical context within which to critically interrogate – and resolve – the relative absence of non-Western thought in the discipline.[4] There are signs, however, that the cross-cultural challenge might be picked up once again (see, for example, Huysmans and Waever 2009). Moreover, a recent series of investigations into Islamic, Chinese and Japanese 'schools' of thought on international relations – past and present – have sought to highlight different meanings of key categories, such as 'sovereignty', as well as deeper philosophical differences related to the concepts of order, justice and change to those presented in the traditional Western canon.[5] Some authors, such as Siba Grovogui (2006a), have undertaken detailed explorations of lineages and genealogies of international thought arising from encounters between intellectuals from the colonized world and the European halls of power. Additionally, intellectuals such as Frantz Fanon, Edward Said, Hommi Bhabha and Ashis Nandy, who in varying degrees have been situated both inside and outside the Western Academy, have been increasingly mobilized in IR scholarship to interrogate the essentialization of cultural identities (for example, Blaney and Inayatullah 1994; Persaud 1997; Jarvis 2001; Agathangelou and Ling 2004; Biswas 2007; Bilgin 2008). Finally, a number of edited collections have been published that emphasize the importance of non-Western experiences of modernity, especially its colonial/imperial dimension (Darby 1997; Neuman 1998; Chan *et al.* 2001; Chowdhry and Nair 2004; Gruffydd Jones 2006a; Acharya and Buzan 2007).

Contributing to these existing conversations, this volume seeks to cultivate an *explicit* and *sustained* critical engagement with non-Western thought on modernity and its importance to the subject matter and theories of IR. The volume sketches out the historical depth and contemporary significance of non-Western thought on modernity, as well as the rich diversity of its individuals, groups, movements and traditions. The main purpose of the volume is to use a set of geo-culturally diverse investigations in order to sketch out the theoretical and substantive contours of an engagement with non-Western thought that refuses to render it superfluous to or simply derivative of the orthodox Western canon of thought. The main aim of the volume is to highlight and explore the *global*, rather than European or Western, context within which knowledge of modernity has been developed. And for this aim, a fundamental assumption is made that imperialism and colonialism have from the start been co-constitutive processes of the typical understood routes into modernity, namely the development of the capitalist world market and the system of states. At a minimum, globalization is not an escape from this historical relationship, but a reordering – and possibly intensification – of it (Barkawi and Laffey 2002). The retrieval of this global context to the knowledge production of modernity in IR might help to provide deeper insights into the contested nature of a global modernity shaped so fundamentally by colonialism and Western expansionism. Now, as ever, these insights are desperately needed for a discipline that is closely implicated in Western foreign policy-making and yet has such a myopic horizon of inquiry.

Organization of the volume

Introductions

The next introductory chapter discusses the perils and prospects of investigating non-Western thought in order to better understand the global context of modernity. The complexities involved in this investigation are significant, especially when the case could be made that the very object to be retrieved has in large part been a construction of colonial/imperial epistemology. Is there – and should we conceive of – such a thing as 'non-Western thought'? And, if there is, how might we encounter this diverse body of thought without in the process assimilating it within an existing archive or rendering it as profoundly 'exotic'? In Chapter 2 I discuss these issues at a general level not to provide a programmatic statement for the collection as a whole, but to clarify the contentious aspects of this book project and to provide the theoretical and conceptual space for engaging with the more specific investigations that follow.

Part I: colonial conditions

That the colonial condition has been more the normal rather than exceptional historical path to modernity is woefully ignored in theories and approaches to IR that tend to bolt imperialism and colonialism onto existing frameworks and narratives that centre upon an idealized European experience. For example, despite their embeddedness within the writings of Hobbes and Locke, imperial and colonial rule have no home in the state of nature/social contract model and its derived dualism as utilized in the core framework of IR theory: anarchy/society. Alternatively, popular historical–sociological narratives of the making of the modern world – Weber's rise of instrumental-rational rule, Marx's primitive accumulation and the liberal appropriation of Kant's 'cosmopolitan point of view' – do not require imperialism or colonialism to be conceived as *core* processes that drive modern social transformation; rather, they are supplementary to, derivative of, or derivations from the rise of the modern state system and/or global capitalist economy. The chapters in Part I seek to address these lacunae by exploring traditions of thought and specific thinkers that have had to engage with the content, meaning, and emergence/divergence of modernity from within a colonial – or more accurately speaking colonized – context. By paying attention to this fundamental global context of modernity each chapter in this part complicates the assumptions of various established theories, concepts and narratives in IR.

In Chapter 3, Gerard Aching engages with issues central to the English School approach to IR. Aching targets the diffusionist narrative of this School that describes the expansion of a European society of states into an international society of states moderated by the 'standard of civilization'. A political community would be judged civilized and hence sovereign by this standard if it met two requisites: one material – a technologically advanced economy – and one politico-ideological – a tradition of individual rights to persons and property. The English School narrative tends to conflate the attainment of 'civilization' judged by this standard with sovereignty, but it is this deterministic conflation that Aching argues is inadequate when studying the slave-holding Americas. Aching shows how, with regards to the nineteenth-century Cuban bourgeoisie, the technical prerequisite was present – an incredibly profitable, productive and complex slave economy – but at the necessary expense of a development of the politico-ideological – a tradition of rights to one's own person. Hence, the Cuban bourgeoisie's adherence to the idea of civilization emanating from Europe was precisely what undermined its legitimacy to pursue sovereign independence from Spain, an entanglement that succeeding Spanish governments took advantage of.

In Chapter 4, Branwen Gruffydd Jones prefigures some of the issues in Part III regarding normative theories that seek to go beyond the container of the nation-state. However, her argument is firmly embedded in the substantive struggles against injustices and racism that took place in colonial Lusophone Africa in the second half of the twentieth century. Gruffydd Jones takes issue with liberal narratives in IR that speak of a progressive and future-oriented entrenchment of cosmopolitan values within international institutions while ignoring the preceding and coterminous struggles over colonial rule that sought to overcome the racial divisions of world order. Instead of abstract and future-oriented notions of fairness and equality, she examines how the thought and practice of the leaders of the Lusophone African anti-colonial movements, Agostinho Neto, Samora Machel, Amílcar Cabral and Eduardo Mondlane, cultivated an internationalism that sought to transcend the colonial logics of racialized revenge or restoration. Taking their prompt from the phenomenal–colonial – rather than noumenal–liberal – world, these intellectuals worked upon a concept of a post-racialized humanity the relationality of which was arguably far denser than that promised by the abstract considerations of liberal cosmopolitanism.

In Chapter 5 Willi Goetschel questions the secularization narrative of Westphalia and the associated rise of modern sovereignty by examining the German-Jewish tradition of political thought, here represented by Baruch Spinoza, Moses Mendelssohn and Heinrich Heine, whom he represents as 'indigenous colonists' within German lands. In this respect, Goetschel argues that the problem of colonialism was entangled within the originating core categories of modern Western political thought. Goetschel explores how these intellectuals thought relationally about their position in the Jewish colonies and the ways in which the rise of the state/civil society complex might turn Jewish colonists into modern German citizens. Following Spinoza's understanding of power in relational rather than possessive terms, Goetschel shows that Mendelssohn and Heine provided a different understanding of secularization that resonates with many contemporary post-colonial challenges to the conceptualization of modernity. Rather than presenting a narrative internal to Christendom of the move from Pope to Prince – traditional hierocratic to modern sovereign rule – these thinkers instead considered secularization to entail the simultaneous recognition of religion and politics – tradition and modern – as discrete but related sites of power that, furthermore, are themselves constituted in multiple forms.

Part II: cultural contexts

In the last few decades most disciplines in the humanities and social sciences have variously experienced a 'cultural turn'. Rather than interrogating the social world from the top down by reference to sweeping universals or unilinear grand narratives, scholars have argued that conceptual and empirical attention must be paid to the particularities of place and the discrete conjunctures of events and conditions that occur therein. In IR (as elsewhere) this move has had proponents and detractors. The former claim that such a turn allows sociological, historical and anthropological sensitivity to be injected into geo-political phenomena that otherwise remain dully abstracted; the latter claim that such a turn leads to cultural reductionism and the abandonment of investigations into global structures of power, which ultimately finishes with Orientalism, that is to say, the exoticizing of 'far away' and 'peculiar' peoples and places. Unsurprisingly, the debate has been most vociferous regarding Samuel Huntington's influential 'clash of civilizations' thesis, one given new life with the ongoing 'war on terror' (for a helpful review, see O'Hagan 2005). Part II speaks to the debates over this turn. But the chapters therein do so by exploring various ways in which culture has been deployed by intellectuals outside Europe and the United States as a resource with which to assimilate, co-opt, resist or transform social–scientific concepts and categories historically associated with Western imperial expansion. Moreover, all of the chapters seek, again in various ways, to engage with non-Western thought on culture in a way that refuses both Orientalism and reverse Orientalism.

In Chapter 6, Sayed Khatab re-examines the importance of Sayyid Qutb's writings on the notion of democracy in Islam. Khatab refuses to follow popular renditions that nowadays place Qutb as an ideologue of terrorism within a canon of Islamic thought that is anti-modern and thus diametrically opposed to Western traditions of democratic thought. Khatab notes the tendency for some actors – Muslim and non-Muslim – to assume that a binary opposition exists between tradition and modernity, religion and secularism, Islamic culture and Western culture. Khatab acknowledges the historical challenge that the imperial West has posed to the Islamic world, but shows how the Muslim response has not necessarily been one of either outright rejection or assimilation. Rather than as an object for studies on terrorism, Khatab presents Qutb's writings as a source in its own right on considerations of constitutional rule, political pluralism and temporal legislation, one that is alternative but nevertheless complementary to sources from the Western canon. Specifically, Khatab focuses upon Qutb's efforts to contain extremism, violence and terrorism in both domestic and international relations by unlocking the many complexities of his central conception of sovereignty: *hakimiyyah*.

In Chapter 7, Kamran Matin also attacks the heart of Orientalist understandings of political Islam as a *sui generis* cultural phenomenon. And in doing so, Matin also fundamentally disrupts the related assumption that political Islam cannot be modern because modernity is defined by a secularization of the political. But while Khatab reinterprets the works of Qutb from within a vibrant Islamic canon of thought, Matin does so by alternatively highlighting the specifically international dimension of modern Islamic knowledge production. Matin investigates the thought of Ali Shariati, widely regarded as the ideologue of Iran's 'Islamic Revolution'. He argues that Shariati's intellectual project was both a product and nemesis of the Pahlavis's 'modernization' programme, an attempt to stave off the loss of geo-political independence that had accompanied the expansion of modernizing – and imperialistic – Russia, Great Britain and France. By this reading, Shariati's 'revolutionary Islam' was not the ideology of an internally pathologized Islamic modernity, but was rather expressive of the attempt to both mediate and repel 'modernity' under the pressure of an encroaching imperialism that itself boasted ownership of modernity.

In Chapter 8, Ryoko Nakano engages with debates in IR regarding the normative basis for international cooperation. Nakano notes how the strategy of 'reverse Orientalism' is still deployed by various Asian leaders in the guise of 'Asian values' in order to legitimize their sovereignty in a Western-dominated world order. However, Nakano is keen to recover traditions of thought with which the normative divide between Western universalism and Eastern cultural particularism could be filled rather than reproduced. Specifically, she recovers the works of the Japanese humanists Uchimura Kanzō and Yanaihara Tadao, who commented on imperial affairs around the *fin de siècle*. These intellectuals interpolated Christianity through Confucian, Daoist and Samurai ethics, and the resulting Japanese humanism, Nakano argues, sought to reconcile universalism with cultural diversity. Key to this humanism was the promotion of a decentralized association of sovereign states and the defence of autonomy as an internationally legitimated norm. In practice, this led Kanzō and Tadao to critique Japanese imperialism through a moral philosophy that was both culturally Japanese and universalistic in its coordinates.

The section finishes with a warning to IR theorists who embrace claims of culturally specific traditions of thought at face value while ignoring the hegemonic knowledge structures of modernity that have originated within Euro-America. All too easily, Arif Dirlik notes in Chapter 9, this embrace can turn into Orientalist reductionism, itself an effect of the fragmentation of the culture of modernity through its global movement. Dirlik examines the recent participation by the Chinese academy in the IR discipline. He argues that the cultural turn has provided the space for writing about the particular philosophical tradition underwriting Chinese IR. Dirlik explores how the idea of IR with 'Chinese characteristics' must contend with a number of different traditions, one recently revolutionary, the other more distant and imperial, and furthermore must balance these contending traditions with the present need to integrate 'harmoniously' into the global capitalist system. Dirlik argues that the later (overriding) concern makes the promotion of 'Chinese characteristics' an incorporative rather than resistive move vis-à-vis dominant epistemological frameworks within the global discourse of IR.

Part III: beyond the national

Since the end of the cold war the IR discipline has been challenged to account for a myriad of processes that, if previously disguised by overriding concerns over superpower conflict and nuclear Armageddon, now reveal themselves by breaking down national boundaries in the political, economic and social spheres. Much has been written on the phenomenon of 'globalization', its putative novelty or historical antecedents, its positive and negative aspects and its sources and causes. In IR some of the most important debates over globalization have interrogated the composition of – and ethical possibilities accompanying – a post-national constellation of global order. In this respect, scholarship has usually focused upon the emanations of these constellations from Western societies, be they concentrated within Western-dominated capitalist institutions of global governance – such as the World Trade Organization (WTO) – or in regional developments – such as the evolving European Union. The chapters in Part III explore non-Western imaginaries and articulations of a post-national constellation arising out of substantive engagements not with a *post-Westphalian* world but with the *post-colonial* condition. It becomes evident that these articulations foundationally confound the assumption that post-national constellations – in theory or practice – can ever be understood as categorically different to and chronologically beyond the national constellation. Rather, both constellations have existed at the same time as potentiality and actuality if we take the global context of modernity to be defined by colonial and imperial practices. This complication of the national and the post-national conditions holds significant ramifications for normative thought in IR that heretofore has focused mainly upon Western emancipatory traditions.

In Chapter 10, Martin Munro and I counterpoise traditions of Francophone Caribbean thought against the popular attribution of cosmopolitical potential to the post-national constellation of new Europe. If cosmopolitanism requires the 'self' to be problematized in a way that pluralizes its identity, we contend that narratives that contextualize this process within intra-European history are insufficient to this task. In contrast, we show how, since the Haitian Revolution, the colonial and slave-holding context of the Francophone Caribbean required thought on the construction of the modern Caribbean 'self' to face the impossibility of any endogenously driven national becoming. Instead, Francophone Caribbean thought had to try and contend with the radically and foundationally pluralized production of the 'self', positioned, as its intellectuals were, between 'savage' Africa and 'enlightened' Europe. We document various currents of Francophone Caribbean thought that have attempted to negotiate the Caribbean position of liminality, and posit Créolité as an alternative – and perhaps more fertile – source for thinking about post-national constellations.

In Chapter 11, Priya Chacko notes that on the rare occasions that India's first premier, Jawaharlal Nehru, is discussed in IR he is placed within existing frameworks such as realism or liberal internationalism. Alternatively, Chacko argues that Nehru strove to be an internationalist nationalist, a position that is nonsensical if rendered through standard frames of reference in IR normative theory. First, Chacko places Nehru's thought in the global context of the anti-colonial movement and explores his similarly global intellectual influences that included Gandhi, Marx, Buddhist philosophy and Rabindranath Tagore. Second, Chacko argues that Nehru's internationalist nationalism rejected the assumption, so fundamental in Western traditions of thought, of the equivalence of the nation and state. Nehru's colonial context prompted recognition of the salience of nation-building for the purpose of self-determination yet also required the moral exercise of power to this end. Hence Nehru sought to mobilize a non-statist nationalism, one that was not predicated upon self-interested and exploitative relations, but an internationalist nationalism that fostered a non-exploitative ethic of relation on the global stage.

In Chapter 12, Anthony Bogues pursues a similar argument highlighting a subtle yet crucial distinction between an ethics of relation of the self and 'other', and the self and *an*other. The former relation derives from colonialism and posits a hierarchical process that distances the self from others; the latter encourages the embrace and touch of distinctiveness between humans. Bogues examines the emergence of this notion of 'human solidarities' among radical black intellectuals and activists in the diaspora and in Africa. Bogues traces this emergence through the International African Services Bureau of the inter-war period, the 'Bandung moment' exemplified by the Tricontinental conferences of the 1960s, and finally in the political thought of Michael Manley and Julius Nyerere in their advocacy for a new international economic order in the 1970s. Bogues contrasts this current of anti-colonial *inter*nationalism with the drive by many post-colonial elites to simply consolidate particular nation-states. Bogues argues that because of their preoccupation with global social and economic justice, the notion of human solidarity bound up in this current of anti-colonial internationalism radically extended the boundaries of liberal procedural equality, boundaries that still limit the purview of much thought on global distributive justice.

Reflections

In Chapter 13, Mustapha Pasha provides some reflections on the project that drives this book. He presents them as 'untimely'. After all, we are supposed to live in a time where Third World consciousness has been consigned (politically and intellectually) to the dustbin of history and wherein the all-incorporating image of globalization has made a pastiche of the 'non-Western' world. Pasha argues, however, that if engaged with through the heuristic device of 'global modernity', this untimeliness reminds us of the originary historical entanglement and conjoining of colonialism and imperialism with the condition described as Western modernity, a description that has been transposed so as to render a present global order. Pasha then draws out the untimely challenges that this book poses to Western IR and clarifies the spaces wherein a non-Western IR might be creatively and critically enacted.

I would like to finish this introduction by commenting upon the limits of the repositioning and reincorporating efforts of this book itself. First, looking back at the completed volume, it is striking that no women thinkers are brought to the fore in any of the chapters. It is trite, but necessary, to state that women thinkers have been central to – and often orginators of – the many projects undertaken to understand and transform a global modernity defined by imperialism and colonialism. A number of the present contributors have, in other works, underscored and investigated these thinkers, which leads me to consider how unexpectedly – but smoothly – the same exclusion of the agency of women enacted by imperial and colonial powers can be unintentionally repeated in projects such as this. Perhaps that is testimony to how deep the hyper-patriarchal dimension of European colonialism remains embedded in imaginings of the non-Western world. Second, and relatedly, the investigations into non-Western thought pursued herein tend to interrogate relatively privileged voices within the institutions of the non-Western world. However, there is a further, monumental, yet just as crucial, requirement to democratize the category of non-Western 'intellectual' beyond the Academy's strictures. I believe that these inadequacies of the volume serve to remind us that, ultimately, global modernity is composed of the considered experiences of many and diverse but related colonized and decolonizing subjects who have drawn upon institutionally unrecognized or marginalized sources and traditions of thought. As the Rastas say, half the story has never been told.

Notes

1 See, for example, three recent forums: Beardsworth (2005), Diez and Steans (2005) and Brassett and Bulley (2007). With regards to the first, note the comments from April Biccum in the following roundtable and the extremely cursory way with which they are dealt. Similar criticism could be made of the lack of investigation in IR of the Dialogue of Civilizations instigated by the ex-Iranian President Mohhamed Khatami. Although see Lynch (2000).

2 See, for example, the chapters on Tahiti and New Zealand in Darwin's *Voyage of the Beagle* (London: Penguin, 1989).

3 For a succinct overview see Dallmayr (2004). See also Larson and Deutsch (1988), Dallmayr (1999), Parel and Keith (1992) and Jung (2002). For a critical retrospect on the 'multiple modernities' literature see Bhambra (2007).

4 Associated with WOMP, for example, was Alker and Beirsteker (1984). For more recent developments see Huang (2007) and Tickner and Waever (2009).

5 On how Ibn Khaldun might speak to IR theory see Cox (1995) and Pasha (1997). On China see Deng (1998), S. Chan (1999), Zhang (2001) and Mitter (2003). On Japan see Williams (2000), Jones (2002), Ong (2004) and Nakano (2007).

2 The perilous but unavoidable terrain of the non-West

Robbie Shilliam

Introduction

In this chapter I argue that an orientation – or perhaps reorientation – towards non-Western thought is a perilous but unavoidable undertaking if international relations scholars wish to explore the global context of modernity. I begin by drawing attention to the inadequacies that are revealed in mainstream understandings of modern subjecthood held by the Western Academy when colonial and imperial route(s) to modernity are brought to the fore of investigation. However, I then explore the significant epistemological difficulties that accompany the engagement with a non-Western archive of thought that at least in part has been constructed through colonially induced forms of representing 'others'. Subsequently, I explore some approaches that might escape the tendency to essentialize and/or exoticize non-Western thought on modernity, specifically 'travelling theory' and 'translating modernity'. What is required, I argue, is a serious engagement with non-Western thought that is nevertheless sensitive to the way in which imperialism and colonialism have carved out the geo-cultural and geo-political terrains of West and non-West. Having made this 'return' to the non-West I suggest how, from this perspective, the ideal of Western modernity might be critically re-examined so as to provide a more adequate appreciation of the global context of modernity, modernity globalized through – and as – colonial and imperial projects.

The inadequacy of Western thought

In the social sciences, modernity refers to a condition of social existence that is radically different to all past forms of human experience that are categorized as 'traditional' and/or 'primitive'. Although IR is largely a derivative discipline to sociology and anthropology when it comes to debates over modernity, these debates – and they have historical roots that reach back into seventeenth-century European thought – have largely provided the framework within which IR theory has developed (for an overview see Shilliam 2010). It is over the question of modernity that the most influential debates have taken place regarding issues of continuity and change within and among societies and the contrasting forms and sequences of change. Moreover, these debates have raised epistemological questions over how to explain the political order formed in the midst of anomie or alienation of the social subject, what kind of knowledge production this subject partakes of when it is impersonalized, desacralized and individualized, and what form of knowledge production is appropriate to understand this modern form of subjecthood.[1]

It is difficult to underplay the influence that these debates have wielded in the Western Academy. But, for the purposes of this chapter, perhaps the most signal effect has been the construction of a consensus that context-free knowledge is universally valid and thus thoroughly modern knowledge, as opposed to context-sensitive systems of thought that remain 'traditional', that is to say personalized, communalized, sacralized and thus 'prejudiced'. This distinction smuggles into the assessment of knowledge production a geo-political and temporal constituency, namely the modern West versus the traditional non-West.[2] Upon this distinction, and through this geo-cultural cleavage, the canon of legitimate social–scientific thought in the Western Academy is constructed and policed. Faced with this distinction, non-Western thought might be considered as a legitimate object of modern inquiry, but not a source through which to construct legitimate knowledge of modern subjecthood.

A prescient example of this geo-cultural division of knowledge production can be found in the recent revival of interrogating the political effect of religious belief. The division of spiritual and profane ways of knowing the world is in large part dependent upon a colonial geo-cultural imaginary, one clearly evident in the traditional comparison of spiritual Indian 'thought' with rational Western 'philosophy' (Krishna 1988). Much thought on modernity in the Western Academy – both mainstream and critical – approaches religious belief having already internalized the Kantian expulsion of religion from practical reason (Hurd 2004). Jürgen Habermas's discourse ethics is perhaps the strongest restatement of this dichotomy. Habermas assumes that *the* problem of pursuing a modern ethical life arises from the loss of the religious basis of moral traditions and the confrontation with profane existence (Habermas 1998).[3]

And yet many routes through which modern subjecthoods were formed display none of the 'disenchantment' presumed by Habermas's moral philosophy. For example, a number of scholars have explored how British colonial rule denied the development of a secular Indian public sphere, which paradoxically led to the cultivation of a 'modern' Indian national identity within personal spheres heavily imbued with religious worldviews (Chatterjee 1986; Chakrabarty 2000, p. 4). Furthermore, in terms of the moral basis of critiquing modernity, many scholars have critically argued through religious – for example Islamic – worldviews about the harmful consequences of Western modernization, especially with regards to its secularization of the public sphere (see, for example, Euben 1997). Similarly, right in the heart of the so-called West – the Americas – there exists an established tradition of thought on black liberation that has offered radical social critiques of the relationship between slavery and modern subjecthood that have nevertheless been made in the religious lexicons of prophesy and redemption (Cone 1970;

Bogues 2003). Thus, when the standpoint is shifted outside of an idealized understanding of European history, profanity is not the only register that facilitates critical examination of modern subjecthood.

Similar issues arise if we consider the racial formation of modern subjecthood produced through imperial projects and colonial rule. By the time that classical political economy tradition had taken root in Scotland, a whole array of non-European cultures, value systems and political communities had started to become homogenized into meta-racialized identities – especially, 'native', 'primitive', 'savage', 'barbarian', 'Negro' – to be contrasted to the superior and more evolved European – and ultimately white – civilization (Quijano 2000; Garner 2007; Blaney and Inayatullah 2010). The Scottish and English scholars of classical political economy and social contract theory made race conveniently absent in their identification of civilizing subjects (Mills 1999). But intellectuals who had been interpolated as something other than civilized and white tended not to. For example, in the late nineteenth century, José Martí attempted to legitimize an independent Cuba by reference to the miscegenation of its population. Martí posited *mestizo* identity as the true emancipatory site of the Americas against homogenizing ideas such as *raza* that had been used by certain Creole elites to justify their rule by reference to a white European heritage (Aching 2005). The syncretism of African and Western modes of life within plantation economies raises the question of whether one can find a pure form of modern subjecthood within that hieroglyph of modernity itself, the United Sates. Alternatively, in the early twentieth century, Marcus Garvey's pan-African political philosophy made an impersonalized but racialized collective, the black diaspora, the agent of transnational self-determination (Shilliam 2006).

Of course, the imperial formation of meta-racialized identities always intersectioned with the gendered dimension of forming colonial subjects (see McCall 2005). European colonizers had a tendency to grant the 'savage' its own special 'nobility' as long as this savage mimicked the martial valour that the colonizers ascribed to themselves. Unfortunately, the proof of such nobility was a suicidal urge to throw oneself upon European muskets and maxim guns, and those of the colonized who decided upon a more prudent (and rational!) course of action were assumed to be feminized peoples, passive and weak. Colonial mentality had to subvert the fact that not all 'native' societies required women to be simply passive property of men; to acknowledge this would be to admit that Europeans might have to learn how to balance the self-determination of subjects with a complex division of labour from savages and barbarians. For example, British intellectuals in Aotearoa New Zealand mapped the complexities, nuances and frictions of gender relations in Māori societies onto a totally inappropriate imaginary of Christian and Victorian patriarchal rule (in general, see Smith 1999). But perhaps the key point to be made here is that the presumed distinction between the modern public sphere of the androgynous citizen and a gendered and affective private life could not coalesce upon a colonial foundation. Rather, as Priya Chacko shows with regards to India, the post-colonial nation came to be recognized in international society as an already gendered female body (Chacko 2008).

The purpose of this section has been to highlight the fact that in the context of imperial and colonial rule, embodied, communal and sacral subjectivities have not been subsumed under the modernist tendency to impersonalize, individualize and make profane. Rather, these subjectivities have formed the very matter of contestations over the modern promise of freedom and self-determination for the majority of the world's population. Thus, if we are concerned with investigating the global context of modernity, that is, modernity globalized through – and as – colonial and imperial projects, no analysis is adequate that makes a categorical distinction between the characteristics of pre-modern and modern subjecthood. This does not mean that Marx, Weber and Habermas are somehow irrelevant to understanding the global context of modernity. What it does mean is that we should be careful not to assume that non-Western categorizations and conceptualizations of modern subjecthood are unsophisticated or even misguided simply because they clash with the epistemological common-sense of the Western Academy. Rather, the clash reveals the fallacy of composition whereby an idealized Western modernity is mistaken for global modernity.

Enrique Dussel provides a useful critique of this fallacy of composition. Dividing the world into centre and periphery, Dussel makes a *general* claim that peripheral subjects – and here he notes the historical existence of a shifting periphery within Europe itself – have had to define themselves against already established 'civilized' images of the human persona, but, as newcomers or outsiders, have enjoyed a critical perspective from which they might be better placed to interrogate the reality of such images (Dussel 1985, p. 4). In Dussel's geo-cultural imaginary, critical thought has just as much (if not more of) a tendency to arise from the periphery than from the centre. Not only does this model suggest that thought from the periphery is more than simply 'derivative' of an 'original', but it also suggests that critical thought from the centre can never really be critical of its own situated experienced if it ignores thought from the periphery (Connell 2007; Walsh 2007).

The perils of representing the non-West

But, as I shall now discuss, there is no simple or direct route into non-Western thought understood as a *sui generis* and transparent archive. I do not wish to downplay the very practical obstacles for scholars who wish to engage with this archive, be it 'mundane' funding problems to language issues where English – and certainly not, for example, Arabic – is the lingua franca of social science (see Mignolo 2000, p. 71; Tickner 2003, p. 301). However, non-Western thought has never really been absent from the Western Academy; and neither should we imagine that its archive is simply waiting to be fully opened, thus revealing a pristine world of discovery. Rather, to use Spivak's terms (Spivak 1988), it is already represented – rather than re-presented – and more often than not in ways that tend to essentialize and exoticize non-Western culture.

For example, debates within the Western Academy have contributed much to the thesis that the success of the East Asian Tigers in the 1980s was due to the preservation of Confucianism (Bell and Chaibong 2003): in short, 'Asian values' are, at least to a certain extent, values inscribed upon 'Asia' by (especially) American scholars. Not just non-Western value systems but identities too have been, in part (but not in whole), constructed by the Academy. Elizabeth Povinelli, for example, makes the case that non-indigenous Australian scholars have inscribed Aboriginal identity as part of a timeless culture worthy of preservation so as to allay liberal guilt about historical illiberal actions. This has produced a paradoxical situation wherein '[n]on–aboriginal Australians enjoy ancient traditions while suspecting the authenticity of the aboriginal subject. Aboriginal Australians enjoy their traditions while suspecting the authenticity of themselves' (Povinelli 1999, p. 31). These examples demonstrate that even when the Western Academy turns its attention towards the 'outside', it is often documenting the fruits of its own (idealized) intellectual labours.

Alternatively, it cannot be assumed that scholars hailing from outside of the Western Academy represent authentic and pristine traditions of non-Western thought. Generally speaking, a body of thought becomes inscribed as 'traditional' only when it is threatened or disturbed by contending bodies of thought. In this respect, any call to embrace tradition as a resource that might oppose, say, Westernization, is itself at least part of the effect of Westernization.[4] Perhaps the most famous example of this process is the embrace in the late nineteenth and early twentieth century by a number of East Asian scholars of the Eurocentric categorization of their own cultures as the exotic 'other'. This 'reverse Orientalism' (Dallmayr 1994, p. 529) is evident, for example, in the Kyoto school of philosophy wherein intellectuals often sought to give value to the East in the global order by virtue of its negative (spiritual) complementarity to the (rational) enlightenment values of the West (Jones 2003, p. 143).

Moreover, the concepts deployed by non-Western intellectuals to guide the creation of post-colonial societies were often inherited from the colonizers' blueprints of modern society and state. For instance, it has been well documented how through a variety of different historical discourses the European concept of the modern state has remained in Indian political thought as an essential – although enigmatic – normative concept (Nandy 1988, p. xi; Chakrabarty 2000, p. 42; Kaviraj 2005). These days, North American approaches to IR tend to dominate national academies in most of the world (see Tickner and Waever 2009). And, of course, many scholars who have filiations to non-Western societies, or hail from racialized communities internal to the West, are themselves gatekeepers in the Western Academy, especially, but not solely, through the carving out of a post-colonial studies niche.[5] Nevertheless, it is disturbing to note that often these intellectuals are either exoticized as curiosities or dismissed as fakirs. The wound of Dubois's 'double consciousness' has yet to heal (Gilroy 1993).

There is, then, a serious myopia involved in representing the archive of non-Western thought as authentic and pristine when it has been constructed through centuries of colonial and imperial relations. But perhaps the greatest effect of this representation is that it must ignore the complexity and heterogeneity of the social worlds and worldviews that imperial forces encountered and in and against which colonial projects proceeded. Moreover, as I have mentioned, the evolution of the disciplines of the Western Academy depended in large part upon the collapsing of this heterogeneity into a gross hierarchy of human conditions mapped, as always, onto a geo-cultural imaginary: the savage, barbarian and civilized. And if this imaginary framed imperial and colonial policy, it also determined the expectations of what kind of capabilities for self-reflection might be encountered amongst certain populations in the world.

Take, for example, Edward Said's celebrated thesis on Orientalism. Orientalism, for Said, is the form of knowledge production of the 'other' that constructs a despotic, sensual and stagnant Orient against the European 'self', a persona typified by reason, enlightenment and progress (Said 1994). The development of the comparative method in eighteenth- and nineteenth-century European universities relied upon the distinctions that Orientalism allowed to be made between areas, while allowing these distinctions to be ranked through a universal narrative of human progression. Alternatively, the intellectual construction of Africa was a far more extreme process of 'othering'. Comparative studies failed to attribute even the faded glory of ancient civilization to Africa, and all things African were cast as the absolute other – the animalistic domain counterpoised to the quintessentially human(e) lands of Europe (Mudimbe 1988). Hegel, at his most charitable, attributed a permanent childhood to Africans; 150 years of learning later, Huntington, at his most charitable, conceded the 'possibility' of a thing called African civilization (Huntington 1996). The silence on Africa in the European comparative studies tradition, in this sense, speaks volumes, and recent collections of comparative studies still woefully under-represent African thought on modernity (see, for example, the selection in Parel and Keith 1992; Jung 2002).

On the other hand, if various regions were historically integrated into the European (and subsequently American) geo-cultural imaginary differentially, so too did the geo-political modes of integration vary, ranging from indirect rule through princely states in South Asia, to direct settler colonization, to the wholesale shipping of Africans into the Americas as part of the creation of an 'Atlantic modernity'. The colonial frontier was (and is) always shifting, blurring and composed of multiple divisions. This variety of integrative processes is important to unpack when one seeks to clarify the particular situatedness from which non-Western intellectuals critically encountered global modernity.

For many intellectuals in the Americas it was the ambiguity of identifying the Americas with Europe that drove investigation of modernity. Walter Mignolo goes so far as to argue that Said's Orientalism thesis partakes in the occlusion of the preceding colonial production of the European 'Occident', which, from the Iberian expansion across the Atlantic, began to include the Americas as a frontier of the European 'West' (Mignolo 2000, pp. 55–60). To their European counterparts, New World colonists were very quickly assessed as contaminated with the savagery of the New World (both putatively found within the Amerindians and imported with Atlantic slavery) (see Pagden and Canny 1989; Garraway 2005). However, Creolization, a concept that addresses the process of 'making native' to the New World and focuses upon the arising ambiguities over geo-cultural identification, has been developed as an emancipatory form of modern subject formation by Caribbean thinkers (Glissant 1989; Bernabé *et al.* 1990).

Alternatively, far removed from the colonial plantation economies lay those regions that might be termed the 'quasi-colonized'. Here, the threat of Western imperial expansion framed intellectual engagements in a specific way, notably via the identification of European modernity as a resource *and* a threat. From the time of Alexander II onwards some Russian intelligentsia embraced their developmental destiny as replicating the recent history of Western Europe in order to avoid 'Asiatic' morass. However, Slavophiles preferred the idea of a 'separate' path for Russia with its claim to the uniqueness and superiority of the Slavic communal spirit (Bassin 1991, p. 9). After the Opium Wars with Britain, Chinese intellectuals struggled in their own way with the need to accommodate, but not be assimilated by, Western imperialism. The maxim, *Zhongxue weiti, Xixue weiyong* (Chinese learning as essence, Western learning as means), resonates even today in the attempt to build an IR theory with 'Chinese characteristics' (Yeh 1998, Chan 1999, p. 173).

The point of this section has been to sketch out the perils of representing non-Western thought when its archive has been constructed so intimately through diverse imperial projects and colonial rule. In the face of these epistemological challenges, any attempt to engage with non-Western thought might seem tragically doomed to merely re-produce the colonizers image of the world. And yet, even with the best of intentions, non-Western thought cannot be so easily dismissed. The Western Academy considers the archive to be, by and large, the repository of derivative, substandard or exotic knowledge, even though it contains originally situated thought upon the experiences of imperialism and colonialism, and even though the Academy's valorization of its own archive is in part a requirement of the very same processes of imperialism and colonialism. But most importantly, these experiences *continue to reverberate* in the present lived experiences of subjects worldwide (to varying degrees of intimacy, of course). Therefore, to acknowledge the perilous nature of the journey (back) to the non-West cannot be misunderstood as an injunction simply to stay at home.

To summarize the argument so far: even having recognized the co-constitution of the archives of Western and non-Western thought through (the threat of) relations of colonial domination, and even after having problematized the authenticity, essentialist nature and pristine character of the non-Western archive itself, it is crucial that we do *not* ignore non-Western thought as a collection of situated outlooks on the modern condition. For it is upon this *uneven* non-Western geo-intellectual terrain – by no means an alien world, yet neither a global commons – that many of the deepest engagements and problematizations of modernity have been produced. Dismissing non-Western thought as an epistemologically suspect archive runs the risk of effacing the global and colonial dimension of the making of modernity, thus lapsing back into a default Eurocentrism. In what now follows, I point out some strategies that might allow for a more adequate navigation of this perilous, but unavoidable, journey.

Reorientation towards the non-West

To begin with, the situated, concrete historical contexts of non-Western thought can never be lost sight of. Non-Western thought must be approached as parts of a relation of a process of domination. For this purpose, however, domination cannot be understood as a one-way relationship comprising the exploitation of a passive victim (Dunch 2002). After all, the colonial relation has always had a negative effect upon the colonizer – and the culture of the 'mother country' – as well as upon the colonized (Nandy 1988; Memmi 1990). With different impacts and to different extents *both* subjects of the colonial relation could conceivably be considered 'victims'. And if this is the case, it follows that so could both colonizer and colonized, again differentially, be considered agents of transformation, or at the very least, possessors of the ability to creatively reason on the mode of transformation.

Indeed, it is simply not possible to explain every non-Western engagement with the West as one of pure and simple colonial domination. For example, and to return to the realm of the 'quasi-colonized', Japan did not come under direct Western domination until the end of the Second World War, and not until attempting its own Western-inspired – if substantively differentiated (Beasley 1987, Chapter 1) – colonial project in Asia, while at the same time attempting an entry into Western-dominated 'international society' (through the League of Nations) as a racial equal. The 'Kyoto school' of philosophy in Japan that formed around Nishida Kitarô in the first half of the twentieth century attempted to critically address Japan's place – and ethico-political mission – in a Western-dominated world. To understand Japanese 'being in the world', Kyoto school intellectuals displayed an interest in Heidegger's works on phenomenology (in general, see Parkes 1987). But it would be hard to then claim that German theory was forced upon the Japanese Academy in an act of cultural domination; and neither is it the case that through this engagement Kyoto phenomenology became a 'Heideggerian' derivative.

Although the Japanese case might be quite particular, it nevertheless alerts us to the fact that the Western script of modernity has never simply been written onto a blank paper to be internalized by the non-Western mind. Non-Western intellectuals (and, of course, populations at large), rather than assimilate the message, have just as much copied this script – out of command, necessity, pre-emption or inventiveness – into existing narratives for pragmatic, political and/or ethical purposes other than what the script was intended for. Therefore, when engaging with non-Western thought we must not only recognize the concrete relations of domination through which such thought has been both created and received, we must also recognize the creative agency that has been deployed in order to construct understandings of an imperially and colonially induced modernity.

Through what conceptual frameworks might it be possible, then, for the Western Academy to enter – or perhaps leave and return to – the terrain of non-Western thought? Two possible frameworks have arisen in recent years: 'travelling theory' and 'translation'.

The idea of theory as travel is by no means new. In both ancient Greek and Islamic thought the act of theorization was closely associated with travel and the dislocation of oneself from one's own context in order to gain a critical perspective on that context (Euben 2004). That travel might be a constitutive act in the production of knowledge has become especially important to anthropology in recent years. After all, ethnographic knowledge is not produced in a direct relationship between the observer and the observed but rather is just as much knowledge produced by the 'travels' – practical and conceptual – of the interlocutor (Clifford 1992). In short, the 'native informant', in order to communicate to both sides, has her/his own history of encounter and discovery. Hence knowledge production of cultural and societal difference is never a comparison of discrete entities; it is itself a practice – a production – of inter-relationships.

As Said pointed out, the origin and destination of a travelling idea might occupy very different socio-political contexts, and depending on the conditions of accepting or tolerating an 'alien' idea, the meaning and use of the idea could be transformed through this incorporation (Said 1984, pp. 226–7). And if ideas travel then they requires translation. Translation is also a generative act of knowledge production rather than simply a technical act of producing a philological fidelity of meaning across discrete lexicons. Ideas do not 'travel' by themselves but are always carried through political projects (Liu 2002, p. 324; Young 2002, pp. 408–9). '[T]he question', Lydia Liu insightfully argues, 'is not whether translation between cultures is possible – people do it anyway, or whether the other is knowable, or even whether an abstruse text is decipherable, but what practical purposes or needs bring an ethnographer to pursue cultural translation' (Liu 2002, p. 306). Here the very practical issue of the nature of colonial domination and the creation of the 'terrain' of non-Western political thought re-arises. So rather than assuming translation to be a predominantly 'cerebral' pursuit quarantined to a privileged stratum of interloping agents (migrants, intellectuals or otherwise), we must understand translation to work more constitutively in the structural reformation or transformation of societies and cultures.[6]

Drawing together the strands of the argument made so far I would argue that translating modernity is not simply an act of assimilating meanings and practices, and neither is it solely an act of resistance. Rather, domination, resistance, appropriation and transformation have to be understood as congenitally entangled in this moment of knowledge production, their entanglement often generating novel meanings of 'modern' categories and concepts. The complexity of this aspect of knowledge production rules out any simplistic and universal ascription of non-Western thought solely as a tradition of resistance or assimilation, and thus guards against the exoticizing of the 'other'. Vincente Rafael's work on Spanish attempts to convert the Tagalog of the Philippines to Christianity is instructive in this regard (Rafael 1988). Rafael documents how Latin words formed areas of untranslatability in the Spanish vernacular of prayers and commandments that were taught to the Tagalog, who then imbued these words with 'inappropriate' indigenous meanings. Submission to the Spanish God could then be performed orally by the Tagalog but minus the meanings of domination that the Spanish idea of conversion assumed. Neither domination nor resistance nor appropriation defined the Tagalog intellectual engagement with Spanish colonialism *in toto.*[7]

Thus stated, an anti- or post-colonial engagement by the Western Academy with non-Western thought requires the cultivation of a set of linked sensitivities. First, we must recognize the determining history of colonial/quasi-colonial cultural and political impingement/domination in modern thought. That is to say, quite simply, that if knowledge is always produced within particular contexts, then (the threat of) colonialism is a meta-context in which knowledge of modernity has been produced. But, second, we must nevertheless be sensitive to the differentiated nature of experiences of imperialism and colonialism. That is to say that non-Western thought has been situated within an array of geo-politically and geo-culturally variegated experiences. However, third, we must remember that this difference has never been unbounded such that all that is required is to list a set of open-ended cultural particulars. We cannot incorporate the archive of non-Western thought into our Academy through a liberal embrace. Rather, we should remember that the variegated contexts within which non-Western thought has produced knowledge of modernity have always been bound to constellations of power that have foisted a *global* imperial and colonial order. Therefore, in the historical–geographical imaginary, the West and non-West operate as positionalities already produced by various intellectual attempts to map and chart a passage through the variegated global experience of colonial modernity. Hence, non-Western thought is *constitutive* of global thought on modernity.

The West viewed from elsewhere

Orienting oneself towards the non-Western side of this relationship might even allow for more adequate critical reflection of the ideal Western experience of modernity, although this should not be taken to be the ultimate purpose of such re-orientation. For this purpose, though, it is expedient to consider engagements in modern European thought with the concept of the 'other' (Bernestein 1991, p. 3; Neumann 1999, p. 1). Two philosophers immediately stand out, who built upon the phenomenological tradition of continental thought (especially Edmund Husserl and Martin Heidegger), namely, Hans-Georg Gadamer and Emmanuel Lévinas. Gadamer's work on 'philosophical hermeneutics' seeks to make explicit the situatedness from which one already receives meanings of the objects of investigation. Dialogue is the key to making visible the 'horizon' of experience to the extent that it allows an expansion of this horizon to a point where it might 'fuse' with differentially situated horizons of experience (Gadamer 2004, pp. 301–5). Here lies Gadamer's contribution to an ethics of difference, that is, that there should be no closure of understanding of the self so that the space always exists for understanding the self in terms of an ethical relation to the other (for example, Dallmayr 1996; pp. 41–8, Shapcott 2001). Alternatively, Lévinas posits a far more radical alterity between the self and the other. Because the other can never be known in and of itself, one cannot make the other into an object of the self. Therefore subjectivity is essentially ethical: the constitution of the self is at the same time a responsibility towards maintaining the integrity of the other (Lévinas 1969).[8]

Gadamer and Lévinas might seem to provide important prompts on how to situate the Western Academy vis-à-vis non-Western thought. And yet it seems as if in both cases the 'other' is effectively contained within the concrete history of European civilization. Indeed, there is a sense that the 'radical' alterity of non-European 'others' is treated more as a threat than as an opportunity for understanding the European 'self'. This bias can be excavated from Gadamer's writings on translation. His fusion of horizons is, at root, a dialogical engagement between diachronic differences within a given society, especially between past and present meanings of social intercourse. However, Gadamer seems to be far more uncomfortable in dealing with the task of translating between presently existing and differentiated systems of meaning. Ultimately, he contains the threat of synchronous (rather than diachronic) difference by claiming rather offhandedly that the task of translating synchronic differences in meaning 'differs only in degrees and not in kind from the general hermeneutical task that any text represents' (Gadamer 2004, pp. 387–99, 438–40).[9] In a similar vein, David Campbell has outlined the problem that the existence of multiple others presents for Lévinas ' ethics (Campbell 1999, pp. 37–8). When having to ethically negotiate relations between the one and the *many*, Lévinas organizes this task by asking 'Who is closest?'. The closest seems to be those who have historically shared a common cultural experience . . . a European (colonial) experience?

The effective bracketing within European civilization of the ethical response to the problem of the 'other' leads to a tendency to treat the problem of difference as one internal to *the* modern subject understood to universally be the 'sovereign individual' of sociological and economic lore. Once this is assumed, there is no reason why an engagement with non-Western thought should be considered an organic requirement of dealing analytically and ethically with the modern problem of the self/other relation. Instead, there is a tacit assumption that the Western archive is sufficient alone for the task. Again, one does not need to leave home to know the world; the world comes into view once we have already constructed a (European) worldview.

This narcissistic tendency can be gleaned in the collection of French intellectuals that have been labelled, imperfectly, as 'poststructuralists' and who have constructed debates about modernity overwhelmingly by reference to the discrete matter of (an idealized) European thought and history. It is all the more peculiar a tendency when one considers the intimate historical relation between the rise in France of structuralist/poststructuralist thought and the pursuit of decolonization in its colonies. For as Robert Young, Pal Ahluwalia and Alina Sajed have noted, the Algerian war of independence formed a crucial part of the political context in which structuralism and then post-structuralism arose as critiques in the French academy. Algeria, more than anything else, revealed the limits of the assimilatory character of the French singular and sovereign subject, the *citoyen*. One might validly question whether critiques of otherness, difference, irony, mimicry, parody and deconstruction of grand narratives are possible, in large part, because of this evolving post-colonial context (Young 2002; Ahluwalia 2005; Sajed 2011). Seminal intellectuals such as Louis Althusser and Jacques Derrida were born in Algeria and spent formative years there, and in his adult life Michel Foucault spent an important sojourn in neighbouring Tunisia.[10]

Poststructuralism cannot be judged solely on the grounds of its colonial lacuna. And neither should one claim – tritely – that it is impossible to critically inter-rogate non-Western thought through the conceptual frameworks of post-structural authors, for example Foucault and Derrida.[11] Instead, the point is quite simple: that critical European thought in general tends to obfuscate perhaps the foun-dational geo-cultural and geo-political context of modern knowledge production itself – imperial rule and colonial domination. I would argue that shorn of this context, the use of critical European thought to interrogate the 'other' on the global stage can tend to produce a 'concept' driven research agenda rather than a 'problem' driven one. The former leads to an abstract engagement with the universal modern condition (albeit interrogated concretely through the European condition) wherein non-Western experiences can be treated as case studies but not as originary sites of legitimate knowledge production (see Neumann 1999, p. 29; Diez and Steans 2005, p. 138; Grosfoguel 2007). And this, perhaps, reveals how insidiously colonial epistemology works in the Western Academy. To put it provocatively: why is it that recent critical responses to the 'war on terror' in IR can so easily, but curiously, evade the non-Western perspectives of this 'war', and instead use its deadly effects to vindicate the writings of various European intellectuals such as Schmitt, Foucault and Agamben?

However, my argument should not be read as an injunction to let the ideal modern subjecthood of the West go un-interrogated. Rather, armed with this appreciation of the colonial context of the production of the 'other' we might better recognize the transformative impact upon – and tainting of – modernizing Europe by its own various colonial ventures. For example, as Ashis Nandy has illustrated, taking on the identity of the hyper-masculinized colonizer abroad also meant tainting the putatively pristine modern character of the mother country's public sphere with the atavistic affectivities of masochism and desire (1988, pp. xv, 2). We might further recognize that different colonial ventures were embarked upon in the context of different trajectories of development between European polities, leading to different forms of colonialism 'outside', and different return-ing effects 'inside'.[12] Diversity in inter-relation is not only the prerogative of the non-West. And armed with this knowledge, we might be better able to appreciate the progressiveness as well as the limits of radical thinkers within Europe and their negotiation of the interlinkages between class, gender and racism. In this regard, the thought and practice of Sylvia Pankhurst could prove very informative (see Davis 1999). Finally, we might be able to better retrieve the history of colonial domination and the production of the 'other' *within* Europe. Ireland, of course, was the first domain to be colonized by Britain (see, for example, Carroll and King 2003). And possibly the most abiding 'other' within (Christian) European civilization was the Jew. Much critical thought on the modern experience within European thought, we might remember, was developed by German-Jewish intellectuals (e.g. Mendelssohn, Hess, Heine, Marx) and, perhaps, made possible by the agonistic nature of this hyphen.[13] Indeed, it was Albert Memmi's liminal position as a 'native' Jew (and not Muslim) in the French protectorate of Tunisia that, he believed, allowed him to personally experience the identities of both colonizer and colonized (see the preface to 1990).

What I have attempted to show in this section is that an engagement with the terrain of non-Western thought does not need to be an exercise in provincialism, any less than an engagement with critical European thought has to be. But that such an engagement has, so far, received woefully inadequate attention must be understood as part of the effect of Eurocentrism. For Eurocentrism is most evident in the unspoken assumption that we do not need to attempt to travel to intellectual terrains outside of the ideal West, and that all that is required to problematize the modern condition can be found within the Western archive. The solution is not to add non-Western thought into the expanding archive of the Western Academy, for that is a continuation in the intellectual sphere of imperial expansion and colonial rule. Rather, the purpose is to undermine the security of an epistemological cartography that quarantines legitimate knowledge production of modernity to one (idealized) geo-cultural site.

Conclusion

In this chapter I have argued that a reorientation towards non-Western thought is a perilous yet unavoidable enterprise if we are to cultivate a more adequate appreciation of the global context of modernity, that is to say modernity globalized through – and as – colonial and imperial projects. To conclude, I would like to point out the concepts and categories that might be problematized in IR theory specifically, and to which many of the subsequent chapters of this book speak.

First, and at the heart of IR theory, is the nature and exercise of political power. In this respect, non-Western thought might provide new perspectives on the interrelated yet multiple forms of modern sovereignty, of rule by law, of hegemonic rule, and in general of the relationship (if any) between *potentia* and *potestas*. For example, much IR theory is devoted to explaining the form of – and intent behind – power exercised through Western institutions, whether this is explained in terms of imperial power, soft power, bio-politics, governmentality, neoliberal governance, etc. Yet IR theory is exceptionally bad at addressing the ways in which these influences have been incorporated, appropriated, resisted and/or transformed in their 'target' societies. In many ways, IR theory depends upon a fallacy of composition to be made between Western and global forms and technologies of political rule. For example, the fact that some Western societies might be governed through technologies of governmentality does not mean that there exists a Foucauldian world order (Joseph 2009).

Second, non-Western thought might provide novel perspectives on the spatial constructions of modern world order, whether these are understood in terms of empire, international society, core/periphery, or a system of states. In the 1970s Hedley Bull mooted the possibility of the replacement of the society of European states by a neo-medieval patchwork of overlapping authorities. Scholars have recently retrieved this idea in order to make sense of the transformations happening within the European Union and in global governance at large (Friedrichs 2001; Zielonka 2006). And yet surely the type of interconnected plurality of (hierarchical) forms of governance that the phrase 'neo-medieval' intonates is not an idea of a future world order in emergence but more accurately an historical and enduring description of the colonial world!

This leads onto the third point, that non-Western thought problematizes – while not ignoring – the proclaimed historical specificity of modernity that is predicated upon a set of temporal dichotomies: traditional–modern, religious–secular, national–post-national, international–global.[14] It is no exaggeration to say that it is our sense of epochs, eras and conjunctures that determines the kind of violence to the movement of things that we perform in theoretical abstraction. If these dichotomies are problematized, along with their implicit grand narratives, political philosophies of internationalism, cosmopolitanism and humanism might take on different characteristics and with that our sense of what is past, what is possible and what is desirable.

Finally, I would argue that the greatest challenge to IR theory is an abiding one that is endemic to the Western Academy as a whole and all who partake in it. It is by no means a challenge that is born of the global war on terror, nor of the rise of the G20. For the social sciences it delineates the horizon of modernity itself. It is the assumption, best articulated by Hegel, that production of knowledge of modernity is, necessarily, self-reflective production of knowledge of our discrete selves, and vice versa. It is hard to underestimate how central this assumption is to the *raison d'être* of the Western Academy: theorizing modernity *is* the production of ourselves as Western subjects being *the* subjects of human history. I would suggest that, as a whole, IR theory is also caught up in this colonially induced hermeneutic circle. In this respect, Jean-Paul Sartre's guide to the European audience reading Fanon's *Wretched of the Earth* remains the most prescient – and as yet unanswered – provocation:

> After a few steps in the night, you will see strangers gathered round a fire, draw closer, listen: they are discussing the fate they have in store for your trading posts, for the mercenaries who defend them. They will see you perhaps, but they will continue to talk among themselves without even lowering their voices. Their indifference strikes at our hearts . . . Standing at a respectful distance, you will feel furtive, nocturnal, chilled to the bone; everyone has their turn; in this darkness out of which will come a new dawn, you are the zombies.
>
> (Sartre 2001, p. 141)

Notes

1 Here we need think only of Max Weber's instrumental–rational ideal type of modern political authority and Karl Marx's explanation of alienation within the capitalist social relation. See Sayer (1991).
2 On the terms 'context-free' and 'context-sensitive' see Ramanujan (1990) and the sympathetic critique offered by Dallmayr (1994).
3 Even Habermas has recently qualified – if not entirely disowned – his own secularization thesis (Habermas 2008). Linklater (2005) shows the effect of the Habermasian assumption on IR theory when he claims that, even though non-Western communities have in principle the resources to embark on Habermasian-style dialogic politics, Western civilization provides the ideal conditions. For an effective response, see Shani (2007).
4 On the invention of traditions in Chinese philosophy see Defoort (2001).
5 For a critique of this niche see Dirlik (1997). For a critical recovery of the post-colonial project see Young (2002).
6 Clifford is very aware of this point, for example, see Clifford (1992, p. 103).
7 On translational issues regarding the Bible and colonialism see Sugirtharajah (2001).
8 For examples of how Lévinas has been productively used to problematize discourses of geo-politics see Campbell (1999) and Howitt (2002).
9 However, see Dallmayr (1996, pp. 41–6) for comments on Gadamer's subsequent development of a more agonistic understanding of the self–other relationship.
10 To this might be added the influence of Maoism on the French left. With regards to Althusser, see Elliot (2006).
11 See, respectively, the post-colonial work of Said and Spivak.
12 German colonialism is, here, an important consideration to the extent that it was embarked upon as a reaction to a German elite sense of 'backwardness' and 'lateness' *within* European civilization itself. On the specificity of German colonial discourse see Berman (1998).
13 See Chapter 5.
14 My own work has been at least partially caught up in these dichotomies. See, for example, Shilliam (2009, p. 201).

Part I
Colonial conditions

3 On colonial modernity

Civilization versus sovereignty in Cuba, c. 1840

Gerard Aching

Introduction

The point of departure for defining "colonial modernity" in this chapter rests on two premises. The first is that modernity is a global phenomenon that came into being with the emergence of Europe's overseas colonies and empires. The second is that the experience of modernity as colonial domination requires a close examination of local resistance to universalizing discourses, as "enlightened" as these may have been, in the extra-European world. This scrutiny is essential if we are to evaluate modernity as a more extensive phenomenon than the provincialism or chauvinism, for instance, with which Hegel remarks in his introduction to *The Philosophy of History* that "what takes place in America, is but an emanation from Europe" (Hegel 2004, pp. 80–2).

As Western European nations assembled their first overseas possessions in the Americas and exerted sovereignty and influence unilaterally from metropolitan centers to colonies within culturally heterogeneous imperial regimes, a common means of articulating social identities resided in associating with and differentiating between large rival empires. Accordingly, a free man in early nineteenth-century Cuba could identify himself as both a subject of and subjected to the Spanish crown. This, in turn, allowed him to distinguish himself, through a select number of traits and markers, from slaves on the island or from free men in the British, French, or Dutch empires. The principal difficulty in arriving at an account of the current world order appears to be how to shift analysis from the vestiges of a nineteenth-century tradition of understanding modernity as teleological discourses of material, social, and moral "progress" that European empires exported to their colonies as enlightened civilization to an idea of modernity that would incorporate the existence and complexity of subjectivities and forms of sovereignty in the extra-European world.[1]

Given the persistence of the teleological tradition, this shift in focus is least effective when it ontologizes experiences of modernity in isolation from colonial encounters like those that decimated native populations and gave rise to local subjectivities that bore troubled relations, classically portrayed through Shakespeare's Caliban, to Western languages and thought. The practice of regarding modernity in the Caribbean and Latin America as inherently marginal versions of a global modernity is both a consequence of Eurocentrism and heavily reliant on positivist notions of culture that confuse the materiality of modernization with modernity or, in more disconcerting scenarios, measure and describe cultural accomplishments in overwhelmingly infrastructural terms. One of the purposes of this chapter is to illustrate how the idea of a colonial modernity goes beyond the conceptual impasse of routinely assigning marginality to the extra-European world.

In this chapter, the term "colonial modernity" should be understood as both a concept and strategy.[2] As a concept, it is meant to contest the absoluteness of certain dichotomies that have informed the English School's theorization of sovereignty in the international order, such as West/non-West, centre–periphery, modern–backward, by illustrating how these binaries are rooted in historical, Eurocentric notions of "civilization." For instance, Gerrit Gong describes and critiques how European states designated which countries belonged to their community of "civilized" nations. Drawing from historical, legal, and political documents, he furnishes what had generally been assumed as the criteria for belonging to this community (fundamental human rights, adherence to the rule of domestic and international laws, freedom of travel and commerce, and a number of European cultural norms). He argues that even though the standard of "civilization" had not been intended as "a legal device to impose European civilization per se" (Gong 1984, p. 21), its requirements still determined which countries could be included within the international society of "civilized" nations. Gong also acknowledges that although the standard of "civilization" eventually emerged as an explicit legal concept, the latter, like the "doctrine of recognition" that it upheld, succumbed to the conceptual inconsistencies of European exceptionalism: "Drawing the fine lines between a universal standard of civilization, a European standard of 'civilization', and a standard of European civilization was one of the problems of defining and applying the standard of 'civilization' " (Gong 1984, pp. 21–2).

Even though he illustrates his claim about the difficulty of defining this standard in his analyses of how "traditional" East Asian countries were subjected to or subjected themselves to a foreign standard of "civilization" for the sake of "modernization," Gong does not go far enough in his critique of the global reach of the Eurocentric standard. Arguably, it may be unfair to assert that his mediations between "traditional," autochthonous standards of "civilization" in East Asia and a "modern," globalizing, Eurocentric standard fail to elucidate the idea of "civilization" that European nations sought to implant in their (former) colonies in the *Americas* – that is, in those areas over which Western Europe extended its sovereignty for over three centuries and where, with few exceptions, no enduring rivalry for defining an autochthonous standard of "civilization" emerged. Though it is certainly reasonable to call for the application of the historical, Eurocentric standard of "civilization" to Europe itself. In what follows, "colonial modernity" describes the relationship between this standard of "civilization" and slavery.

In order to go beyond binary oppositions that, under the guise of objectivity, camouflage the prevalence of a Eurocentric standard of "civilization" in the assessment of extra-European sovereignties, I employ "colonial modernity" to

interrogate the absence of a teleological or causal link between the global extension of this standard and the creation of a sovereign state, specifically focusing on
Cuba around 1840. My definition of "colonial modernity" can thus be considered
a strategic approach to extra-European sovereignty that partly relies on archival
work in order to render Creole or local attempts to articulate an autochthonous
standard of "civilization" more visible. As such, "colonial modernity" not only
suggests that it is possible to expand and deepen our view of global modernity by
looking towards a colonial past but also that archives, like empirical research and
philosophical reflection, are crucial for the production of theory.

In extending the "modernity" in "colonial modernity" backward instead of
relentlessly forward, it becomes feasible to propose a conception of modernity
that avoids exclusively positivist notions of culture and overdetermined metaphors
of modernizing infrastructures in regional accounts of what constitutes "civilization," national sovereignty, and the modern. "Colonial modernity" does not mean
discarding the importance of modernizing projects, such as nation building; it
simply places them in dialogue with other pertinent factors. As a stance against
the Eurocentric standard of "civilization," "colonial modernity" is intelligible not
as an assertion of absolute dichotomies such as "civilization" versus "barbarism"
(a traditional juxtaposition in Latin American and Caribbean letters), but, in concert with Shilliam's call in the introduction to this volume for recognizing the
co-constitution of Western and non-Western thought, in the close examination
of how the "civilized" and the "uncivilized" emerge simultaneously as both a
local and global phenomenon and as a foundational duplicity. This duplicity is not
inherently Latin American or Caribbean; rather, it originates in a historical hypocrisy that traveled with the European promotion of a standard of "civilization"
in the Americas. Specifically, the simultaneously *legal* and *immoral* nature of
chattel slavery presented an ethical challenge to Spanish sovereignty in the "New
World" for roughly three centuries after the debates about Europe's simultaneous
promotion of Christian doctrine and human bondage in its first overseas colonies.
My study illustrates how Cuba's reformist Creole bourgeoisie grappled with this
inherited hypocrisy and, in perceiving itself as unable to live up to the prevailing
Eurocentric standard of "civilization," rejected national sovereignty.

Although tracing the historical evolution of this foundational duplicity
lies well beyond the scope of this study, it would be worthwhile to point out
some of the contemporary ways in which certain binary oppositions that aim to
describe the Caribbean's and Latin America's place in the world have structured
the regions' intellectual traditions. In light of the advances in science, technology, and a wide range of human activities and knowledge that arose primarily
in Western Europe until around the late eighteenth century, initial attempts at
creating collective identities posited the Americas as Europe's Western frontier
– a designation that loosely conflated notions of physical extension, bounty, and
technical advances with those of limits, thresholds, and insufficiency (Alonso
1998, pp. 8–19; Mignolo 2000, pp. 132–6). Since the early twentieth century, the
cumulative result of this view has been the tendency to define modernity in the
Caribbean and Latin America in terms of hybridities and asymmetries. One of the

contemporary ways in which the field has been simplified can be found in the idea that the perceived heterogeneity that characterizes social life in the Caribbean and Latin America presents evidence of a *peripheral* modernity. It is difficult to overemphasize the degree to which this fundamentally positivist notion of a peripheral modernity continues to occupy the attention of contemporary thinkers, from policy-makers to artists and literary critics in Latin America, the Caribbean, and international forums that devote themselves to researching these regions in a variety of academic disciplines.

How does attention to a so-called peripheral modernity organize thinking about the relationship between the Caribbean, Latin America, and the "developed" world? "Peripheral modernity" postulates two sets of opposed yet interrelated associations. First, when marginality is regarded affirmatively as the regions' most salient feature, foundational discourses have employed keywords such as hybridity, Creolization, and other epistemological categories denotative of heterogeneity and asymmetry in order to measure and assert a relative cultural autonomy.[3] So long as peripheral modernity represents an acknowledgment of the existence and history of uneven relations with the metropolitan center's putatively pure and fully developed modernity, the concept can be used to define a difference that resists that center. "The distinction," according to Carlos Alonso in his study of the rhetoric of cultural discourse in Spanish America, "lies on how to interpret the difference that is characteristic of Spanish American cultural production: is this difference the symptom of an incapacity to fully deploy a given model of development, or is it the trace of an enabling maneuver to negotiate a way out of the strictures imposed by that model?" (Alonso 1998, p. 48). As either "symptom" or "trace," this attitudinal and methodological distinctiveness is understandably reactive since it emerges from colonial contexts that could not entirely transform local difference into metropolitan sameness. Like Alonso, García Canclini understands the failure of adapting to metropolitan models as an erroneous measurement of Latin America's modernity against "optimized images" of modernizing processes in metropolitan centers (Canclini 2005, p. 44). In this sense, a peripheral modernity, then, reiterates the shifting, ambiguous confluence of insufficiency and excess at the same time that the term may be employed to invoke an enabling difference. This first set of connotations posits the peripheral as an unprecedented site and temporality for establishing an autochthonous and empowering notion of the modern beyond center–periphery and modern–backward distinctions by blurring, as Shilliam asserts in the introduction with regard to Creolization, the geo-cultural boundaries of the West and the non-West.

The perceived asymmetries of Western modernity's American frontiers also inform the second set of meanings that the term "peripheral" generates. However, this assessment of the regions' apparently uneven development interprets the simultaneous presence of surpluses and scarcities as evidence of faulty or failed projects of modernization. In contradistinction to Martí's optimistic account of the novelty of "advanced and consolidated" nations having come into being in "less historical time," a negative view of peripheral modernity would consider the Cuban intellectual's observations as proof of temporal disjunctures and material insufficiencies that hinder and destabilize "proper" development. Consequently, pre-modern vestiges, instances of technical obsolescence, and other objects and phenomena purportedly lying outside the forward march of modern "civilization" were considered obstacles, especially during the second half of the nineteenth century and the early half of the twentieth, to the creation of modernizing projects whose temporal and material uniformity would be analogous to those of Western metropolitan centres.[4] This negative assessment is more prone than the first view of peripheral modernity to considering "the modern" to be external to the historical experiences of the Caribbean and Latin America. As long as asymmetries are persistently cited as inadequacies in this disapproving view, these regions remain subjected to the perennial recruitment of social and economic resources in order to attain the status of the "developed world." "Like Sisyphus," Gong remarks, "the less 'civilized' were doomed to work towards an equality which an elastic standard of 'civilization' put forever beyond their reach" (Gong 1984, p. 63).

The principal shortcoming of the idea of peripheral modernity in its current usage is not its ambiguity per se – for this has clearly been instrumental in generating debates about the meanings of progress – but its weak duplicity. The idea fails to address how progress is rendered intelligible in the western hemisphere and, in failing to do so, ends up reproducing itself as "an inverted Eurocentrism that cannot resolve the crisis of inequality" (San Juan 2002, p. 229). When Fredric Jameson claims that Jürgen Habermas's view of modernity as an unfinished project is "usefully ambiguous," the former refers in the first instance to the inability of the middle class and its modes of production to complete this project and, by extension, to the incomplete status of the Enlightenment's emancipatory goals (Jameson 2002, p. 11). This notion of incompleteness coheres as a strong ambiguity because it allows for critiques of modernity that range widely, for example, from Walter Benjamin's reminder that the documents of modern civilization also portend barbarism to Robert Bernasconi's and Susan Buck-Morss's more recent arguments that even though Enlightenment thinkers did not engage with pervasive social practices that patently contradicted their ideas, such as racism and slavery, their emancipatory ideals are still worth pursuing (see Benjamin's seventh thesis in 1985; Buck-Morss 2000, pp. 821–65; Bernasconi 2003, pp. 13–22). By contrast, the current theoretical weakness of "peripheral modernity" arises from its inability to go beyond descriptive, teleological statements about material progress: it offers no concerted philosophical project that accounts for and critiques experiences of modernity in the Caribbean and Latin America.[5] Rather, the instrumentality of its ambiguities has been geared toward locating and measuring these regions according to a scale of modern achievements whose referents are limited to Europe and North America; the idea still remains removed from any consistent and rigorous critique of regional attachments to a global modernity in the making.

This chapter does not propose a philosophical project that engages with non-metropolitan views of modernity, "civilization," and sovereignty, for such a worthwhile undertaking exceeds this study's potential contribution to the analytical shift from Eurocentric to global modernity that I mentioned earlier. In what follows, my argument proceeds in three stages. First, I examine the claim that European empires exported an idea of modern civilization that was instrumental for establishing models of national sovereignty in the extra-European world. Second, I describe and interrogate the meaning of modern civilization as Cuba's Creole reformist bourgeoisie reflected on the pitfalls of national sovereignty during the 1840s; for the sake of historical accuracy, the term that the Creole bourgeoisie employed to evaluate the peculiar configurations of the universal and the particular that emerged in their colonial environment was not "modernity" but "civilization" (Mazlish 2004, p. 12). Finally, I close by briefly placing the Cuban example in the broader field of colonial modernity in the Atlantic world.

Civilization and colonialism

In *Beyond the Anarchical Society*, Edward Keene argues for a more comprehensive understanding of the modern international order than that which the influential English School of international relations began elaborating in the 1950s.[6] Drawing from its historical studies of European states systems, the English School theorized the organization of international affairs on the basis of this continent's experience of nation formation and global dominance, and concluded that the "normative structure" of the modern world order relied on a "principle of internal freedom" whereby states established agreements that respected "their common interest in mutual independence" (Keene 2002, p. 22). The mutual toleration of territorial sovereignty lay at the heart of this modern view of world order, and Keene's study goes beyond Gong's by introducing the practice of toleration into his description of an international order. In addition to critiquing the English School's projection of idealized relations between European states as a model for organizing international affairs in the rest of the world, Keene makes a convincing case for the existence and importance of a second pattern of international order that was predicated not on toleration but on the promotion of "civilization" in the extra-European world:

> The concept of civilization performed two roles in international legal thought: it defined the border between the two patterns of modern international order, and it described the ultimate purposes that the extra-European order was for. This vision of a bifurcated world was fully developed by the middle of the nineteenth century, and one can see in international legal texts from that period a widely accepted distinction between the family of civilized nations and the backward or uncivilized world beyond.
>
> (Keene 2002, pp. 6–7)

The international political and legal order was thus split into two patterns whose purposes – toleration or civilization – were (and are) frequently at odds; this opposition was especially the case, as I show later, in the designation of which communities belonged to the "family of civilized nations" or to the "uncivilized world beyond" Europe.

In order to appreciate what belonging to this "family" implied, it is necessary to understand what was meant by "civilization." Citing John Stuart Mill's work as a point of departure, Keene states that the two main elements that informed the nineteenth-century understanding of civilization were material development (economic and technological progress) and a moral component that relied on the presence of an educated, refined population and good government based on just and effective political, judicial, and administrative systems (Keene 2002, p. 112). According to Keene, the material and moral aspects of the idea of civilization that Europe exported to its colonies underwrote imperial and colonial systems that divided sovereignty across borders and enforced individuals' rights to their "persons and property" (Keene 2002, p. 6). Moreover, both elements were assumed to be constitutive of civilization either as a state of affairs – as for example in Europe, where these aspects were purportedly achieved in full – or as a process in which the material and moral dimensions of civilization remained perennially elusive. Needless to say, as Keene shows, the borders of the civilized world were constantly in flux as new nations entered the "family of civilized nations" in the nineteenth and twentieth centuries and as racial theories increasingly became the pseudo-scientific means by which the frontiers of "civilization" or its potential could be drawn or withdrawn.

Keene persuasively argues that orthodox theories of international order fail to explain modern world politics when they focus too narrowly on the European states system. This argument implicitly critiques Gong's distinction between "traditional" and "modern." But although Keene's contention that the world was divided into two patterns of order represents a significant contribution to understanding configurations of sovereignty outside Europe, it cannot be assumed that the idea of civilization that the extra-European world assimilated necessarily led to nation-building projects or political autonomy and sovereignty. This statement does not refute Keene's argument that toleration and civilization were "fundamentally different purposes of international order, and the effort to realize both at the same time has led to serious tensions, or even contradictions' (Keene 2002, p. 148). But a supplemental claim is required: that the promotion of "civilization," especially in colonized areas of the western hemisphere during the nineteenth century such as Cuba, could also be internally destructive to nation-building and attempts at establishing sovereignty. The island's prosperous Creole bourgeoisie, which was the community that most clearly possessed the wealth to pursue political autonomy and membership to the "family of civilized nations" in the 1840s, consistently refused to strike out for independence.

One of the clues to this paradox lay in the stark contrast between Cuba's relatively high degree of material and technological modernization and its colonial status. This contrast serves as a counterpoint to the notions that modernization invariably emanates from Europe and serves as an adequate measure of modernity. For instance, Manuel Moreno Fraginals describes the suppression of the island's bid for its (and Spanish America's) first university chair in political economy in 1818 as the Creole bourgeoisie's first major setback as a class (he lyrically refers to its dilemma as the problem of possessing a "soaring bourgeois consciousness with clipped wings"[7]). It rearranges contemporary mental maps of the modern to discover that this episode occurred seven years before the first chair in this field was established at an English university (Oxford) (Hilton 2001, p. 41). The importance of this reference to political economy cannot be overemphasized. If wealth determined access to modern civilization, then, by most mid-century economic indicators, the island's Creole bourgeoisie certainly had good reason to want to examine its own economic expansion. Because of the enormous wealth that poured into Cuba as it replaced Haiti as the world's largest sugar producer, the Creole bourgeoisie began by the 1830s to compete with its Spanish counterparts, both on the island and in the Peninsula, and soon established close commercial ties with English, French, and American manufacturing and trade networks. Such was the rivalry between the Creole bourgeoisie and the Spanish colonial administration that Captain-General Tacón opposed railway construction in Havana during his administration because he was determined that the colony should not enjoy this technology before Spain did. Nevertheless, Latin America's first railway was constructed in Cuba.

Rather than simply offer evidence of modernization, the material advances that I have just mentioned cannot be fully appreciated without incorporating the Creole bourgeoisie's awareness of the gap between its economic prowess and colonial subjugation. In *Spectres of the Atlantic*, Ian Baucom couples material wealth and self-reflection when he avers that even though it is certain that the birth of the modern subject in the Enlightenment may be attributed to the emergence of abstract speculative reason, its birthplace is the speculative finance capital that characterized the circum-Atlantic trade in manufactured goods, slaves, and primary commodities that we call the Great Triangle (Baucom 2005, p. 55). According to Baucom, both forms of speculation represent conditions of possibility for "an overarching speculative revolution" that organizes abstract reason and finance capital (Baucom 2005, p. 56). The slave trade provided the engine for this financial revolution because slaves functioned as commodities for sale as well as the "reserve deposits of a loosely organized, decentered, but vast trans-Atlantic banking system" (Baucom 2005, pp. 61–2). Because this system was historically constructed as a *circuit* of transactions and influences, the place of the Caribbean in this system during the nineteenth century does not render the region peripheral to or backward within this speculative revolution. In other words, the problem that Cuba's Creole bourgeoisie faced in locating itself within modern civilization was not economic and technical underdevelopment, but how to equip their evident wherewithal with speculative reason worthy of their place and circumstances. Herein lies a second clue to the Creole bourgeoisie's paradoxical political behavior: chattel slavery, the very labor regime that helped to provide the bourgeoisie with its enormous margins of profit, was also the Achilles heel of its prospects for political autonomy.

The Creole bourgeoisie, and especially its reformist sector, did not speculate openly about slavery and universal freedom because, on one hand, the colonial government did not permit it to do so and, on the other, because it refrained from addressing slavery's moral issues at the expense of its own bids to negotiate greater, but not absolute, political autonomy from Spain. The local bourgeoisie was unwilling to fathom universal freedom if the latter meant that it would need to divest itself of its rights to the ownership of human property. If, as Keene asserts, spreading the idea of civilization across the globe involved attaching individuals' rights to "persons and property," then these economic rights to human property also rationalized the relationship between civilization and slavery in Cuba. Legal codes defined slaves as property, and property within commercial liberalism constituted the very foundation of the bourgeoisie's economic "freedom."[8] Several Spanish governments knowingly took advantage of this economic and moral entanglement by encouraging the contraband slave trade and thereby furthering their geo-political approaches to Cuba.[9] In 1837, the Spanish minister, Calatrava, was reported to have said that preserving slavery in Cuba was analogous to having an army of 100,000 men there to deter Cuba from seeking independence (Corwin 1967, pp. 65–6). Cuba's reformist Creole bourgeoisie could not separate the simultaneously *legal* and *immoral* nature of a significant portion of its income from its bid to join "the family of civilized nations." Its "clipped wings" can thus be seen as the result of colonial domination and a self-inflicted wound: this sector of the local bourgeoisie refused to consider emancipating its slaves as a means of freeing itself from Madrid's ploy to keep the island supplied with slaves, and Spanish governments counted on this refusal in order to retain the colony. As this volume frequently shows, such circumstances of colonial domination need to be taken into consideration if we are to evaluate the local and global production of knowledge about modernity, "civilization," and sovereignty and require a different narrative from that proffered by the English School and even by Keene's critical stance of the latter. In the following section, I interrogate how the bourgeoisie's adherence to the idea of modern civilization that it assimilated from European sources created a stumbling block for nation building and sovereignty.

"Civilized" nationhood versus sovereignty

In a letter that they wrote from New York on September 12, 1834, the Cuban exiles Félix Varela (a philosophy professor and priest) and Tomás Gener (a wealthy Catalonian plantation owner) strongly advised Domingo del Monte against translating and publishing Charles Comte's *Traité de legislation* in Cuba.[10] Comte, a respected law professor and Permanent Secretary of the Académie des Sciences Morales et Politiques in Paris, published his treatise in 1826 on the purported natural and moral laws that determined the conditions for the advancement of peoples across the globe. Del Monte, a wealthy patrician and reformist member of the Creole bourgeoisie, probably became familiar with sections of the treatise at the gatherings of Cuban intellectuals around Varela in New York and Philadelphia in 1829. Apart from Comte's assertion that warm climates do not produce the effects on people that have been attributed to them and that the inhabitants of cold countries are generally no freer, more active, nor more virtuous than those from warmer climes, the most important section of the study for del Monte and his colleagues was the last book of the treatise which tackles the subject of slavery. During Captain-General Miguel Tacón's administration (1834–1838), writing about slavery in Cuba was practically outlawed. According to Varela's and Gener's letter, del Monte had expressed interest in translating Comte's study in order to slip the discussion of slavery into the open and canvas enlightened support for abolishing the slave trade on the island.

The importance of Varela's and Gener's letter resides in the clarity with which it reveals the moral quagmire in which the Creole reformists found themselves on the question of slavery. Even though this influential minority within the local bourgeoisie opposed the contraband slave trade, it is crucial to underscore that they did not entertain an abolitionist agenda.[11] This refusal to accept abolitionism is significant because it distinguished the Creole reformists, as members of the local bourgeoisie, from the abolitionist Quaker bourgeoisie in England and the United States. Given the fact that abolitionism is normally regarded as responsible for stimulating subsequent democratic liberalisms and movements that are identified with modernity, such as women's suffrage and working-class rights in the Anglo-American context, the Cuban Creole bourgeoisie's dilemmas have not, to my knowledge, been approached as a manifestation of the same modernity. The required level of abstraction in order to belong to the modern world is also a crucial consideration here: whereas many abolitionists in the United States and England conceived of legally enslaved subjects *in other places* in abstract terms, the Creole bourgeoisie lived in close proximity to their slaves. Varela and Gener capture the difficulty of sustaining this proximity in two statements that they juxtapose in their missive. In the first of these, they maintain: "in many places, it is openly said that it is an injustice to claim freedom for whites and deny it to blacks" (del Monte 2002, p. 368);[12] in the second statement, they assert, as they put it, the widely known but suppressed truth that in Cuba "the blacks' enslavement is the cause of the whites' enslavement. The people know it all too well, and the government knows it all too well" (del Monte 2002, p. 368).

This conscious move from, on one hand, acknowledging the debate about the universal extension of freedoms to, on the other, affirming that chattel slavery enslaved the island's white population articulates a necessarily ambiguous response to the spread of a modern notion of civilization across the Atlantic world. The Creole bourgeoisie's experience of cultural domination did not allow them to assume the critical distance from and abstract engagement with slavery that their socioeconomic counterparts enjoyed in the metropolis. It was not the case that Valera and Gener were less enlightened or "civilized" than metropolitan politicians and intellectuals; as exiled colonials, they were routinely denied the status of being regarded as pertinent contributors to the definition of their community.

As members of a wealthy and informed Creole bourgeoisie that was cosmopolitan in its outlook and commerce, these "young liberals," as they liked to call themselves, possessed the wherewithal to weigh in on such debates. However, rather than eagerly join a discussion that would have allowed them to assume their place as members of a revolutionary, international bourgeoisie – as Marx and Engels would unambiguously refer to this class fourteen years later in the first *Communist Manifesto* – they chose, instead, to assume a moral position that they substantiated on the basis of local circumstances and experience. Their rhetorical move thus contests the commonplace that colonies seamlessly constitute a *telos* for the uncontested expansion of Enlightenment liberalisms. The "young liberals" were, after all, slave owners *and* colonial subjects, who blamed slavery and colonialism for subjugating their class. Yet it is not coincidental that at the same time that the Creole reformists refused to emancipate their slaves, thereby curtailing the full extension of the emancipatory discourses with which they became familiar, they also rejected political autonomy as they deliberated between conserving their colonial status and promoting annexation to the United States.[13] Let us examine this entanglement more closely.

The reformists' willingness to place sovereignty in the hands of other nations appears as a social contradiction in *El Ingenio* (*The Sugar Mill*), Moreno Fraginals's seminal economic history of the Cuban sugar industry. Describing the first element of this contradiction, Fraginals writes

> thanks to his political savvy and wealth, José Luis Alfonso, the Creole sugarocracy's preeminent figure, can be found spearheading a movement of annexation to the United States at the start of the 1840s in light of the fear that the conservative English government might oblige Spain to adopt an abolitionist attitude toward slavery.
>
> (Fraginals 2001, p. 459)

It is worth noting that the reformist bourgeoisie calls for annexation from a position of great economic strength and technical modernization. Alfonso belonged to the Alfonso-Aldama clan, a prominent family of the Creole bourgeoisie whose economic clout had little to envy its American and English counterparts. By 1860, this family's third generation had diversified its economic ties and interests; it owned forty sugar plantations with no fewer than 15,000 slaves as well as banking, insurance, railway, and shipping firms. The family possessed ten titles of nobility and married into wealthy European families, including that of the Bourbon royal house in Spain. In outlook and attitude, the Alfonso-Aldama family and similar clans acted like the bourgeoisie from other parts of the world. The wealth that these families moved and the leadership of several of them in the humanitarian effort against the slave trade (but never against slavery itself) were analogous to the wherewithal of the Quaker businessmen in London, whose anti-slavery committee meetings took place after the Royal Exchange closed at the end of every business day.

Solid economic reasons encouraged the Creole bourgeoisie to promote the annexation to the United States at this time. Not only was its northern neighbor Cuba's most significant market in the hemisphere, but it was one of its main partners in the economic liberalism that the island's sugarocracy fomented in spite of its colonial status – that is, it was American ships supplying Cuba with slaves that gave the Creole bourgeoisie some of its most extensive experience in free trade up to that time. According to Fraginals, the fear of an expanding abolitionism in Europe urged Alfonso and the rest of the Creole reformists to pursue annexation.

And there were clear signs that abolitionism was gaining ground in Europe: Britain abolished slavery in its overseas colonies in 1834, and Spain eliminated its last vestiges on the Peninsula in 1836. When it became clear that Spain's remaining provinces of the Philippines, Cuba, and Puerto Rico would henceforth be banned from the Cortes and ruled as colonies beginning in 1834, the Creole bourgeoisie realized that they had lost their constitutional ability to represent and defend its slavery-based economic welfare in Madrid. In this scenario, the Creole bourgeoisie chose not to strike out for political autonomy from Spain, but to explore annexation to the United States.

Alfonso's activism also provides the second element of the contradiction that Fraginals cites in his study. The historian notes

> Toward the end of the same 1840s, with the free trade policy already inaugurated and the antislavery movement beginning to be dismantled [in Cuba], one finds the same José Luis Alfonso paying for the publication of antiannexationist pamphlets, thereby abandoning the ship that he captained and leaving the literary annexationists penniless.
>
> (Fraginals 2001, p. 459)

When it had become clear that Spanish economic reforms facilitated more free trade opportunities for Cuban sugar producers and the colonial administration had brutally eliminated the anti-slavery threat that allegedly gave rise to the so-called Escalera Conspiracy of 1844, the Creole bourgeoisie settled back into the imperial fold.[14] That Alfonso began the decade promoting annexation to the United States and ended it reaffirming Cuba's colonial relationship with Spain is typically explained as the bourgeoisie's hypocritical and opportunistic attitude toward the nation-state. From Marx's and Engels's statement in the *Communist Manifesto* that the bourgeoisie's "need of a constantly expanding market for its products chases [it] over the entire surface of the globe" to Franz Fanon's more contemporary claims that the bourgeoisie is a *hesitant* nation builder, there is a long tradition of social analysis that posits this class as frequently more concerned with its economic welfare than with patriotism and political sovereignty (Marx and Engels 2005, pp. 32–3).[15] But there is more to this paradox than mere duplicity: even though Alfonso's shift from annexation to the reassertion of Cuba's colonial status appears to be a classic case of bourgeois hypocrisy, it is essential to point out that political autonomy was out of the question during this period so long as the Creole bourgeoisie remained convinced that independence would mean sharing power with a sizable number of former slaves and free blacks and mulattos.

The Creole bourgeoisie's notion of "civilized" nationhood foreclosed the possibility of sharing political power with these sectors of the local population because, even though the material requirements for introducing Cuba into the "family of civilized nations" were evidently fulfilled, significant moral issues remain unresolved. What the idea of civilization as the undisturbed, global spread of certain ideals of material and moral "progress" emanating from Europe hides from view is the degree to which these ideals encountered resistance from communities that were even the most materially prepared to embrace them. Stated more specifically, on what civilizing, moral grounds could the reformist bourgeoisie stand if it continued to enslave human beings? The "young liberals" avoided resolving this inherited dilemma directly. As they could not assume an abolitionist stance without committing financial suicide, reformism – that is, the plan to abolish the slave trade but not slavery – allowed them to negotiate a degree of civility without substantially impairing their economic welfare. Reform not only slowed the spread of enlightened, abolitionist thinking on the island, but also gave its adherents time to prepare for a moment in the future when the struggle for independence would become feasible. In the meantime, they eluded the moral question of universal freedom by turning to local, technical measures that would purportedly have allowed them to ready themselves for political autonomy. As early as 1835, José Antonio Saco, the Creole bourgeoisie's most outspoken ideologue, asserted that any thought of abolishing the slave trade would need to be accompanied by an effective program of white settlement because "upon it depends the advancement of agriculture, artistic perfection, in a word, Cuban prosperity in all branches" (Saco 1935a, p. 32). Such was Saco's desire for Cuba to belong to the advanced, "civilized" nations of the world that two years later, in pronouncing against Spanish colonialism, he wistfully envied Canada's "chain of golden links" under British rule (Saco 1935b, pp. 35–6). In effect, what the Creole reformists unquestioningly conceded was that it was to whiteness, which they associated with prosperity and moral uprightness, that modern civilization accrued.

As the "young liberals" saw it, one of the pressing challenges that they faced became that of imagining Cuban nationhood given the racially heterogeneous, colonial society to which they belonged. There were no paradigms for considering this degree of racial heterogeneity and range of legally free and enslaved subjects and communities in the universalizing discourses about civilization that they adopted from Europe. Yet even the idea of modern civilization with which the reformists engaged as they speculated about the island's future was neither pure nor seamless. Mazlish documents how shortly after the modern notion of civilization appeared in Europe during the Enlightenment, a notion of culture arose to compete with it. In the early stages of the new usage, "civilization" was identified with the "cold, calculating, mechanical, and universalizing way of thinking embodied, supposedly, in the Enlightenment and in revolutionary France," whereas *Kultur*, as philosophers such as Johann Herder conceived it, was "rooted in the blood, land, and unique history of a particular people, the *Volk*" (Mazlish 2004, p. 21). According to Mazlish, both terms constituted attempts to "restore meaning" to societies in the throes of radical socioeconomic transformations at the end of the eighteenth century (Mazlish 2004, p. 21). Hence, the distinction between a hegemonic universalism and a resistant, cultural particularity was already associated with the modern usage of "civilization" before it became exportable to other regions of the world. What, then, was required in order to render "civilization" an exportable colonial ideology?

By the first decades of the nineteenth century, two significant changes had taken place within the concept of civilization. First, the tolerant eighteenth-century cosmopolitanism that acknowledged and compared civilizations gradually gave way to a Eurocentric racism, such as Gobineau's in *Essai sur l'inégalité des races humaines* (1853–1855), which turned the concept of civilization into "an obstacle to any real understanding of the other" (Mazlish 2004, p. 46). Second, as Keene implies in his reference to Mill's ideas on civilization, the term appears to have absorbed the conflict between the material and the moral that respectively pitted "civilization" against "culture" in Europe during the Enlightenment. By relegating European cultural specificities to the background, the concept assumed a level of abstraction and "universality" that facilitated its export. A consequence of the engagement with this abstraction by local communities such as that of Cuba's Creole bourgeoisie was the creation of an autochthonous, white "fictive ethnicity," the purpose of which was not to specify racial features – this would come later in the century with the emergence of pseudo-scientific racism – but to promote socioeconomic agendas that would advance "civilization" and indigenize it for the local bourgeoisie.[16]

A second consequence of engaging with an abstract notion of enlightened civilization was the "young liberals' " concerted efforts to create a local counter-discourse (like Herder's association of blood, land, and the unique history of a people with *Kultur*) that would allow them to assume and represent a unique identity within the "family of civilized nations." These reformists strove unsuccessfully to liberate their literary activities from official censorship, but they were, from within the private sanctuary of Domingo del Monte's literary circle, responsible for the island's first collective experiments to produce a local literature that would attest to the civility that they required for national sovereignty and, at the same time, provide critiques of colonialism and slavery. As I previously mentioned, the reformists saw themselves as the primary victims of colonial rule, and it is on this basis that they refrained from accepting responsibility for maintaining their slaves in bondage.

It is therefore by no means arbitrary that the claim that slavery enslaved the Creole bourgeoisie also gave rise to memorable protagonists in Cuba's first novels. I would contend that the internal contradiction that hindered the Creole reformist bourgeoisie from attaining "civilized" nationhood finds its exact representation in ambiguous yet stoic characters like Anselmo Suárez y Romero's Francisco (from *Francisco*, New York, 1880), Gertrudis Gómez de Avellaneda's Sab (from *Sab*, Madrid, 1841), and Antonio Zambrana's Francisco (from *El negro Francisco*, Santiago de Chile, 1873). These narratives found their inspiration in Juan Francisco Manzano's *Autobiography of a Slave* (London, 1840), which is the only slave narrative that has thus far surfaced in the Spanish-speaking world. With their attention to local landscapes, plantation life, slavery, and the moral dilemmas that slavery presented, the novels that the circle's members wrote were published in several countries, but not in Cuba until the twentieth century. This literary outburst has been described as the Creole bourgeoisie's swan song because it captured the complex internal contradictions of a community that failed, despite its economic prowess and splendor, to achieve autonomy for the island. Rather than providing evidence of a marginal modernity, this failure makes sense in light of an idea of "civilization" that promoted moral uprightness in the colony at the same time that it made a national sovereignty, shared with former slaves and free blacks and mulattos, an undesirable means of collective self-realization.

The Atlantic space of colonial modernity

The modernity that I have described as colonial is definable not as stark oppositions between center and periphery, metropolis and colony, but through circuits of social and economic activities, transactions, and influences. To imagine colonial modernity in these terms allows us to avoid the problems of one-sidedness in Eurocentric accounts of modernity, as E. San Juan, Jr. argues (2002, pp. 223–4), by theorizing "[p]arallel or coeval modernities . . . within a differentiated, not centralized, ontology of determinate and concrete social formations." Such circuits are built on relations of power in multiple sites. Even though Fredric Jameson declares that the fundamental meaning of modernity is global capitalism, his view of global modernities is concerned less with their simultaneous existence in multiple sites than with the arguments for difference that the "ideologues of 'modernity' " champion:

> The answer is simple: you can talk about 'alternative' or 'alternative' modernities. Everyone knows the formula by now: this means that there can be a modernity for everybody which is different from the standard or hegemonic Anglo-Saxon model. Whatever you dislike about the latter, including the subaltern position it leaves you in, can be effaced by the reassuring and 'cultural' notion that you can fashion your own modernity differently, so that there can be a Latin-American kind, or an Indian kind or an African kind, and so forth.
> (Jameson 2002, p. 12)

Despite its cynical delivery, Jameson's point about the pitfalls of autonomous difference is well taken. But in my view, the concept of colonial modernity retains a critique of capitalism at the same time that it is inclusive of the ways in which modern life has historically been experienced in multiple areas of the globe. Historians of the Atlantic world have never lost sight of these circuits; and seminal works, such as James's *The Black Jacobins* (1938/1962), Benítez-Rojo's *La isla que se repite* (1989), Glissant's *Poétique de la relation* (1990), Gilroy's *The Black Atlantic* (1993), and Baucom's *Spectres of the Atlantic* (2005) provide powerful reminders that the movement of bodies, goods, finance, and ideas substantiated the centrality of the Atlantic world in studies of modernity. Yet, as I have shown, it is not enough to limit our understanding of colonial modernity to the reach of modern infrastructures, no matter how decentralized and competitive these modernizing projects might have been. I would like to close this chapter by summarizing two claims that elucidate this assertion.

The first claim to which I have gestured and now wish to state outright is that the Atlantic world in which Western Europe established its first overseas colonies emerged as a social space that was subjected to special laws. Rather than being viewed as potentially sovereign lands with autonomous colonial subjects, these colonies were treated as proto-states of exception in which, for example, activities such as slavery that eventually became illegal in the metropolis were sanctioned in the colonies for purely economic reasons.[17] Cuba's Creole bourgeoisie directly experienced the impact of the distinction between, on one hand, the growing opinion in Europe that slavery was both immoral *and* illegal and, on the other, the protection that the practice enjoyed under colonial rule; yet this community refused to consider the abolition of slaves as a means of freeing itself from the hypocrisy of a distinction that was imposed from Madrid and ultimately lucrative for what remained of the Spanish empire and for itself in the 1840s. In other words, this hypocrisy is shared, mutually though unevenly constitutive of the relations between metropolis and colony, and illustrative of the unsustainability of absolute distinctions between "center" and "periphery" within a transatlantic network of, as Baucom puts it, an "overarching speculative revolution." Keene's discussion of the extension of "civilizing" projects to Europe's colonies clearly sets the stage for analyses such as the one above, but it does not fathom how calls for enlightened moral conduct in the Americas also led to competing proposals for sovereignty. In *Moral Capital*, Christopher Brown documents how the Philadelphia Quakers in 1775 were the first group in the Anglo-Atlantic world to dedicate itself to anti-slavery principles (Brown 2006, p. 108). The year is significant because it shows how the North American campaign for independence increasingly made chattel slavery a moral issue, especially as the advocates of independence understood the degree to which slavery constituted a political liability against the English. Hence, when Varela and Gener declared from their exile in New York in the 1820s that the discussion of freedom for both blacks and whites was being heard "in many places" – through and along, as it were, a network of transatlantic relations – it should not be assumed that this debate either originated in or referred solely to Europe.

The final claim about colonial modernity that I want to clarify is that because internal contradictions are constitutive of it, these duplicities provide windows of opportunity for assessing the affective distance between a community's ideals of its autonomy and its inability to attain them. Colonial modernity can thus be conceived as an experience of subjugation – analogous to but not a mere duplicate of a "universal" modern subjectivity – that presses communities and individuals to reflect on and define their place in the world. Unique bids for and experiments with sovereignty emerged from the frustrations of a colonial bourgeoisie that saw itself enslaved by slavery, in the case of mid-nineteenth-century Cuba, or vilified, in the Anglo-American context, as "degenerate American colonists" on whom the moral responsibility for slavery lay, which is to say, "only on the western side of the Atlantic" (Brown 2006, p. 152). Consequently, colonial modernity is not an inherently peripheral version of "metropolitan modernity" but an experience of subjugation, thwarted contestation, and similar engagements between rulers and their subjects that held out perilous yet creative possibilities for autonomous action and for sovereignty.

Notes

1 Bruce Mazlish (2004, pp. 1–19) documents how, even though the reified noun "civilization" had its roots in European colonial expansion, the term became a neologism during the Enlightenment.

2 Mignolo employs the term "coloniality" to refer to the "coexistence and the intersection of both modern colonialisms and colonial modernities . . . from the perspective of people and local histories that have to confront modern colonialism"; he also calls coloniality the "reverse and unavoidable side of 'modernity' – its darker side . . ." (Mignolo 2000, p.22). In my usage of the term "colonial modernity," I do not distinguish between modernity and colonialism, which brings the term closer to Mignolo's theorization of "coloniality."

3 These concepts represent some of the most frequently cited commonplaces in the region's intellectual and artistic production. García Canclini (2005) provides a useful discussion of some of these terms. An important contribution to the positive valorization of heterogeneous cultural formations was Fernando Ortiz's (1963) introduction of the term *"transculturación"* (transculturation) in order to deepen discussions of a cultural anthropology of the late 1930s that understood cultural encounters and interrelations from the purview of the term "acculturation." Other seminal elaborations of or commentaries on this line of thought include Glissant (1981, 1990), Rama (1982), Benítez-Rojo (1998), and Bernabé *et al.* (1989).

4 For a discussion of the emergence of this purview, see Larrain (2000, pp. 70–91). The perception in both Americas during the nineteenth century that "progress" implied the immediate or gradual elimination of sectors of the national population (such as the wars against indigenous communities in the United States, Argentina, and elsewhere and the agendas to introduce European immigrants in order to whiten the local population in Cuba and in politically autonomous regions in the Americas) as well as the idealizing aestheticization of the autochthonous from romanticism to the avant-garde represent *treatments* of national "others" in the name of modernizing and civilizing projects of nationhood. In his critique of the post-colonial fetishism of hybridity, Creolization, and syncretism, San Juan (2002, p. 232) argues that "unsynchronized and asymmetrical formation" provided an ideal context for magical realism.

5 Liberation theology is one of the few areas that undertook, as Enrique Dussel avers, a critical philosophy that located itself self-consciously on the periphery. See Dussel (2001, p. 442).

6 Keene does not propose that critiquing the English School means refuting their historical sources outright; he returns to Hugo Grotius's seventeenth-century account of the law of nations in order to transcend the conventional uses to which the Dutch lawyer's seminal ideas about international relations had been put, and he provides a reading of Grotius's ideas that would instead be applicable to a world political order in which colonial experiences can be taken into consideration.

7 See Fraginals (2001, p. 115). The late Moreno Fraginals, Cuba's renowned economic historian, also alluded to the sugarocracy's disillusionment in these terms: " . . . not being able to teach the true economics of the period in it [America] demonstrates the terrible frustration of a class that tried but could not be bourgeois." All translations from this text are mine.

8 According to David Brion Davis, this conflation made it extremely difficult for abolitionists to push for the separation of property and human rights. See Davis (1975, pp. 267–8).

9 Spain and England signed a treaty abolishing the Atlantic slave trade in 1817. For more on this treaty and the intricacies of the Anglo-Spanish diplomatic negotiations over the slave trade, consult Corwin (1967) and Murray (2002, Chapters 4–6).

10 The full title of Comte's treatise is *Traité de Legislation, ou Exposition des Lois*

Générales suivant lesquelles les peuples prospèrent, dépérissent, ou restent stationnaires.

11 For more on the relation between abolitionism and the political liberalisms that the former helped to generate, see Brown (2006) and Hochschild (2006).

12 All quotes from this text are my translation.

13 According to Rafael Rojas, even though independence was not among the liberals' aims, "colonial liberalism in Cuban political culture, like that of a monarchical liberalism in English, French, and Spanish political cultures, is perfectly imaginable and demonstrable." See Rojas (1998, p. 40; my translation). In other words, colonial liberalism without independence was not a deficiency but a studied option and agenda.

14 Backed by the British and Foreign Anti-Slavery Society, David Turnbull was appointed the British consul in Havana in 1840. His activities in Cuba as well as the general alarm at the presence of this influential abolitionist on the island were partly responsible for setting off a chain of events that ended in the so-called Escalera (Ladder) Conspiracy of 1844. A contingency of geopolitical events at that time caused the colonial government to crack down on anyone it considered to have abolitionist sympathies of any sort. The result of the brutality included the torture of slaves and many influential members of the growing free black community and the imprisonment of others. The debate over whether there had been a conspiracy at all still continues. For more on this episode, see Murray (2002, Chapters 8 and 9).

15 Also see Fanon (1968, p. 152). The Creole reformist bourgeoisie were responsible for facilitating the birth of the Cuban novel, and this is one example among several that indicate how cosmopolitanism and patriotism are not mutually exclusive. For more on this subject, see Robbins (1998, pp. 1–19).

16 Étienne Balibar defines "fictive ethnicity" as the conceptual means by which the idealism of national and transnational discourses is rendered less arbitrary and more relevant to localities. This kind of racism exemplifies what Balibar calls "doctrinal" or "theoretical" racism, which he describes as a practice that has been closely tied to humanist–universalist ideologies for over two hundred years. See Balibar (1998, pp. 96, 58 respectively.).

17 Owing to space considerations, I am unable to elaborate my argument that the first conceptual discussion of a colonial modernity can probably be traced to the debates in the sixteenth-century Spanish court between Bartolomé de las Casas and Juan Ginés de Sepúlveda over whether the Indian had a soul or was a "natural slave" according to Aristotle's precepts and, consequently, could legally be subjected to a "just" war and the dispossession of lands. These debates have been recognized as foundational for modern international law and comparative ethnology and were eventually decided in favor of Las Casas and the Indians. Although the moral argument triumphed in Spain, the imperial project determined that colonial subjects were in need of Europe's "tutelage." For a thorough treatment of these debates and their significance, consult Pagden (1982).

4   Anti-racism and emancipation in the thought and practice of Cabral, Neto, Mondlane and Machel

Branwen Gruffydd Jones

I do not think that the national liberation struggle is directed towards inverting systems of oppression in such as way that the master of today will be the slave of tomorrow. To think in this way is to go against the current of history. Attitudes of social revenge can never be what we want, which is the freedom of men.

Agostinho Neto (Neto 1974, p. 19)

It could be objected that the language of autonomy and self-determination has limited cross-culture validity because of its Western origins.

David Held (Held 2003, p. 472)

Introduction[1]

Contemporary International Relations (IR) scholarship contains contradictory strands and tendencies that reflect the discipline's historical and geopolitical origins and development. Mainstream IR scholarship remains essentially conservative, connected with the maintenance of state power. Critical IR seeks explicitly to expose the historical structures of international power and develop knowledge that might contribute to the progressive and emancipatory transformation of world order (Wyn Jones 2001). However, much critical IR scholarship remains limited by a deeply rooted eurocentrism that structures the whole of the western academy, and *especially* the discipline of IR (Gruffydd Jones 2006b). Efforts in critical IR to articulate normative challenges to the global status quo remain limited as a result of overlooking both the imperial nature of international order and the global history of anti-imperial and non-Western struggles and discourses. The critical project in IR remains hampered by its partial selection of resources of critique, and reproduces long-entrenched certitudes regarding the benign and progressive character of Western modernity. Within international political economy, scholars concerned with problems of oppression, the maintenance of hegemonic world orders and possibilities of global transformation, have turned fruitfully to the insights of Marx and Gramsci, but persistently overlook other sources of critique such as Frantz Fanon and Amílcar Cabral. Within normative debate, those concerned with the possibilities of a more just social and international order turn, by habit and instinct, to the Western canon of political thought. Cosmopolitan theory within IR is used in this chapter as an exemplar of well-intentioned debate that falls woefully short of disciplinary claims to provide understanding of international source and relevance.

A richer understanding of the deep challenges that confront any attempt at progressive global transformation is possible if, instead of starting from Western philosophy, we learn from a broader, global range of experiences, including radical internationalist, feminist and anti-colonial struggles. This chapter explores the liberation struggles that developed against Portuguese colonial rule in Africa in the mid-twentieth century. A commitment to anti-racism and internationalism was an integral component of the thought and practice of the leading figures in these liberation struggles – Agostinho Neto, Amílcar Cabral, Eduardo Mondlane and Samora Machel. The chapter explores how these two defining features arose from the analysis and experience of colonial oppression, as well as from critical engagement with existing traditions of revolutionary thought and practice from other contexts.

For some critics, across various positions, such an exercise of retrieval would seem at best idealist, at worst irrelevant. Today, under conditions of global neo-liberal hegemony, the war on terror and the rise of China, what is the point of dwelling on the anti-colonial radicalism of the 1970s? Surely, to do so could only be to indulge in romantic nostalgia. Many critics, including some post-colonial critics, see little merit in 'Afro-radicalism' with its modernist visions and monolithic utopian politics.[2] It would seem that while the thought of Cabral *et al.* might have been momentarily effective four decades ago, it has long passed its use-by date. Of course, the current global conjuncture is very different to that of the 1960s or 1970s. Yet, while in Africa colonialism as such is no longer the problem, the deepening and strengthening of relations of global domination under the supremely technocratic guise of finance and multilateral development aid has not altogether invalidated the basic analysis of *neo*colonialism articulated by such thinkers. The purpose of this chapter, however, is not to explore the contemporary relevance of these struggles and their discourses. While no doubt important, such an exercise requires first that these struggles are examined in their own right. They should be recognized as important moments in the global repertoire of struggles occasioned by the contradictions of modernity in the twentieth century. In the context of the discipline of IR, with which this book engages, such recognition is both necessary and inherently radical, given the weight of the academy's eurocentric amnesia and wilful silence regarding the existence, originality and worth of political discourse of African origin. (Rarely does one read that Machiavelli or Hobbes is no longer worthy of study.) Analysis of these struggles also contributes to the ongoing and much broader critical analysis of the global history of black radicalism (Edwards 2001; Bogues 2003).

The analysis set out here is not an idealist, textual celebration articulated in abstraction from historical context or consequence, but an attempt to examine the relationship between historically specific experiences and relations, and emergent forms of practice and thought. While foregrounding the colonial context within which luso-African anti-colonial discourse emerged, it is fundamentally important that such an inquiry does not presume from the outset the content of this discourse. In his reflections on the intellectual terrain of the 'non-West', Shilliam highlights the question of subjecthood as a central but complex issue at the heart of struggles against identities and positions imposed through colonial domination. He also cautions against the perils of seeking to represent the non-West, especially if efforts are led by abstract theory rather than concrete historical investigation attuned to the creative agency of the colonised. Finally, Shilliam persistently returns to remind us of the enormously variegated breadth and form of the colonial and anti-colonial experience. Heeding such cautions, we must be attentive to the actual historical specificity of the visions of alternative subjecthood that arose in the context of different anti-colonial struggles.

This chapter highlights in particular the anti-racism and internationalism embedded within the luso-African anti-colonial struggles. The structure of Portuguese colonial oppression in Africa was profoundly racialized. In such a heavily structured context, what forms of resistance and what alternative conceptions of subjecthood are possible? Pius Adesanmi has argued that,

> because whiteness has always predicated its own historical agency on a Hegelian, master-slave negation of its racialized others, the subalternized entity could only launch itself on the tortuous path to agency in two ways. First was to name and assign the appropriate responsibilities to the sign of its negation, hence the emergence and the consolidation of the white-European oppressor category in African historicist discourses. Second was to come to terms with the equation of its own color with all things negative and its consequent containment within demonized geospatial territories; hence, the emergence of an oppositional black-victim category within the same context. This *prise de conscience* is the foundation of the philosophy of struggle inherent in African discourses and constitutes the informing spirit of the praxes represented by African nationalist and liberationist struggles.
>
> (Adesanmi 2004, pp. 42–3)

Yet at different historical moments and contexts, emancipatory struggles have emerged which deliberately attempted to go beyond the logic of racialization, and to imagine the anti-colonial and post-colonial subject without a defining reference to race (Grovogui 2006a). It is important to remember these cases in themselves, as historically existing forms of struggle that sought to transcend logics of racialized revenge or restoration, evidence which contradicts the conflation of emancipation with race as a matter of necessity. As this chapter underlines, the liberation struggles of the Portuguese African colonies explicitly refused categories of both 'white European oppressor' and 'black victim'. The very possibility of constructing anti-racist social orders in a racialized global order is shot with contradiction. However, the difficulties of subsequently realizing an anti-racist post-colonial society is a related but distinct question, beyond the scope and purpose of the present chapter.

Cosmopolitanism in IR theory

One of the many important strands of critical IR is the development of a cosmopolitan project. This seeks to theorize and identify possibilities for the realization of a cosmopolitan world order, or world society, in which all people (as individuals) are treated equally and the equal rights and moral status of all are recognized and realized.[3] The debates explore the question of the possible and best forms of relationship between bounded political communities which prioritize members over outsiders, and the universal ethical and equitable treatment and interaction of all individuals in the world, as moral agents of equal worth. Cosmopolitan theory promotes values of universal moral equality, universal dialogue, and democracy and justice. It is argued that for the realization of such principles, the social order must be organized to facilitate the participation of all voices in discussion and dialogue on an equitable, unconstrained basis where participation is not hindered by material inequalities. Cosmopolitan theory advocates that the social and international order should be designed on the principle of not doing, or minimizing, harm (intentional and unintentional) to others, including distant strangers (Linklater 2001, 2002).

The objectives of this project are laudable and, on their own terms, progressive. However, the limitations of this project become apparent when it is considered in and against a broader global context, both theoretical and historical – most importantly, the global context of colonial modernity. In raising profound questions of the appropriate treatment of members of a political community and 'others' or 'distant strangers', IR theorists draw on Western classical and contemporary political thought, from Pufendorf, Vattel and Kant to Habermas, Rawls and Beitz. In turning thus to what Shilliam calls its own internal resources, IR treats the Western canon not as *a* body or tradition of thought, but *the* tradition of thought. Andrew Linklater, outlining 'the classical approach to political community', writes 'The classical approach has dominated political theory and practice for more than three centuries. . . . My assumption is that the majority of the world's population accepts some version of the classical approach' (Linklater 2002, pp. 138–9).

IR theory about cosmopolitanism, its normative discourse and implications for institutional design and political practice are developed with reference to a specific understanding of world history, as well as a specific set of references of political thought and experience. What is assumed, usually implicitly and sometimes explicitly, is the Western provenance and the progressive character of cosmopolitanism. There is an assumed fit and unique integral consistency between notions of 'modernity', 'democracy', 'equality', 'justice', 'progress', 'rights' and their historical referents located in the Western experience (for example,

Linklater 2002, p. 144; Held 2003, pp. 471–2). The literature identifies a progressive entrenchment of cosmopolitan values within the institutions of international order, in particular from the mid-twentieth century. Albeit with various qualifications, IR cosmopolitans imply a narrative of world historical progress towards a cosmopolitan ideal, embedded in the development and expansion of 'international society' (Linklater 2002, p. 146). The emergence of cosmopolitan values in the institutions and practice of international relations is characteristically identified in the post-Second World War institutional complex of the United Nations (Held 2002; Held 2003, pp. 473–5).

Cosmopolitan literature in IR essentially grapples with how bounded political communities, existing in an international states system and international society can and should best balance and integrate rights and duties, obligations and preferences, towards members of one's own community and 'others', 'foreigners' or 'distant strangers', especially distant strangers who are suffering. Yet it rarely gives explicit consideration to the history and continuation of imperial structures and practices, or to non-Western experiences, political institutions or bodies of thought, many of which have arisen in and against imperial oppression. It is not simply that IR theory has inadvertently overlooked a rich source of historical and theoretical insight into the normative questions being posed. The very questions posed by cosmopolitan theory in IR make little substantive sense when considered in abstraction from the imperial context of global modernity. Or, perhaps, they make sense *only* when the global context of modernity is overlooked. For at the heart of imperial order is precisely the deliberate establishment and legitimation of political boundaries, essentialized cultures and traditions, norms of inclusion and exclusion, and the differential treatment of 'selves' and 'others'.

When imperialism and the rest of the world are brought into view, the historical narrative of international moral progress emergent from the West becomes unsustainable. The orthodox narrative of the progressive entrenchment of cosmopolitan norms with the expansion of international society from Europe to the rest of the world overlooks, for example, the profound struggles over the establishment of the UN system and the imperial world context that heavily shaped those struggles. In particular, it overlooks the centrality of struggles over race and colonialism that were waged within and without the UN system from its very beginnings. Organizations and individuals representing African-Americans and colonized peoples campaigned to extend, strengthen and broaden the formulation and institutionalization of 'rights' discourse in this context. Their efforts were consistently marginalized and undermined by the leading Western powers and diplomats (Ledwidge 2007). The subsequent formal institutionalization of further progressive international norms, such as UN Resolution 1514 of December 1960 (the Declaration on the Granting of Independence to Colonial Countries and Peoples) and Resolution 1904 of November 1963, (the Declaration on the Elimination of All Forms of Racial Discrimination) came about on the insistence of the formerly colonized and non-Western members of the international community. Major Western powers – the United States, Britain, France, Belgium and Australia – abstained from Resolution 1514 (Ince 1974, Chapter 1; Sud 1983,

Chapter 3). The orthodox narrative also overlooks the continued racial oppression, colonial subjugation and counter-revolutionary terror that endured in the practice of the 'great' Western powers long after the formal institutionalization of the UN principles of universal rights.

In the rest of this chapter I examine the forms of political thought and practice arising from one of the often forgotten moments of twentieth-century global modernity – the Portuguese colonial wars and anti-colonial struggles. Against IR cosmopolitanism's appropriation of universal values for the West and partial reading of political thought, I highlight the values of internationalism, solidarity and anti-racism that emerged within and were integral to these anti-colonial struggles.

Anti-racism and internationalism in the thought and practice of Neto, Cabral, Mondlane and Machel

This section examines the thought and practice of four African revolutionaries in historical, global context. There is a substantial literature addressing separately the thought and achievements of Neto, Cabral, Mondlane and Machel.[4] Here, however, their contributions are analysed together and in relation to each other. This serves to illuminate better the important relationships between the struggles and their leaders, and the broader context of global modernity in the twentieth century.

The political thought and practice of these key revolutionary figures was the product of a distinct set of experiences, conditions and imperatives which were rooted in the structures of global imperial modernity. The early political consciousness of Mondlane, Machel, Neto, Cabral and other leading figures in the independence movements was formed originally through direct experience and witnessing of racial oppression and discrimination, hardship and dispossession that characterized the Portuguese colonial social order. Each had their own individual experiences, as well as witnessing and hearing about the sufferings of family members, neighbours, fellow workers, students and colleagues, and learning about the experiences of their ancestors. The conditions they experienced and witnessed, which informed their understanding of colonialism, included the routine, daily humiliations and suffering foundational to the lived colonial order, as well as the specific practices of colonial war and counter-revolution, from surveillance, imprisonment and torture to massacres, bombardment and assassinations.

The various experiences of the humiliations and brutalities of colonial oppression suffered and witnessed by Mondlane, Machel, Neto and Cabral, in Africa and Portugal, constituted a vital foundation as their understanding and consciousness developed in the course of the liberation struggles. Yet the analysis here highlights how these experiences and the struggles to transform the basis of colonial oppression and achieve liberation led to an understanding and a set of normative commitments that sought not to match, but to transcend, the logics and exclusions of imperial order. The racism, humiliation, collusions, intimidation, practices of torture and assassination were met with deliberate efforts to forge an explicitly anti-racist set of norms and practices, extending solidarity and respect to all, and seeking to instil discipline and humane practice in the conduct of liberation war.

The emergence of connected struggles and shared consciousness

The struggles for African independence always included an important international and shared dimension. This was embodied explicitly in the Pan-African movement, which, from the 1930s/1940s, focused increasingly on African decolonization and was increasingly influenced by Africans as well as African-Americans. In many African colonies the post-war period of the 1950s and 1960s was characterised by an opening of political space and the formation of African associations, movements and parties which organized and campaigned for independence. The fascist colonial rule of Salazar resisted any such opening, however. Political parties and organizations were banned; the African cultural, sport and educational clubs, networks and associations which emerged, mainly in urban areas, were subject to increasing surveillance and interference; and any manifestation of open resistance was met with immediate, brutal repression. All appeals for peaceful political negotiations leading to independence were refused. Political organizing and mobilization were thus necessarily clandestine, and much of the initial activity which led to the establishment of the liberation movements took place abroad, in neighbouring countries and in Europe. This gave an important international dimension to the experiences and consciousness of the leading figures of the various national struggles.

Neto, Cabral, Mondlane and many others met initially in Portugal, while studying. In the 1940s and 1950s African students studying in Lisbon and Coimbra became involved in the political resistance against fascism, participating in meetings and activities of student organizations, the Peace Movement, the MUD Juvenil (Democratic Unity Movement – Youth) and the Portuguese Communist Party.[5] In addition, they began to organize their own activities and groups alongside, but distinct from, the Portuguese democratic movement (de Andrade 1980, pp. xxiii–xxiv). An important component were various cultural, literary and sporting initiatives organized among African students in Portugal. Given the weight of Portuguese racial ideology, centring on the negation of black African worth, such activities were in themselves inherently political, vehicles for individually and collectively affirming and enriching African identity, agency and critique in the colonial context.

Many leading African nationalists including Neto and Cabral were active in running the Casa dos Estudantes do Império (CEI) and published essays and poems in the CEI journal *Mensagem*. Other important institutions of cultural and political organisation were the Casa de África, the Clube Marítimo Africano and the Centro de Estudos Africanos (CEA). This was an important time and context in the forging of solidarity and unity among the leaders of the anti-colonial movements (Mateus 1999, Chapter 3). The shared experiences, activities and discussions in Lisbon and elsewhere were significant in shaping the developing political consciousness of Neto, Cabral, Mondlane and other leading nationalist figures, and constituted the early phase of an enduring and later more formalized relationship of unity and solidarity among the movements. Mário de Andrade recalled:

> In 1950 . . . we were so many that it was already possible at that time to set up two football teams . . . Cabral himself played, and me – I didn't know how to play, but I also played. But this *confraternização*, this manner of being together, playing football, this was only one of the ways of camouflaging our objective, which was to organise cultural meetings, which necessarily later had to change to political meetings, and even to political organizations.
>
> (de Andrade 1973, p. 10)

There were many and enduring points of collaboration between the leaders and movements. Cabral was active alongside Neto in the establishment of the first anti-colonial movements and later the MPLA (Movimento Popular de Libertação de Angola) in Angola, and it seems that he also helped in or gave support to the creation of FRELIMO (Frente de Libertação de Moçambique) (Mateus 1999, p. 91). In 1957, Cabral met in Paris with five other comrades from Mozambique, Angola and São Tomé, where they held a study seminar, called 'Meeting of Consultation and Study for the Development of the Struggle in the Portuguese Colonies'. From there, Cabral returned to Lisbon and established the Movimento Anti-Colonialista (MAC). The MAC later evolved into FRAIN (Frente Revulunionária Africana para a Independência das Colónias Portuguesas), which finally gave way to the Conferência das Organizações Nacionalistas das Colónias Portuguesas (CONCP). CONCP was established in 1961, with its headquarters in Rabat, and remained an important organization playing a crucial role in sustaining the unity and cooperation of the movements throughout the duration of the wars (Vieira 1988). Its first conference was held in April 1961 in Casablanca, with support from the Kingdom of Morocco, to promote the cause of independence and the unity of the national movements (Bell 1971; Cruz e Silva 1998, p. 210; Costa Pinto 2001, p. 40). At the second conference, held in October 1965 in Dar es Salaam, Cabral highlighted the significance of their cooperation and unity:

> We must strengthen our unity, not only within each country but also between us, the peoples of the Portuguese colonies. The CONCP has a very special meaning for us. We have the same colonial past, we have all learned to speak and write Portuguese, but we have an even greater, perhaps even more historic, strength: it is the fact that we began the struggle together. It is the struggle that binds comrades, the companions for the present and the future. The CONCP is for us a fundamental strength of the struggle. The CONCP is in the heart of every combatant in our country, in Angola, in Mozambique. The CONCP must also represent, we are proud to say, an example for the peoples of Africa. For in this glorious struggle against imperialism and colonialism in

Africa, we are the first colonies to have joined together, to discuss together, to plan together, to study together the problems concerning the development of their struggle. This cannot fail to be a very interesting contribution to the history of Africa and to the history of our peoples.

(Cabral 1980, p. 258)

The processes of decolonization in the rest of Africa had a major influence on the leading figures fighting for independence from Portugal. The high period of African decolonization in the 1960s brought inspiration and hope. The early experiences of African independence also brought lessons and warnings, however, regarding both the parasitic corruption of the post-colonial elites, described and analysed by Fanon and Dumont, and the determined and disastrous machinations of neocolonialism. Mondlane, Neto, Cabral and Machel closely followed the experiences of the Congo, Ghana, Algeria and elsewhere. They were deeply affected by the struggles in the Congo and the assassination of Lumumba, and the experiences of post-colonial Ghana and the overthrow of Nkrumah (Depelchin 1983, p. 78; Munslow 1983, pp. 102–3; Khazanov 1986, p. 81; Ganhão 2001, p. 12).

They also learned from the *global* canon of anti-colonial and revolutionary thought and experience. They read widely, including the political and cultural literature of the Negritude movement, the pan-African movement and socialist, communist and anti-imperial movements from all regions. They read and discussed political thought, literature and poetry from Latin America, Russia and France, the writings of the Harlem Renaissance, and the Paris-based journal *Presence Africaine*. They discussed the works of James Aggrey, Leopold Senghor, Karl Marx, Aimé Césaire, Leo Tolstoy, Jorge Amado, Jean-Paul Sartre, Pablo Neruda, Nicolás Guillén and Langston Hughes (Shore 1983, p. xxiv; Chilcote 1991, p. 9; Laranjeira 1995; Carreira 1996, p. 45; Cruz e Silva 1998, p. 196; Mateus 1999, pp. 97–105; Ganhão 2001, p. 14; Campbell 2006). Neto in particular read Black American literature and poetry, 'whose struggles and writings decisively influenced the process of decolonisation of African intellectuality' (Mateus 1999, p. 100; see also Torres 1977, pp. 191–213; Martinho 1980).

Perhaps most important of all however was the way in which their understanding and consciousness was informed by the conditions and struggles of their own societies. The relationship between lived experience, concrete conditions, and political consciousness was an explicit component central to the developed political thought of all four (see, in particular, Cabral 1969; Neto 1974; see also Gruffydd Jones 2008). The revolutionary character of these struggles, and the thought and practice of the leaders, cannot therefore be understood simply in terms of an 'application' in the African context of existing notions or traditions of revolution already developed elsewhere. These struggles certainly learnt from the global heritage of revolutionary tradition; as Depelchin observed, 'Far from FRELIMO's leaders was the idea that they had invented the Mozambican revolution without drawing from other revolutionary experiences' (Depelchin 1983, p. 82). Yet they must be understood fundamentally as emerging from the context of colonial oppression and the contradictions of liberation, and as providing an original contribution to the global revolutionary canon.

The intransigence of the Portuguese colonial regime, the mounting violence and brutality of colonial war and the numerous efforts on the part of the Portuguese to undermine, infiltrate, co-opt and fragment the liberation movements made it imperative to confront a series of problems and contradictions of political and armed struggle. The anti-colonial leaders faced problems of maintaining unity within their movements, mobilizing the largely rural population inside the colonies, seeking international support and assistance while avoiding manipulation by powerful global forces, and defending the legitimacy of their cause in the wider international context. Resolving such problems required increasing clarity and depth of understanding regarding the character of 'the enemy' – what they were fighting against and why – and the strategy and aims of liberation. The experiences of colonial oppression and the imperatives of the extended political and armed struggle gave rise to rich and searching reflections, debates and normative discourse regarding profound and fundamental aspects of the interactions and inter-relations among and between peoples, and possibilities for transforming social relations to build a more just social and international order. Two important and related dimensions emerged as central features of the anti-colonial struggles of the Portuguese colonies: anti-racism and internationalism.

Anti-racism and internationalism

The question of race in the struggle for liberation and independence was confronted directly in the course of FRELIMO's war, and resolved through a difficult and bitter period of internal disagreement and rivalry within FRELIMO, from 1968 to 1970 (Depelchin 1983; Munslow 1983, pp. 102–11; Vieira 1988; Christie 1989, pp. 48–60). Serious disagreements had arisen within FRELIMO over the strategic conduct of the war, and the political and economic organization of life in the liberated zones, resting ultimately on different understandings of what they were fighting against and what they were fighting for. Against the 'cultural-nationalists', principally Simango, Nkavandame and Ngwenjere, Mondlane and Machel were insistent that the struggle must be waged against the Portuguese colonial system, not against the Portuguese *people* or against the white race. Machel had defended this position during debates in Algeria, as leader of the second group of FRELIMO soldiers to go for military training. Christie records that 'The race issue would return again and again in Machel's career as a soldier and a politician, and was a point on which he was never prepared to compromise' (Christie 1989, p. 25). They were equally insistent in their determination to transcend ethnic and regional identity as coalescing factors informing the purpose of the struggle. Mondlane insisted on these principles at FRELIMO's second congress in 1968, and was endorsed. After the assassination of Mondlane in 1969, by PIDE (Polícia Internacional e de Defesa do Estado) secret agents, Machel was elected as President of FRELIMO and thus the principled commitment to an anti-racist position was consolidated. He explained:

We are not fighting to become Portuguese with black skins. We are fighting to affirm ourselves as Mozambicans, without this meaning contempt for the Portuguese people or any other people. In this respect, FRELIMO reaffirms its wish to fully co-operate with all peoples in the world on a basis of independence, equality, respect and mutual interest. FRELIMO also reaffirms that the definition of a Mozambican has nothing to do with skin colour or racial, ethnic, religious or any other origin. Members of FRELIMO are all Mozambicans who adhere to its programme of struggle against Portuguese colonialism, for the independence of Mozambique. FRELIMO is not a racialist organisation and is not waging a racialist war.

(Machel 1982, p. 36)

Neto also held an unswerving commitment to an anti-racial understanding of the liberation struggle. Problems of rivalry, factionalism and division afflicted the Angolan liberation struggle to a far greater extent than in Mozambique, both within the MPLA and between the MPLA and rival movements. Both UNITA (União Nacional para a Independência Total de Angola) and FNLA (Frente Nacional de Libertação de Angola) waged their struggles on regional and ethnic lines, and the endurance, depth and devastation of the divisions that wrecked the liberation struggle and post-independence attempts to build Angolan society were largely due to the external support received by FNLA and UNITA from the United States, South Africa and other powers, including Mobutu's Zaire. Neto, however, was always insistent on the position of anti-racism. He recognized the logical appeal of a racial understanding of oppression and struggle:

It is common to confuse the enemy of Africa with the white man. The colour of skin is still an element for many in determining the enemy. There are historical and social reasons, lived facts which consolidate this idea in our continent.

(Neto 1974, p. 17)

Nevertheless he insisted:

In our countries we are not making a racial war. Our objective is not to fight against the white man solely because he is white. It is that we fight against those who support the colonial regime. . . . if there exists in some of our combatants the idea of a war against the white man, it is necessary that it be immediately substituted by the idea of a war against colonialism and against imperialism; a war against oppression, for the liberty and for the dignity of all men in the world. This idea will fortify our struggle. It will offer more guarantees and new prospects that open up a brilliant future for all men. In a time of hatred we will have fraternity and understanding.

(Neto 1982, p. 172)

Cabral was likewise explicit and insistent regarding the need to transcend a racial understanding of the struggle for liberation. In addition to confronting this issue as a problem for the developing political consciousness of Guineans fighting for their independence, he also addressed the challenges and contradictions of forms of international solidarity constructed on the grounds of race, as manifest in notions of Negritude and Pan-Africanism (Cabral 1973; Hill 1984).[6]

This leads to the inherently related dimensions of solidarity and international-ism which emerged as firm and explicit planks in the thought *and practice* of all four independence leaders. These principles of solidarity and internationalism are located in a broader, global tradition, yet they were also the specific product of the particular circumstances and imperatives of the struggle against Portuguese colonialism, and the broader relations of imperialism sustaining the Portuguese colonial system. Neto, Cabral, Mondlane and Machel shared a clear understand-ing of Portuguese colonialism as a structured system of oppressive social relations rooted in and sustained by global imperial relations and the structures of global capitalism. This analysis was based on direct and keen awareness of the long historical dependence of Portuguese colonialism on the imperial power of Britain, France, Germany and America, a dependence that was both financial and military and took on new forms and heightened significance in the context of Nato support for Portugal's colonial wars. They were equally determined in their principled support of non-alignment and their determination not to let their struggles become subordinated to the Sino-Soviet split and rivalry.

All branches of the shared struggles for liberation from Portuguese colonialism were recipients of internationalist support. The support of neighbouring Guinea-Conakry, under Sekou-Touré, was vital for the success of the PAIGC (Partido Africano da Independência da Guiné e Cabo Verde); Guinea also provided sup-port for the MPLA. Tanzania, under the leadership of Nyerere, provided essential support for the liberation of southern Africa, above all for FRELIMO (Ishemo 2000; see also Bogues 2003). Nyerere's support was crucial at all stages, from the initial establishment of FRELIMO and the emergence of unity among the various independence movements to the provision of a base for military training and for establishing the first fronts in Niassa and Cabo Delgado, and remained constant throughout the war. Tanzania suffered directly for this principled support, when in 1971 during the 'Gordian Knot' offensive the Portuguese army bombed villages within Tanzania (Ishemo 2000, pp. 85–6). Mondlane and Machel were keenly aware of the risks and costs that such solidarity carried, and of the courage of Nyerere's principled and committed support for their struggle (Mondlane 1969, p. 128; Ishemo 2000, p. 87). As individuals, they also benefited from important acts of solidarity. Machel, for example, received vital support from people in Botswana and from the ANC (African National Congress) during his flight from Mozambique to join FRELIMO in Dar es Salaam in 1963 (Christie 1989, pp. 16, 23). In 1962 the Portuguese Communist Party arranged for Neto and his family to escape from Portugal, after his release from prison (Somerville 1986, p. 26; Mateus 1999, pp. 112–13). The following month, Neto sent a 'fraternal embrace' to the Portuguese democratic and progressive organizations to which he owed his freedom (Mateus 1999, p. 113), affirming that he was 'conscious that the struggle against the exploitation of man by man in whatever part of the world is a direct contribution to our liberation.' (cited in Mateus 1999, p. 113)

They upheld the principles of internationalism in practice, often at great cost. This was manifest most directly in their determined support for other African liberation struggles – especially those of Zimbabwe, South Africa and Namibia. Mozambique, in particular, extended very concrete solidarity to the peoples of Zimbabwe and South Africa in their long and bitter struggles for liberation, and Mozambican society and economy suffered tremendously over many years as a result of this principled and enduring commitment (Machel 1979, 1980). The liberation movements also provided moral and diplomatic support for oppressed peoples and liberation struggles around the world, from Vietnam to Palestine, western Sahara to East Timor (Cabral 1980, pp. 255–6; Machel 1980; Vieira 1988).

These values of anti-racism, internationalism and solidarity rested on a firm, confident and defiant conviction of their historical moral agency and the legitimacy of their cause, their right to sovereignty, independence and freedom as individuals, as peoples, and as historically constituted African nations. They understood their struggles as the struggle to *re*-gain their freedom, and thus refused any idea of asking for their freedom. Neto and Cabral explained of their struggles:

> This experience is simply an expression of a need experienced in Africa over the past five centuries, and most especially in the last decades, the need for each and every one of us to feel free. It is also a broader expression of the common desire of men in this world to regard themselves as free, *as capable of releasing themselves* from the shackles of a society in which they weaken and die as human beings.
>
> (Neto 1974, p. 11, emphasis added)

> We, as peaceful peoples but proud of our love of freedom, proud of our attachment to the ideal of progress in the twentieth century, took up arms with determination and unshakably; we took up arms to defend our rights, given that there was no law in the world which could do it for us. . . . we do not love war, but war, armed struggle for liberation, was the only way out that Portuguese colonialism left us for the regaining of our dignity as an African people, our human dignity. . . . What is the most striking manifestation of civilization and culture if not that shown by a people who take up arms to defend their country, to defend their right to life, progress, work and happiness?
>
> (Cabral 1980, pp. 252–3)

Accordingly they spurned any patronising spirit of charity and philanthropy, insisting on solidarity and internationalism on their own terms. This is expressed in FRELIMO's poem:

Brother from the West
Brother from the West –
(How can we explain that you are our brother?)
the world does not end at the threshold of your house
nor at the stream which marks the border of your country
nor in the sea
in whose vastness you sometimes think
that you have discovered the meaning of the infinite.
Beyond your threshold, beyond the sea
the great struggle continues.
Men with warm eyes and hands as hard as the earth
at night embrace their children
and depart before the dawn.
Many will not return.
What does it matter?
We are men tired of shackles. For us
Freedom is worth more than life.
From you, brother, we expect
and to you we offer
not the hand of charity
which misleads and humiliates
but the hand of comradeship
committed, conscious,
How can you refuse, brother from the West?

(FRELIMO, 1973)

After the fall of the fascist regime in 1974, FRELIMO's discussions with the Portuguese government rested on three principles: recognition of the unconditional right to immediate and full independence; recognition of FRELIMO as the sole legitimate representative of the Mozambican people; and acceptance by Portugal of the transfer of the powers that it still exercised to FRELIMO, as the representative of the people (Vieira 1988, p. 8). When the Portuguese government refused to accept these principles, insisting on a ceasefire first and a subsequent referendum on independence, 'Samora Machel replied that it was not up to the slave-owner to ask his slaves if they would like to be free – particularly when they had already picked up guns to free themselves' (Vieira 1988, p. 9).

These components of normative discourse and practice are related. They rest on an expanded vision of humanity and a confident understanding of the rightful historical place of African peoples as equal members, along with all other peoples, of humanity. The leaders of the liberation movements explicitly understood and advocated the contribution that their struggles were making not only to the liberation of their own peoples, and to Africa more broadly, but to the whole of humanity, and to moral and material *progress* on a world scale (Neto 1974, pp. 15, 19; Cabral 1980, p. 253; Machel, in Munslow 1985, pp. 66, 67). Cabral argued 'We must regard ourselves as soldiers, often anonymous, but *soldiers of mankind* in this vast front of struggle that Africa is in our times' (Cabral 1980, p. 253, emphasis added). Frequently, references to 'us' or 'our people' were followed directly by reference to all other peoples. This was a conception not of a bounded political community essentially distinguished from others on the grounds of cultural or other difference, but of historically differentiated peoples who share humanity in common. At all times they were careful to distinguish between the Portuguese colonial system and fascist government, and the Portuguese *people* (for example, Cabral 1980, pp. 257, 271). This was a firm principle informing their policy and practice. In insisting on this distinction they were able to acknowledge the humanity they shared with their oppressors: 'deep in their hearts both the watchdog [of colonial fascism] and the exploited nonetheless felt themselves slaves of the system as a whole' (Neto 1974, p. 18).

Conclusion

In conclusion, it is instructive to briefly contrast the norms arising from the anti-colonial liberation movements, as expressed in particular by their leaders Neto, Cabral, Mondlane and Machel, with those developed by the Western cosmopolitan tradition, especially in its current manifestations in recent IR literature.

The first point of contrast regards the underlying concept of political community. The cosmopolitan tradition, while upholding the principle of the moral equality of all individuals in the world, nevertheless presumes that mechanisms for realising equal treatment need to allow for equal participation of different cultures, and to mediate moral equality with the right to cultural difference. It retains an assumed notion of 'the other' and radical difference or essential cultural specificity; this appears to be the logical corollary of the assumed notion of the 'bounded political community'. The African liberation movements fighting against Portuguese colonialism also recognized the significance of culture, but they understood their struggles, agency and rights as arising from a common, shared human condition. They articulated an expanded concept of humanity that transcended notions of race, religion and essentialized culture.

The second point is related, and regards the implications for normative practice arising from each approach. The cosmopolitan project rightly seeks to confront the injustices of inequality and suffering in the global system. However, while developing elaborate modes of philosophical argument about different forms of distributive justice (Lu 2005), the solution advocated is essentially limited to *philanthropy* and *altruism*. This contrasts starkly with the norms of practice regarding global conditions of inequality and suffering arising from the African liberation movements. Their strong ethic of international solidarity demonstrated a deep commitment to transforming the *structures of oppression* throughout the world, and working alongside others in a shared emancipatory endeavour.

These more expanded values arose from the shared personal and societal experiences of racism and oppression, of a policy based on the total negation of African identity, culture, agency and history, a policy aimed at gradually (over centuries) 'assimilating' and 'civilising' black Africans into the Portuguese civilization.

The normative discourse of the liberation movements was developed not simply through intellectual debate and contemplation, but through the imperatives and experiences of struggle. Perhaps this accounts for the differing social ontologies underlying the two normative discourses. The liberation struggles, in seeking to change the conditions of their own suffering – not through asking or waiting for help from distant strangers, but through their own dignified agency – were compelled to identify the *causes* of their suffering.

One of the distinctive features of the thought of these four revolutionaries was their conviction in highlighting the structured relations of colonialism, imperialism and capitalism as the cause of their peoples' oppression. This enabled them to identify equally with all other peoples, regardless of culture, race, ethnicity, religion or nationality, and to recognize the humanity they shared with the Portuguese people, always distinguishing the Portuguese people from the colonial system and fascist regime. The cosmopolitan project upholds noble values but fails to fully explore or develop a causal explanation for the conditions of injustice and inequality in the modern world. Instead, a social ontology of individuals, bounded communities and cultural difference is assumed. This is an atomistic and ahistorical social ontology, and its logical outcome is the normative impulse to philanthropy and altruism that safely overlooks questions of structural oppression, the historical and contemporary causal relationship between global wealth and global poverty, and the need for structural change.

It is, at the very least, ironic that a theoretical approach so concerned to create an all-inclusive dialogic community can so consistently exclude from its conversations all but the Western canon of thought and experience. I would go further, however, to argue that this is not simply ironic oversight. The contemporary debates in critical normative IR theory remain structured by underlying assumptions and logics whose roots lie far back in European thought and experience. This underlying structure arose in the global historical context of European expansion and encounters with non-European peoples in the Americas, Africa and Asia. Notions of bounded political communities, of radical, essential cultural or political difference, of 'the other', of distant strangers are central to cosmopolitan debates in IR theory. These are contemporary permutations of ideas that are not transhistorical but, on the contrary, historically very specific to the ascendancy of European supremacy. From the sixteenth through to the nineteenth centuries, the imperatives of European expansion and colonialism were reflected and refracted in bodies of political, philosophical and legal thought. These changing and cumulative traditions sought to differentiate the European self (white, rational, Christian, bearer of rights and civilization) from the non-European other (non-white, irrational, heathen, barbaric, uncivilized) and thus rationalize the differential treatment of Europeans and non-Europeans, as individuals and peoples. Shilliam has exposed the routine and unexamined assumption of a Western subjecthood as *the* subject informing even critical strands of Western thought. Today's debates in cosmopolitan IR profess the most noble of progressive ambitions, yet their assumptions and manner of discussion, and their inclusions and exclusions, betray their status as the sanitized successor of this long tradition of what Grovogui has called 'racialised international thought' (Grovogui 2006b).

Notes

1 Many thanks to Robbie Shilliam for his excellent editorial guidance and patience, and to our hosts at Wadham College and all participants for a wonderful workshop at the University of Oxford in June 2007.
2 For different strands of criticism see Mbembe (2000) and Scott (2004).
3 See, for example, Archibugi and Held (1995), Linklater (2001, 2002), Shapcott (2001), Held (2002, 2003), Cabrera (2006) and Sutch (2006).
4 An important exception is the recent study by Mateus (1999). Fobanjong (2006) also emphasizes the need to 'cross-reference' the liberation struggles. Book-length studies include Chabal (1983), McCulloch (1983), Ribeiro (1983), Khazanov (1986), Christie (1989), Mwenda (1985), Munslow (1985), Trigo (1989), Chilcote (1991), Carreira (1996), Sopa (2001) and Fobanjong and Ranuga (2006).
5 Neto in particular was active in the Portuguese political movements (de Andrade 1973, p. 11; Mateus 1999, pp. 84–8; Barradas 2005). Cabral associated with them but never joined them (Chilcote 1991, pp. 8–9).
6 Although sympathetic, Neto also came to criticize the understanding of race embodied within Negritude. See Laranjeira (1995).

5 Voices from the "Jewish colony"

Sovereignty, power, secularization, and the outside within

Willi Goetschel

Introduction

In international relations (IR) as well as in political discourse in general, state, power, and sovereignty have come to assume fundamental importance. Seen as primordial concepts, which define and determine the conceptual framework of the current debates, they figure as conditions of the possibility for the life form of local and global politics as we know it, thus exerting a quasi-fundamentalist exigency on the theoretical context that defines the playing field of IR, or so it seems. If the cold war did not prove it, critics maintain that the post-Soviet world demonstrates that the state has become by now the only show in town. To be a state, to be recognized as sovereign, is what all constituencies seek to aspire to, or so the argument goes.[1] Consequently, power is in this context conceived as force, be it military, economic, or in any of its kinder versions such as diplomacy or discursive persuasion. But to view the political world this way is a relatively new phenomenon that has been contingent on a vision of modernity that claims a universal outlook, which, however, upon closer examination turns out to have only a limited purchase. Deployed as constitutive for the discourse of IR, the normative claim of these concepts, even in their weakest forms, seems to pre-empt any critical examination that would delimit their universal hold.

This chapter explores an alternative line in the history of political philosophy. It is a line of theorists who not only engaged critically with classic forms of modern political thought from Machiavelli to Hobbes, Locke, and the Enlightenment, but who were studied by their contemporaries though mainly in a manner that was distinguished by a mostly disowning attitude. Suspiciously eyed as outsiders, Jewish philosophers, especially Baruch de Spinoza and Moses Mendelssohn, would be granted admission to the discursive universe of modern thought only by way of an assimilation that would at the same time both assimilate and "other" them. Although their reception was thus contingent on the universal features that contemporaries sought to identify in their thought, the reception remained curiously preoccupied with at the same time retaining them as distinctly "other." Jewish philosophers were thus subject to a sort of assimilation that denied them the very status of philosophers. Ironically, the very moment of critical independence that would otherwise have distinguished their philosophical authority was in their case turned into proof of a betrayal of Christian sensitivities, especially during a time when they underwent a process of secularization transforming Christian values into universal ethical norms. As a consequence, the critical potential of modern Jewish thought in the Enlightenment was buried, disfigured, and sedimented by readings that remained oblivious of the challenge it would articulate. Attention to the critical dissonances that the Jewish philosophers of the Enlightenment express – but which have been disowned, if not ignored, by most of their critics – might help us rethink some of the foundational concepts at the center of IR.

In making Westphalia the standard narrative for theorizing the modern state, IR has rightly identified the age of secularization as critical for the formation of modern political arrangements.[2] But in singling out Westphalia as the representative model, the surrounding factors that produced the constellation of Westphalia have been downplayed if not completely ignored. If Westphalia has thus become conventionally understood as the secular answer to the deadlock of political conflicts that issued from the challenge of the Reformation, addressing modern secularization in terms of inner-Christian conflicts can no longer satisfy critical explanations.[3] Theories of secularization turn out to be problematic as they are often just secularized variations of a Christian perspective wherein secularization is viewed as a development internal to Christian religions. The "Jewish Question" is just one of its products, whereas "Jewish," and other non-Christian questions, fall outside the scope of such narratives. If traditional secularization theories are therefore limited in terms of a global compass, the problem of a limited scope applies also to the way in which the Westphalian paradigm defines the state, sovereignty, and civil society as secular entities. For post-colonial as well as post-national sensitivities, "secularization" no longer provides an answer but poses questions that require attention. If the secular state and current concepts of civil society no longer serve the purpose of modern political conflict resolution, it might prove helpful to recall those philosophical projects that addressed the question of secularization, civil society, the state, and power from a different perspective.

There are two ways to look at borders: one is to look beyond them at the other side and see how the excluded "outside" reflects back onto the "inside"; another way is to examine how the distinctions set up at the "center" construct a logic of self-legitimation. Distinctions continuously replicate themselves on each side of the divide (for example, Luhmann 2002, Chapter 3). With regard to the question of the place of the Jews in modernity, it may be helpful to look "the other way," as it were, from the "outside" in. If the view back from the periphery to the center is one that provides the opportunity to turn an apparently disadvantaged position of disenfranchisement into critical leverage, Mendelssohn gives this return of the gaze an additional critical turn. Mendelssohn's plea for emancipation suggests more than just a call for social and political equality. It also suggests a principal critique of key concepts of modern political philosophy that resonates suggestively with current post-colonial sensibilities and highlights their critical significance.

Mendelssohn's examination of the conceptual foundations at the very center of political theory suggests that these foundations are themselves based on distinctions that duplicate themselves at the moment borders are drawn. As a distinction that cannot be limited to one side of the border but always points beyond its marks to the other side, any form of demarcation or border drawing implies some form of colonization.[4] To better understand the fuller implications of key concepts in political philosophy and respond to the challenge of rethinking globalization in a critical key, a fresh look back at the European discourse on center and periphery, the domestic arrangement, and the problem of Europe's internal colonies may provide firmer grasp of the internal tensions informing the particular logic that governs the discourse of political theory. This chapter explores the way in which Mendelssohn's discussion of the Jewish situation in eighteenth-century Prussia addresses some of the more problematic implications of concepts such as sovereignty, state, secularization, and power.

With the striking phrase of the "Jewish colonist," Mendelssohn positions his plea for the emancipation of Jews boldly at the center of the Enlightenment debate of Empire, the modern nation-state, and the role of Europe in the age of colonialism. His intervention critically suggests that the question of colonialism is from the outset not just a foreign affair but grounded in domestic arrangements. The conflicted dialectics of inclusion and exclusion is thus one that informs in often uncanny ways the very constitution of how the state and the sovereign are imagined. Turning the eyes from the periphery back onto the center, the periphery becomes in Mendelssohn's discussion legible as the outside that is already inscribed in the very construction of the center. Mendelssohn thus exposes one of the most conflicted complexes at the heart of Western culture. There is no other tradition that played the same kind of formative and enduring role in the history of the formation of Western civilization and its cultural canon, and could thus be seen as being more at the center, than the Jewish tradition. Yet it seems at the same time peculiar that this prominent role came with the costs of a brutal fixation of the Jewish people as the total other at the very root, core, or ground of the West. It usually takes non-Western minds to recognize the oddity of this anomaly – if it is one – but its constitutive moment poses questions concerning the kind of logic that informs a discourse that systematically disavows any forms of acknowledgment of "Jewish roots" at the heart of its conceptual construction of the West, a disavowal troubled by a deep-seated repression of the other within.

A gruesome illustration of how this repression has become an integral part of the architectonic fixture of the political and religious discourse is the case of the Frankfurt Jews. Site of the election of the emperor, Frankfurt and its ghetto have come to play a curiously central role in Europe's history. Claimed as early as 1236 by Frederick II as his personal property and domestics – "servi camerae nostri" – the Jews of the Holy Roman Empire of the German nation became a century later pawns in Karl IV's financing scheme for the acquisition of the imperial crown. In order to provide for the large sums of cash required for his election, Karl IV mortgaged his tax claims on the Jews against cash advances from numerous German cities. He even went so far as to grant in advance amnesty should Jews in the process come to death. It did not take long until the cities availed themselves of this sort of quick solution to secure the outstanding debts (Breuer and Graetz 1996, pp. 28–45). But this is where the story begins. When a century later Frankfurt built its cathedral, tombstones of the fourteenth-century fatalities were used. They did become part not only of the altar's foundation, but also of the cathedral's gothic ceiling. Although the pieces of the altar's foundation were retrieved in the twentieth century when they were discovered, the stones that became elements of the ceiling's structure remain irretrievably part of the construction.[5] This case of integration of the excluded at the heart of the construction of Western canonical architecture exemplifies the constituent role of the dynamics of the distinction between inside and outside at the ground level of the foundation of the discourse of the West.

If Frankfurt Cathedral and the history of its construction are a stark reminder of the Jewish experience in Europe, its staggering image represents also an architectonic model of the conflicted grounds on which Europe built power and sovereignty. Read this way, Frankfurt Cathedral takes on paradigmatic significance for understanding a discourse of silence and repression that, if only for a moment, surfaces with critical force in Mendelssohn's call for emancipation as one that is not just self-interested but carries wider significance for the universal emancipation of humanity in any kinds of colonies as well as domestically.

I shall first examine Mendelssohn's strikingly unusual discussion of the Jews as "indigenous colonists" and the critique of key political concepts that this expression suggests, especially sovereignty, the state, and civil society. But to fully understand the implications of Mendelssohn's political thought requires attention to Spinoza, whose sophisticated philosophical framework offers a liberating alternative to the normative theories of Machiavelli, Hobbes, and others. Reading Mendelssohn with Spinoza will highlight the critical implications that Mendelssohn's political theory has for the conception of secularization. Turning then to Heine, the critical force of the trajectory in Spinoza and Mendelssohn assumes further illumination in the way Heine stages the problem of the concept itself. The chapter concludes with Heine's critical use of the word "modernity," which, rather submitting to a discourse of hegemonic assumptions, opens up the possibilities for defining modernity as the site of critical renegotiation of contending claims.

"Indigenous colonists"

When in 1782 Moses Mendelssohn published the German translation of Manasseh ben Israel's *Vindication of the Jews* – the seventeenth-century Amsterdam rabbi's call for the legal recognition of the rights of the Jews in England – he added a preface that marked his first explicit and public political intervention in print, i.e. in the forum of the republic of letters. At that time, Mendelssohn was already 52 years old and internationally renowned for his eloquent and authoritative Jewish representation in cases of imminent expulsion, persecution, and disenfranchisement. A seasoned and experienced spokesperson on Jewish affairs, Mendelssohn had assumed the stature of Europe's elder statesman of the Jewish nation. His steadfast diplomatic service gave him probably a more intimate experience with the ropes of power than he possibly would have cared for. But the exposure to the world of politics also provided a more intimate familiarity with regard to how power worked in the corridors of the state and its institutions than most political theorists of the period could claim. Mendelssohn's preface thus reflects the rare combination in eighteenth-century Germany of the voice of a critically committed Enlightenment philosopher and an expert public spokesman in finely tuned political intervention.

In Prussia, and German lands in general, Jews were at that time "tolerated" under specific laws that defined their rights and privileges. The communities were treated as corporative entities that negotiated with the authorities and were responsible for their constituency as a whole. Any privileges granted to individuals were attached to their specific status as Jews. Often described as a "nation," the Jews remained until their emancipation in the nineteenth century and often longer still distinguished as a distinct group isolated from the "Germans." When Mendelssohn, for instance, arrived in Berlin from Dessau as a young student he, like other Jews, had to proceed to the gate next to the Jewish quarters and pay the toll imposed on Jews and cattle. "The Jew of Berlin," as Mendelssohn was soon to be called, or, alternatively, the "German Socrates" because of the stunning literary success of his updated version of Plato's *Phaidon*, quickly assumed prominent stature as one of the most distinguished champions of the German Enlightenment.

With the preface, Mendelssohn initiated the political discourse of Jewish emancipation on his own terms. Circumspectly announced as an appendix to Christian Wilhelm Dohm's *On the Civic Improvement of the Jews*, Manasseh ben Israel's *Vindication of the Jews* and Mendelssohn's preface were, however, published separately. Flagging them as an "appendix" to Dohm, Mendelssohn thus marked his intervention in a telling manner as a second, yet at the same time autonomous, step in the discourse of Jewish emancipation had been effectively inaugurated by Dohm's bold and enlightened plea for "civic improvement." In a way the appendix was designed as an amendment that was as much an endorsement, as it was a critical commentary. The historic Jewish voice of one of the most enlightened rabbi of the most advanced and enlightened European city in the previous century – seventeenth-century Amsterdam – thus framed, but also resonated with, Mendelssohn's own voice. The full force of the significance of Mendelssohn's argument becomes clear only if we notice the critical dynamics of this exceptionally pointed and self-conscious move of political self-positioning. Situating himself as advocate and mediator of Manasseh ben Israel, Mendelssohn's own voice signals, rather than just claiming to speak for himself, the Berlin Jews, the German Jews, or the European Jews for that matter, that he is articulating the concerns, both past and present, of Jewry as a whole.

Providing the legitimacy for Mendelssohn's voice, the appendix's positional arrangement reflects with mimetic precision the narrow margin of the title conceded to the colonist who seeks to address the motherland and its central discourse. Highlighting the predicament of the situation in which Jews find themselves under the regime of European rule, Mendelssohn exposes at the same time the logic of rule in general. The question of the emancipation of Jews is the challenge of the state to turn, as Mendelssohn puts it, "these indigenous colonists into its citizens."[6] In framing the question of the legal status of Jews in the terms of colonial discourse – and more precisely a colonial project within the borders and territories of the motherland – Mendelssohn presents the issue as one that is directly linked to the problem of the conception of the modern state. At the heart of the problem, Mendelssohn's line of argument suggests, thus stands not the issue of how to fit the Jews into the scheme of the modern nation-state but, on the contrary, the question of the problematic assumptions of a political philosophy whose notion of the nation-state remains informed by concepts of power, sovereignty, and legitimacy that warrant critical examination in the first place. As Mendelssohn invokes Jewish emancipation as the project of turning "indigenous colonists into [a modern nation-state's] citizens," he highlights that the entanglement of the colonial and domestic issues is one that represents a constituent link that political discourse has yet to address.

With Mendelssohn, the problem of colonies comes into view as not just one existing abroad, but one residing at the very heart of the political foundation of the modern European nation. The critical impetus of Mendelssohn's approach to couch the Jewish experience in terms of a colonialist experience exposes the deeply problematic implications of notions of statehood, government, sovereignty, and legitimacy that rely on a homogeneous conception of civil society and its citizens. In addressing the state's functions and limits in terms of its relation to its domestic colonies, Mendelssohn's argument sheds light on the inner conflicts and tension that define the logic of the modern nation-state. For the problem of this logic is that it claims sovereignty and legitimacy on the grounds of a dialectic of self-determination that is contingent on the distinction of self and other, but which hinges paradoxically at the same time on the suppression of perceived "others" at home and abroad. The case of the colonist becomes, in Mendelssohn's return of the gaze, the colonialist case of the state, i.e. the case of the problematic nexus of colonialist discourse and the foundation of the modern nation-state.

Dohm, in his call for the emancipation of the Jews, argues that the state's willingness to offer generous economic incentives for the colonists it welcomes contrasts curiously with the treatment of domestic Jews who, unlike the foreign colonists, have a different loyalty to the state in whose lands they have resided in since times immemorial, a fact that suggests that the Jews deserve at least the same consideration foreign colonists such as the Huguenots were given (Dohm 1973, pp. 89, 113–15, 133). Mendelssohn, in a critical move, reminds Dohm and his readers that the legal status of the Jews was that of a domestic colony. In taking up this issue critically, Mendelssohn shows how the particular role that the concept of the domestic colony plays for theorizing the legal status of the Jews poses questions of principal importance with regard to the way in which the concepts of state sovereignty and legitimacy are constructed. For Mendelssohn, theorizing the Jews (these "indigenous colonists") in a way that reminds the reader of their domestic provenance exposes the problem of theorizing the foundation, sovereignty, and legitimacy of the state on a model of exclusion with subtle yet unassuming eloquence. Addressing the Jews as colonists, Mendelssohn's argument reveals a paradox at the center of the problem with undeniable distinctiveness. Making the Jew the "indigenous," but also the colonist in his own land, the distinction between colonist and indigenous is "re-entered," exposing the problem that every indigenous claim is already itself a form of colonization. In reclaiming the colonialist terms as the historically accurate framework to describe the domestic arrangements of the Jews in medieval society, Mendelssohn reminds us not only that the medieval order continues to inform the *modern* nation-state, but also that this is the cause of the permutation of the same problems in modernity. Whereas the corporate existence of the Jews as a people with its own forms of internal self-government seamlessly integrated in the medieval social order ruled along corporate identities, the transition to modernity led to the challenge to imagine the Jews in a post-corporate world. As Jews were now seen and expected to act as individuals while their right to individuality on their own terms was denied, the appropriate category of subsumption to theorize the place of Jews in modernity, Mendelssohn suggests, became the colony.

If the modern state's task must be to succeed in making its "indigenous colonists" equal citizens, Mendelssohn's argument highlights an inherent problem at the core of the construction of the state. The mere existence of "indigenous colonists" reminds us that the grounds on which the state stands are more conflicted than the fictional founding narratives would concede. Critical attention to the issue of the status of domestic colonies – even as deterritorialized as that of Jews in German lands – poses the question of the dependency of the motherland, its legitimacy and sovereignty, from domestic arrangements that might ultimately challenge the very construction of legitimacy and sovereignty on which the discourse on the modern nation-state is based. Furthermore, a closer look at the domestic arrangements poses the question of the legal and political grounds on which they are made in critical manner. If the borders and criteria for in- and ex-clusion are unilaterally drawn, are they really borders? Mendelssohn's discussion of the jurisdiction of the colonizing motherland addresses this question with critical urgency. If there exist, in fact, "indigenous colonies" within the territories of a "mother nation," then the premise of the formation of the state out of a homogeneous space and population seems to lack the consistency that is supposed to secure its claim for legitimacy. Contrary to that logic, the existence of "indigenous colonies" indicates an inconsistency as sovereignty is claimed as a self-identical concept thought to be co-extensive with the territory over which it holds rule. Putting pressure on this narrative, Mendelssohn exposes its fallacy.

Mendelssohn's argument, however, is cautiously couched in terms of how to disentangle the theological from the political concerns in civil society. This is the explicit aspect of the argument. The question at the time for which Mendelssohn had also been commissioned to provide expert opinion on was whether the Jews had a right to their own authority for jurisdiction concerning religious matters or whether religious institutions and traditions were like all other aspects of civil life to be considered subject to Prussian law. Mendelssohn's answer was clear and unambiguous: the state had no authority to interfere with issues of faith and religion. Whereas Prussian courts with non-Jewish judges presented no problem for Mendelssohn when it came to the question of who would be sitting on issues concerning matters of Jewish religion, the courts and judges would in these cases bound to be follow Jewish law the state would be obliged to respect (Mendelssohn 1929–2011, 8, pp. 16–17; Mendelssohn 2002, pp. 100–3).

In terms of granting autonomy to a colony, Mendelssohn argues that there are two areas of concern: civil matters on the one hand and religion and church affairs on the other. The first matter, as Mendelssohn argues, can be conducted entirely on the terms of the colonies' own traditions, laws, and customs that determine the relationships and which are all contractual. With regard to church matters and religion, however, the colonist's argument now suggests that his religious beliefs trumps the motherland's claims because, as Mendelssohn observes, theoretically speaking there does not exist any form of rightful claim to jurisdiction at all concerning matters of church and religion. Religious difference, in others words, can produce no difference in title, legal or political (Mendelssohn 1929–2011, 8, pp. 16–19; Mendelssohn 2002, pp. 100–5).

Mendelssohn's argument consists in pointing out that the motherland cannot concede any law to its colonies that it lacks the power and legitimacy to grant to its own citizens (Mendelssohn 1929–2011, 8, p. 20; Mendelssohn 2002, p. 108). The point that underlies Mendelssohn's argument, and which he introduces here, is that any claim to a right that does not exist already in the state of nature is devoid of legitimation (Mendelssohn 1929–2011, 8, p. 19; Mendelssohn 2002, p. 106). In the preface to Manasseh ben Israel, Mendelssohn concludes that the "mother nation" has therefore no authority to privilege any religious faith or doctrine by awarding any goods or benefits, to reward or punish their acceptance or rejection. The explicit and openly addressed issue in Mendelssohn's argument against Dohm concerns Mendelssohn's view that there is no political right for the state in matters of religion. The "mother nation" cannot confer any rightful authority in ecclesiastic or religious matters to its colonies since no claim to such a right exists with regard to the "mother nation" itself.

So far, the explicit line of the argument. But there exists a more critical implication. Mendelssohn's discussion suggests that what counts as a right of a colony counts consequently also as one for the motherland. Turning the tables, Mendelssohn thus makes critical use of the colonial discourse to flesh out the equal "rights of humanity" or human rights for the motherland and its colonies (Mendelssohn 1929–2011, 8, p. 17). The rights of each colony, "and the Jews in particular," cannot be different from the rights of the motherland, this argument implies. While pointing out that what the "mother nation" does not possess she cannot grant to her colony, Mendelssohn confronts his readers with the problem that while the relationship between "mother nation" and colony is framed in such a way as to correspond with the relationship between the state and its citizen, a careful examination of the domestic arrangements points to the hidden but crucial presupposition that the notion of an "indigenous colony" is an unexamined, but centrally fundamental, assumption of the modern nation-state:

> Thus the mother-nation itself is not qualified to attach the enjoyment of any worldly good or privilege to a doctrine particularly pleasing to it, or to reward

or punish the adopting or rejecting thereof; and how can it concede to the colony that which is not in its one power?

(Mendelssohn 1929–2011, 8, pp. 20–1; Mendelssohn 2002, p. 108)

In a critical move, Mendelssohn addresses this blind spot of modern political thought by highlighting the problem of the "indigenous colony" as a critical reminder of the limits of authority of the "mother nation." Mendelssohn's argument advances the issue in an illuminating way in addressing the problem of political rights not through a direct analysis of state power and sovereignty, but by way of a discussion of the relationship between "mother nation" and "indigenous colony." Mendelssohn is studiously unassuming in articulating his argument, but the critical significance of its implications will become clearer when Mendelssohn develops a full-fledged formulation of his views on political philosophy in *Jerusalem or on Religious Power and Judaism.*

Couching his argument in terms of the colonist's viewpoint, Mendelssohn's critical impetus has often been misunderstood as an apologetic, even assimilationist, stance. But rather than sanctioning any discourse on the assumption of an "indigenous colony," Mendelssohn's argument highlights the point that the interdependence between the "mother nation" and its "indigenous colony" does not and cannot foreclose the innate natural right that informs the constitution of any rightful state, be it in the motherland or in any of its colonies. As the colonial situation is legally one that is derived from the motherland's, this derivative constellation does not create a surplus or excess of claims or rights but, rather, brings out the problem more pointedly as it presents itself with regard to the claims of the motherland to consider autonomy and sovereignty as a purely domestic and internal matter. For the question then arises on what notions exactly are the concepts of domestic autonomy and membership of the nation grounded.

For Mendelssohn, the view from the colony thus not only confirms the rightful claim to the innate right of the colony to self-determination with regard to all civil law and religious matters, but also outlines the parameters for the rightful condition that would legitimate recognition as motherland and "mother nation." Mirroring back the colony's view regarding the constitution that, in order to be rightful, must be derived from the motherland, the colony's legal structure and government remains contingent on the civil state of the motherland. The principle of this relationship, the argument implies in no uncertain terms, can only be one of equality. Consequently, the distinction between "motherland" and "indigenous colony" is ultimately problematic if not altogether spurious as far as any legal and political claims are concerned, or so Mendelssohn's line of argument suggests. The logic of sovereignty is thus put under further pressure. Not only can no "mother nation" establish any form of right that is inconsistent with its own domestic arrangements, but these domestic arrangements come now under critical scrutiny from the colonist perspective. In this perspective, the state's claims to sovereignty are now subject to the critical examination of a public discourse that is no longer constituted by the exclusive membership of citizens but includes now anyone over which the state claims its authority.

If the challenge of domestic arrangements cannot be separated from the challenge of the situation in the colony, the "domestic" colonies in the heartland of the "mother nation" provide a reminder that colonialism is always already a matter of domestic politics. The fact that the colonies that Mendelssohn is talking about – the ones of Jews and the French Huguenots in eighteenth-century Prussia – do not have territorial borders but operate as legal constructs in a state of estates only brings home the point more poignantly: the deeply embedded function of colonialist thought for the construction of the modern nation-state, sovereignty, power, and social contract. Changing the position of the observer, Mendelssohn's critical angle directs attention back to the question of the conception of the "mother land" as one defined by the problem of internal difference it seeks to project onto external as well as internal others. The problem of the claim of a self-identical conception of nation-state and sovereignty is thus shifted to external and internal border disputes that complicate and continually displace the problem of the identity of the sovereign through the refraction of the figure of the colonist within.

Mendelssohn's preface to Manasseh ben Israel's *Vindication of the Jews* reminds its readers that the notion of the indigenous colonist is structurally tied up with the problem of the construction of the nation-state and its concept of sovereignty. The problem of citizenship and civil society poses problems that neither the nation-state nor the colonial model can resolve on its own. Rather, the two models turn out to be intertwined, each defined by an exclusionary approach to citizenship and civil society. Critical against the conceptual force of the approach these models mandate, Mendelssohn's argument serves as a critical reminder that the nation-state is based on a concept of national homogeneity that presupposes the colony for internal distinction in order to stabilize the boundaries of enclosure. The aporetic challenge consists in the problem that any move to self-determination in the framework of national discourse reproduces the inside–outside divide and, as a consequence, links autonomy with a heteronomous moment of arbitrating the exclusion of others. Any state that divides civil society along the lines of class, nation, religion, or any other criterion thus undermines the claim to sovereignty and self-legitimacy so long as it excludes others that it makes part of its sovereign sphere of rule. Emancipation must therefore be understood as a principal demand not of individual constituents of the groups that are excluded but of the state itself in its very own interest.

Power, state, and sovereignty in Spinoza and Mendelssohn

Mendelssohn's view from the "indigenous colony" is a position that frames the question of state, power, and sovereignty in critical difference to traditional accounts. This decentered view is defined by the exclusion of the indigenous colonist from an "inside," an exclusion that at the same time seeks to lock up and contain the other. These constitutively contradictory terms of the Jewish experience at the moment of the emergent modern state lead Mendelssohn to examine the terms of modern political thought in principle. Mendelssohn thus critically challenges both the paternalist approach that defines the political philosophy of

Christian Wolff, the exponent of German Enlightenment rationalism, and the con-tract-based theories of Hobbes and Locke that remain inadequate when it comes to theorizing state, power, and the question of sovereignty. If they had devel-oped valuable paradigmatic frameworks for political thought, Mendelssohn's *Jerusalem or on Religious Power and Judaism* reminds its readers that Hobbes and Locke remain hostage to visions of political freedom and self-realization that are contingent on a restrictively mechanic understanding of political power.

Mendelssohn's alternative approach, on the other hand, is informed by the kind of critical reasoning that Spinoza advances. Departing from Machiavelli, Hobbes, and Descartes in critical manner, Spinoza articulates an alternative approach to rethinking power, state, and sovereignty. Spinoza resists instrumentalization and the claim of sovereign control by theorizing power as a dynamic configuration of power potentials whereby power is no longer understood as an entity but function-ally as geometrically ever-changing and infinite possibilities. Spinoza's critical approach prepares the theoretical groundwork for Mendelssohn. For this reason, this section will explore Mendelssohn's thought with an eye on Spinoza to high-light the critical impulse of Mendelssohn's views.[7]

For Spinoza (an "echo of the Orient," as Hegel dubbed his thought) and Mendelssohn, political power is to be understood in terms of power in general. Rather than following the cue of political power or a particular form of its theo-retical reconstruction to formulate a philosophical notion of power, they both proceed in the opposite direction by framing political power in terms of a more general theory of power. In grounding the concept of power in the context of their larger philosophical frameworks they signal a critical intervention equal only to Kant's insistence that theory and practice cannot be wrenched apart. With regard to the question of the theory of sovereignty at stake here they respond with a provocatively modern claim to the sovereignty of theory or, more precisely, they understand the profound link that interconnects the theory of sovereignty with the question of the sovereignty of theory. Power then can no longer be theorized "sovereignly," from either the throne or the philosopher's armchair, but comes into view as a determining relationship that constitutes all human activity, desire, and aspiration. Consequently, power is no longer imagined as residing in distinct places but understood as ubiquitous.

For Spinoza, not the least critical consequences of his ontology based on his concept of substance is to comprehend power itself not as substance, but as its modifications. Spinoza defines individuals as so many infinitely possible forms of modifications; hence, there are as many forms of powers as there are individuals, i.e. modifications of substance or nature. In addition, just as any individual has no more right to exist than the power to do so, so no power has more legitimacy or normative force than it is capable of enforcing. Spinoza's notorious formula that power equals right goes both ways. It ascribes only as much right to power as there is power. However, the concept of power is, for Spinoza, defined not by representation but merely by function. Power can thus claim only what it can actually enforce. Spinoza does understands power not as an entity but a relational phenomenon, i.e. in terms of functionality.

With regard to human relations, Spinoza thinks of power as distinctly rela-tional. If political power is institutional, its force is based on compliance and is consequently not localizable in a particular place or authority. In other words, political power rests on agreement, persuasion, obedience, and compliance. Political authority and legitimacy are defined by this confluence of effects, and no theory of political power can abstract from this constitutive nexus that defines the formation of power. For Spinoza and Mendelssohn, the mythical birth of Athena – the armed Goddess champion of reason – is just that: the brainchild of Zeus and his mythologists, who created a fantasy of sovereign power that can produce its own legitimacy by recourse to self-referentiality. Against such an uncritical conception that ignores the complex functional interdependence that constitutes power, Spinoza reminds us to attend to the particular dynamics that determines the economy of power. According to this understanding, power is not only unsta-ble and in flux but resists, therefore, brute control, transfer, or containment.

In summary, Spinoza's immanent approach does not comprehend power as residing in individuals, institutions, or other forms of political life but locates it as the connecting agent between them. Power's mercurial character defines the hydraulic rather than static laws of the dynamics that define the nature of power. Approaching Spinoza via Mendelssohn not only reflects a particularly illuminat-ing trajectory of historical reception that has long been considered a "minor" line, but makes it possible to flesh out the critical impetus of Spinoza's theory of power. With Spinoza, not only does Mendelssohn's view on power emerge as the idi-osyncratic attitude to which it has been reduced, but its ramifications can now be recognized in their own sophisticated philosophical impetus.

Mendelssohn signals his move to differentiate forms of power with regard to their different forms of manifestation already in the title of his, we might as well call it, "theological-political treatise," *Jerusalem or on Religious Power and Judaism*. Rather than merely arguing that religion presents a power of its own, Mendelssohn's *Jerusalem* suggests that power per se, as abstract or "pure" form does not exist. Power exists instead only in specific historical configuration, i.e. in the form of the specificity of its historical particularity. Political power there-fore cannot simply be balanced or offset against religious power. The functional disparity of the two opposed powers illustrates the theological–political differ-ence, which encodes the power dispositives in each case in incommensurably different fashion. The radical alterity between politics and religion presents for Mendelssohn the reminder that political and religious power are not to be con-fused but must be kept apart, and that the difference in their competences must be recognized in order to avoid the short-circuiting of different forms of power. For Mendelssohn, this calls for, among other things, the consistent emancipation of political theory from the overt and covert influence of religion that proves resistant to secularization yet so profoundly informs modernity's political power discourse.

Power is thus neither "primitive," primary, nor originary, but always already mediated and conditioned by history, i.e. social interaction. In other words, power appears only in one or another specific form, i.e. the power of a particular state or some form of religious power or other political institution. And behind it we do not have to imagine some reified concept of power per se, but historically particular forms of a state, religion, and civil society, none of which represents ultimate and unconditional grounds but all of which require continuous renegotiation. Mendelssohn's rethinking of the concept of power makes it possible to address the marginalization and exclusion of the Jews from politics and society as a normative prescription that contradicts the claim of classical political philosophy that its assumptions are devoid of metaphysics. But for Mendelssohn this points far beyond what may be misunderstood as a parochial argument for tolerance, acceptance, and recognition, which would merely amount to a correction as far as the arrangements of power and law are concerned. Mendelssohn calls for a rethinking of a more profound and deeper seated problem of the dominant notion of power of which the Jewish "state of exception" is simply a stark reminder. Consequently, Mendelssohn welcomes Dohm's efforts to call for the emancipation and equality of the Jews not as an act of mercy and equity, but based on the insight that the demand of equal rights presents a necessary condition for politically enlightened reason as well as state's reason:

> And fortunate will it be for us [Jews] if that cause [of emancipation and equality] become at once ours; if there be no such thing as urging the rights of mankind, without at once claiming ours.
>
> (Mendelssohn, preface to Manasseh ben Israel, Mendelssohn 1929–2011, 8, p. 5; Mendelssohn 2002, p. 80)

In the light of Spinoza we can appreciate Mendelssohn's approach in *Jerusalem* as the project to secularize the concept of power in such a way that its theological implications no longer need to be concealed and suppressed but can be addressed without making philosophy the hostage of hidden theological claims. Spinoza's consistently descriptive concept of power, devoid of teleological implications, makes it possible to formulate an analytic of power that remains resistant to normative pressures. This is because Spinoza never conceives power in abstract terms, but always "geometrically," that is, functionally as the interplay of forces that does not create any normative surplus.

Spinoza and Mendelssohn reconceptualize power in a resolutely alternative fashion to conventional theories of power. Central to both is the insight not only that power as *potentia* is juxtaposed to power as *potestas,* but that this distinction makes it impossible to ontologize power, i.e. to reify it.[8] Where power is staged in the form of official violence, coercive right, punishment, and other forms of brute and structural force, Spinoza's and Mendelssohn's approach suggests that, as with any case enforcing power, there is not so much power itself at work but rather its opposite, powerlessness, caused by the sheer need of its realization that ultimately signals the lack of power rather than force. We all are familiar with this phenomenon: it is at the moment of crisis rather than strength when one reaches for the mattresses, for rifles, and for other weapons. Violence steps onto the scene where power proves impotent. To wish to define power through the display of power and violence would mean to put the cart before the horse, i.e. to identify power with the forms of its decay; but this is possible only so long as the fiction of a lasting and irrevocable power transfer is maintained, a notion that both Mendelssohn and Spinoza vehemently reject. Optimized forms of power are to be found where the display of power is superfluous, whereas the need for force serves as an indicator and symptom of powerlessness. Mistaking the display of force for a paradigm represents a profound misrecognition of the dynamics of power in general.

As a consequence, Mendelssohn, just like Spinoza, theorizes the state differently than his contemporaries. To construct a state, the political theorist cannot rely on stable building elements solidified by rationalist certainties (a lost proposition in light of Spinoza's and Mendelssohn's concept of power). Spinoza sets political theory on a footing distinctly different from Machiavelli, Hobbes, and Locke by insisting that political thought must ground its reasoning in a critical consideration of the constitutive role of the psychodynamic economy of the affects. Following Spinoza's insight in the *Political Treatise* and the *Ethics* that the affects represent the central force that defines political power, Mendelssohn highlights the dynamics of human development as self-empowerment – or self-realization – as the central moment in the construction of the state envisioned as a structure for political self-government. Mendelssohn thus identifies the individual as the irreducible constituent of civil society that provides the resources on which the state is run.

Understanding the state as the organ of civil society's self-organization, Spinoza and Mendelssohn view the dynamics of the economy of power as the formative force that makes the political structure of the state possible in the first place, which, consequently, rests on the dynamic equilibrium of the social forces that constitute it. This requires the recognition of the state as a function of power that remains inseparably linked to the constituents of civil society from which it originates. The state, on this view, is thus less an arrangement for settling the claims between its parties, and more a community-based structure to provide the necessary framework for peace and freedom. In this way, the state comes into focus as an entity that rests on an economy of power dynamics that constitutes and therefore defines its structure rather than the other way around. The state's purpose, function, and tasks are thus established by the concept of power that makes the state the organ of the civil society as the site in which political power originates. As a political organ the state cannot serve as source for self-legitimation as classic political philosophy would have it.

Locating the site of the source of power outside the structure of the state, Mendelssohn and Spinoza expose the self-referential circuit of the logics of legitimation used for rationalizing political power through the logics of the preservation of the state based on the confusion of power and violence as its form of decay. Instead, by recognizing power as the conditioning force that constitutes the legitimacy of the political state, its function, purpose, and tasks emerge in a new light. The notion of the provisional nature of any transfer of power to the state or any other representative of sovereignty for that matter requires the state to be thought of as continuous rather than discontinuous with human needs and desires. Thus, Mendelssohn's disenfranchised position provides the critical lever for theorizing state, power, and sovereignty. His view from the "indigenous colony," the "periphery within," prompts him to rethink the discourse of the state and sovereignty from the position of a decentered centrality that turns the subject position of disempowerment into a liberating force of critique.[9]

This particular shift in the accentuation of the legal framework of the conception of the state advances a vision profoundly different from both contract-based, as well as traditional feudal versions. Mendelssohn's and Spinoza's approach differs from the model of the administrative state, whose self-proclaimed interest of best practice envisions an optimization of administrative power driven by the kind of functionality of the machine paradigm that Kant had already exposed as ill-conceived. In opposition to these available notions of the state, Spinoza and Mendelssohn advance an alternative conception that envisions the state as a dynamic political institution designed for the sole purpose of political life in a civil society, i.e. to provide a lasting and rightful framework for human life to thrive, what Spinoza calls "peace." In critical distinction to Hobbes's view of peace as simply the absence of war – ultimately a dismal vision of solitude and desert-like state of stasis – Spinoza's biblically inspired view of peace carries the connotation of the Hebrew word for peace and its Messianic force of *shalom* as wholeness. For Spinoza, peace is the comprehensive purpose of the state as a state of intactness and freedom aligned with virtue as fortitude (*fortitudo*) and reason (Spinoza 2000, Chapter 5, §§4–5). This means that the state's purpose is to optimize the conditions conducive for people to become autonomous, self-determining, and self-empowered.

Likewise, Mendelssohn formulates a theory of the state in striking contrast to the customs of political philosophy. Equally wary of assumptions of moral normativity and the political realist variety, Mendelssohn accentuates the educative aspect of the state over and against the coercive one. Irreducible to a simply coercive institution, the state's strength shows when its educative function renders the coercive one superfluous. For Mendelssohn however, education is not a euphemism for paternalist control but signifies the dynamic notion of human development by directing the affects toward perfection. At the heart of Mendelssohn's moral, esthetic, and political philosophy, *Bildung* presents the central notion for rethinking the purpose of the state. The state's mandate for education as the complementary and ultimately more effective and promising road to achieve its purpose is further grounded in Mendelssohn's *Jerusalem* as a balancing act between state and church that theorizes both institutions as deriving their legitimacy from the mutual acceptance of each other. Following Spinoza's *Theological–Political Treatise* and its recognition of the theological–political complex as constitutive in defining the political moment, Mendelssohn recognizes that both the political and the religious powers that be resist any form of reduction of one to the other, but are to be understood as providing legitimacy of either one only in tandem. Mendelssohn's unique conception of the theological–political balancing act as the constitutive ground for political legitimacy makes the moment of *Bildung* (or education) the central guiding concept capable of serving as a criterion for defining the proper functioning of the state as political and the church as religious. As civil society gives rise to these two forms of power, political and religious, it does so by linking them at the same time reciprocally. If Mendelssohn were able to articulate his critique through a critical view back from the colony, we could call his stance Mendelssohn's own "post-colonial" vantage point.

Sovereignty and secularization in Mendelssohn and Heine

The recognition of this reciprocal interdependency of state and church leads Mendelssohn to articulate a theory of sovereignty that follows Spinoza. Both stress the autonomy of state and church as properly guaranteed only if the other's is recognized in its irreducible rights. Mendelssohn develops this further in grounding the authority of state and church in a division of labor, competence, and authority, thus addressing at the same time the issues of both sovereignty and secularization. Against the confusion of political sovereignty and sanctity, Mendelssohn's *Jerusalem* highlights the difficult linkage that traditional notions of state and power suggest. Exposing the confusion of the political and the religious as cause for the failure to understand the nature of civil society and its attendant dynamics of power, Mendelssohn's approach indicates that the question of sovereignty cannot be separated from the examination of religious power and secularization. And secularization is on these terms understood as a movement that cannot be isolated from the theological–political context whose result it is just as much as is the institution of the church.

In terms of the critical theory of secularization that Mendelssohn advances in *Jerusalem,* sovereignty of the state can be adequately theorized only if seen in balance with the religious dimension. If this balance is unhinged, both state and church are in jeopardy. Secularization therefore does not imply the denial of representation of religious needs in the public sphere but, on the contrary, the recognition of the legitimacy of religion as a constitutive part of human nature and therefore a legitimate part of life in civil society. The task and challenge is thus not the indictment of religion, but to sort out the contending competences between politics and religion or, in other words, to disentangle the theological–political knot. Secularization is the stage where the mutual recognition of state and religion is recognized as the condition for the grounding of state sovereignty in legitimacy. In other words, Mendelssohn avoids the self-referentially tautological claim of classic theories of sovereignty, which relies on the logic of short-circuiting power and the divine, be it in the openly explicit claim of aristocratic legitimacy or in the arcane fig-leafed fashion of "political theology." Instead, his approach argues that secularization is maintained only if religion is given its adequate and meaningful place in civil society and that denial of such a claim would be not secularization but its dangerous reverse.

With Spinoza and Mendelssohn, secularization comes into focus as an intrinsically religious category itself. Secularization does not indicate a departure from religion or its end, but rather the recognition of religion's formative significance, the particular and profound yet often ignored role that religions and their traditions continue to play in a post-Enlightenment age. In agreement with the literal meaning of "secularization," they understand that this process does anything but neutralize religion because it signifies religion's powerful, if unacknowledged, return to social and political life. As a consequence, secularization becomes discernible as a process that cannot be easily differentiated from religion, but rather is a process of religion. The desire to separate the two reflects the desire to cut through the complicated interdependence of the theological–political complex, i.e. the process of secularization is another name for this complex.

Maybe no one has understood this better and expressed it more eloquently than the post-Romantic German Jewish poet Heinrich Heine. Secularization emerges in both his critical and literary work as anything but a final point of closure. Rather, secularization is faced with the continuing challenge of confronting the theological–political tensions that inform the experience of modernity. Heine provocatively foregrounds the striking nexus that constitutes the secular and religious as mutually constitutive aspects of the human condition. Heine makes this his explicitly critical point in *On the History of Religion and Philosophy in Germany*. It is significant, though rarely recognized, that this first original approach to intellectual history was to define its genre in a lasting manner by advancing a bold and trailblazing theory of secularization that still warrants adequate appreciation. The conceptual framework relies in critical manner on the philosopher discussed at the heart of this essay, Spinoza (Goetschel 2004a, pp. 253–65). Written in a Spinozist key, this intellectual history presents the unlikely couple of spiritualism and materialism, mind and body as the protagonists of a quest. Heine's sequel, his literary history, *The Romantic School*, restaged the Cervantes-like drama of mind (Don Quichotte) and body (Sancho Pansa) by acting out the comedy of their mutual dependence. As Heine suggests in both essays, secularization and religion depend in equal measure on each other, just like Don Quichotte and Sancho Pansa do, as each rests on the condition of the other's existence.

This approach allows Heine to critically expose Christianity's continuing claim for hegemony, accompanied by an equally continuing challenge by the heretic, yet vital, alternative traditions on which Christianity rests but which it seeks to deny and exclude. Judaism, paganism, and materialism not only come into view as vital forces that threaten to assert their force the more they are repressed, but also serve as a critical reminder that Christianity itself is profoundly shot through and dependent on these heterogeneous traditions. On Heine's reading, Christianity emerges as one of the first and formative forms of secularization (see part 1 of Heine 2007). If Heine anticipates important insights of nineteenth century-materialist and Marxist critique of religion, his approach remains in critical manner true to Spinoza in that he resists the foolish temptation of throwing out the baby with the bathwater. Like Spinoza, Heine understands that secularization is not the solution to the problem of religion, but is itself part of the problem.

In his *Travel Pictures*, Heine presents the two dominant Christian confessions in illuminating alignment with the economic fault lines of Protestant and Catholic forms of capitalism. The Jewish comedy, however, does not serve as triumphant contrast of a luckier religion that would allow for the secularization that Christianity's two corporate branches resist. Instead, Heine's Jewish comedy highlights the subliminal hold of religion in all its manifestations, in other words that any form of secularization remains an eminently religious process (see Prawer 1985). If conversion to another religion and denial of one's own religion proves an impossible embarrassment – i.e. the pressure of Jewish assimilation – that leads to comic forms of the return of the repressed: Christian desire for the claim to universalism is reminded of its Jewish sources.[10] Secularization, then, is what defines religion. It is a religious category. Heine's conception of the post-Enlightenment condition is thus pointedly conscious of the constitutive nexus of secularization and its religious traditions.

As a result, the task of rethinking the problem of secularization requires a critical revision of the Westphalian narrative. Secularization is no longer sufficiently analysed in terms of the confessional conflicts of early modern Europe. Unless the issue of the "indigenous colony" comes into focus as a problem that informs modern political theorizing (if often only in subliminal forms) secularization is reduced to an inter-confessional problem, whereas its far-reaching critical significance is ignored. Such a reduction has unfortunate implications for our understanding of the dynamics of modernity. Mendelssohn's discussion of the "indigenous colony" serves as a critical reminder that "inside" the Westphalian model there still resides the larger issue of the problem of the Jewish–Christian relationship. Unless the dynamics of this relationship receives critical attention, the discourse on secularization and modernity will remain parochially Eurocentric at best and will ultimately fail to explain the European situation itself. Secularization, in other words, cannot shed its religious history of the appropriation of religious property and contents for non-religious ends and intents. But this does not mean that we are locked inside the ecclesiastic cage. On the contrary, Heine's joyous celebration of religious difference signals a vision of liberation that breaks open the constraints of the secular field of vision as it recalls the so ancient and thus so post-contemporary biblical vision of universal liberation of all of humanity, a vision that secularization still has to appreciate as the ground upon which its own modernity rests.

If the history of Frankfurt Cathedral presents as a stark reminder of the structural entrenchment of Jews as outsiders within the construction of the discourse of the "West," Mendelssohn's critique brings home the point that the nation cannot serve as a stable referent that the claims of the state and sovereign require it to be. Rather, civil society is always already multinational. As a result, the notion of the indigenous colonist, as Mendelssohn's preface to Manasseh ben Israel's *Vindication of the Jews* reminds its readers, is structurally tied up with the problem of the construction of the nation-state and its concept of sovereignty. Citizenship and civil society poses problems that neither the nation-state nor the colonial model can resolve on its own. Rather, the two models turn out to be intertwined, each defined by an exclusionary approach to citizenship and civil society. Mendelssohn's argument serves as critical reminder that the nation-state is based on a concept of national homogeneity that presupposes the colony for internal distinction to stabilize the boundaries of enclosure. The aporetic challenge consists in the problem that any move to self-determination in the framework of national discourse reproduces the inside–outside divide, and, as a consequence, links autonomy with a heteronymous moment of arbitrating the exclusion of others. Any state that divides civil society along the lines of class, nation, religion, or any other criterion thus undermines the claim to sovereignty and self-legitimacy as long as it excludes others that it makes part of its sovereign sphere of rule. Emancipation must therefore be understood as a principal demand not of individual constituents of the groups that are excluded, but of the state itself in its very own interest.

Contentious modernity

In the current context of the discussion about how to define modernity – historically, locally, globally, theoretically – it might be helpful to return to the scene of the term's appearance. Attention to this historical and theoretical specificity allows us to grasp a critical approach to this question that opens up the debate at a moment of fierce contention over the challenge of how to theorize the concept. Whether we can speak of "one" modernity or whether we would be better advised to do so in terms of a plurality (and how many such modernities we could then envision) and whether modernity is a "Western" concept that has become a universally applied template whose particular origins, however impaired the universalism it seeks to impose, are questions that are, in an illuminating way, already addressed at the moment this term is introduced.

Introducing the word "*Modernität*" in his *Travel Pictures* in 1827, Heine's creation of the word gained wide currency and theoretical appreciation with the translation of the *Travel Pictures* into French, from where the notion would enter Baudelaire's world. But, although Baudelaire has assumed paradigmatic importance in the project of deciphering the meaning of modernity, the scene of the notion's initial creation has remained curiously unexamined. The subsequent career of the word exemplifies the attempts at its appropriation, but it also offers, on the other hand, the opportunity for reclaiming the critical moment that has been nearly erased by scholarship and criticism alike. Attending to the specificity in which Heine approached modernity suggests ways to recover the concept's liberating potential that has become illegible by committing modernity to readings seemingly oblivious to the concept's own critical potential.

In Heine, "modernity" enters the scene in the context of a critically significant juxtaposition of Walter Scott with Lord Byron. The pair come to represent two different, but complementary, ways to grasp the spirit of the age: the contention between the restorative and the innovative impulse. The particular spirit of Napoleon as a man of modern times, Heine notes, can be adequately captured only by creatively negotiating the differences between Scott and Byron. Although the idea of modernity seems out of place in the world of Scott's backwards-looking historical novels, eccentrically clashing with the blinding aura of the new Napoleonic age, Byron's hard-charging approach falls equally short in its bid to capture modernity as it lacks the ability to preserve those non-contemporary elements of the past that so profoundly inform the push toward progress and innovation. Byron's radicalism thus threatens to nip modernity in the bud with esthetic charms that tend to ignore the underside of history that Scott knows how to address. Modernity, Heine suggests, is nothing that can be captured by one or the other, but represents the moment where the old and the new come together in a creative antagonism, whose dynamics informs, defines, and thus comes to constitute the present.

Modernity, on this reading – or rather, these contending styles of writing – represents not the "modern" or the past, but that particular moment of their exchange where they conflict, clash, destroy, but also create, a new constellation through their tensions and contention. In Heine's vocabulary, modernity carries no normative implications and imposes no ethics other than that of a dialogue in which the liberating forces of contradiction give voice to rather than silence the problems and difficulties the constellation of modernity brings to the fore. As a dialogical concept, this notion of modernity does not give rise to particular forms of universal claims but serves as the scene for exchange, transaction, contention, and critique. Its emancipatory charge carries a weak form of messianism the liberating openness of which resists the temptation for closure: its universal vision stubbornly resists the imposition of any particular form of universalism with its fatal consequence of erasure of other forms of particularity.

Heine reminds us that theories of modernization lack universal application because of modernity's double-faced nature. Defined by the process of negotiation between the old and new, modernity's "universal" challenge consists in each and every case of presenting a unique configuration between old and new – which may promise analogy, but no conceptual identity. However, with Heine we do not need to forsake modernity as a bad form of universalism. Instead, we can appreciate the concept's universal appeal no longer in terms of an imposed proposition that can only be accepted or rejected, but as the description of a universal condition whose specificity makes each situation particular. As a consequence, every moment of modernity can be understood as a distinctly particular call for attention to the specific constellation of that modernity which in each particular case will give rise to yet another negotiation of the concept. Heine, in other words, gives voice to a concept of modernity that is universal because he liberates it from any semantic occupation. Arguing for a concept of modernity that makes difference and alterity its central concerns, the concept becomes now universally accessible because it no longer rests on the exclusion of the particular.

With Heine, it becomes possible to recognize the spurious grounds of the invidious alternative to read modernity as Western (and thus either subject all of humanity to an administered concept of modernity) or else disown the "non-Western" world from traditions claimed as exclusively European. In the "English Fragments," the concluding book of *Travel Pictures*, Heine offers a striking illustration of the way modernity negotiates its emancipatory visions outside of this false alternative. Strolling along the Thames, Heine visits a ship importing goods from India. Lacking any means of communication with the Muslim sailors he encounters from India, Arabia, and Africa, Heine welcomes them with the greeting "Mohammed!," which is enthusiastically returned by the sailors with the equally joyful salutation of "Bonaparte!" (Heine 1906, p. 452) Both liberating and revolutionary, these battle-cries give voice to the fact that the spirit of universal liberation only be expressed can in particulars, and at the same time more than that: the fact that the human difference in which the universal resides remains communicable by human beings, though only in the name of the other.

Notes

1 See, for example, Mervyn Frost (1996, p. 212) for a "secular interpretation" of Hegel, curiously oblivious of the implications secularization might entail for theorizing the state. It is no surprise then that Frost proposes the state as the solution rather than the object of critical examination (Frost 1996, p. 148). If individuality is according to Frost and by courtesy of Hegel constituted by the state (Frost 1996, p. 158), Hegel had turned the tables on Mendelssohn, who insisted on the primacy of individuality. The argument in this chapter suggests that Hegel's turn has not been altogether assuring.

2 For a concise summary of the rules on engagement of the Westphalian model see Watson (1992, Chapter 17).

3 Philpott (2000) cogently argues for the role of the crisis that the Reformation triggered as the driving impulse for the emergence of the Westphalian model of state sovereignty. His succinct political analysis ignores, however, the larger theological background of confessional conflict in the difficult relationship of Christianity to its "mother" religion, Judaism. Although references to Jewish sources of the Christian tradition surface in this context among others also, for instance in Max Weber's *Protestant Ethics*, the role of the Jewish context in the question of secularization is curiously enough mostly ignored. I thank Warren Montag for having pointed out to me the particular role that the citation of Jewish sources plays in Weber.

4 For a discussion of the nexus between colonization and epistemology see Goetschel (1999).

5 I would like to thank Raphael Gross, director of the Jewish Museum Frankfurt am Main, for bringing this part of the story to my attention.

6 See Mendelssohn (1929–2011). The full reference information for the collection is Moses Mendelssohn, *Gesammelte Schriften: Jubiläumsausgabe*, eds. Ismar Elbogen, Julius Guttmann, and Eugen Mittwoch, in association with Fritz Bamberger, Haim Borodianksi, Simon Rawidowicz, Bruno Strauß, and Leo Strauß, continued by Alexander Altmann in association with Haim Bar-Dayan, Eva J. Engel, Leo Strauß, and Werner Weinberg. 25 in 38 vols (Berlin: Akademie Verlag, 1929–32; Breslau: S. Münzs, 1938; Stuttgart-Bad Cannstatt: F. Frommann, 1971–2011) (hereafter cited by mentioning the volume and page number of the passage in question). For an English translation see Mendelssohn (2002, p. 80). Samuel, however, translates the passage: "those native aliens into citizens."

7 For a more detailed discussion of the theoretical context in which Spinoza and Mendelssohn develop their ideas and a discussion of the relevant literature see Goetschel (2004a, 2007).

8 For Spinoza's important distinction between *potentia* and *potestas* see his *Political Treatise*, in which he consistently maintains the distinction between the two. *Potentia* relates to *potestas* there as *natura naturans* does to *narura naturata* in the *Ethics*. See also Goetschel (2004a, pp. 76–8).

9 Editor's note: it would be interesting to compare and contrast Goetschel's representation of Mendelssohn here with Enrique Dussel's "philosophy of liberation."

10 For a detailed discussion of Heine's acting out of this two-pronged problem see Goetschel (2004b).

Part II
Cultural contexts

6 International relations of modernity in Sayyid Qutb's thoughts on sovereignty

The notion of democratic participation in the Islamic canon

Sayed Khatab

Introduction

It is frequently argued that because many Islamic countries are traditional monarchies or dictatorships, or because of those events that have taken place in these countries, Islam is not compatible with either modernity or democracy. Some would maintain that Islamic culture is itself a stumbling block to a democratic polity and modernistic society and can accommodate neither. To maintain such a position is to misunderstand not only religion, but society, history, and the operation of social forces. Nevertheless, various political stances compete for attention in these academic and media discussions. In this competition Sayyid Qutb's writings, and in particular his concept of sovereignty, is routinely considered as a threat to an orderly international relations (Tibi 1998, p. 42; Kepel 2002, pp. 27–8, 62–3; Zimmerman 2004, pp. 224–6). In terms of defining certain issues for the Muslim intelligentsia, Qutb (d. 1966) charted the renewal of Islamic thought of which a large number of the current radical Islamic organizations are the legatees. His thought on sovereignty was constituted in such a way that is attractive to many Islamist organizations, and the potential for militants to draw strength from Qutb's writings and influence domestic and international relations is significant. Some publications extend beyond Qutb's writings at times and beyond the "canon" at other times; and overall they take varying approaches of which each is colored by world politics.

After 1990, the international debate on Islam's relation to modernity, by and large, was an expression of post-Soviet representations. Following the catastrophic events of September 11, Islam has become one of the top priorities on the agenda of global security (Haas 1999, pp. 88–90; Rubin 2002, pp. 42–5). The discipline of international relations (IR), enshrined by modernity, has been grappling with the tasks of how to conceptualize the Islamic concept of sovereignty in the institutions of modernity. As a result, Islam's compatibility with democracy and its commitment to world peace and coexistence with the West and the rest have come to be the subject of colorful discussions by governments, politicians, intellectuals, cartoonists, and political commentators, with the clash of civilizations thesis never far from mind (Huntington 1996, pp. 21, 215, 239; Zimmerman 2004,

p. 238). This sense of urgency and relevance resulted from the realization by some decision-makers that the problems occupying IR – transnational terrorism, local and regional conflicts, proliferation of armies, influx of refugees, social dislocation and deprivation, cultural disintegration, and economic hopelessness – were not confined to individuals or groups, but also applied to Islam. The tragedy of September 11 made it difficult, for some, to distinguish between Islam and terror. Islam and Muslims thus became presented in the media as celebrity models and world stars.

It is not surprising then that there is a proliferation of cartoons, books, and other writings in Arabic and European languages about Islam. Much of this material is used to speak of Islam in terms of certain binary opposites: tradition as opposed to modernity; resurgence as opposed to decline; and decadence as opposed to renewal. This paradigm has become more complex as concepts such as secularization, Westernization, and globalization have been added to this pattern and language of superiority and inferiority (Davis 1987, pp. 36–8; Esposito and Voll 1996, p. 14; Kepel 2002, pp. 27–28, 62–3; Zimmerman 2004, pp. 224–6). As a result, there has been an appalling failure to systemically treat the main issues at hand, conceptually and theoretically. The main dynamic behind the binary opposites is a swing from resentment to resentment; from jihad to crusade; from division between neighbors to division between nations and between civilizations; between Islam and modernity; between here and there; between Islam and the West; between them and us; between our values and their values; between the heaven and the earth; and between this world and the other. The influence of these notions on domestic and international relations is profoundly critical to world peace.

Contributing to the debate, this chapter investigates Islamic responses to modernity. It examines whether or not Islam is compatible with democracy, the most positive connotation of modernity. It is widely considered that democracy and modernity go hand in hand. The investigation focuses on the thought of Qutb, the Islamist, who is widely considered "the godfather" of Islamic political thought and movements in the modern world. Exposing this influential current in Islamic thought, and demonstrating that neither Islam nor Qutb rejects modernity or democracy, the chapter also provides the Islamic conception of the two key terms in question. Starting with a brief background outlining the Muslim response to modernity in the past two centuries, this chapter will examine Qutb's concept of sovereignty (*hakimiyyah*) and its orientation toward IR, and will place a special focus on the notion of democracy in the Islamic canon of thought. It seeks to generate new understandings of this political thought with regards to extremism, violence, and terrorism by unlocking the many complexities of Islam's relation to the polity with special focus on the conception of sovereignty and its relations to modernity's constitutional rule: pluralism, elections, and temporal legislation.

Modernity: challenges and Muslim responses

The definition of modernity's nature and sources is routinely considered in connection with Western societal and cultural qualifications. Progress in sciences and technologies has made rationalization and efficiency the key concepts of modernity and the emblems of our epoch, so much so that the fact of modernity is very often confused with what appears to be the ideology of modernism. As emphasized by Shilliam in the introduction to this book, modernity is usually defined only through the prism of Western experience in which the West versus the rest is a key theme. Neither Islam nor its culture and thought were seen as important to the canonical thought of modernity. "Non-Western thought," Shilliam says, was "rarely considered to be a source through which to construct legitimate knowledge of the modern world." Modernity is thus seen as a condition of European history, and is characterized by the rise of the nation-state, industrialization, capitalism, socialism, democracy, science, and technology. Modernity is embodied in the processes of European reform which emerged, to some extent, from religious revolt against the Vatican in the fifteenth century and which were followed by the eighteenth-century's Enlightenment. It is these processes of reform that influenced religion's relation to polity and society in Europe and which changed and embraced all angles of human life. It contains all the greatest human achievements that influenced all societal spheres including industrialization, autonomization, democratization, and pluralization (Rundell 1987; Giddens 1990; Habermas 1994).

Modernity's institutional elements, such as the nation-state, capitalism, and industrialization, infiltrated into the Muslim world in many ways. Most important, however, were the imperial and colonial relations that in the last two centuries impacted upon Muslim communities through various social, political, and cultural ideas, the bulk of which were Western in origin (Samarah 1991, pp. 5–6). In short, Muslims came into contact with modernity through Western military, commercial, and colonial expansionism. Equipped by the Industrial Revolution and prompted by necessity, European powers invaded the Muslim world to safeguard their economic, political, and ideological interests. An influx of Europeans engaged in a range of pursuits in the Muslin world from raw materials extraction to banking, education, administration, governance, law, and commerce. Such dramatic involvement in the affairs of Muslim society debilitated its traditional economic and political institutions and forced the gate wide open for a massive infusion of modern ideas that manifested itself in the patterns of Muslim life (Lewis 1993, pp. 23–5, 28–32). In other words, the lack of strong economic and political institutions capable of regulating Western influence led to the rapid distortion of traditional patterns leading to the collapse of the Ottoman Empire and eventually the rapid assertion of direct Western colonial control of Muslim countries. Protected by such military expansionism, modernity challenged Muslim society's canon with the transformation from self-rule to European colonial rule (Husayn 1985, pp. 14–16; Lewis 2002, pp. 14–16).

The social dislocation that ensued was traumatic and led to debates on the cultural and socio-political role that Islam should play in dealing with this challenge. It is critical to compare two worlds of which one was constantly stirred by modernity's technological effervescence while the other was invariably stilted in memories of a flourished past and clung to old traditions which mixed local cultures with Qur'anic references. For one might ask about Islam's commitment and inclination toward modernization, "Who assures us that the Muslim world is capable of acceding to modernity and modernizing Muslim society without denying the foundations of Islam?" In this respect, Muslims' response to modernity can be divided in three categories, of each which found currency among Muslims during the nineteenth and twentieth centuries.

1. *Imitative traditional response.* This response follows the traditional or historical method, *taqlid* (imitation), i.e. to imitate the Muslims' history or Muslim ancestors, in what they said or did, to apply the Islamic tradition, regardless of considerations of relevance in terms of place, space or generation. It disregards temporal consideration and legal reasoning (*ijtihad*). This category has proven a failure as it has not been able to meet the challenges of modern life (Abu Zahrah 1957, pp. 474–523; Al-Bardisi 1985, pp. 169–216).

2. *Imitative modern response.* This was often called the foreign solution (*al-hall al-khariji*) and meant the imitation of the modern West by borrowing its ideas and directly implementing them. This approach was appreciated and practiced by the Ottoman caliphate when confronted by Europe's military might. The Ottomans focused mainly on what was immediate and visible, such as military, weaponry, warfare tactics, economy, and governance. They were determined to accomplish their plan to regain their power, but their method was to imitate Europe indiscriminately and to fashion Muslim society according to European norms rather than to select what suits Muslim society. Their imitation included Western lifestyle and fashions to the extent that the Ottomans replaced the "turban" with the "Roman fez" (Gurel 1990, pp. 87–8) and declared European dresses the official dress of the state's workforce, military or civil. They then reformed their judiciary system, personal law, banking and interests, toward the end of the period known as the "age of reform" (*'asr al-tanzimat*) (Husayn 1985, pp. 15–18). In this connection, Bernard Lewis emphasized that the Ottomans were borrowing Western laws and ideas that were actually "developed in different circumstances" and by ways "different from their own way of doing things" (Lewis 2002, p. 64). Because attempts were made to import, rather than to learn and develop knowledge, the Ottomans entered a cycle of emptiness, weakness, and loss of vision because of the millstone of imitation. In this connection, Montesquieu could be said to have recommended for Muslims seeking modernity what the Qur'an had recommended for their ancestors in the seventh century. The Qur'anic advice to Muslims preparing be citizens of a modern state was to learn: to seek education and acquire knowledge if it was in China (Qur'an, 96: 1–5). Even with the passing of that era, the principle remained the same and continued to be considered an essential quality of modern society and its governance. As Montesquieu states: "The laws of education are the first we receive . . . these prepare us to be citizens . . ." (Montesquieu 1989, p. 31). ". . . Education bears on all these things to make what is called the *honnété*

hommé, who has all the qualities and all the virtues required in this government" (Montesquieu 1989, p. 33 and ff. (*b*)).

3. This theme is very important in the thought of Montesquieu and also Qutb. Both men emphasized the importance of learning for governance and the stability of modern society. Both thinkers stipulated that systems and laws should originate in the culture of the country where they were intended to work (Montesquieu 1989, p. 8). The Ottomans responded to modernity through all stages with imitation and importation. Neither these nor the Roman fez or the European dress helped the caliphate to regain power: its decline continued unabated. Patriotism and nationalism added a new dimension to the challenge of modernity and accelerated the decline of the caliphate, bringing it to an end in 1924.

4. *Rational modern response.* This approach calls for legal reasoning (*ijtihad*) and the rational assessment of Western ideas, to adopt from them whatever is consistent with Islamic culture and is able to develop Muslim society. The Egyptians used this approach to modernize their society. Egypt's modern period is conventionally dated from the time of Muhammad Ali. Immediately after assuming power in 1805, Ali began his modernization program and focused mainly on culture, industrialization, modern administrative institutions, and a modern army. He did not follow the Ottomans' imitative method. One reasons for this was his intention to affirm Egyptian identity and to differentiate Egypt from the Ottoman rule. Ali centered his program, mainly, on France, to which he sent educational missions to learn about the modern world's nature of governance, industries, and democracies. The rise of the Egyptian press, industrialization, and a strong army were certainly not possible without the help of Europe, and France in particular. Ali also established a Representative Council, promulgated the "State Basic Law," and replaced the Consultation (*shurah*) Council with the Special and the General Legislative Councils. In this respect, scholars of Islam in the East and the West do not consider Ali's philosophy of modernization to be inconsistent with *Shari'ah* (Schacht and Bosworth 1960, pp. 404–5; Watt 1961, pp. 178–80; Weiss 1980, pp. 1–4, 15–22; Mawdudi n.d., pp. 40–6).

Modernization on the basis of *Shari'ah* was continued by Ali's successors. Isma'il Pasha, for example, established the modern parliament and electoral system (one person–one vote), called on to separate the three authorities, and modernized laws within the fold of Islam. Pressured by modernity's forces in the East, Isma'il (ruled 1863–1879) established a committee to translate the law of Europe (Napoleonic Codes) and compare it with the Islamic law. Napoleonic Codes I and II were translated and compared with *Shari'ah*. The *Application of the French Civil and Criminal Law to the Law of Imam Malik* found that Napoleon's Codes were taken from King Lewis's Code, which originated in and was mainly taken from the Maliki School of Islamic Law. These comparative volumes were developed to include Hanafi and Shafi'i law and worked as a guiding model for recoding the *Shari'ah* and writing the Egyptian civil and criminal law. These laws have been examined by special committees in France and Egypt and the final result, entitled *Comparative Legislations*, was published in Cairo by the Sorbonne and Cairo Universities.[1]

Egypt's experience confirms the capacity and inclination of the *Shari'ah* toward modernity, democracy, and human rights. The *Shari'ah* which established what Antony Black called a New Nation in Medina (Black 2001, pp. 13–14) is the *Shari'ah* that established modern Egypt. The *Shari'ah*'s constant and flexible nature, which facilitated King Lewis's and Napoleon's extractions for their Codes, is the *Shari'ah* that facilitated the extraction by Egyptians of Egypt's civil, criminal, and constitutional laws, a response to the needs of modern society.

Egypt's *Shari'ah*-based constitution of 1923 was consulted with the advanced constitutions of the most developed countries (Fahmi 1963, p. 138). It was under this constitution that the largest Islamist movement was established and developed, and reached its political and intellectual maturity. The Muslim Brotherhood was established, in 1928, by al-Banna, who stated the Islamicity of the 1923 constitution as follows:

> Those who drafted this Egyptian constitution, despite having based it on the most advanced principles and highest constitutional opinions, took great care to make sure that is nothing could be in conflict, in any way, with Islamic foundations. The texts were made either to confirm the Islamic foundations directly such as this text which says "Islam is the religion of the State" or interpretably to confirm the Islamic foundations, such as the text which says "The freedom of belief is guaranteed."
>
> (Al-Banna 1992, pp. 321–2)

To al-Banna, Egypt's modern constitution of 1923 was "not in conflict with the foundations of Islam; and not far from the Islamic system; and not strange to it" (Al-Banna 1992, pp. 321–2). If this is so, it would be logical to enquire about al-Banna's position and opposition at this period of time. In this regard, al-Banna says:

> Despite the parliamentary system and Egypt's Constitution, in their fundamental principles, do not have any conflict with what Islam laid down in the system of government, we would announce that there is misapplication and failure in the protection of the Constitution's fundamental principles which are also Islamic. This resulted into what we complain about of corruption and of what we have from all this unstable parliamentary life.
>
> (Al-Banna 1992, p. 322)

Thus, the area of this Islamist's oppositional discourse, until he died in 1949, was within the theme and framework of the practice or the application of the law, not the law itself. The difference is obvious.

The 1923 constitution was updated in 1949 and 1971, but the problem of "corruption," outlined by al-Banna, remained to provide a fertile ground for opposition and to generate new arguments about the application of the law. After al-Banna, Qutb developed his concept of *hakimiyyah* (sovereignty) in order to eliminate those factors that provided for the misapplication of the law in Egypt.

Qutb's response

Modernity has also been characterized by Anthony Giddens as a distinctive pattern of change that breaks all previous bounds (Giddens 1990, p. 2). Democracy, pluralism, human rights, and industrialization have achieved a great momentum in today's most popular fashions, and they express the most positive connotations of modernity. There is no difference between the fashions of clothes and the fashions of ideas. Hence the society of our present is also modern in comparison with the previous one. However, "the modes of life brought into being by modernity," Giddens maintained, "have swept us away from all traditional types of social order" (Giddens 1990, p. 4). The changes that appeared in the later decades of the twentieth century were also considered by Giddens as a crossing bridge to a new social order that is focused "largely upon issues of philosophy and epistemology" (Giddens 1990, p. 2).

To Montesquieu, society is not a society without law; law is not law unless implemented; and implementing the law needs a government (Montesquieu 1989, p. 3). A society, first and last, is the patterned relationships of human beings, and their pulses are the pulses of the society. To Qutb, Islam also has something to say about society. Islamic law came with its ethical insights and eternal vision to reform the society: to correct its behavior and harmonize its pulses. Qutb considers that the first society established by Islam was modern in comparison with the pre-Islamic one (Qutb 1983, pp. 83–4). The pre-Islamic society changed from *Jahiliyyah* to Islam, which guaranteed social justice, freedom, equality, and human rights, and limited governmental power to the rule of law or *hakimiyyah* (Qutb 1992, p. 904). Whether this change has to conform to modernity and democracy is for Qutb but a matter of words. To him, democracy is not reduced to a dry and limited meaning expressed through the lexicon and dictionary terms. It is, rather, a comprehensive concept with qualifications and values regarding the self and the other, and a combination of the socio-political conditions necessary for social justice, universal peace, intercultural relations, and the formation and development of the welfare of the individual and of society.

In this context, the question about Islam's capacity and inclination toward these changes is critical. In many post-9/11 publications, Islam has captured the imagination through connotations of terrorism, anti-modernity, anti-democracy, and anti-human rights. As far as modernity, democracy, and sovereignty are concerned, the jihadis seem to have their own theory. Their opposition – even hostility – to democracy stems from their own understanding. Bin Laden's lieutenant Ayman al-Zawahiri, for example, understands modernity as a threat to Islamic culture and values. Thus, "the battle against modernity," he says, "cannot be fought on a regional level without considering the global hostility towards us" (Al-Zawahiri 2002, p. 10). This theme gave birth to al-Qa'ida's "global jihad" and continues to nourish its tactical framework. Hence, the contour of al-Qa'ida's jihad is not regional, but global. In what follows, the jihadis' writings are taken as a point of departure because they mobilize Qutb's concept of sovereignty as a threat to global security. The logic here is to outline these jihadis' view and then demonstrate Qutb's response to these views.

Al-Zawahiri understands democracy as a Western idolatrous idea especially designed against Islam. For him, democracy is a form of "*shirk bi Allah*," or associating partners with God. Islam renders sovereignty to God, whereas democracy renders sovereignty to the people. In democracy the legislator is human beings, whereas in Islam the legislator is the Almighty God. Hence, democracy is a blasphemous idea that usurps God's right to legislation and gives it to the people (Al-Zawahiri 2002, p. 98; Al-Zawahiri n.d., pp. 7–9). Al-Zawahiri considers democracy as a new "religion" based on deifying humans by virtue of awarding them the right to legislate without being bound by another authority. As democracy gives sovereignty to humans, it would have to mean the denial of God's "sovereignty" (*hakimiyyah*). Here, al-Zawahiri uses Qutb's construct (*hakimiyyah*), but criticizes Qutb's advocacy of constitutional democratic rule as part of *hakimiyyah*. Al-Zawahiri considers the parliamentarians as "idols" and those who elect them commit, by doing so, the arch-sin of *shirk*. Thus, participating in elections or other democratic processes is forbidden (*haram*), and those who do so are apostates who must be killed (Al-Zawahiri n.d., pp. 12–14). Here is an important jihadi trend: the belief that jihad is the only means by which to first establish a caliphate in one country and then enlarge it through taking over other countries.

For example, the Islamic Liberation Party (Hizb al-Tahrir al-Islami, HT) was established in Jerusalem in 1952 by the Palestinian scholar and member of the Brotherhood, Taqiyy al-Din al-Nabahani (Al-Kilani 1995, p. 15). During the past five decades, HT has expanded, and it currently has its own blueprints, journal, and website, with headquarters in more than fifty countries including Britain, the United States, and Australia. It has also gained great momentum in Indonesia, Malaysia, and the Asia-Pacific region, as well as in former Soviet Muslim states in Central Asia. The HT has been suspended in some countries, for example Germany and Denmark, but not in the United States, Britain, and Australia. Whatever its reasons might be, HT's proclaimed aim, as stated in English, is to establish a "caliphate" in which

> The ruler is accepted on condition that he conveys Islam as a message to the world through *da'wah* and *jihad*. . . . It also aims to bring back the Islamic guidance for mankind and to lead the *ummah* into a struggle with *Kufr*, its systems and its thoughts so that Islam encapsulates the world . . . The field of work for it [is] in one country, or a few countries, until it is consolidated there and the Islamic State is established.[2]

Conveying Islam as "a message to the world through *da'wah*" makes sense, but I find it difficult to understand the meaning of conveying Islam as a message to the world through jihad. The word "*da'wah*" and the phrase "struggle with *Kufr*" are carefully chosen. This is one of the HT's tactics: the trickery and tricky relations between these phrases are explained not only in words, but also in deeds.

In April 1974, the HT, led by the Palestinian Dr Salih Siriyya, obtained some weapons and made a failed attempt to seize control of the Military Technical Academy in Cairo. It was the first time a Muslim organization had openly announced its aim to overthrow a government by force, an aim repeatedly rejected by al-Banna and Qutb (Khatab 2001, pp. 451–80). Because of its aim of *Khilafah*, HT does not accept the modern state or its institutions and borders (Al-Quds al-Arabi 2007). This challenge is still on the HT's agenda and is frequently reported in the media and scholarly works. According to Lentini, the HT is a "threat to the states" (Lentini 2004, pp. 128–48). Despite the fact that HT has benefited greatly from democracy, and established headquarters in many Western democracies, HT still brands democracy with *kufr*. Yet HT's founder, al-Nabahani, himself stood for election, and lost, in 1951, and in both 1954 and 1956 only one of the HT's candidates won (Hourani 1983, p. 17; Tamimi 2003, p. 3). This confirms the HT's hypocrisy in its belief that democracy contradicts Islam's code in all issues, major or minor. In an interview, a dissident affiliated with *Hizb ut-Tahrir* told a Radio Free Europe analyst: "People are tired of democracy . . . Our people are Muslims and they yearn for Allah and to live by his laws" (Akbarzadeh 2004, p. 121).

Similarly, the Jama'a Islamiyya (JI) understands democracy as *shirk* and blasphemy. This position also applies to all militant groups worldwide. All of them agree that the systems of the present Muslim states are not different from Western democracies of *kufr*. They want to establish a caliphate ruled by their own terms of *shari'ah*, and they agree on jihad in order to overthrow governments. In short, the militants have the same goal but different approaches to it. Differences between them should not obscure their tactical and ideological affinity. Some might prefer to act immediately if they are well established. Others might opt for a tactical discretion vis-à-vis their opponent while they still weak. Silence (i.e. sleeping cells) is a key strategy, buying them time to prepare their inner strength. Therefore, all militant groups' infrastructural models are based mainly on the metamorphoses strategy of fission, division, cleavage, mitosis, and meiosis, and thus appear under titles and personal names that are not familiar to the modern era.

Furthermore, militants do not trust Western democracies. They argue that when their Algerian brothers were winning the presidential election Western democracies interfered and brought the election to halt and kept the corrupt regime in power. It was at this point that the opposition turned militant. This also applies to many Muslim countries, as their regimes are not democratic, but came to power through military coups. Speaking of the Central Asia's radical groups, Lentini has outlined what could be considered as part of the problem:

Additionally, the presence of democratic countries' troops in Central Asia has not really improved these countries' human rights records. In some cases, these countries have used the "War against Terrorism" as an excuse to accelerate repression. Again, this tends to feed into dissident, militant and terrorist groups' hands.

(Lentini 2004, p. 1 36)

Consequently, militants have to find whatever exists in their culture to support their position against those particular democracies that might support despotism and dictatorship. In so doing, they draw strength from Muslim authorities, selectively, to support their ideological position.

The militants' argument against democracy is apparently based on some of Qutb's key concepts and centered mainly on sovereignty (*hakimiyyah*). They, however, do not understand it, and what Qutb meant by *hakimiyyah*. They read his writings but do not follow his program. They draw strength from Qutb's writings only to influence domestic and international opinions. Such tactics have contributed much to misunderstanding Qutb's works. It is therefore not surprising to find many publications that deal with militants' literature through the prism of 9/11 and therefore conclude that Qutb's writings are a threat to democracy and global security.

Take, for example, Zimmerman's article about al-Zawahiri. Zimmerman considers Qutb's writings as a justification to "overthrowing all world governments, including those governed by Muslims, by means of a worldwide holy war" (Zimmerman 2004, p. 223). Such a theme is difficult not only to understand but to establish, yet no reference to this claim is provided. This statement in words and language diverges completely from Qutb's ideological position, as there is no reference to such statement in Qutb's works, including his last *Milestones*. For this and the like claims, Qutb's educational program says:

(3) The Islamic movement must begin from the people to educate the people. (4) The Islamic movement should not Waste its time by engaging in the current political affairs, or try to overthrow the governments or to establish the Islamic system by force. The people themselves will ask to establish the Islamic system when they understand the correct meaning of the Islamic creed.

(Khatab 2001, p. 468)

Zimmerman also claims that "Qutb in 1964 added to his Islamic writings *the need to overthrow all existing governments by force if necessary and the necessity of subjecting all non-Muslims to Shari'ah*" (Zimmerman 2004, p. 223, emphasis added). Once again, no reference is provided, but on this topic Qutb stated:

The freedom, justice and equality that were granted by Islam are comprehensive and encompassing all affairs of human life. Islamic system is universal and widely opens its society for all people irrespective of their ethnicity, color, language, and religion or creed. Islam's universality does not mean to discriminate against others because of their faith, color, language or other privilege.

(Khatab 2002, pp. 168, 186)

Islam has abstained from all forms of compulsion, even the mental compulsion implicit in the miracles that accompanied the earlier religions. Islam is the religion that respects the cognitive and emotional faculties of man and is content to address them without compulsion and without miracles that break the laws of nature.

(Qutb 1983, p. 146)

The right to freedom of belief is the basic characteristic of human liberation. Without the freedom to think of religion, man cannot be identified as a human being. The freedom of belief is the first right that gives to and secures for this creature [man] his human quality and human identity.

(Qutb 1992, p. 291)

Qutb's idea about Islam's universal applicability cannot therefore mean "force" or "worldwide holy war."

Those militants who deny Islam's commitment to democracy usually lack knowledge of their religion and make it, like their faith, rigid and limited in time and space. In addition to their lack of knowledge in the humanities, militants are indoctrinated with some shallow Islamic literature. They define things literally with extreme simplicity. For instance, they consider the Islamic state to be only a huge state "caliphate" whose ruler must be called "caliph" and must assume power through "allegiance."[3] However, none of these is an obligatory form to which Muslims must conform. The caliphate was itself divided and subdivided, and the caliphs fought each other bitterly. Qutb never defined Islamic rule as a caliphate: he speaks only of Islamic society. He left it to Muslims to decide for themselves the best form of state (Qutb 1983, pp. 75–86).

Militants draw on Qutb's construct *hakimiyyah* (sovereignty) to mean "God's rule." Not only is this a loose translation, but militants further interpret it as meaning "government by God" (see Faraj 1981, pp. 15–17) and this concept is central to their discourse against democracy. They try to shape their opinion along Qutb's comprehensive lines. Not only are the issues of politics too complex to be simplified in this manner, but the concept of "government by God" or even "God's rule"' is totally misunderstood. None of this tallies with Qutb's concept of *hakimiyyah* and state, and such analyses lack due attention to language, the philosophy of law, and socio-political context. Militants should understand that "government by God" or "God's rule," in Qutb's view, is but "theocracy," which, with its entire forms, flags, and colors, Qutb totally rejects. According to Qutb, based on several Qur'anic verses (i.e. 2:229; 4:59), "government in Islam is limited to regulations laid down in the Qur'an and *sunnah*, the primary sources of *shari'ah* law" (Qutb 1993a, pp. 151–2). Limiting the government to law is not synonymous with theocracy or autocracy, but implies democracy in its widest sense. According to scholars of political theory, "limitation of governmental power, in regulating the affairs of the people, to the law is the central principle of constitutional rule" (Al-Zalabani 1947, p. 130). To communicate constitutional rule, Qutb described the limitation of governmental power in one word: "*hakimiyyah*."

Qutb derived the word *hakimiyyah* from the Qur'anic word *hukm* (to govern and to rule). As far as I am aware there is no accurate English translation of *al-hakimiyyah* that does not lose its force and intent; hence I shall describe and characterize. *Hakimiyyah*, as defined by Qutb, is "the highest governmental and legal authority" (Qutb 1992, p. 210; Qutb 1993b, pp. 21, 68, 92,126). Based on this definition, "*hakimiyyah*" could be translated as the word "sovereignty." However, Qutb uses this term "*hakimiyyatu* Allah," meaning "Allah is the highest governmental and legal authority" (Qutb 1992; Qutb 1993b, pp. 21, 68, 92, 126, 146). Thus, militants have come to understand *hakimiyyah* as meaning "God." However, Qutb did not say that *hakimiyyah* is God nor even leave room for speculation; rather he defined the concept as follows:

> The *hakimiyyah* means that the *shari'ah* of Allah is the foundation of legislation. Allah does not descend Himself to govern, but sent down His *shari'ah* to govern.[4]

Examination of this text reveals two key points: (i) *hakimiyyah*, in Qutb's view, is not Allah, but the *shari'ah*; and (ii) Qutb's reference to *shari'ah* does not prohibit people from legislating for themselves. This shows militants' profound misunderstanding not only of Qutb's ideas, but also of their religion and the Qur'an. They take the immediate meaning of what they read, which is out of context. Considering these remarks, al-Qurtubi (d. 671/1272) emphasized that the *shari'ah* is not Allah, but it has come into being by Allah's command. In his writings, Qutb frequently uses the term "*hakimiyyatu* Allah", but never says that *hakimiyyah* is God (Qutb 1992, pp. 279, 889–91, 893, 897). In using this expression, Qutb is simply imitating similar Qur'anic expressions such as "*ardu Allah*" (earth of Allah), "*sama'u Allah*" (heaven of Allah), "*naqatu Allah*" (she-camel of Allah), "*shahru Allah*" (month of Allah), "*rasulu Allah*" (messenger of Allah), "*mala'ikatu Allah*" (angels of Allah), and "*ruhu Allah*" (spirit of Allah). Imitating these expressions, Qutb said "*hakimiyyatu Allah*" (the s*hari'ah* of Allah). Neither the *Shari'ah* nor these Qur'anic expressions is God, but have "come to being by Allah's command" (Al-Qurtubi 1985, Vol. 15, p. 24; Vol. 6, p. 41). Thus, militants should consider that neither the "she-camel" nor the "*hakimiyyah*" is God. The *hakimiyyah* is in practice the sovereignty of law. This law limits governmental power and regulates its functions. Limiting governmental power to the law implies not theocracy or autocracy, but democracy. Thus, Qutb considers *hakimiyyah* not to be against democracy, as such, but compatible with it.

Legislation is another key issue linked to *hakimiyyah* and frequently used by al-Qa'ida and militant groups to substantiate their claim that the legislators are humans in democracy, but God in Islam. According to them, humans cannot legislate for themselves; hence the human mind is but a recipient. This claim is not in line with Qutb's way of thinking despite the jihadis extracting such a meaning from Qutb's frequently used expression, "Allah is the Creator and Legislator." Qutb uses this phrase in a context that never deprives people of their right to legislate in any place, space, and generation. This is justified by Qutb's reference to *shari'ah* as the foundation of legislation. This means that people can legislate for themselves on the basis of *shari'ah*. Anyone familiar with Qutb's sophisticated system of thought and his stand against despotic tyrants will knows of his strong belief in the power of the people. For Qutb, reform comes not from the top, but from the people, who will ask for it provided they understand their rights and do not fear "tyrant":

> I told my friend that if I were in charge, I would open twice as many schools as there already existed in Egypt to teach this generation one thing – *sukht* (anger) in the face of the corrupt and distorted reality which dominates this generation . . .
>
> (Qutb 1946)

With this in mind, Qutb does not seek to deprive people of the right to legislate for what they need on the basis of *shari'ah*. First, Qutb presents "Islam" as a "comprehensive system that is able to respond to societal development at any time, place, and generation" (Qutb 1992, Vol. 5, pp. 2826–30; Qutb 1993c, pp. 60–2). Second, the "*shari'ah*," Qutb says, "did not give detail on everything in this life," but remains silent on some issues, including "government form," the "consultation method", and other matters that lie the heart of the state's structure and functions, including relations between the state and its citizens, among the citizens themselves, and between the state and outside world. On these grounds at least, the rights of the people to legislate for themselves are as wide in Qutb's view as the needs of the people are in any place, time, and generation (Qutb 1983, pp. 84, 119–25).

The *shari'ah*'s deliberate silence on these matters is suggestive of the need for continuous temporal legislation. Qutb contends that Muslims are allowed to legislate in areas not touched upon by the *shari'ah*, as well as on matters on which the *shari'ah* provides only broad basic principles with no detailed laws (Qutb 1992, Vol. 4, pp. 2010–11; Qutb 1993a, pp. 46–61, 150–1; Qutb 1993d, p. 122). In either case, it is up to the people of any Muslim country to "enunciate legal opinions" when they need detailed "legislation based on the spirit of *shari'ah*." It is thus clear that legislation in an Islamic state cannot be in "contravention" of the spirit of the *shari'ah*. Thus, when Qutb says "the *shari'ah* of Allah is the foundation of legislation" (Jawhar 1977, pp. 111–46; Qutb 1992, Vol. 1, p. 297; Vol. 2, pp. 1123–4), he is not rejecting continuous temporal legislation, but confirming "the *Shari'ah*'s capacity to establish a modern society and respond to its affairs of growth and renewal" (Qutb 1950; Qutb 1983, p. 26).

Militants, however, take Qutb's expression literally, rejecting temporal legislation entirely. The interweaving of their own words with Qutb's makes it difficult,
for some writers, to distinguish Qutb's view from al-Qa'ida's (Zimmerman 2004,
pp. 238–40). But Qutb's writings, including *Social Justice* (1949), detail the
shari'ah's capacity to establish a modern society of justice, equality, fraternity,
and human rights. To him, Islam did not come devoid of laws, but explained much
of the foundation of legislation and legal rules, whether materialistic or criminal,
commercial, or international. The Qur'an and *hadith* and the law books are full of
this (Qutb 1992, Vol. 2, pp. 891, 904–5, 1083; Vol. 4, pp. 1991–3; Qutb 1993c, p.
60). The *shari'ah*'s capacity to establish a democratic society was acknowledged
in the Lehigh International Convention of 1938 and again in the Washington
Convention of 1945; and there were representatives at the Bench of International
Court under the title Islamic *shari'ah* (Al-Banna 1992, pp. 139, 267).

To Qutb, legislation should stem from the country where the laws are intended
to work (Qutb 1993a, pp. 54–6). Prostheses from here and there will not help to
develop society as it should (Qutb 1993c, pp. 60–1). However, Qutb does not
reject the experience of other nations: "The *shari'ah* has the capacity to respond
to modern life's growth and renewal. We should utilize our own experience as
well as the experience of all nations in whatever is in harmony with the general
idea of Islam and its principles about life" (Qutb 1993c, p. 60). Thus, utilizing
modern Western democracies' experience in making laws is not *shirk*; temporal
legislation is not *shirk*. Portraying the Islamic society that he seeks to establish,
Qutb advises Muslims to legislate for themselves whenever they need to and for
whatever they want:

> This Islamic society is a new and dynamic society that is continually on the
> move towards human liberty; all types of liberality and development . . .
> Questions about the criteria of rulership; consultation methods . . . to the end
> of the list are on the agenda of the researchers of Islam . . . they try to address
> these important questions . . . but they do their research in a vacuum . . .
> they have no example of a true Islamic society existing before their eyes . . .
> Legislation cannot successfully result in good laws, before a physically
> established true Islamic society to know, at least, what we need and what
> we need not. Islamic jurisprudence cannot emerge or grow in vacuum, and
> it cannot live in vacuum as well. The required laws cannot exist in the mind
> and papers, but emerge from the living reality of life that is precisely the life
> of the true Islamic society. Thus, Islamic society must be firstly established,
> with its physical and natural structures to be the actual environment which
> creates its appropriate Islamic jurisprudence that is able to deal with the new
> society and its affairs in the reality of daily life. Here, this new society might
> need banks; insurance companies . . . etc. and might need not. We cannot
> assume what laws that this society will exactly need; we do not know the
> volume or the shapes of the laws that this society needs; so, we cannot legis-
> late to it in advance.
>
> (Qutb 1992, Vol. 4, p. 2010)

This means that the Islamic system, like democracy, allows a group of people (experts) to legislate for the entire people. In either case, human beings use their talent and expertise to legislate and make laws through independent reasoning (*ijtihad*). Thus, there is no scope for militants to draw on Qutb to support their rejection of democracy, or to support their assertion that Islam does not allow Muslims to legislate for themselves.

Furthermore, as militants assert that the people in Islam should legislate on the basis of the spirit of *shari'ah*, whereas those in Western democracies legislate on the basis of the spirit of *humanity* (not necessarily based on religion at all), those militants must come to terms with the fact that Islam is the religion of reason in the discourse of Abduh and Qutb (Muhammad 1931, pp. 210–13; Qutb 1992, Vol. 2, 1112–21; Vol. 3, pp. 1187, 1218–19, 1255, 1753). For Qutb, the spirit of *shari'ah* is not against the spirit of *humanity*, but in harmony with it (Qutb 1992, Vol. 2, p. 801). Qutb maintains that *shari'ah,* with its spirit, has come to deal with "human reasoning" and to "communicate with human intellect" and the "spirit of *humanity*." These are the "foundations" upon which Qutb's entire political and economic theories are based: "(i) absolute liberation of the inward soul; (ii) complete human equality; and (iii) firm social solidarity" (Qutb 1983, p. 32). For Qutb, the *shari'ah* does not dictate but communicates and addresses "human reason and emotional faculties without compulsion and without miracles that break the laws of human nature" (Qutb 1983, p. 146). In short, legislation on the basis of the spirit of *Shari'ah* or the spirit of *humanity* should not be the cause of enmity between Islam and democracy, but should, if anything, increase their compatibility.

Militants turn a blind eye to these facts and reject legislation by humans while utilizing modern democracies' aircrafts, video/audio tapes, computers, weaponry, and communication technologies achieved through the spirit of humanity. These things were not *sunnah* created or used by their Muslim ancestors. Militants consider their own turbans and dress style as *sunnah*. This also is not Qutb's view: there are no "special clothes," or "'men of religion," or "sheikhs and dervishes" in Islam (Qutb 1993c, pp. 63, 69–75, 85, 105–6). This dress style is but an Arabian custom and has nothing to do with Islam. Focusing on the legislative power, Qutb outlines some examples from Islam's early period: Muhammad himself "consulted" his Arab and non-Arab companions, males and females, "before deciding" on matters not touched by *shari'ah* or broadly outlined without specific details. Additionally, among the "tens of hundreds of examples" is the Persian Salman's view of defending Medina against the Confederates, the view of the women in the al-Hudaybiyya Treaty, and Abu Baker and 'Umar's views on the prisoners of Badr war. These were all also political decisions. Submitting the matter to his people and considering their advice, Muhammad wanted the people to "share freely" in the decision (Haykal 1976, p. 235), and this practice was followed by his successors, in varying style and forms. These examples, Qutb asserts, are not "obligatory," and it is not mandatory for a Muslim community to conform to any of them (Qutb 1992, Vol. 5, p. 3165; Al-Nawawi 1993, pp. 878–4).

Temporal legislation, Qutb maintains, can be vested in an "individual" or a "limited number" of people, who constitute the "legislative body." The people might choose to use a "general public vote" (one person–one-vote) or the vote of "one House or two Houses" or any other system that "suits the nation's circumstance" at a particular time and in a particular place (i.e. a system that suits Indonesia may not applicable to Egypt). The people "should decide which vote system suits them: should it be vocal or in writing? Should it include all affairs of politics, defense and others, or only some affairs?" Muslims should also choose the "authority" that observes and is responsible for these procedures: is it the responsibility of the elected president and his Cabinet? Is it the Judiciary's responsibility? Or the People's Assembly? These channels are not prescribed in Islam's authoritative texts. Thus, it would thus appear that the form of government, the form of consultation, the type of legislature, and the election procedures may all differ from one country to another and may include some alterations and adjustments from time to time with no compromise to the Islamic nature of these arrangements (Qutb 1993a, pp. 141–3). In this way Qutb outlined not only Islam's similarity to democracy but also its difference, and suggested that Islam is an independent system. "It may happen in the development of human systems that they coincide with Islam sometimes and diverge from it sometimes, but Islam is a complete and independent system" (Qutb 1983, p. 76; Ahmad 1962, pp. 83–104).

Qutb's thoughts on sovereignty bring the state's authority under the realm of *hakimiyyah*. As *hakimiyyah* is "the highest governmental and legal authority," which is the law, the sovereignty is thus the sovereignty of law. On this basis, Qutb shifts the derivation of the authority or the legitimacy of the elected government away from its electoral majority and places it within the realm of the executive power, namely the law. To Qutb, after an election, the elected government derives its legitimacy from its activity in facilitating the application of law, not from its majority or as the result of elections (Qutb 1983, pp. 14, 15, 82; Qutb 1993d, p. 123). With this in mind, the government (i.e. the ruling party) cannot pass laws on the basis of its majority support among the electorate or its majority in parliament or in the senate, but must do so through the entire people or their representatives. Nor can a president pass laws on his own authority and he has no power of veto. Thus, *hakimiyyah* limits the power of the ruling party while enhancing the power of the people. In this way, laws and policies will not be in the specific interest of the elected party or its ideology (i.e. labour or liberal, democratic or republican), but reflect the interest of all the people, that is all parties (Qutb 1992, Vol. 4, p. 1990). In so doing, Qutb does not deny the rights of the people or the electorate, but enhances the power of the entire population while limiting the power of the elected party. This means that the concept of *hakimiyyah* leads to the elected government being responsible to the entire people rather than to the party or to a majority with a particular interest or ideology. Thus, once the government is elected by the people, it derives its legitimacy not from the electoral majority, but from the governmental activity of facilitating the application of the law.

Furthermore, impeaching a government, as emphasized by *hakimiyyah*, cannot be instigated by a minority or a particular opposition party, but is the responsibility of the entire people. The law gives the people full rights to choose their government, to watch and evaluate its activity, and to support or reject and impeach it through legitimate means (Qutb 1983, pp. 84–5). Thus, Qutb's thoughts on *hakimiyyah* confirm Islam's compatibility with democracy, and that *hakimiyyah* is the main principle of constitutional rule that is able to limit governmental power.

With regards to Western democracies, Dicey and Wade describe England's constitution as follows:

> Constitutional Law, as the term used in England, appears to include all rules which directly or indirectly affect the distribution or exercise of the sovereign power in the state. Hence it includes (among other things) all rules which define the members of the sovereign power, all rules which regulate the relation of such members to each other, or which determine the mode in which the sovereign power, or the members thereof, exercise their authority.
>
> (Dicey and Wade 1941)

Defining the constitution's intention, Strong notes "The objects of a constitution, in short, are to limit the arbitrary action of the government, to guarantee the rights to the governed, and to define the operation of the sovereign power" (Strong 1963, p. 10). This is simply what Qutb meant by *hakimiyyah*. He wants to limit governmental activity to the sphere of law. This principle, Qutb asserts, is a Qur'anic (2: 229) order lucidly expressed in legal terms such as "do this and do not do that." The Prophet himself was not empowered to exceed or over-step these limits (Al-Mawardi 1966, pp. 10–12; Qutb 1992, vol. 1, pp. 248–9; Vol. 2, pp. 685–87; Qutb 1983, pp. 80–1). Confirming the *hakimiyyah*'s emphasis on constitutional rule and the limitation of governmental power in Egypt, immediately after the July Revolution (1952) Qutb sent an open letter to President Muhammad Naguib urging him to eradicate corruption and prepare for a new constitution within six months. With his sense of humour, Qutb also ironically described the process of cleaning up as a "just dictatorship." He said:

> The Constitution of 1923 had brought about the corruption of not only the King and his collaterals, but also the political parties and politicians. This Constitution will not be able to protect us from the return of corruption if you have not established a comprehensive program to prevent those corrupted figures from further parliamentary activity. . . . Should not the people, who have suffered the oppressive dictatorship for decades, be able to tolerate six months of a just dictatorship? We are assuming any action of cleaning-up is but a dictatorship anyway.
>
> (Hammudah 1990, p. 112)

President Naguib was delighted with this ironic missive, laughing and showing it to his inner circle, and thereafter describing himself as a "just dictator" (Muhammad 1931, p. 113) and describing Qutb as "the master of the Revolution" (Al-Khalidi 1994, p. 303). While demonstrating Qutb's sense of humor and ability to give constructive criticism, this also illustrates his ideological position that constitutional rule is legitimate in Islam and rests at the core of *hakimiyyah*.

In this way, Qutb understood *hakimiyyah* as essential to the organs of the state and its identity and its domestic and international relations (Qutb 1992, Vol. 1, p. 501; Vol. 2, p. 3165). Indeed, among the many principles of *hakimiyyah* is an emphasis on the unity of humanity in terms of race, nature, and origins. This reflects the teaching of *tawhid*, upon which *hakimiyyah* is based, as a fundamental code that provides for the foundation and identity of state and its national and international relations (Qutb 1983, pp. 80–6). If the sovereignty (*hakimiyyah*) of the law is accepted, the government should observe justice, freedom, power sharing, human rights, and consultation between the ruler and the ruled.

Furthermore, in regards to the relations between Islamic and non-Islamic cultures or civilizations, Qutb's appreciation of his culture or civilization is clearly visible in his style, language, and even in his vocabulary: "the question for me is my honour, my language, and my culture" (Calvert 2000, pp. 90–1). However, his appreciation of his own culture does not prohibit intercultural relations but rather supports them. As a literary critic by profession, his thought, in a sense, seems to stem from his understanding of literature. To him, literature or arts is not beyond the framework of *hakimiyyah*'s philosophy, or beyond any sphere of human life, political, religious, or other:

> Literature (arts) is the emotional commentary on life and it issues from the wellspring to which all the philosophies, religious belief, experiences and influences in a given environment have contributed. Literature perhaps has the strongest influence in creating the inward emotional idea of life and in giving the human soul a particular character . . . Literature – like the other arts – is an inspired expression of living values which stir the artist's conscience. These values may differ from one soul to another, from one environment to another, and from one age to another, but in every case they issue from a specific conception of life and of the ties between humankind and the universe and between some men and others . . . It is foolish to try to separate literature or arts generally from the values they try to express directly or whose effect on human feeling they try to express. Even if we succeeded – and that is impossible – in separating them from these values, all we would have left would be empty expressions, meaningless lines, bare sounds or lifeless lumps. . . . Islam came to develop and evaluate life, not to accept the existing situation at any time or in any place, and not merely to record its impulses and restraints, its inclinations and limitations, whether at a particular time or over a long period. The task of Islam is always to stimulate life toward self-renewal, growth and development and to stimulate human capacities toward creation, freedom and upward development . . . The literature or arts that issues from the Islamic conception is a literature or an art that provides guidance by virtue of the fact that Islam is a movement for the continual renewal and advancement of life and is not content with the existing reality in any moment or generation and does not excuse it or beatify it simply because it is the reality. Its principal task is to change this reality and improve it and continually to inspire the movement to create ever new forms of life.
>
> (Qutb 1983, pp. 205–6)

It is within this framework Qutb thinks of intercultural relations. In doing so he leaves the door wide open to borrow from Western cultures to develop and modernize. But, before doing so, Qutb consults his culture and "if I find that I must borrow from European ideas, I would do so if this idea would develop the culture without manipulation or assumption" (Qutb 1993e, p.8; see also Qutb 1993b, p. 143). This is an important principle in Qutb's thought, including his political theory:

> In the world of economics, an individual who already has funds does not resort to borrowing before reviewing his funds to see whether or not they are sufficient. And, likewise, a state does not resort to importing before reviewing its financial resources and calculating its raw materials. Should not spiritual capital, intellectual resources and the heritage of heart and soul be treated the same as goods and money are in human life? Of course they should! But in this so-called "Islamic world" do not review their own spiritual or intellectual heritage before they think about importing principles and plans and borrowing systems and laws from across the deserts and beyond the seas!
>
> (Qutb 1983, p. 7)

Thus, Qutb is not against Western culture or civilization. The issue for him, as it is for Montesquieu, is that laws and systems should originate in the culture of the country in which they intended to work (Montesquieu 1989, p. 8). In Muslim countries, Qutb says, the decision to borrow is usually made by only a few individuals, if not a single individual drawn from despotic rulers. Paying back this kind of debt does not affect this or that particular individual, but affects all the people, the culture, and identity of the entire nation for generations to come. Reviewing the assets of cultural heritage is important for someone like Qutb, who never hides his appreciation of his language and culture. But nor does he hide his appreciation of European and American culture. Recounting on his visit to North America, Qutb praises the United States' civilization as follows:

> America – the New World which captures the imagination of all humankind, occupies more mental space than America's vast plot occupies on the Planet! This New World has captured the hearts of peoples from every corner of the Globe; all races and colours with varying interests, aims and dreams. America – this vast area from the Atlantic to the Pacific; the inexhaustible materials and resources; the powers and men; the great industries which are not known to any other civilization. America – the countless variety of productions; the innumerable educational institutions and laboratories; the brilliant planning and management which stimulate the mind and admiration. America – the luxurious dream of the promised paradise; the fascinating putty of nature. America – the embodied dream in the place and space.'
>
> (Qutb 1951, pp. 1245–7)

Yet Qutb adds that:

America has forgotten one thing: one thing has no value here – the spirit (*ruh*). Here, a PhD student submitting a thesis on the best method of washing the dishes. This is more important than a thesis on the Bible, if not more important than the Bible itself . . . America is good as a workshop for the world . . .

(Al-Khalidi 1994, pp. 201–2)

Nevertheless, Qutb encourages Muslims to benefit from this fascinating civilization. He even compares America with his own country and stresses his conviction as follows:

The United States utilized and continues to utilize its capital assets (intellectual heritage). Egypt, however, is ignoring its capital as if Egypt has nothing or has gone bankrupt. The reality of present life in Egypt cannot be accepted by anyone. The capacity of Egypt is enormous, if only Egypt believed in its heritage.

(Qutb 1950, p. 756)

Qutb here reflects on all spheres of American civilization. This "luxurious dream of the promised paradise; the fascinating putty of nature; and the embodied dream in the place and space" is the result of "brilliant planning and management." The Americans worked hard to "develop" their civilization from their own "cultural heritage," not by importing "from overseas." This, however, does not apply to any country in the Muslim World. Among the many examples mentioned by Qutb is Egypt:

Egyptians ignored their own heritage, casting aside their spiritual and intellectual capital . . . Egypt imported principles, systems, theories, laws and solutions . . . Because they stopped believing in their cultural heritage, Egyptians thought this imported mix would solve their problems.'

(Qutb 1983, p. 7)

Conclusion

The issue for Qutb, then, is not the word "modernity" or "democracy" as such, but the true meaning of these key concepts. Qutb believes that Islam is not against either modernity or democracy. Islam can modernize and accept the new even from outside its own tradition. Qutb does not view modernity in terms of a break with the past. Modernity means new and better technology and an improved standard of human life. Unlike in Western thought, Islamic thought on modernity also means a *renewal* with the *past*, a return to the original ethos of Islam. If militant individuals or groups have serious problems with the knowledge of modernity and democracy, then these do not stem from Islam. Their intolerance is political.

Islam's similarity to democracy will not change the Islamic system's nature.

There is "similarity" between them, but each system has its own "specifics and precisions" which illustrate its "nature and identity" (Qutb 1983, pp. 86–7). Islam, as asserted by Qutb, is not against the positive attitude and achievements of Western democracy. His *hakimiyyah* concept in fact means the rule of law. It enhances Islam's compatibility with democracy, and promotes Islam's international relations in all spheres of human life with great emphasis on the unity of humanity in race, nature, and origins. Relations with the West and borrowing from it for development and renewal are not prohibited. *Hakimiyyah* is not a concept designed to "separate Muslims" from the "caravan"' of life, or to reject great achievements of humanity. It, too, stresses peace through law, peace of conscience (human or society), peace at home, peace in society (civil or political), and peace in the world. In *hakimiyyah*, world peace is rooted in local or regional peace. If democracy, freedom, pluralism, and human rights are among the most positive connotations of democracy, Islam can do them better.

Hence, Islamic thought, as emphasized by Shilliam in the introduction, "is not just an object of inquiry for modern thought, but a legitimate source of knowledge for explanation of modernity." The number of militant Islamic movements calling for an Islamic state and the end of Western influence is relatively small. Nevertheless, these groups are causing great fear among people in the Middle East and the West. Finding a way to allay this fear will depend not only on how Islam deals with concepts such as modernity or democracy, but on how the West deals with Islam.

Notes

1 These comparative legislations were completed and published in Cairo by Makhluf Muhammad al-Minyawi (d. 1878) under the title *Tatbiq al-Qanun [al-Faransawi] al-Madani wa-alJjina'i 'ala Madhhab al-Imam Malik (The Application of [the French] Civil and Criminal Law to the Law of Imam Malik)*. This is recently republished in two volumes by (Jum'ah and Siraj 1999). Professor Ali Jum'ah has been Egypt's mufti since 2006.

2 See the party's website: www.hizb-ut-tahrir.org/english/english.html (accessed August 21, 2005).

3 See their website: www.hizb-ut-tahrir.org/english/english.html (accessed August 21, 2005.

4 See Qutb's Testimony on December 19, 1965, in Jawhar (1977) and Qutb (1992, pp. 297, 1123–4).

7 Decoding political Islam

Uneven and combined development and Ali Shariati's political thought

Kamran Matin

My Lord . . . tell my people that the only path towards you passes through the earth, and show me a shortcut.

Ali Shariati

If there are obstacles the shortest line between two points may well be a crooked line.

Bertolt Brecht

Introduction[1]

Ali Shariati is widely regarded as the ideological architect of the Iranian Revolution (Abrahamian 1982; Sachedina 1983; Esposito 1986; Abedi 1986; Burgess 1988, p. 6). The extant approaches to Shariati's political thought highlight his creative appropriation of modern Western political philosophies in his politicized re-imagination of the Shi'a Islam. Accordingly, Shariati's ideology of 'revolutionary Islam',[2] an influential variety of the wider phenomenon of 'political Islam', has been categorized under the rubrics of 'liberation theology', Third World populism or 'Islamic fundamentalism' (Keddie 1981, p. 217; Esposito 1986, p. xi). However, these ideological typologies or discursive deconstructions, illuminating as they might be, arguably provide only a political morphology and not a theoretical comprehension. What seems to be lacking is a social theoretical explanation of political Islam as part of a wider theory of the development of modern non-Western political thought.[3]

In this chapter, I attempt to provide such an explanation through a critical development of the theory of uneven and combined development (Trotsky 1985; Rosenberg 2006, 2007; Matin 2006, 2007). This is the intellectual substance of the idea of an 'international historical sociology' of Shariati's political thought (Rosenberg 2006). I argue that Shariati's politico-intellectual project of revolutionary Islam was part of a wider Islamic discourse of 'radical authenticity' (see Mirsepaasi 1994, 2000) that was generated by the Pahlavi modernization project as part of the wider process of modern uneven and combined development in Iran (Matin 2009). Crucially, the Pahlavi modernization was international in both origin and substance. Accordingly, I shall demonstrate that Shariati's 'revolutionary Islam' was largely driven by the identification and mobilization of the appropriate *agency* for operating in the context of Iran's internationally transmutated social milieu in order to achieve a socio-political transformation broadly resonant with the Iranian radical left's political strategy. The chapter seeks to show how an international theoretical sensitivity can provide an intellectual antidote to the mystification of political Islam by orthodox approaches, both within and outside IR, that see it as a cultural phenomenon to be studied *sui generis* (see *inter alia* Huntington 1996; Lewis 2002).

I present the argument in three main parts. First, I show why despite its profound international origins and impact non-Western political thought has been marginal within IR. Second, I provide a brief history of the relation between Islam and politics in terms of the *ulama*'s attitude towards the state. This forms the background against which both the continuity and ruptures in the formation of political Islam, as a modern ideology, become evident. Third, I critically examine Ali Shari'ati's political thought and show how his innovative appropriation of modern Western political thought aimed at laying the intellectual foundation for a new agency capable of overcoming Iran's socio-economic ills through a social revolution.

International relations of/and non-Western political thought

Bassam Tibi makes the poignant argument that, unlike their Western ancestors, Third World ideologies, including 'political Islam', cannot be domesticated (Tibi 1986, p. 19). Put symbolically, there is no non-Western equivalent of *Die Deutsche Ideologie* (Tibi 1986, p. 17). Although the intellectual nativism of even this Marxist classic is contestable (Shilliam 2006), the issue Tibi highlights is crucial with respect to the theoretical comprehension of non-Western political thought. For it highlights a specifically international dimension of modern intellectual production in the non-Western world that has often remained theoretically undigested.

This causal dimension can be sketched as follows. Capitalism is inherently claustrophobic. Moving away from its European epicentre through colonial and imperial projects, of which it was both an engine and a product, Western capitalism, and various ideologies associated with it, continuously and fundamentally became implicated in the development of social, economic, cultural, intellectual and ideological forms in all non-Western societies. What Marshall Hodgson called 'the great Western transmutation' became the pressure point on the Islamic world too (Dabashi 1984, p. 673). Thus, despite persistent claims to authenticity, ideational purity, nativism, etc., what the West/non-West encounters actually involved in ideological terms were synthesis, hybridity and amalgamation (Roy 1994, 2004).[4] In short, the 'structural heterogeneity' of (semi)colonial societies, resulting from their externally induced incorporation into modern world economy, has also had a clearly ideological–intellectual element overdetermined by these societies' modern international relations. It is, indeed, impossible to find any ideology in modern(ized) non-Western societies which is explicable by exclusive reference to internal social dynamic, not even Islam (Tibi 1986, p. 19). There is therefore a distinctly *international* dimension to non-Western political thought and ideology that strongly inveighs against their comprehension in purely sociological–cultural, or more generally internalist, terms.

Logically it follows that IR can be an, if not *the*, ideal intellectual site for analysis and interrogation of non-Western political thought. However, the dominant approaches within IR have paid scant attention to non-Western political thought in both their theorizations and theory-constructions. This is highly curious given the fact that, for much of its history, IR has been directly concerned with non-Western geopolitical and developmental challenges with distinct intellectual and political articulations. The institutional reason for this has long been recognized (Hoffmann 1987; cf. Smith 2000). More recently, it has been shown that classical political theory, on which IR systematically, albeit uncritically, draws, occludes, distorts and suppresses cultural difference through its monolinear schemas of historical progress away from a pre-historical 'state of nature' (for example, Jahn 2000; Blaney and Inayatullah 2004). The resulting Eurocentric 'historicism' construes all instances of developmental difference as 'aberrations', 'deviations' or 'anomalies', which are, consequently, reduced to diachronically anterior, and normatively inferior, modes of rationality and civilization.[5] Societies that display such forms of 'development' can, Eurocentric pundits argue, be elevated on the ladder of history through 'civilizing' missions carried out by Western bearers of reason (Dussel 1993, pp. 67–8; Eze 1997; Chakrabarty 2000; Blaney and Inayatullah 2002; see also Dallmayr 2004, p. 250).

But within both the West and its colonies, the intellectual challenges to the West's Procrustesian universal history, composed and narrated by the modern singular subject, were coeval with, and largely produced by, concrete socio-political struggles which they supplied with intellectual compass and ideological edge. For the 'effacement of heteronomy' (Odysseos 2007, p. xxix) that modern historicism envisaged theoretically also mandated concrete socio-political projects of change, e.g. colonial administration or 'modernization' programmes. A key element of these projects was the multifaceted processes of 'primitive accumulation': the process whereby direct producers, most often the peasantry, were separated from their means of reproduction, the land. This was often introduced by indigenous ruling elites, who viewed it as central to their industrialization strategies aimed at maintaining geo-political and economic independence in the face of the imperial onslaught of the modern West.

These instances of 'conservative revolution' also involved a general process of ethical estrangement and cultural corrosion. In some cases, they imploded into the kind of intellectual responses that involved the invention of *Ubermensch* and *volk*, arguably the most consequential substitutes for the slain God of *tradition* at the hands of *modern* reason (Herf 1984; Giesen 1998). These were German prototypes of a new discourse of authenticity in response to the socio-cultural and economic upheavals that were brought to a cataclysmic culmination with Germany's defeat in the First World War (Jones 1992). Similar discursive and ideological projects that sought to mediate the tension between 'culture' and industry became the hallmarks of various strategies of national revival in almost all (semi) colonial societies, including Iran. Nonetheless, the resulting 'native' shield of authenticity against modernity became the spear of modernity itself. Crucially, these emergent discourses of authenticity were indeed strategies for successful being-in-the-(*modern*)-world and not exiting from it. Discourses and ideologies of heterogeneous and culturally authentic existence and universal homogeneity of modernity were co-constitutive.[6]

The discernment and conceptualization of this mutually constitutive relation between 'tradition' and 'modernity' – generating various unintended but consequential *métissage* and simulacra – has been a defining character of the subaltern and post-colonial studies.[7] The main argument of such studies is that the ideas of the abstract or the universal are subverted or mutated precisely when they are *actually* implemented, i.e. when they are imposed on, or adopted by, a society other than, and different from, their original one. For this actualization involves the process whereby the analytically distinguishable dimensions of a concept, i.e. its discursive aspect represented by the apparent semantic purity, merges with, and is reconstituted by, its figurative dimension, that is, its practical visualization and enactment in a different time and space (Chakrabarty 2000, p. xii).[8] Yet although these critiques do successfully reveal the violent character of modern Western 'civilization', camouflaged and justified by its universalistic claims and historicist ontology (Mill 1929), they tend to gloss over or shy away from analytical consideration and theoretical incorporation of the condition of possibility of Eurocentrism to become a hegemonic discourse and practice with an undeniable universal impact. Relations between the 'global north' and 'global south' should not be overculturalized as though these relations are primarily about 'discourse, language or identity [and] not armaments, commodities, exploitation, migrant realities, debt, drugs' (Dunch 2002, pp. 303–4; Eagleton 2003, p. 161).

The above discussion was intended to highlight two, in my view, crucial considerations with respect to the analysis of non-Western political thought as a result of modern international relations. The first consideration concerns the danger of essentialism that lurks behind any inside/outside binary opposition. The second consideration concerns the centrality of power relations in the processes of Western modernity's expansion. This international power asymmetry has consistently given rise to intellectual and political resistance, which have, in turn, overdetermined the process, forms and trajectory of modernity itself. In short, there is, in modernity, a transformative tension between the abstract and the concrete that is activated most clearly and consequentially on the plane of 'the international'.

The theory of uneven and combined development best captures the dynamics of this historical process through its conceptualization of 'the international' and 'the social' as coextensive and co-constitutive. Accordingly, the specificities of the modern non-Western political thought could not be derived from hermetically conceived cultural traits and idioms – even though these are always appropriated for reasons to do with the construction and mobilization of an effective agency, as I shall argue below with relation to Shariati. Nor would they be seen as representing a mere resistance to cultural corrosion and religious erosion – again even though these are also very real phenomena and always part of the process. Rather, modern non-Western political thought, including political Islam, should be rethought as essentially attempts to mediate capitalist modernity, as an international and intercultural process, through the rearticulation of Western intellectual products and their transformative incorporation into the native cultural, ideological and political discourses. From the perspective of their immediate subjects, such attempts are formulated as discourses of authenticity intended to protect an allegedly pristine culture (see *inter alia* Roy 1994; Qutb 2007, pp. 9–13 and *passim*). But in practice, as it was intimated above, such ideological strategies often synthesize the 'traditional' and 'modern', reconstituting them in unintended ways and forms. Shariati's 'revolutionary Islam' is an important and illuminating instance of this process.

The politico-historical context of the emergence of political Islam in Iran

The idea that Islam has a tendency towards seizing state power further fresh support following the Iranian Revolution. Neo-Orientalism has generalized this into a basic claim regarding the inseparability of Islam and politics.[9] But this claim is fundamentally deficient on two accounts. First, as Oliver Roy correctly argues, 'Islam and Muslim societies [are not] one global, timeless cultural system' (Roy 1994, p. vii); they contain a rich and vast cultural and historical diversity. Moreover, ideologically, Islam has, since the death of the prophet Mohammed, been internally heterogeneous. Furthermore, politically too, the praxis of the *ulama*, the ideological/religious cadre of Muslim societies, has been subject to spatio-temporal modality. Second, the generic and abstract character of the claim regarding the inseparability of Islam and politics renders it of little use in understanding the historically varying forms of the relations between Islamic dogma and practices, on the one hand, and the state, or more generally political authority, on the other. After all, religions – even when they are institutionally separated from states – are arguably political to the extent that they form ethereal structures of normative socio-cultural sensibility and subjectivity within which the political assumes its concrete forms (Dabashi 2002; Hurd 2004). As such, Islam's alleged thrust towards seizing the state power is as political as Christianity's post-medieval seclusion from the state power and public sphere more generally. Political abstention, by force or choice, is political and has political ramifications.

Thus, the intellectually more pertinent and important question is the historical character, determinants and modalities of the relation between Islam, in its doctrinal and institutional diversity, and the state. Such an approach to Islam(s) and politics yields a rather complex picture.

To start with, there are important differences between the Sunni majority and the Shi'a minority with respect to the conditions of the legitimate rule.[10] Shi'ism attributes the post-prophetic right of rule to a particular line of Mohammed's male descendants, or imams. However, the legitimate right to rule was, according to the Shi'as, usurped by the Sunni caliphs. Sunnism, in contrast, adopts a more impersonal view of the conditions of legitimate rule that is accordingly decided through elections based on consultation (*shura*) and *ijma* (consensus) and affirmed by *bay'ah* (oath of allegiance). Thus, from the outset the idea that the legitimacy of rule necessarily arises from the prophetic descent was absent from the Sunni dogma. Rational and pragmatic considerations and the general expediency of the Muslim community, contested as it was and remains, were seen as the overriding factors in determining the leadership of the Muslim community. In short, Shi'ism is, in Weberian terms, the expression of, and based upon, the institutionalized perpetuation of charismatic authority in the doctrine of *imamate* (Arjomand 1996). The belief in the occultation of the last imam is, therefore, essentially a device for pre-empting routinization of the charisma. In contrast, Sunnism routinizes charismatic authority in its theory of caliphate, whose institutional procedures are heavily influenced by the pre-Islamic Arab tribal conventions (Arjomand 1996, Chapters 5 and 6).

More generally, classical Islamic thought had an in-built mechanism that (re) produced the discursive dynamism that partially underlay the *ulama*'s tendency to collaborate with, if not submit to, the existing political authorities. This mechanism was the result of the belief in the absolute comprehensiveness of the Shari'a (Hodgson 1993, p. 14). This totalization has historically tended to subvert the intellectual differentiation of a separate branch of political philosophy or political theory within Islamic thought, hence the assignment of political rule, the state and governance to the related disciplines of *fiqh* (jurisprudence) and *kalam* (theology) as subfields of the Shari'a. This theological feature of Islam itself indicates the underlying abstract view of the overall unity of Islam as a complete way of life subsuming the political or the state (Tibi 1986, p. 16). It is this axiom that has been taken at face value by neo-Orientalist scholars in their analyses of Islam and its relation with the state. Yet this formal/theoretical adherence to the idea of the unity of the religious and temporal authorities was continuously subverted by the concrete actions and functions of the state, hence the recurrent tension between the Islamic thought and practice. More often than not the *ulama*, self-professed guardians of Islam's call for justice, legitimized despotic secular governments. Nevertheless, this was highly conducive to 'ministerial authority' that is 'inclined to sustain its own legitimacy via its institutional recognition by the political establishment' (Dabashi 2006, p. 102). For the most part of Islamic history, the theoretical 'co-extensiveness of religious and political spheres in Islam' (Akhavi 1983, p. 197) was in practice a shifting combination of symbiotic and parasitic relationship between Islam and the existing states. *Raison d'état* tended to overdetermine the Shari'a.

It is in this context that Shi'ism's abstract doctrinal disposition to reject the temporal powers in the absence of the twelfth imam, Mahdi, has to be viewed. Shi'ism was elevated to official religion by the Safavids (1501–1721) and the

Shi'a *ulama* acquired considerable power and influence during the reign of the weak monarchs of the Qajar dynasty (1791–1925). However, with the rise of the Pahlavi monarchs to power, the situation began to change radically. Reacting to Iran's increasing loss of (geo)political independence, the Pahlavis embarked on modernization projects. Consequently, the Shi'a establishment was increasingly forced to review its approach to, and relation with, the state.[11] But crucially, this change occurred in the context of a decidedly polyvocal politics which had followed the commencement of Iran's modern uneven and combined development. This political–ideological plurality assumed its organizational form during the constitutional period (1905–1911) (Matin 2006). Three broad political tendencies, with unequal and fluctuating socio-political weight, co-existed: Shi'i modernism, liberal nationalism and socialism. Two fundamental and inter-related issues more than once brought these trends into political cooperation: foreign domination and monarchical autocracy. The Constitutional Revolution and Oil Nationalization Movement were important instances of such successful, albeit temporary, cooperation.

However, with the commencement of the rapid and radical land reforms and industrialization programme by the second Pahlavi Shah (1960s to 1970s), the ranks of two new classes, the urban middle class and the working class, began to swell rapidly. Yet, the top-down and inflective nature of the externally induced Pahlavi modernization subverted the correspondence between these new classes' objective foundations and subjective self-understanding as Western 'historicism' stipulated and modernization and development theories presumed. In short, the socio-cultural alienation ushered in by the state-led primitive accumulation, and accompanied by a pervasive depoliticalization, tended to reinforce the popular desire for a new existential ideology. The contest for the construction of a fresh and hegemonic 'discourse of authenticity' pitted Shi'ism and secular forces, including the Pahlavi monarchy, against each other. It was on this ideological terrain that the contradictions of the modern uneven and combined development were perhaps most clearly played out.[12]

At the same time momentous political developments on the international stage, e.g. the cold war, anti-colonial and nationalist revolutions and revolts across the Third World, forced all three trends into ideological and theoretical retrospection. The stakes were high as all of them vied for the same social constituencies, most important of which was arguably the new educated youth, the product of modernization programmes. Thus, the tendency that could best communicate with and organize these emergent modern social classes would be able to place its ideological stamp on the revolutionary movement that was already in active gestation. The ideological discourse that could attract, enervate and mobilize this agency was therefore of enormous importance.

As it turned out the 'Islamists' were most successful in offering precisely such an ideology. Surely, compared with their secular rivals, the Islamists were in a much more favourable position owing to the extremely harsh political circumstances under which the seculars, the left in particular, operated. Nonetheless, it is also crucial to note that the structural depth of Shi'ism's intellectual retrospection and ideological reinterpretation far exceeded that of the Left's.[13] And, arguably, it was precisely this critical reflexivity that largely accounts for the success of radical Shi'ism in securing ideological and consequently political hegemony over the Iranian Revolution. The leading figure in this new genre of Islamic modernism in Iran was Ali Shariati.

Ali Shariati: the ascetic ideologue of social revolution

> It is in becoming that we can be. It is in action that truth manifests itself. . . . Faith is [to be] turned into a conscientious ideology.
>
>   Ali Shariati (cited in Dabashi 2006, pp. 114, 130)

Dr Ali Shariati (1933–1977) was born into an old professional religious family reputed for their piety, social service and asceticism.[14] He received a bachelor's degree in French and Arabic from Mashhad University in 1960 and then went to Paris, where he obtained a doctorate in sociology and religious history. While in Paris Shariati avidly read Western socio-political thought and philosophy and was highly influenced by Marx, Sartre, Gurvitch and Louis Massignon. Shariati also actively participated in the student movements in support of anti-colonial struggles in the Third World, Algeria in particular. He was also deeply involved in the anti-Pahlavi activities of the Iranian students abroad. Upon his return to Iran in 1965, Shariati was briefly imprisoned. Shortly after his release, Shariati took up a lectureship at Mashhad University, where his politically charged lectures attracted large student crowds. In 1967 he moved to Tehran, where he became the principal lecturer–preacher at Hosseyniyyeh'i Ershad, a newly founded religious institution that strove to introduce a modernized Islamic curriculum. Shariati's lectures at Hosseyniyyeh were hugely popular not only with the religiously minded high-school and university students, but also with many secular leftist intellectuals. In 1972, he was imprisoned, but upon interventions by the French and Algerian governments was released in 1975. In May 1977 he was allowed to leave Iran for London, where he died of a heart attack in June that year.[15] Shariati's collected works number thirty-five volumes, mostly transcripts of his lectures published posthumously.

In so far as Shariati's ideology of 'revolutionary Islam' can be *methodologically* typified, it has arguably both structural and discursive affinity with post-colonialism. For they both share in a specifically international politico-cultural temporality that supplies their political content and the conceptual sinew. This dynamic international dimension essentially consists in a particular spatio-historical positionality that is concretely manifest in synthetic socio-political forms (Chakrabarty 1992). There is, however, an important difference between Shariati's political thought and (academic) post-colonialism. The latter tends to deconstruct the systematized and normatively unequal dichotomies of the imperial–colonial subject. Shariati, on the other hand, construes a novel revolutionary praxis that is derived precisely from the heterogeneity of socio-cultural and political-historical experiences constantly regenerated by the dynamics of modernity as a dialectical international process. Thus, the post-colonial project tends to (re)affirm intersocietal and cultural difference *sui generis,* but seeks to evacuate the Eurocentric undertone that inferiorizes it vis-à-vis the West (see Blaney and Inayatullah 2002). On the other hand, although Shariati too recognizes developmental/cultural difference as constitutive of the social, he seeks to comprehend, challenge and possibly transcend it through radical political praxis aiming at bringing it into *partial,* i.e. socio-economic, confluence with the West. Thus, ever present in Shariati's *oeuvre* is a relentless articulation of not only the possibility, but the acute necessity, of a *modern/Western* radical politicality that he unproblematically, some say paradoxically, sustains by a universal socialist utopia, which, crucially, remains ontologically anchored in an Islamic cosmology. In other words, Shariati believed that the 'true' Islam is intrinsically egalitarian and hence superior to socialism in the sense that it has the additional quality of possessing a profound ethical dimension that supplies normative meaning and moral orientation to social and individual life. Thus, Islam, Shariati thought, had a universal appeal and was capable of accommodating all forms of cultural and national diversity. But why did Shariati, a layman lacking Shi'i authorial credibility, insist on this philosophical synthesis given the immensity of the intellectual and political challenges it involved?

The reason can be sought in Shariati's acute awareness of the political consequences of inter-societal difference for the formation of revolutionary agency in a colonial-modernizing society. The driving force of Shariati's intellectual life was a supremely political goal. This political project was, in the simplest terms, the foundation of a universal 'monotheistic classless society' (*jame-ye bi-tabaqe-ye tauhidi*) in which 'oppression', in all its manifestations, would be abolished – a project that Shariati's religious–conservative detractors considered to be only semantically different from socialism, hence the common epithet of 'Islamic Marxism'. Nonetheless, to this end Shariati knew all too well what was needed: a revolutionary mass movement. Indispensable to the formation of this revolutionary agency was a political ideology capable of engaging and positively provoking the cultural–emotional sensibilities of the principal agency of the revolution, 'the people' and *not* the proletariat or 'national bourgeoisie'. For Shariati believed, and constantly argued with the Iranian left in mind, that despite appearances modern classes (both bourgeoisie and proletariat) did not exist in Iran as they had historically developed in the West (Shariati 1979b). In this contention he consistently deployed arguments that effectively invoked developmental unevenness and hence the reality of difference (combination).[16] Thus, a radical, egalitarian and action-inspiring political ideology could not appeal to the class-consciousness of the proletariat *á la* Lukács, but to that of 'the people', 'the oppressed'.

However, the popular consciousness of the 'oppressed' multitude or 'the people' – including the working class, petit-bourgeoisie and peasantry – was overdetermined by a 'traditional' Islamic political imagination. This was due to the specificity of the modern transformation in Iran, which had bypassed the economic power base of the unproductive mercantile bourgeoisie (the bazaar). It had also produced a modern working class that was both numerically small and organizationally fragmented owing to the predominance of the small workshops in the Iranian economy (Shariati 1977a, 1986, p. 18). However, both classes, especially their younger generation, were exposed to, and to varying degrees influenced by, Western culture and education. This recognition, Shariati continuously argued, highlighted the indispensability of a 'modern' language with an effervescent and enervating 'traditional' accent. Only this, Shariati insisted, would secure the vital requirement of a revolutionary ideology popular in agency, but class-conscious and elitist in leadership. This was the political leitmotif and the distinctive character of Shariati's 'revolutionary Islam'.[17]

This intellectual enterprise immediately confronted two main contenders: the traditional institutions and authority of the Shi'a *ulama*, and the secular forces. Shi'ism's historical complicity with the state was discussed in the previous section. Shariati ruthlessly indicted the Shi'a *ulama* for cultivating a socio-political imagination and disposition permeated by passivity, resignation and fatalism, ills that Shariati attributed to the formation and domination in Iran of an 'evil triangle' of 'wealth, force and deceit', his euphemism for the historical collaboration of the Shi'a *ulama*, the monarchy and the bazaar (petit)-bourgeoisie.[18] The secular radical left was, however, a different matter. Intellectually, Shariati had a deeply ambivalent attitude towards Marxism, oscillating between admiration and ethical–philosophical critique.[19] Marxism, Shariati argued, remained unidimensional, unbalanced and incomplete in its interpretation and evaluation of man on the sole basis of production (Hanson 1983, p. 16); it essentially retained 'the world-view of Western bourgeoisie' (Shariati 1979a, p. 117). Politically, Shariati had, however, deep sympathy for the Iranian new left. He shared its goals and admired the ideological devotion and revolutionary zeal of its followers. But he criticized their strategy, obscure language, inability to communicate with the masses and cultural aloofness, which, he argued, detained them within a political practice and discourse incestuous in their mode and audience. Nonetheless, Shariati believed that the new left, unlike the traditional Shi'a *ulama*, was an important force to be allied with and hence engaged with them. And it is this consideration that partially explains Shariati's appropriation of Marxist, and more generally modern, political and philosophical vocabulary. For Shariati did believe, probably owing to his misreading of the Leninist tactic of 'the vanguard party', that the revolutionary leadership must be at the hands of the 'committed intellectuals' and hence the pivotal importance of the university and college students in his political action plan (Shariati 1977a, 1980a, 1986, p. 46 and *passim*).[20]

* * *

At this point let us look more closely at Shariati's revolutionary Islam.[21] Shariati consistently argued that inter-societal difference means that radical intellectuals of the Third World societies must bear in mind that they cannot imitate Western experiences of modern socio-economic development. Because

> [The] European intellectual is dealing with a worker who has gone through three centuries of the Middle Ages and two centuries of Renaissance. . . . [and] lives in an atmosphere not dominated by a religious spirit. . . . He lives in a well-developed industrial bourgeois system . . . and has attained a higher stage of growth and self-consciousness . . . [European industrial proletariat] has formed a . . . distinct and independent class. . . . I live in a society in which the bourgeoisie, except in big cities, is in its nascent stage. The comprador bourgeoisie is a middle-man, not a bourgeoisie of the genuine producing system. . . . We still do not have a workers' class in our society. What we have are just groups.
>
> (Shariati 1977a, p. 1; see also Shariati 1986, pp. 9–23)

Human aspirations can, Shariati believed, have universal credence and reach, but developmental and cultural difference (unevenness) subverts universality of any particular notion of the political deployed for the realization of those aspirations. This means the need for specific political strategies with respect to the most effective agency they seek to mobilize for realizing those political strategies. This polychromic conception of political strategy logically necessitates (a) 'native' instances of 'revolutionary ideology'; (b) ideologies that combine and convey universal human ideals and culturally specific collective imagination through the articulation of what is entrenched and present in order to supersede the political status quo; and (c) a supersession that by definition also supersedes all linear conceptions of how it is historically achieved. Thus he argued that 'a conscious and alert individual [could] grab history by the collar [and] propel it from feudalism to socialism' (cited in Rahnema 2000, p. 291).

Crucially, this transformative consciousness was, for Shariati, a product of ideology. This ideology was Islam: 'Islam as an ideology is not a scientific specialization but is the feeling one has in regard to a school of thought as a belief system and not as a culture' (Shariati 1968, p. 5). And any ideology, Shariati argued, required two fundamental elements: a world-view and a philosophy of history (Shariati 1968, introduction). It was his attempt to derive these two elements from Islamic thought and history that led him to re-read Islamic sources with what could safely be described as a Marxist lens. This re-reading involved a translational translucence that rendered the resulting image non-coincidental with either Marxism or pre-existing 'Islam'. But, crucially, this new image was still readily visualizable through an Islamic imagination and was painted on the cultural canvass of Islamic ethics and cosmology. Shariati described his strategy for this reinterpretation as one that retained the traditional form of the Shi'i-Islamic theological and philosophical categories and discourse, but reconstituted their content in the service of a revolutionary praxis. This strategy was particularly facilitated by Islam's 'symbolical language' (Shariati 1979a, p. 71). This intellectual device, he argued, was also used by the prophet Mohammad in relation to the traditions and customs of the pre-Islamic Arab society. Two crucial instances that demonstrate the working of this intellectual device concern his reinterpretation of the story of 'Cain and Abel' and the Shi'i concept of *imamate*, which as a result were infused with strikingly radical and modern overtones.

Hitherto seen merely as an ethical anecdote on the consequences of greed, the story of Cain and Abel in Shariati's reinterpretation becomes the source of the essential material for an Islamic philosophy of history.[22] In this anecdote Shariati discerns a certain 'historical determinism' generated by 'dialectical contradiction' between 'two hostile and contradictory elements'. The story of Cain and Abel, Shariati argued, essentially shows that 'the history of man, God's vice-regent on earth, began with contradiction'. In elaborating on this contention Shariati introduces modified forms of the Marxian concepts of mode of production and class struggle. He argues that

> Abel represents the age of a pasture-based economy, of the primitive socialism that preceded ownership and Cain represents the system of agriculture, and individual or monopoly ownership. . . . Abel the pastoralist was killed by Cain the landowner; the period of common ownership of the sources of production. . . . [t]he spirit of brotherhood and true faith, came to an end and was replaced by age of agriculture and the establishment of the system of private ownership, together with religious trickery . . .
>
> (Shariati 1979a, pp. 98–9)

Keenly aware of the Marxian echoes of his argument, Shariati immediately distinguishes his approach by arguing that contra Marx, the transformation of the egalitarian pastoralist society into an in-egalitarian, class-divided and property-based agriculture was the result not of the development of productive forces or division of labour, but of *power* only (Shariati 1979a, p. 100). This contention is crucial to Shariati's overall project because it involves two modifications of the Marxist categories. On the one hand, it becomes the basis for Shariati's attribution of primary causality to the political (as he (mis)understood him). And, on the other hand, by legitimizing the 'political' category of 'oppression' – derived from the centrality of power in historical movement – as opposed to the 'economic' category of 'exploitation' – he allows the articulation of 'the people', 'the ruled', 'the oppressed' to jettison the (working) class.[23] And all this was ultimately driven by Shariati's assessment of the overall socio-political and economic conditions in contemporary Iran in terms of a revolutionary praxis.

The other important example in Shariati's practice of 'retaining the form and changing the content' concerns the Shi'i principle of *imamate*. The double and paradoxical function of this concept, as a doctrinal basis for both political oppositionism and quietism, was discussed in the previous section. In short, for much of the history of Shi'ism, and especially since its adoption by the Safavid state as the state religion, *imamate* – in conjunction with the concept of *ghayba* (occultation) – was transformed into the theological basis for a de facto legitimation of tyranny and oppression (*zulm va jowr*).

> The burden of the trust of *tauhid* was entrusted in history, after the Prophet himself . . . with the institution of Imamate, with Ali and his descendents. But in the course of time, Shi'ism, which had begun as a protest . . . became a tool in the hands of the possessors of money and might. . . . its true visage became hidden beneath the dust of opportunism, vacillation, and misinterpretation.
>
> (Shariati 1979a, p. 30)

Shariati argued that, contrary to the passivity and fatalism of 'awaiting', which the *ulama* have made into a maxim based on the notion of occultation (of the twelfth imam), this is (or should be) the basis for conscious action in order to prepare the last imam's return and the realization of Islam's 'ideal society – the umma' (Shariati 1979a, p. 119), hence the idea of *entezaar, mazhab-e e'teraz* (awaiting is the religion of protest) (Shariati 1979c). It is the revolutionary prosecution of this uninterrupted and conscious action that requires *leadership* that is, Shariati argued, the true and expanded meaning of *imamate*.

Moreover, in an ingenious move, Shariati also tries to dilute the exclusively Shi'i connotation of the concept of *imamate*. He does this through the etymology of the word '*umma*', which he identifies as Islam's ideal society. He argues that the root of *umma* is *amm*, meaning both path and intention (Shariati 1979a, p. 119). Shariati argues that the combination of path and intention rendered Islam's normative goal universal and hence beyond and above particularism of blood and soil, i.e. nationalism (Shariati 1986, p. 15).[24] Moreover, the infrastructure of *umma* is the economy. For 'whoever has no worldly life has no spiritual life' (Shariati 1979a, p. 119). *Umma* is thus based on 'equity and justice and ownership by people – a classless society – the revival of the system of Abel' (Shariati 1979a, p. 119).[25] At this point of his ideological exegesis Shariati introduces the concept of *imamate* in a clearly reconstructed form:

> The political philosophy and the form of regime of the umma is not the democracy of heads, not irresponsible and directionless liberalism which is a plaything of contesting social forces, not putrid aristocracy, not anti-popular dictatorship, not a self-imposing oligarchy. It consists rather of 'purity of leadership' *not the leader*, (for that would be fascism), committed and revolutionary leadership, responsible for the movement and growth of society on the basis of its worldview and ideology, and for the realization of the divine destiny of man in the plan of creation. This is the true meaning of imamate!
>
> (Shariati 1979a, pp. 119–20)[26]

De-emphasizing the personal dimension of the imamate and stressing the 'path and intention', Shariati seems to be trying to widen his audience and engage Sunni Muslims as well as the seculars. Moreover, by stressing the crucial role of the 'responsibility' and 'commitment' of the intellectuals, Shariati skillfully appropriated Sartre's existentialism, which he readily subsumed under Eastern mysticism (Shariati 1977b, p. 1). Thus, unlike Sartre's existentialism, which is derived from the lack or abandonment of metaphysical truth, Shariati's existentialism of responsibility and commitment is based precisely on religious truth, though with largely similar motivations and consequences. Moreover, permeating Shariati's discourse is the recurrent deployment of a re-apprehended and politicized form of *irfan* (Islamic mysticism). Shariati had always been attached to *irfan*, but it gained renewed significance for him as a result of his acquaintance with Louis Massignon (Shariati 1970).[27]

The foregoing shows that Shariati made a series of theoretical and political substitutions; a phenomenon that is a common feature of the processes of uneven and combined development (Knei-Paz 1978, pp. 192–8). Thus, in Shariati's discourse, a Marxist activist in the Iran of 1970s was likely to see a programme of Islamic camouflaging of Marxist vocabulary: 'committed intellectual' (the modern surrogate for the absent imam); to lead 'the people' (a substitute for the absent proletariat); towards the ideal society of *umma* (the equivalent of socialism). Young and educated Iranians from a more traditional background, but still with strong religious sensibility, felt that they had finally found a radical and modern, yet still Islamic, alternative to leftist politics. Displaying an extraordinary degree of conviction and devotion Shariati therefore had largely succeeded at reconstructing the dominant, but largely conservative and passive, discourse of Shi'ism into a modern popular ideological force marked by an innovative combination of modern revolutionary zeal and a radically reformed sense of Muslimhood: 'revolutionary Islam'.

Conclusion

Reporting on the Iranian Revolution, Michel Foucault, the master historicizer, made the following statement in 1978:

> Astonishing destiny of Persia. At the dawn of history, it invented administration and the state: it entrusted the recipe to Islam and its administrators supplied the Arab empire with civil servants. But from this same Islam it has derived a religion [Shi'ism] which has not ceased, through the *centuries*, to provide an *irreducible* force to all that which, at the base of a people, can oppose the power of a state.
>
> (Cited in Almond 2004, p. 17, my italics; see also Aysha 2006)

Foucault failed to see how this purportedly anti-state Islam produced one of Iran's most bureaucratic and repressive states in which Islam is continuously, sometimes radically, (re)adapted – often subordinated – to the interests of the state. But Foucault's approach to the Iranian (political) Islam is of a wider intellectual significance. For if the preceding analysis is plausible, the attitude of the critical Western scholars such as Foucault towards Islam indicates that Orientalism's 'epistemological finitude' is far more entrenched in Western intellectual imagination than what critical Western scholarship suggests (Berman 1998, p. 6; Young 2002).

This entrenchment is, I argue, the result of the *spatially* dichotomous and self-contained conception of modernity (West vis-á-vis non/extra-West) that remains operative even in the radical Western intellectual traditions such as postmodernism and post-structuralism. This is, of course, not to overlook these intellectual projects' enormous challenge to Western singular 'self' and its self-understanding as the unique and singular site of 'civilization' and 'reason'. But their perception of, and reaction to, other non-European, particularly Islamic, societies suggest that their critique of European modernity is primarily driven by intellectual alertness to an essentially intra-European temporality, i.e. they are preoccupied with the ways in which social, political and cultural forms have changed diachronically *within* Europe. Accordingly, European development is identified and conceptualized in terms of, and with reference to, the specifically European historical time and forms of subjecthood in isolation from, or in spite of, Europe's constant encounters and interactions with 'other' non-European societies and civilizations. As Shilliam in his contribution to this volume shows, this attitude even marks the work of astute thinkers such as Gadamer and Lévinas, who pioneered the themes of difference and alterity in modern Western philosophy. This is highly significant. For as I have argued, inter-societal relations and interactions, from which successive Western traditions of thought have abstracted, constitute a distinct and constitutive dimension of historic process and social reality. A conceptual incorporation of this specifically international dimension of social change, which is central to the theory of uneven and combined development, would construe modernity as an integrated and integrative totality while also affirming its internal differentiation, dialectical dynamics and significant variations across times and spaces.

This intellectual move has a crucial implication for the category of 'non-Western thought'. For once re-viewed as an international category, the negative definition of 'non-Western thought' – constructed with reference to a singular and discreet West – will instead signify a positive and mutually constitutive inter-relation. In other words, the very notions of the 'West' and the 'East' that represent concrete instances of socio-cultural constellations turn out to be permeated by each other at all levels. Consequently, ideological, intellectual and political products that arise from these constellations also need to be understood in terms of this basic condition of ontological co-constitution, which is what actually renders them resistant to comprehension through singular categories and linear histories. Shariati's political thought eminently testifies to this reality. His reconstruction of the 'actually existing Islam' in Iran was strategically driven by dynamics only partially internal to Iran, and the final product of this reconstruction, the idea of 'revolutionary Islam' that is inscribed on the Iranian Revolution and its ongoing evolution, has had crucial consequences far beyond Iran.

The recognition and conceptual integration of the international dimension of social change has wider and important implications for IR as an academic discipline. For more than two decades now, the detractors of the mainstream IR theory have invoked social (domestic) determinations of international relations and geopolitics in order to challenge the purported timelessness of the behavioural logic of states generated by 'anarchy', i.e. the multiplicity of political communities, which is the basis of the mainstream IR's paradigmatic self-definition contra sociological studies. Yet, in their concentrated attempt to de-reify anarchy as a supra-social category, they have tended to neglect a serious engagement with, and social theorization of, anarchy as a distinct field of causality. This recognition, however, needs not to re-entrap us in the mainstream IR's ontological inside/outside duality. Rather, it essentially invites us to conceive of 'the international' and 'the social' as inter-related and mutually constitutive without rendering the causal significance of either of them derivative of, or reducible to, the other. This would enable a deep socialization of 'anarchy' and pose a much stronger challenge to the mainstream IR. This chapter is a small contribution to these collective efforts.

Notes

1 Thanks to Karim Cubert and Robbie Shilliam for their valuable comments.
2 I use the terms 'Islamic modernism' and 'political Islam' interchangeably. On 'Islamic modernism' see Rahman (1970, 1982).
3 Moaddel (1992, 1993) makes such an attempt but his analysis remains largely 'sociological' and under-appreciative of the degree of transformation that ideology itself undergoes.
4 Keddie (1983), for example, elaborates on the influence of both Ibn-Khaldun and Guizot on Jamal ad-Din al-Afghani.
5 Even in 2004 a Western commentator could say: 'I still see the Iranian Revolution as a 'deviant' case' (Kurzman 2004, p. vii).
6 For example, Heidegger's philosophy can be read in these terms (Heidegger 1996).
7 But the representation of this interactive relation has been insufficiently affirmative. An important example, and in many ways trend-setter, is Said (1994). For IR-related literature see Darby (1997).
8 See also Shilliam's discussion (Chapter 2) of 'travelling theory' and 'translation' as alternative ways of rethinking the world-wide spread and modality of modernity.
9 Influential authors writing within this paradigm include Lewis (1993, 1998, 2002), Huntington (1996) and Ajami (1992).
10 Even a cursory treatment of the numerous smaller 'sects' within both the Shi'a and Sunni Islam is beyond the scope and purpose of this chapter.
11 Sunni political activism has been of marginal importance in Iran generally subsumed under the wider ethnic and nationalist movements.
12 For a more detailed discussion of this argument and the concept of the 'citizen-subject' on which it is based see Matin (2009).
13 The main development in the Iranian left, was the emergence of the militant Maoist and neo-Stalinist groups following the 1953 coup. These groups challenged the traditional monopoly of the pro-Soviet Tudeh Party over leftist politics. But because of the brutal anti-communism of the Shah's regime, these groups from their inception adopted underground armed struggle. Consequently, Iran's new left lacked the necessary preconditions for becoming a popular movement similar to Islamism. See Zabih (1986), Behrooz (1999) and Greason (2005).
14 Rahnema (2000) provides the best and most comprehensive political biography of Shariati.
15 The Iranian opposition groups and Shariati's followers always maintained that he was killed by SAVAK, the Iranian secret police.
16 Shariati (n.d.) used the metaphor of' 'cameleopard' (*shotorpalang*) to describe the hybrid nature of colonial societies and subjects.

17　Shariati (1971, 1972) often uses epithets 'revolutionary', Alavi (pertaining to Ali) and 'red' interchangeably for his articulation of the radical ('true') Islam.

18　For Shariati's vehement attacks on the Shi'a *ulama* see Shariati (1971, 1972, 1977c).

19　Shariati (1980b) provides his most sustained critique of Marxism. For a counter-critique see Bayat (1990). On Shariati's dilemmatic relation with Marxism see Dabashi (2006, pp. 135–40).

20　Mojahedin-e Khalq, more than any other political group, represented the organizational expression of Shariati's ideas (Abrahamian 1989).

21　The following discussion draws on Shariati (1977a,d, 1979).

22　This part of the discussion draws from Shariati (1979a, pp. 97–110).

23　Shariati equates 'the people' in his discourse with the Qur'anic word *al-nas* (Shariati 1979a, p. 49).

24　Shariati accepts that nationalism has been positive 'at certain historical conjuncture in Europe'. For the complex, often mutually reinforcing, relation between 'Iranian nationalism' and 'revolutionary Islamic ideology' see Paul (1999).

25　Shariati immediately adds that, contra Marxists, this infrastructure is only a means and not the end.

26　Shariati even argued that Protestantism was essentially an attempt at the Islamisation of Christianity (Shariati 1979b, p. 56).

27　On 'committed intellectual' see Shariati (1986, Chapter 1). Shariati admired Massignon's masterpiece, a biography of the sufi saint Mansur Hallaj (Massignon 1994).

8 Beyond Orientalism and "reverse Orientalism"

Through the looking glass of Japanese humanism

Ryoko Nakano

Introduction

The study of international relations has increasingly sought to transcend the normative divide between the universalizing cultural pretentions of the West and the diversity of cultures outside it. At the same time, the difficulties that diverse societies have faced in building shared norms has hampered the ability of states to solve collective action problems, such as how best to protect human rights, safeguard the global environment, and combat international terrorism.[1] A slow progress of policy coordination and implementation in multilateral institutions raises not only practical questions about the limit of institutions in delivering outcomes, but also normative questions about the relative importance of global norms and local cultural values. The Bangkok Declaration of 1993 pronounced a growing Asian resentment of Western-style political liberalism.[2] Although this declaration asserts that the Western conceptualization of human rights should not be taken as inherently universal, critics could also claim that the discourse of Asian values is simply a tactic used by authoritarian regimes to divert criticism of their human rights record (Hurrell 1999).

Debates on the universality of Western values may be increasingly prevalent in the post-cold war world, but they are not new. Rein Raud has shown that the contemporary "Asian values" debate of the 1990s and Japanese "overcoming modernity" debate of 1942 have encountered the same pitfall (Raud 2007). In this volume, this pitfall is described as "reverse Orientalism," a cultural perspective that gives higher value to the East by relying upon exaggerated Orientalist dichotomies of center–periphery, rational–spiritual, and modern–pre-(or post) modern. As Robbie Shilliam argues in Chapter 2 of this volume, many non-Western thinkers have been drawn to these dichotomies in representing themselves and "merely re-produce the colonizers image of the world." In imperial Japan, parallel discourses of Orientalism and reverse Orientalism often reinforced each other. Following the Meiji Restoration (1868–1869), the political leaders who signed the so-called "unequal treaties" with the Western powers attached the highest priority to the survival of the nation through the management of political, social, and cultural integration. This "modernization and Westernization" project introduced the most common Orientalist dichotomies to Japanese populations, instilling in them the image of following the cultural lead of the West. At the same time, a reverse discourse also emerged as Japan's success in modernization, the outcome of which was most vividly observed in the Russo-Japanese War (1904–1905), implied the great potential of Asian or non-Western civilizations (Aydin 2007). In this context, the ideological vision of Asian *dōbun* (cultural affinity) became increasingly a code-word for Japanese domination in Asia: the policy pronouncement of the New Order in East Asia of 1938 most prominently reflected Japan's self-image as the leader and embodiment of Asia. Although Japanese aggrandizement policy under the heading of the Greater East Asian Co-existence and Co-prosperity Sphere came to an end in 1945, reverse Orientalism continues to shape the discourse that glorified the uniqueness of the Japanese as manifested in *Nihonjin-ron* (a theory of the Japanese) (Faure 1995).

This chapter explores the Japanese search for an alternative vision to Orientalism and reverse Orientalism through the writings of Uchimura Kanzō (1861–1930) and his disciple, Yanaihara Tadao (1893–1961).[3] Both of them represented a school of thought that I would like to call *Japanese humanism*. Their innovative reconstruction of moral philosophy constituted an original strand of thinking that was deeply humanistic and unquestionably Japanese. Emphasizing intrinsic human qualities, both Uchimura and Yanaihara correlated Christian moral convictions with Japanese moral traditions such as Buddhist compassion, Confucian paternalism, and imperial benevolence. How both thinkers tried to escape from the two extremes of Orientalism and reverse Orientalism is a major question in this chapter. For a number of reasons, Uchimura and Yanaihara have received only minor scholarly attention in the study of international relations. First, unlike the pan-Asian movement which became influential in political circles in the 1930s, their writings had little impact on Japanese foreign policy. Second, both Uchimura and Yanaihara had a strong preference for order and stability so that their critique tended to be moderate and did not cause major political or social turmoil.[4] Third, unlike the Kyoto School that advocated a distinct Japanese philosophy to counter Western universalism, Uchimura and Yanaihara were not perceived as "Japanese" thinkers. Instead, many saw them a peculiar "Christian" minority, which was strongly influenced by Western ideas and had left "Japanese" traditions behind.

There are two major reasons to re-examine the writings of Uchimura and Yanaihara. First, Japanese humanism is a good example of "translating modernity." Shilliam argues that translating Western ideas is a "generative act of knowledge production rather than simply a technical act of producing a philological fidelity of modernity." Both Uchimura and Yanaihara were Japanese nationalists who used elements of invention to draw authority from past local traditions in order to legitimize new moral principles.[5] They never rejected a shared belief in transcendental spirituality specifically attributed to native Japanese. With a strong sense of respect and loyalty to the emperor, they were keen to integrate Japanese traditions and Christian teachings. The birth of *mukyōkai* (non-church) Christianity, which originated in Uchimura's rejection of the missionaries, signified the creation of a new type of Japanese Christian ecclesia, in which each individual should relocate his or her own faith to a direct relationship with God. Because of their efforts to adjust to foreign ideas and find a better fit with existing belief and practices, the work of Uchimura and Yanaihara should be treated as part and parcel of a Japanese endeavor to fill in the normative divide between the universal cultural pretentions of the West and cultural diversity outside the West.

Second, Uchimura and Yanaihara aimed to reconcile statecraft with moral ends. Like Western philosophers who sought universal moral traditions that are applicable to international relations, Uchimura and Yanaihara were committed to establishing moral foundations that could guide not only human conduct, but also statecraft. For them, what was required for building such foundations was not only Japanese traditional authority, but also a more rational method of ethical reasoning. Viewing political affairs from a humanist standpoint, they cast doubt on imperial slogans, such as *chūshin aikoku* (loyalty and patriotism) and *kyōson kyōei* (co-existence and co-prosperity), which were often used for the justification of Japan's hegemonic hierarchy. Since both critically searched for an alternative to the path of imposing Japanese values on those outside the territory, it is worth drawing lessons from their political thought for the study of international relations.

The chapter consists of three parts. The first examines the development of the Japanese Orientalist/reverse Orientalist discourse in the aftermath of Japan's opening to foreign trade and diplomatic relations in the mid-nineteenth century. The second focuses on Uchimura's pacifist critique of imperial Japan from a viewpoint embracing both Japan's moral tradition of *bushidō* and Christian ethics. The third explains Yanaihara's attention to the principle of autonomy as an internationally legitimated norm, and suggests that Japanese humanism warned that tolerating a view of binary opposition would hinder the process of establishing international cooperation.

Orientalism and reverse Orientalism in modern Japan

Japan encountered the Great Powers (the United States, Britain, France, the Netherlands, and Russia) in the turbulent final years of the declining Tokugawa government (1853–1867). The new Meiji government used the sense of insecurity created by this encounter to enact political reforms aimed at strengthening the military structure and economy. The driving force of this "modernization and Westernization" project was twofold: the fear of falling into the hands of the Great Powers, especially having witnessed the recent defeat of China in the two Opium Wars; and the humiliating experience of being forced into an "unequal treaty" system in which Japan accepted both restrictions on its tariff autonomy and its jurisdiction over foreign residents. Given this immediate danger to the very existence of the nation, Japanese politicians and intellectuals argued that a series of political reforms by the Meiji government was required for the maintenance of its independence. Somewhat ironically, Japan made an artificial return to the past in its national project of modernization and Westernization. With the traditional authority of the imperial house on their side, the Meiji government set out to create an image of essential Japanese tradition. From elementary schools to religious, social, and economic institutions, various local agents were integrated into the national political regime in which members developed a sense of togetherness, along with an appreciation of common culture, language and traditions, national history, and imperial myth.[6]

The self-image of Japan as a rising power in Asia evolved nationally and internationally between the Sino-Japanese (1894–1895) and the Russo-Japanese Wars (1904–1905). Along with the realist perspective of Yamagata Aritomo, who argued the importance of Korea as a strategic buffer zone, Japanese military advancement into Asia was promoted in the name of the "salvation of backward Asia." When the Korean kingdom requested China's assistance in suppressing the Tonghak insurgency, the Meiji government promptly decided to intervene. The Japanese government and media described military interference as a legitimate effort to overthrow the Sinocentric regional order which was, in the Japanese view, corrupt, backward, and stubbornly resistant toward modernization. It was no coincidence that a new discourse of *tōyōshi* (the history of the East) came into existence during that time. According to Stephan Tanaka, *tōyōshi* established "modern Japan's equivalence with Europe, as the most advanced nation of Asia, and also the distinction from and cultural, intellectual, and structural superiority over China" (Tanaka 1993, p. 12). Japan's victory in the Russo-Japanese War further strengthened Japanese self-confidence as a leader of Asia in overcoming a sense of white racial supremacy and the backwardness of the East.[7] While the Japanese political agenda was still locked into the project of modernization and Westernization, Asianism became the major force of justification for the use of force against the Asian "others" in the name of liberation.

Within the Japanese colonial empire, which eventually came to include Taiwan, the Korean peninsula, Karafuto (southern Sakhalin Island), and the Kwantung Leased Territory, the classification of populations represented the notion that native Japanese were considered to be the bearers of superior culture and technology. The ideological vision of *dōbun* (cultural affinity) created slogans such as *kyōson kyōei* (co-existence and co-prosperity) and *isshi dojin* (equal benevolence of the emperor). At a policy level, this vision was translated into the principle of assimilation, which aimed at integrating the colonized into Japanese society and culture.[8] Yet the unequal treatment of the colonized under Japanese imperial rule reflected the dominance of Orientalist dichotomies of center–periphery, rational–spiritual, and modern–pre-modern, borrowed from the thesis of the White Man's Burden and the Manifest Destiny. Japanese policies based on this Orientalist notion were intended to serve not only to create a prosperous regional community, but also to integrate the region into the Japanese sphere of interest. Japan never eliminated the discriminatory practices against, among, or between nations, histories, and cultures within the Japanese empire. As Michael Weiner argues, in addition to the transfer of wealth from the peripheries to the center, Japan "gained important ideological benefits from territorial expansion. The mere existence of empire provided final confirmation of Japan's status as a Great Power, engaged in the glorious task of bringing civilisation to the 'lesser' peoples of Asia" (Weiner 1994, p. 25). While anthropologists, philosophers, and political scientists facilitated a particular national image of Japan, the imperial discourse of Asian unity continued as the undercurrent of Japanese colonial domination, supported especially by those who either ignored or discounted the nature of anti-Japanese nationalist resistance in Korea and Taiwan.

A strong sense of Japanese exceptionalism dominated/inspired the pan-Asianism of the 1930s. As Japan searched for an alternative to the crisis of the international political and economic system, pan-Asianism entered the official discourse as a means of stressing Japan's strategic and cultural connection with China, and later Southeast Asia, beyond its existing colonial empire. Despite a political and ideological challenge, especially coming from growing Chinese nationalism, pan-Asianism functioned as a tool for providing the Japanese mission in Asia with an air of legitimacy, suggesting that Asia could not be integrated easily into the global reconfiguration of the West. In the name of the New Order in East Asia (1938), which could be contrasted with the failed Western international system and Western imperialism, Japan's commitment to the imperial project took a moral and even universalistic tone. The Showa Research Association (SRA) was directly involved in the state political project of imperialism. Philosophers such as Miki Kiyoshi, a member of SRA, and Tanabe Hajime, his senior, provided the ethical promise of cosmopolitan freedom in a way that would promote imperial domination (Kim 2007). Although these philosophers aimed to provide the antithesis of Western imperialism, their perspective provided an ideological weapon which reinforced the confrontation between the West and Asia. This is the paradox of "reverse Orientalism." In Naoki Sakai's words, "Japan's uniqueness and identity are provided insofar as Japan stands out as a particular object in the universal field of the West. Only when it is integrated into Western universalism does it gain its own identity as a particularity" (Sakai 1989, p105). In the mirror showing the West as imperial powers, they saw a new Asian order as their own creation, which was to be recognized by the West.

Japan's vision of an East Asian order reflects, therefore, the polarity of the Orientalist picture. This polarity could reinforce both images of Japan's distinct and exceptional character: as a follower of the West and as the leader of Asia. Those who argued for the latter direction emphasized Japan's authentic cultural traditions and inferred that Western powers could not create a good society in Asia. However, such a discourse falsely assumed the homogeneity of the Japanese nation and empire. Is there any alternative approach to Orientalism and reverse Orientalism other than the binary categories of Japan and the West? The following section will examine how Uchimura and Yanaihara resisted such a bifurcated perception.

Uchimura Kanzō: departure from Orientalism and "reverse Orientalism"

Born into a samurai family in 1874, Uchimura Kanzō encountered Christianity at Sapporo Agricultural College under the guidance of the Christian vice-president

William S. Clark, and acquired a deeper understanding of Christian faith during his days in Amherst College, Massachusetts. The "disloyalty incident" (*fukei iiken*) of 1891 made his name well known to the Japanese public. When Uchimura was teaching at Tokyo First Higher School, he did not make a profound bow to a copy of the *Imperial Rescript of Education* (*Kyōiku Chokugo*) because of an instinctive thought: if the act of bowing was meant to be in worship of the emperor, it would offend his Christian conscience. Although he later reconsidered, coming to believe that bowing was not worship but simply a mark of respect for the emperor, public criticism of his "disloyal" conduct grew. Inoue Tetsujirō and Katō Hiroyuki, senior professors in Tokyo Imperial University, criticized Christianity as incompatible with national polity: Buddhist journals specifically targeted Uchimura as a disloyal Christian. As the Meiji government undermined the importance of Buddhism in order to strengthen the relationship between the state and Shintō institutions, Japanese Buddhists were eager to present themselves as the defenders of the Japanese nation. Criticism of Christianity was the means of restoring links between Buddhism and the state (Snodgrass 2003, pp. 127–9).[9] As a result, Uchimura left Tokyo First Higher School. This incident consolidated the image of Uchimura as a major Christian opponent to Japanese loyalty to the emperor.

Another source of controversy was Uchimura's absolute pacifism at the time of the Russo-Japanese War (1904–1905). Total opposition to all wars marked the character of his writings after the outbreak of the Sino-Japanese War (1894–1895), which he had formerly supported. He severely criticized the oligarchic Meiji government as the major culprit of the aggressive war. Uchimura also cooperated with socialists such as Kōtoku Shūsui and Sakai Toshihiko when they organised the Risōdan (Band of Idealists) in 1901, and politically aspired to achieve radical social reforms. Both Uchimura and Kōtoku worked as editorial writers at *Yorozu Chōhō*, the major Tokyo daily newspaper, and presented a critical opinion on the elevation of a small privileged minority at the expense of workers and farmers, the worst consequence of which was found in the Ashio Copper Mine incident.[10] When the possibility of war with Russia emerged, both Uchimura and Kōtoku adopted a pacifist line and objected to the predatory nature of Japan's approach to neighboring countries. When *Yorozu Chohō* demonstrated its open support for the war in 1903, Uchimura announced his resignation, followed by the resignation of Kōtoku.

The image drawn from the above was that Uchimura was the opponent of national authority. However, Uchimura identified himself as nationalist as well as Christian. One of the distinct characteristics of Uchimura's work and activities was a persistent resistance to Christian missionaries who aimed to teach Christianity as a "universal" religion to the Japanese without any knowledge of local cultures and traditions in Japan. For Uchimura, the missionaries taught their own interpretations of Christianity rather than the content of the Bible because they saw very clearly the discontinuity between the Gospel and Japanese traditional values. Their one-sided method of teaching was not able to build a bridge between universalism and particularism.[11] Uchimura thus strived to find "Christianity received by

Japanese directly from God without any foreign intermediary" (Uchimura 1920, p. 592). This gave rise to *mukyōkai* (non-church) Christianity, which advocated teachings grounded in local culture and traditions that should go beyond the knowledge attained through the missionaries. The rejection of missionaries was Uchimura's effort to place Japan outside the Orientalist vision.

Uchimura's vigorous attempt to establish a foundation for Christianity based on Japanese moral and cultural traditions can be found in his numerous works on Japanese moral figures and traditions (Mullins 1998, Chapter 4). The Japanese moral foundation of *bushidō* was of particular importance to him. Having a Confucianist father and samurai family tradition, Uchimura maintained a strong sense of Confucian and samurai ethics even after he became Christian. *Japan and the Japanese* (later re-entitled *Representative Japanese*) was Uchimura's major work that described the traditional Japanese ethos which can be found in the teaching of national figures such as Nichiren and Saigō Takamori. Uchimura argued that, although Saigō left the Meiji government in protest over its Korean policy, he was a man of righteousness (*gishi*), who had diligent virtue and modesty. Uchimura's understanding of Christianity can be summarized by Caldarola's words: for Uchimura, "Christianity grafted upon Bushido will be the finest religious expression in modern history" (Caldarola 1979, p. 57).

The departure from Orientalism does not mean that Uchimura immediately escaped from the Orientalist polarity. His original perspective of Japan and the West had much in common with Japanese late nineteenth-century thinking, namely the early foundation of "reverse Orientalism." Questioning how the Western powers, despite the ideals that they proclaimed, could justify the takeover of others' lands, Uchimura suggested that Japan should be an entity "to reconcile the East with the West" and be the "advocate of the East to the West" (Uchimura 1892). Just before the outbreak of the Sino-Japanese War, he argued for the righteousness of fighting against China and the removal of Chinese influence from the Korean peninsula, primarily because China's backward policies were the impediment to Korea's opening up to the external world (Uchimura 1894, p. 39). Uchimura wrote, "We have [a] right to interfere, and it is our duty to interfere, when they are dying of hunger, when they are attacked by robbers, when our plain common-sense shows us that they are rapidly going toward the brink of destruction" (Uchimura 1894, p. 42). Knowing that Saigō Takamori, a former samurai and one of the leaders of Meiji Restoration, insisted on the necessity of opening a new diplomatic relationship with Korea (*sei-Kan ron*) within the context of "Heaven's laws," Uchimura explained that Saigō's intention in seeking an appointment with the chief envoy to Korea was not to "crush the weak" but to "lead them against the strong" (Uchimura 1894, p. 194). Korea needed to be guided properly lest it should be insolent to the Japanese envoys. What is evident in this writing is that Uchimura had a faith in the righteousness of Japan's intervention in the Korean affairs. His description of Japan and Korea was Manichean: Koreans were "helpless," "ignorant," and "defenceless," on the one hand, and Japanese were "lovers of Freedom and ardent admirers of human rights," on the other (Uchimura 1894, p. 41).

However, once the Sino-Japanese War broke out, Uchimura immediately realized that the Japanese government had little interest in hearing the voice of the Koreans and Chinese. The Treaty of Shimonoseki (1895) was a symbol of Japan's aggressiveness: it was "not a treaty of peace" but a "treaty of many successive wars that were to devastate the Far East for many years to come" (Uchimura 1897, p. 191). Uchimura expressed his shame at having supported the war. He lamented for the Koreans, who were not fully liberated because of Russia, and for the Formosans, who fell under the Japanese control after the war. The structure of his world vision here was neither "Japan versus the West" nor "Japan versus Asia" but "a just Japan versus an unjust Japan." This shift is important in the sense that he viewed Japan's war from the standpoint of humanism, not Orientalism. Maruyama Masao saw Uchimura's critique of the Japanese nation as a positive light within imperial Japan (Maruyama 1998, pp. 92–7). The national recon-figuration of Japanese society was quick and widespread throughout indigenous social structures and cultural values so that individuals were inclined to shift their allegiance from local norms to the concept of the nation. Although Japan's nation-making project in the Meiji period allowed little space for the develop-ment of humanist and socialist traditions, Uchimura criticized the Japanese national authority and system from a moral standpoint, synthesizing Christian and Japanese notions of human qualities and dignity. This critique was meant not just as an expression of a Christian perspective, but as the duty of a Japanese citizen, who held a higher loyalty to the emperor. In this way, Uchimura put more importance on the "liberation" of the poor and the weak than strengthening of a national pride and superiority.

In a nutshell, Uchimura incorporated Christianity into Japanese moral traditions. As a Christian humanist, he gave priority to the respect for human qualities and individual life. At the same time, his strong attachment to *bushidō* and the emperor never wavered. In the sense that he restructured both Christian and Japanese moral traditions, Uchimura indeed played a prominent role in developing Japanese humanism. His critical reflections on Japanese deeds in the Sino-Japanese War marked his departing point from the Orientalist vision of dichotomies. His perspective influenced a limited number of people through the Bible studies class: some considered the Christian faith totally separate from politics; others saw the need to translate Christian faith into a policy vision. The next section examines the work of Yanaihara Tadao, one of Uchimura's prominent disciples, who was deeply engaged in a challenging task on how to govern diverse but interconnected communities within the imperial political regime.

Yanaihara Tadao: the principle of autonomy as an internationally legitimated norm

In 1923, Yanaihara was appointed to the Chair of Colonial Policy at Tokyo Imperial University. His academic position was the product of Japan's political need to develop effective colonial rule and management. After Japan acquired control of Taiwan and Korea with a large number of ethnically different popula-tions, Japanese policy-makers and political thinkers were faced with the question of how to govern these colonies effectively under the ideological vision of *dōbun*. Yet, Yanaihara took his own path as a social scientist in search of the best means of achieving the goal of constructing an imperial order in which every human dignity would be respected regardless of race, class, and ethnicity. Following the example of Uchimura, Yanaihara organized Bible study classes and performed evangelical activities in Japan while he was working in academia. Several remarks on Christian ethics in his academic writings implied that his scholarly work was deeply connected to his Christian faith.

One manifestation of Yanaihara's humanism was his criticism of Japanese colonial policy, which restricted the freedom and diversity of populations in colonies under the principle of assimilation. The first rationale of his criticism was not particularly humanist. He suggested that it was nothing but a rational act for Japan to give political rights of autonomy to Koreans and Taiwanese. Without these rights, colonial resistance to Japanese domination would inevitably occur, as had already happened in the March First Movement in 1919. This proposal for colonial autonomy seemed distinctively liberal in Japan, where assimilation dominated the discourse of Japanese colonial management. At the same time, in the sense that self-rule can be a cost-efficient colonial policy, it could be even imperialist. However, as his article on Korea explicitly demonstrated, the second rationale of his criticism, justice, implied humanism (Yanaihara 1926). He regarded as unjust the racial and ethnic discrimination embedded in Japanese nationals and colonial institutions. With great sympathy toward the Korean outcry for independence, he argued that the key to bringing justice to Korea was to "respect the autonomy of individual personality," and the shared sense of community (in his own English words, "Group Personality"). It was morally correct to replace discriminatory practices with political rights of autonomy. By using the Confucianist and Daoist term *michi* (the right way), Yanaihara demonstrated that the respectful treatment of colonial subjects did not contradict Japanese moral sprit and paternalism (Yanaihara 1926, p. 742). Unlike Uchimura, he did not have a strong attachment to samurai ethics, but he nevertheless saw that Confucianism and Christianity were complementary and that the moral foundation of each should not be denied. Thus, the colonial administration should tolerate societal and cultural diversity in colonies; the redistribution of wealth should be redirected to the political and economic developments of a colonial society.

With regard to colonial independence, Yanaihara made a rather modest statement that national independence would not be the ultimate objective for the Koreans (Yanaihara 1926, pp. 742–3). The meaning behind these words is that even formal independence would not change the subordinate status of Koreans vis-à-vis Japan. This view reflected Japanese experiences in the international states system. Although the post-World War I international order seemed to be reorganized by the principle of equal state membership under the auspices of the League of Nations, the hierarchy among the states did not disappear. On the contrary, as Japan's proposal to eliminate the racial inequality clause was turned down, the realities of Great Power politics cut across the non-Western status of formal equality. Furthermore, as Konoe Fumimaro, who later became the Prime

Minister (1937–1939, 1940–1941), expressed, the League of Nations was insufficiently attentive to the inherent tension between status quo and "revisionist" states (Konoe 1918). Because of the harsh realities of Great Power hierarchy, Yanaihara emphasized the importance of formulating colonial policies under the principle of autonomy, rather than focusing on the legal independence of Korea.

Why did Yanaihara consider that the principle of autonomy was the best means of bringing justice? The principle of autonomy was based on his decentralized vision of the world in which each societal group could exercise its own right to self-government. His scope of analysis widely covered the history of population migration from ancient times to the age of imperialism. In Yanaihara's view, the study of *shokumin* should be extended to include the interaction between the colonizers and colonized, and between the state and the colonized, as well as among the social groups outside the direct influence of the state.[12] He regarded the third type of interaction as the origin of human awareness that needed to reconcile the competing demands of the colonizers and colonized in order to attain the development of the world economy and world politics (Yanaihara 1929, pp. 165–6). Here the principle of autonomy served as a means of holding together diverse cultural and ethnic impulses.

Yanaihara placed great emphasis on the principle of autonomy as a foundation of social justice through which the local peoples could preserve their culture in order to improve their material conditions and to make their voice heard. The implementation of this principle might vary according to the solidarity and level of development of colonized populations. Yet, the point here is that, because empire needed to handle the tension between an imperial dominance and cultural diversity, the principle of autonomy, which would make the "politics of difference" possible, became part and parcel of an imperial system. Indeed, in the 1920s there was a new model of a free trade-based imperial system, which should be distinguished from a territory-based imperialism in the nineteenth century (Sakai 2007, pp. 206–11). The change of imperial perspectives cannot be understood in isolation from the emergence of the British commonwealth system and the mandate system of the League of Nations, both of which were particular interests of Yanaihara's. Since he credited the emergence of these institutions with a historical significance, let us see in detail how he described the implications of each institution.

First, Britain came to adopt the principle of autonomy through the formation of the dominion system, in which former colonies (Canada, Australia, New Zealand, and the Union of South Africa) had the right to self-government while maintaining the British monarch as head of state. In reference to Anne Robert Jacques Turgot's words that "colonies are like fruits which only cling till they ripen," Yanaihara emphasized that the integration of the British Empire was strengthened as if it were "forests of the ripened and fallen fruits" (Yanaihara 1937a, pp. 289–90). This did not mean that he was blind to the exclusion of non-White populations in the British Commonwealth (Oguma 1998, pp. 188–92). Indeed, he pointed out that the dominion status of British white colonies was not the product of ethical concerns with the autonomous nature of colonies but a pragmatic decision based on the practical purpose of organizing empire. Nevertheless, he valued highly the changing characteristic of the British Empire as forming "a voluntary association" in which a "shared sense of community" (group personality) outside the British Isles was to be respected. Here Yanaihara saw the compromise between an interest-based approach and social justice.

Second, the mandate system of the League of Nations has a historical significance in the sense that it offered the prospect of setting down the principle of autonomy to guide the behavior of imperial states toward former colonies. Yanaihara understood that the mandate system was adopted in only a limited number of areas, and that the supervisory role of the League was insufficiently defined. However, he explained that Article 22 of the Covenant of the League of Nations ensured the responsibility of the mandatory states to administer mandated territories so as to prepare them for self-government under principles such as non-annexation, freedom of commerce, and the tutelage of the people. These constraints on mandated states implied that a new international norm was created to protect the wealth and development of those who were formerly designated merely colonized populations. In this sense, the system of the League of Nations was a budding international force that pursued social justice by reconciling the competing demands of the colonizers and the colonized. He wrote that "were a war to break out in the near future, this would ultimately lead to a more advanced international institution for the development of colonial populations" (Yanaihara 1937a, p. 195).

Yanaihara's strong adherence to the principle of autonomy runs directly counter to the other voices in the pan-Asianist discourse in the 1930s. By 1930, Japanese Sinologists such as Uchida Ryōhei and Naitō Konan had already argued that China as a whole was merely a civilization, not a state, and, in particular, that Chiang Kai-shek was not the state leader but just one of the warlords who used a policy of bourgeois nationalism (Miwa 1990, pp. 135–8). In the aftermath of the Manchurian Incident in 1931, these descriptions were rapidly incorporated into the official rhetoric used by Japan to extend its paternalistic duty toward China (Crowley 1974, p. 272). In opposition, Yanaihara looked at the strong nationalist sentiment in China which was fully engaged in the norm of self-determination and sovereignty. He compared China's chaotic situation with what the Meiji leaders of Japan once had to confront, and insisted that "although the Meiji government was a feudal one and had a sufficient reason to be accused in terms of a lack of democracy, it cannot be denied that the Meiji government achieved national unification" (Yanaihara 1937b, p. 332). Japan, therefore, should respect the Chinese national ideology that emerged under the leadership of Chiang's Kuomintang.

In Yanaihara's view, the recognition of Chinese sovereignty would not contradict what was commonly acknowledged as an "internationalist" approach, namely peaceful diplomacy in cooperation with Western powers. He urged Japan to find a way to avoid a war with China and to "promote friendly relations between Japan and Britain, the United States, Soviet Union and China" (Yanaihara 1937c, p. 105). Just before the outbreak of the second Sino-Japanese War in 1937, he predicted that Japan's war against China would directly cause international repercussions and even a conflict between Japan and Western powers. In contrast to pan-Asianists such as Rōyama Masamichi, who sought the formation of a new East Asian to oppose the Anglo-American international states system, Yanaihara did not find any legitimacy within this self-proclaimed order, which would damage both Japanese moral traditions and the legacy of the internationalist approach within the League of Nations, the Geneva Convention, and the Kellogg–Briand Pact (the Pact of Paris).

Although Yanaihara shared a future vision of East Asian unification with pan-Asianists and a sense of Japanese spirituality with the Kyoto School, he was not hesitant to criticize each presumption consolidating the prevailing hegemonic relations. His rejection of the grandiose project of East Asian order and the philosophical provision of Japanese spirituality implied that Japan could not take leadership in Asia without winning the trust of, and obtaining consent from, its counterparts in Asia. In this sense, the principle of autonomy provides the basis for making the distinction between just and unjust state conduct and advancing in these directions to facilitate the pursuit of accommodation. The lesson drawn from this section is that, although it was undoubtedly necessary for the non-West to overcome the Orientalist perspective and formulate a new form of order other than Western imperialism, any efforts to overcome Orientalism should not end in a reverse Orientalism that placed Japanese values and qualities in a privileged position over other Asian nations. Defending China's sovereignty was a key to avoiding such pitfalls, because a decentralized association of sovereign states would prevent Japan from pursuing the extreme path of reverse Orientalism.

Conclusion

This chapter has examined how Uchimura Kanzō and Yanaihara Tadao, as Japanese humanists, aimed to overcome the limits of Orientalism and reverse Orientalism. They sought to overcome the difficulties created by the Orientalist view that privileges the center over periphery, the rational over the spiritual, and the modern over the pre-modern. Although both Uchimura and Yanaihara decided to adopt Christianity as the core foundation of morality, they recognized that spirituality also exists within Western rationalism and that rationalism exists within non-Western traditions. They rejected the assumption that "universal" values drawn from the Christian missionaries were readily accessible to populations in the non-West, and also refused to take sides, pitting "being Japanese" against being "not Japanese." In particular, Uchimura pursued a way of addressing and attaining complementary moral ethics based on both Japanese moral traditions and the Bible. By doing so, he rejected the fictional universal authenticity promoted by the missionaries, but at the same time viewed Japanese actions through a Japanese ethical lens.

His successor, Yanaihara, made a scholarly effort to rebuild a moral foundation of imperial order. As the Japanese colonial empire came to include non-native Japanese as its imperial subjects, he saw the need to expand beyond an imperial order constructed only in terms of Japan's inwardly constituted spirituality or the romantic ideal of the Japanese feudal ethos. Yanaihara argued that the rules of proper conduct within culturally diverse communities needed to be built under the principle of autonomy and social justice in order to win the trust and consent of the colonized. In this sense, Yanaihara's defense of the state sovereignty of China also meant a defense of the principle of autonomy as an internationally legitimated norm. In a nutshell, Japanese humanism put the primary importance on developing a moral philosophy in a way that would reconcile universalism and cultural diversity.

What implication does Japanese humanism have for the study of international relations? Indeed, the idea of "universality" often found in Western literature is a potential problem because it may lead to the unilateral imposition of values on other states (in both the West and non-West) and eventually hinder cross-regional and intra-regional cooperation. Yet, in the same way, emphasizing cultural particularity is also problematic. As there are no values that are self-evidently universal to people across the globe, it is extremely important not to consolidate cultural particularities as a way of marginalizing external others. In particular, Japanese humanism warns of the risk that tolerating a view of binary opposition would hinder the process of establishing international cooperation: if the state appropriates the process of adopting external ideas to avoid external criticism, it may end up with the fate of reverse Orientalism. For this very reason, we should note that so-called Asian values, as represented by the Bangkok Declaration of 1993, may not be a solution to the universalizing pretentions of the West. Neither coercion nor resentment of universally proclaimed values would help us work together on the multifaceted global challenges. Instead we need to reduce the danger of creating another form of reverse Orientalism. This is the first and foremost step to resolve tensions in the relationship between cross-regional and intra-regional interpretations of global norms such as democracy and human rights.

Notes

1 For instance, Miller (2007) develops a political theory of global justice for a world of different self-determining national communities.

2 The "Bangkok Declaration," signed by thirty-four Asian and Middle Eastern countries at the Regional Meeting for Asia of the World, placed more importance on economic and social rights than on civil and political rights.

3 Japanese names are presented in the traditional order, with surname first, except when cited for English-language literature.

4 Having no attachment to sacramental rituals in church or any other establishment functioned as a convenient way of defending individual faith under the censorship of imperial Japan. In contrast to church members, non-church Christians were relatively free from oppression by the authorities because there was no formal organization. Ōta Yūzō criticized their lack of political activism and direct confrontation with the authorities (Ōta 1977).

5 "An element of invention" is not peculiar to Uchimura and Yanaihara, because, as Nardin correctly argues, traditions that draws authority from their past "characteristically legitimize change by minimizing it" (Nardin 1992, p. 7).

6 According to Gluck (1985), the "Meiji ideology" was produced for the integration of Japan as a nation.

7 Aydin (2007) examines the profound impact of the Russo-Japanese War on the wider discourse of non-Western intellectuals.

8 In Japanese colonial policy, the meaning of assimilation varied, depending on time, place, history, and the material culture of colonial subjects. In the case of Koreans and the Han Chinese in Taiwan, assimilation largely meant copying Japanese language and culture. In the less populated areas, it meant inspiring native culture with a vague "Japanese spirit."

9 According to Tabata (1959), Katō's ultra-nationalistic criticism of Christianity enhanced the widespread attack on Christianity. It was influential not only on an individual Christian but also on the churches. Later, Japanese churches became nationalistic.

10 Kōtoku advocated the need to protect the rights of the farmers who suffered from pollution caused by the Ashio Cooper Mine. See Asukai (1978, pp. 135–6).

11 Caldarola (1979, p. 49) describes Uchimura's non-church movement as "a challenge to the superiority of the West."

12 In the early twentieth century, the term "*shokumin*" was often understood as equivalent to the English term "colonization" and implied that a particular agent or a state enforced or encouraged the movement of population from the original state territory to its colonized areas. See Nakano (2006, 2007).

9 Culture in contemporary IR theory

The Chinese provocation

Arif Dirlik

Introduction[1]

The diffusion of the ideology and practices of globalization over the last two decades has been accompanied by proliferating cultural claims on modernity that are audible in calls for the recognition of multiple and alternative modernities. It is ironic that modernity globalized – global modernity – calls modernity into question as a coherent cultural concept. The questioning of modernity also challenges modernity's ways of knowing, including the claims to universality of knowledge produced under the sign of science, which now appears as only one among many ways of knowing. As the globalization of modernity erodes the centrality to it of its Euro/American origins, its epistemology, too, loses its hegemony, and retreats into parochialism as the product of one cultural province among others of modernity. Theory, an essential tool in the production of such knowledge, and one of its foremost symbols, follows the fragmentation of knowledge into fragmentary spaces of culture (see Dirlik 2007, pp. 70–9).

IR theory would seem to be no exception. Since the 1990s, the question of culture has moved to the forefront in discussions of IR. Newcomers to IR theory, such as academics from the People's Republic of China (PRC), have qualified their desire to participate in the global discourse on IR with the condition that their particular concerns and outlook be part of any such discourse. Discussions of theory in the original homeland of IR in the United States have on their part repeatedly raised the question of its parochialism, and the need to incorporate in it the voices of others if it is indeed to live up to its universalist pretensions. Some authors have seen in "the return of culture" the revival of questions that were part of IR theory at an earlier stage (in the 1930s and 1940s).[2] Culture was indeed quite prominent in the US social sciences in general in an earlier period, most importantly in discourses of development informed by Weberian assumptions. The present needs to be distinguished from the past, nevertheless, for the vastly different part culture has come to play. Earlier discussions deployed culture in the consolidation of Euro/American hegemony, in explanations of backwardness that viewed backwardness as a function of inherited cultural traditions. Those same cultural traditions are deployed presently by the "backward," now competitors in modernity, not only to explain their success but to challenge the hegemony of Euro/America.

I take up in this discussion problems presented by the "cultural turn" in IR theory with specific reference to the PRC. IR in the PRC is a relatively new discipline, going back to the beginnings of the "reform and opening" initiated after 1978. Chinese academics deplore the underdevelopment of IR theory in the PRC, and express a determination to become part of global theoretical discussions. On the other hand, uncertainties about the future of IR in the global IR establishment provide openings for alternative approaches, making this a propitious time for newcomers such as the PRC. China appears to some, moreover, as "the most obvious candidate for an independent IR tradition based on a unique philosophical tradition" (Waever 1998, p. 696). What then might be problematic about Chinese entry into the global discourse on IR theory, or the assimilation of IR theory in the PRC?

The answers to these questions may have much to reveal about problems of IR as a disciplinary undertaking in general, and the PRC orientation to it in particular. It is quite obvious from contemporary discussions that IR is a deeply divided discipline, raising questions for any newcomer on where and how to find the most effective entry into its domain. On the other hand, consideration of what scholars from the PRC or other Chinese societies may have to contribute to IR theory needs to guard against the pitfalls of Orientalist reductionism. Chinese scholars are by no means unanimous in their attitudes toward IR theory – or even on what may constitute theory. Furthermore, there is nothing obvious about China's so-called "unique philosophical tradition," or the relationship of that tradition to contemporary Chinese perceptions of the world and the policies that issue from them. Indeed, on the basis of evidence available, if one were forced to choose between a future for IR theory of greater universalism made possible by the assimilation of diverse traditions, such as the Chinese, or fragmentation under the pressures of difference, it would seem wiser to bet on the latter rather than the former. Where theory (in contrast to policy) is concerned, moreover, with the intensified transnationalization of education (among other things, including class and ethnic and gender interests and alignments), divisions in approach that cut across national boundaries may be at least as significant as differences between national groupings of scholarship. Still, this very predicament of fragmentation may contribute to further disciplinary development by bringing to IR theorization a more critical sense of history both in disciplinary practice and in the discipline's consciousness of its own development and limitations.

IR theory with "Chinese characteristics"

There is an irony to the study of IR in the PRC. Like their Euro/American counterparts, Chinese scholars wish to globalize. But globalization does not carry the same meaning for all concerned. To Euro/American scholars, the globalization of IR means to incorporate in it difference, including Chinese difference, to make IR more universal. Chinese scholars, on the other hand, desire above all to "Westernize," to become part of a "Western" discourse on IR, while retaining an identity of their own. The irony presents the analyst with a basic question: What is the difference that difference makes?

IR in the PRC is so far a dependent discipline with little claim to originality. Ever since Deng Xiaoping declared plans for a "socialism with Chinese characteristics" as the goal of post-1978 reforms, Chinese politicians and academics have gotten into the habit of attaching "Chinese characteristics" to everything from the most significant to the most trivial. A cynical reading would suggest that the phrase serves as a cover to disguise mimicry of the "advanced" societies of Europe and America that has been the core of developmental policy since the 1980s, a cover that works because of a persistent Orientalist fascination with Chinese difference. More charitably, it points to a search that has been under way for over a century now for a Chinese essence that may give the country a unique present and future even as it is transformed radically by forces from abroad. Both readings have some validity, and account not only for oscillations between universalism and parochialism that have marked modern Chinese history, but also the contradictions that have played an important part in dynamizing it. The contradiction may also help us grasp some of the issues in Chinese perceptions of the world, and the way they may help shape the course of IR as academic undertaking.

IR in China is a new discipline, going back to the 'reform and opening' in the early 1980s. As the standard account goes,

> Before the 1980s no real IR theory was taught in China. The so-called theory of international politics before then was just interpretation of the viewpoints of Marx, Engels, Lenin, Stalin, and Mao Zedong . . . University courses were just to explain theories of imperialism, colonialism, national liberation movements, and war and peace.
>
> (Song 2001, p. 63)[3]

This situation has changed drastically since the 1980s, when IR came into its own as an autonomous discipline. In the early 1960s, only the People's University in Beijing and Fudan University in Shanghai had departments of foreign affairs. These universities were joined from the late 1980s by Nankai University in Tianjin and the Foreign Affairs College in Beijing in the teaching of IR theory, which now began to include Western IR theory. IR theory was also taught in government and party institutions, as well as in the Chinese Academy of Social Sciences (CASS). Universities around the country began to offer courses on contemporary world politics, stimulating the market for textbooks. Initially poor in quality, and mostly copied from one another, the textbooks have considerably improved in quality over the years since then.

Access to foreign writings on IR has also improved, and China now compares favorably with the United States in this respect. A recent study on IR by Fudan University professors Zhao Kejin and Ni Shixiong includes in its bibliography, in addition to the most important US publications on IR in English and Chinese translation, Chinese translations of works translated from German, French, Italian, Swedish, and Japanese (Zhao and Ni 2007). Journals and journal publications have proliferated in tandem. However, developments in IR theory have not been commensurate with these institutional developments in research and teaching. Gerald Chan wrote in 1999 that,

The Chinese theory of IR, if there is a coherent one at all, does not pose any significant challenge to existing (Western) theories of IR. In the foreseeable future it is likely that the Chinese theory will only add marginally to and complement current theories, making IR theory more pluralistic, more representative, and more interesting, as will the theories or perspectives of other major countries.

(G. Chan 1999, p. 3)

It is safe to say that the situation has not changed much over the last decade and, despite brave talk of "Chinese characteristics," Chinese writings on IR remain derivative. This could still be explained as a consequence of the time lag in entry into the disciplinary realm of IR, but in order to assess the potential of the discipline for intellectual and theoretical breakthroughs, we need to consider other possible obstacles to the development of a "Chinese theory" that are internal to the institutional and ideological development of IR in the PRC over the last two decades. These include fetishization of development, and the dependency it has created on Euro/American, especially American, intellectual models that are barely disguised by recourse to the cover of Chinese characteristics. They include, contradictorily, the persistence of the legacies of the revolution, however distorted, that haunt post-revolutionary developments – which is most evident in the ambivalence toward theory. They also include the problem of how to define "Chinese characteristics," and to integrate it in theoretical work. The latter also involves the fundamental question of how "Chinese characteristics" may be relevant not just to theory or IR as a discipline, but to what we might call the actually existing world which, after all, must be the ultimate referent for all theoretical work if the latter is to be anything other than academic entertainment.

The problems thrown up by these tendencies are already visible in debates among Chinese scholars over the development and nature of IR. Song Xinning, himself a leader in efforts to establish IR theory in the PRC,[4] has attributed disciplinary divisions mostly, if not wholly, to generational differences, implicitly holding an older generation for the inertia in the field. Song wrote in 2001 that,

Most Chinese scholars, especially the younger ones, are optimistic about the future development of IR studies in China. First, the domestic political atmosphere is improving, although there are still limitations. As long as the open-door policy continues, China's IR scholars will have more freedom to express their views both within the profession and in public forums. Secondly, due to the implementation of the enforced retirement system, those conservative, senior university professors will eventually withdraw from their positions in IR studies. More and more junior scholars who have received academic training in foreign institutions of higher education are taking over important academic and administrative posts.[5]

Divisions have been primarily over the understanding of theory, and the question of "Chinese characteristics." Aside from the issue of Chinese characteristics, which I will discuss below, Chinese scholars have been divided over the nature and function of theory. In the words of Geeraerts and Men Jing,

> The basic concept of theory in China differs markedly from the one found in mainstream Western epistemology. While according to the latter, the function of theory consists in explaining and predicting, theory in the Chinese conception has to serve the purpose of socialist revolution and construction. Such a conception stresses both a theory's ideological content and effectiveness in application. Thus theories are strongly ideologically oriented and must be able to instruct practice the 'right' way. Ideological soundness as well as effectiveness in guiding policy-making are paramount in judging a theory's value.
>
> (Geeraerts and Jing 2001, p. 252)

From this perspective, "the research conducted by Western IR scholars is unavoidably restricted by the national and cultural environment in which they are nested" (Yuan Ming, cited in Geeraerts and Jing 2001, p. 252). In a broad sense, there are only two types of IR theories, Western bourgeois and Marxist–Leninist (G. Chan 1999, pp. 7–8; Geeraerts and Jing 2001, p. 253).[6]

These views are associated in the literature with an older group of scholars, such as Huan Xiang, Liang Shoude, and Feng Tejun, who, regardless of their own reservations, must be considered the first generation of post-revolutionary IR scholars. Their efforts to integrate IR theory with the legacies (and goals) of socialist revolution appear outmoded from the perspective of a younger generation alienated from the socialist revolutionary past, and more in sympathy with (if not products of) "Western" understanding of science, in contrast to the older generation's equation of "scientific" with Marxism–Leninism, including its Chinese incarnations in Mao Zedong thought (Mao Zedong *sixiang*) and Deng Xiaoping theory (Deng Xiaoping *lilun*), as ideological orthodoxy has enshrined them. This younger generation, desirous of participation in the most "advanced" intellectual trends in the world, seems to have no problems with the global scope assumed by "Western" theory, its claims to transcend particular interests of nation, class or gender, and its aspirations to universal validity.

As Song Xinning's qualification (cited above, fn. 8) suggests, however, these generational differences should not be understood totalistically, as characteristics of every member of the generation, but only as historical markers that may be used to distinguish one generation from another. Equally important may be the political differences that cut across generations, producing intra-generational disagreements, and keeping alive seemingly outmoded ideas that may be resurrected once again if circumstances warrant it. In the case of the PRC, the very persistence of rule by the Communist Party has given staying power to Marxism as a referent for theory. Although Marxism has receded to the background of theoretical discussions with academic liberalization and greater educational transnationalism, it has by no means disappeared.

Most commentators, Chinese and foreign, focusing on disciplinary developments, take for granted a break in the 1980s between a pre-IR and post-IR theory periodization, accompanied by a teleological assumption that Chinese scholarship must follow an inevitable path from its revolutionary past to greater integration with "Western" scientific theory. This may or may not be the case, but both the understanding of the break and of its aftermath may be misleading in ignoring the contradiction that persist, which are the contradictions of a post-socialist society. Clearly there were international relations, as well as IR thinking, before the 1980s. The appearance of another kind of IR thinking, consistent with the turn away from revolutionary socialism to accommodation with capitalism, did not merely write a script on a blank sheet of paper.[7] The beginning was not just a beginning, but also a suppression of something that existed earlier. Although suppressed in order that IR can become an academic discipline (within a broader political context), this earlier thinking that is the legacy of revolution has refused to go away, and continues to haunt post-socialist thinking. It is, in fact, one important sense of the phrase "Chinese characteristics." And if it shows more strongly with the first post-revolutionary generation in IR theory, it has not disappeared from later thinking. Nor is there any reason to expect its ultimate demise with time, at least not in the immediately foreseeable future (on postsocialism see Dirlik 1989; see also Yuan 2007).

More interesting have been changes in the content of Marxism. IR theory in China has been bound not only to "Marxism," but to a Marxism that is subject to reinterpretation with changes in policy. Since the 1990s, new interpretations have been added to it as a changing leadership adds its own signatures to the theory. More recent works on IR theory in the PRC have sought to accommodate themselves to Jiang Zemin's "Three Represents" (*sange daibiao*) and Hu Jintao's "harmonious society" (*hexie shehui*) or "harmonious world" (*hexie shijie*). It is possible to speak of a progressive compromising of Marxist theory as a radical sociology as it is forced into ever-intensifying accommodation of capitalism, and the emergence of a class society in the PRC, but even this requires great caution, judging by the greater attention given to social problems of development and ideological rejuvenation under the current leadership.[8] What is more directly pertinent here is the way in which these changes have transformed the idea of "Chinese characteristics" as well.

Reference to "Chinese characteristics" immediately invokes thought of "an independent IR tradition based on a unique philosophical tradition," in the words of Waever, cited above. It is probably fair to say that Chinese have been a great deal more ambivalent about that tradition than their Euro/American admirers (or, for that matter, critics). Although there is a good case to be made that, as socialism has receded, the "unique philosophical tradition'" has moved to the foreground of Chinese self-identification, reference to "Chinese characteristics" still retains an ambiguity, referring, depending on the speaker, sometimes to the philosophical traditions of imperial China and sometimes to the socialist revolutionary tradition. Indeed, writers on IR in the PRC for the most part agree that it was the socialist tradition that was foremost in the minds of the first post-revolutionary generation, who argued for an IR theory that would be consistent with China's circumstances as a socialist society. The IR theory that these scholars sought to create was one that would integrate the insights of "Western" theory with Marxism as it had been interpreted by Mao Zedong, and subsequently Deng Xiaoping, to account for the special circumstances of Chinese society. Chinese scholars claimed that Chinese IR research before the 1980s had concentrated on

> imperialism, national liberation movements, international solidarity, and principles of peaceful coexistence. From the beginning of the 1970s, [they] probed into theories of interdependence, international cooperation, diplomatic strategy, and cultural elements in international relations.
>
> (Geeraerts and Jing 2001, p. 256)

A popular text often cited listed Chinese contributions as the "five principles of co-existence,"[9] "strategic division of the Three Worlds,"[10] "peace and development in the world," (*heping fazhan*), and the new international political order (Tejun and Xinning 1992, pp. 36–7, cited in Chan 1998, p. 13). More generally, IR theory as conceived by these scholars was to be attentive to the *guoqing*, a term that does not exclude culture, but is not reducible to it either, as it captures simultaneously material conditions and the intangible elements that make up a nation's particularity (G. Chan 1999, pp. 151–2).

This very contemporary sense of "'Chinese characteristics," which includes the past as a constituent of the present, but as only one element among others, has been accompanied from the beginning by another, more distinctly cultural-ist, sense of "Chinese characteristics" that looks to the past for the definition of "Chineseness" and an "IR with Chinese characteristics." The two senses of "Chinese characteristics" are related, and yet also fundamentally contradictory, as the one views the past through the lens of a socialist revolutionary tradition, whereas the other is deployed, more often than not, in the negation of revolution by the resurrection of a cultural tradition which the revolution had set out to abolish. This latter sense of "Chinese tradition," symbolized most importantly by the Confucian tradition, has moved to the forefront as Chinese society has been progressively derevolutionized over the last two decades.

It is this sense of "Chinese characteristics" that most foreign observers have when they refer to "a unique philosophical tradition." The Chinese have been much more divided over the issue not only because of the problematic relationship of contemporary China to its imperial past, but also because of the complexities of that past, which yields not one but many traditions, and resists efforts to create a single tradition, or define a "national essence." The difficulty is resolved, more often than not, by a reductionist distillation of complex and historically changing philosophical traditions to a few simple ideas that can then be made to stand in for something called a Chinese cultural tradition.[11]

Song Xinning provides us with a list of concepts and orientations that have been raised by Chinese scholars as fundamental to grasping "Chinese understanding of the world order and China's position in the world community" (Song 2001, p. 70). Topping the list are terms related to geo-politics that place the imperial house at the center of world order: *huaxia zhongxin zhuyi* (*huaxia*-centrism), *huayi zhixu* (*hua-yi* order), *tianchao lizhi* (ritual order of the heavenly dynasty), and *chaogong tizhi* (dynastic tribute system). Then comes terms that pertain to the nature of government in general: *renyi daode* (humane righteous morality) and *renzheng* (humane government), which distinguish kingly rule (*wangdao*) from despotic rule (*badao*), which, though less desirable, is nevertheless preferable to disorder or chaos. Finally, but perhaps most fundamentally, are terms that indicate a basic orientation to life in general, for example *hehe* (two different characters, one suggesting harmonious blending and one peace), which found its most popular expression in the phrase *tianren heyi* (unity of heaven or nature and human). From this orientation derives the representation of the Chinese commitment to peaceful resolutions over resort to force and the military. This, of course, is only part of the story. Song notes that these characteristics, associated with Confucianism and Daoism, found a less idealistic counterpart in the legacy of the legalists (*fajia*), who, less convinced of the goodness of humans, believed in law and punishment (against ritual and cultivation) in containing evil, closer in spirit to the realist school in IR (Song 2001, p. 70).

As this last qualification suggests, there was no single Chinese theory of IR. And the norms suggested by the ideas above represent ideals rather than the realities of imperial dynasties' interactions with their neighbors. The ideals, and the texts from which they are derived, were products of the "Warring States" period, corresponding roughly to the second half of the first millennium BCE, when the ideal of unity under the Zhou Dynasty gave way to a number of states contending for power, which would result in reunification under an imperial government the end of the third century BCE.

The terms "*hua*" and "*huaxia*" are often translated as China, as Song does in his discussion, to be contrasted with *yi*, which is rendered into barbarian, especially in English usage, which, Song, to his credit, eschews in favor of the more neutral term, "tribal societies." These usages, including the identification of *hua* or *huaxia* with China, are products of the nineteenth century, and the reinterpretation of the vocabulary of imperial China for nationalist purposes.[12] The terms "*hua*" and "*huaxia*" referred originally to the tribal societies that inhabited the central Yellow River region, who by the end of the first millennium BCE came to distinguish themselves from those outside the area as the 'central kingdoms' (also *Zhongguo*). These kingdoms, moreover, evolved different terms for different groups of outsiders, to distinguish other tribal societies from one another. Together these societies constituted *tianxia*, or all-under-heaven, which connoted not the whole world, but the world that counted. Although the Chinese were quite aware from the Han Dynasty (206 BCE to 220 AD) on of the existence of other societies as far as Imperial Rome, it was the societies that came to constitute an Eastern Asian ecumene that counted in the unfolding of inter-state relations, with a geographically expanding *huaxia* at the center – most importantly, the rulers who ruled over *huaxia*, with further pretensions to ruling all-under-heaven. It is important to draw attention to these problems of terminology to reveal the complexity of these relationships, and the manner in which they confound notions of the unitary state, as well as of ideas of the inside and the outside. Much is lost in the translation. It is in modern usage that both China and "barbarian" are reduced to the singular terms, *Zhongguo* and *yi*. It is also modern nationalism that has reduced the complex notion of open sovereignty that may be implicit in a term such as "all-under-heaven" into rule over bounded territory, which converts reciprocal relations of the "tribute system," however hierarchical, into the colonialist claims of the modern nation-state.[13]

For a large part of the first millennium of imperial history, the area designated "China" was too divided to have a coherent foreign policy. Between 1000 and 1300 AD, roughly speaking, a number of major kingdoms co-existed, leading historians to write of "China Among Equals" against clichés of a Sinocentric world order (Rossabi 1983). It was only with the last three dynasties, the Yuan (1275–1368), the Ming (1368–1644), and the Qing (1644–1911) that a sufficiently cohesive and coherent unity was achieved to speak of an inside and an outside. And two of these dynasties, the Yuan and the Ming, were ruled by "outsiders" (Mongols and Manchus, respectively). In other words, even after sustained imperial unity was achieved, the distinction between "Chinese" and "foreigner" was still blurred, which is evident also in the part played by Jesuit missionaries in the official circles of the very "han" Ming Dynasty, which further underlines the centrality to the "middle kingdom" of the ruler, who remained the subject of inter-state relations. Still, the realization of sustained unity under the Ming and the Qing enables glimpses into the actualities rather than the textualities of imperial conceptions of inter-state relations, and the role of violence in the conduct of foreign affairs. A recent study by Alastair Johnston suggest not only that "realism" was implicit in the classical military texts produced during the late Zhou, but that Ming policy was quite in keeping with the "parabellum paradigm" implicit in these texts, which assumed that "warfare and conflict are relatively constant features of inter-state affairs, that conflict with an enemy tends toward zero-sum stakes, and consequently that violence is a highly efficacious means for dealing with conflict" (Johnston 1995, p. 61).[14]

Johnston's conclusion derives additional plausibility from long-standing evaluations of the imperial state which, Confucian in ideology, owed much to the principles of the legalists in the organization and conduct of government. Any assessment of "Chinese characteristics" derived from the imperial past or from the more recent revolutionary tradition needs to be attentive to the gap between ideal and actuality, and what it may have to contribute to a global discussion on IR. One would be hard put to argue that for all the talk about moral rule, it was morality rather than power that motivated dynastic ruler, or that philosophical assumptions of 'unity between heaven and humans' made the Chinese relationship to nature any more harmonious than anyone else's. The latter, which has acquired renewed currency in recent years, sounds cruelly ironic at the present with the unprecedented ecological destruction that has accompanied China's development. Jurgen Osterhammel has written that,

A genuine Chinese paradigm for the understanding of international relations seems to be lacking. Chinese tradition offers a variety of normative ideas on the conduct of relations between the empire and its neighbours, but none has much relevance for understanding the post-imperial world. Marxism, in whatever form, has never offered a strong analysis of international relations. . . . Chinese Marxist thought on the principles of international relations has advanced little beyond Lenin's theory of imperialism. An updated Sino-Marxist paradigm of international theory may be under construction, but it does not appear to be available at the present time.

(Osterhammel 1992, p. 129)[15]

The question raised by Osterhammel is what part there is to be played in a contemporary world by concepts that were products of a different world, marked by different arrangements of states and societies. With the forceful opening to commerce and diplomatic intercourse in the middle of the nineteenth century, Qing leaders and their successors in the Republic and the People's Republic came to operate within a new framework of international relations in which the principle of sovereign, and nominally equal, states replaced the hierarchical ecumenical assumptions of *tianxia*, and formal legal regulation of relations between sovereign states replaced the ritual order that had guided the tributary system of the Ming and the Qing.[16] The new system assumed "an internal political hierarchy [therefore, order] and external geopolitical anarchy [therefore, disorder]," which is also the assumption that has guided realist approaches to international relations, with the sovereign state as its unit (Teschke 2003, p. 3).[17] This was the system challenged by socialist revolutions inspired by Marxism. Now that world, too, recedes to the past, as a brave new world of global modernity challenges into question the social and political arrangements of modernity, including Marxism.

Over the last decade and a half, globalization has provided much of the inspiration for the policies of development that the PRC has pursued, to the point at which policy-makers see in globalization the continued success of the impressive development the country has registered during these years.[18] At the same time, contrary to those who would see in globalization the erosion of the nation-state, or notions of sovereignty based on the nation-state, the communist state is almost fanatical in its insistence on sovereignty, which guides its activities globally, and motivates its unwavering internal colonialism in territories it deems to be Chinese. As long as socialist revolution remained a paramount concern, emphasis on state sovereignty was modified somewhat by considerations of anti-imperialist alliances and international class solidarity in the cause of revolution. These concerns have receded to the background in post-socialist China, where incorporation in global capitalism is viewed as the key to development. Ironically, going global economically has also brought with it questions of political and cultural sovereignty, which are the contradictions of contemporary Chinese modernity, and also help account for attitudes toward IR theory.

Chinese scholars may insist on making distinctions based on memories of an earlier revolutionary experience, or the textual legacies of an imperial past, but their foremost goal has been to accommodate, and integrate into, mainstream IR theory, much as the PRC seeks to integrate into a global system through which it seeks to achieve the goal of "peaceful development" (*heping fazhan*). Under these circumstances, the insistence on "Chinese characteristics" reads not as a challenge to "Western" IR theory, but as a nativistic self-assertion to guard against loss of identity within it – what William Callahan has referred to as "realism with Chinese characteristics" (Callahan 2001, p. 80). So long as they are recognized a voice of their own – and whether out of a disposition to scientism that is a legacy of "scientific" Marxism or because of an enchantment with the "advanced" social sciences of the "West" as represented by its mainstream (and influential) representatives – Chinese scholars seem quite prepared to fall in with the universalistic assumptions of Euro/American IR theory, which seeks to incorporate other cultural perspectives not to qualify but to consolidate its hegemony.[19]

Theory under siege: IR theory in Chinese perspective

In their recent discussion of IR theory in the PRC, Zhao Kejin and Ni Shixiong write that, "no matter what country or region, all must obey the universal laws of historical development." But, they continue, because each country is placed differently historically, geographically, and in interactions with others, they each "must seek their own particular laws, and construct theories that accord with their own special characteristics, their habits, customs and styles" (Zhao and Ni 2007, p. 1). They also reaffirm, by way of conclusion, that, "the foremost task of Chinese theory is to resolve the problems that confronts the path of peaceful development the country confronts" (Zhao and Ni 2007, p. 377). Although practice must be the point of departure for theory, theory will not emerge spontaneously but requires effort and appropriate circumstances. Among the obstacles to theoretical development they cite are absence of free exchange of ideas, political dependency (to be distinguished from political relevance and involvement), and the commodification of the academy (Zhao and Ni 2007, pp. 380–2).

Although Zhao and Ni are associated with the more liberal "Shanghai school," their attitudes toward the issue of theory would seem to be characteristic of IR work in the PRC. It may not be possible to speak of a "single" Chinese IR without forcing Chinese scholars into an Orientalist mold, but it seems less problematic to speak of a general practical orientation to issues of theory, driven by an emphasis on Chinese particularities within a broader context of universality that is associated increasingly with globalization. Zhao and Ni are clearly guided by policies indicated by Jiang Zemin's "Three Represents" and Hu Jintao's "harmonious world." They are also less anxious than others in discovering "Chinese characteristics," except in an existential sense, in terms of China's placement in the world rather than abstract cultural criteria derived from the distant past, or the lessons of a revolutionary past that may no longer be relevant to the present. Their work is exemplary, nevertheless, of the emphasis on "peaceful development" that has been a staple of Chinese foreign policy since the beginning of "reform and opening," and which guides most discussions of IR.

Peaceful development includes, at least formally, a concern internally for the welfare of the population ("harmonious world" goes with "harmonious society"), and a concern for the welfare and balanced development of the people of the whole world. As the official statement on the "scientific outlook on development" puts it,

> To pursue the path of peaceful development, it is necessary to unify internal development with opening to the outside, bind together Chinese and world development, integrate the basic interests of the Chinese people with the common interests of the world's people. China upholds harmonious development internally, and peaceful development externally; the two are related as parts of an organic whole, toward the creation of long-term peace, common prosperity and a harmonious world. . . . [In foreign policy] we need to advance international relations on the basis of the Five Principles of Mutual Coexistence. We must advance further to strengthen unity and cooperation with developing countries as the firm basis of foreign policy work . . . we must continue to try hard to develop partnership with neighboring countries . . . we must improve relations of mutual benefit and cooperation with all powerful countries. . . . A harmonious world ought to be a democratic world, a neighborly, just and inclusive world. A new idea of security needs to be established upon mutual trust and interest, equality and association. It must safeguard civilizational diversity, and multiple paradigms of development.
>
> (Anon. 2006, pp. 132–3)

If the goal of theory for Chinese practitioners is to facilitate the realization of the ideals expressed in such a program, is this IR theory? Apparently not, according to most commentators on the development of IR; Gerald Chan writes that,

> I deliberately use the word "perspectives" instead of "theory" in the title of this book because I doubt whether the Chinese have indeed a theory of IR and also because the word "theory" in China has a meaning different from our general understanding of the word.
>
> (G. Chan 1999, p. xii)

Indeed, one gets the impression from most discussions of IR theory in China, including some by Chinese scholars, that whereas "we" have IR theory, they have ideology and culture, at least they claim to. And the issue is not just the "word," or its translation from one context to another. The Chinese term for theory, "*lilun*," literally translates as "discourse on principle," which is not that far removed from the word "theory" in its general usage.[20] In addition, the term in its modern sense has been in use now for a century, and it would be the height of arrogance to assume that Chinese are misreading a foreign word. If there is misreading, there is a good reason for it.

That being the case, is it possible to reverse the question, and ask not why Chinese do not have theory, or do not seem to be willing to do theory like "we" do, as if that were a failure, and ask instead why "we" have theory and do theory the way "we" do? Instead of subjecting Chinese ways of doing things to the scrutiny of "our" ways, and judging them by the standards of "our"' practices, is it possible to inquire if the way they do things may have something to tell us about the nature and shortcomings of the ways "we" do things. Perhaps Chinese contribution to IR theory may ultimately be most important not for introducing new "cultural" perspectives, but in bringing to the discussion an alternative cultural practice of politically and historically informed scholarship that may bring additional critical perspectives on IR theory in its mainstream development in the "West."

There is no question that Chinese IR scholarship, like much else, is open to criticism for its ideological subjection to policies that change with each change in leadership, as well as its predisposition to a "nativism" that unfortunately phrases theoretical questions in the culturalist language of "Chinese characteristics." These, in turn, confirm predispositions among foreign observers (regardless of origin), who are prepared to find ideological dogmatism among scholars of a post-revolutionary society, or conversely (and contradictorily) unchanging cultural legacies of the "five thousand-year-old civilization of China." Nevertheless, it is quite evident from critical scholarship on IR in general that some of the critique that has been directed insistently at IR in China is characteristic of IR in general, which is indeed a field deeply divided not only along ideological divides, but also along national styles. One wonders if in some of these critiques China does not play the part of "the other," whose difference may be quite useful in covering up the divisions of "our" field, and sustaining some kind of illusory unity. Unfortunately, Chinese practitioners of IR, who have been anxious to escape from a past that incarcerated them within the prison-house of ideology, and importunate in their desire to be accepted by the hegemonic scholarly establishments of the United States and Europe, have indeed played their own part in nourishing such illusions.

Indeed, the suggestion (by Zhao and Ni, for instance) that each country has its own IR theory in accordance with its own particular circumstances is one that Chinese scholars have most likely learned from their readings in Euro/American IR literature, which is replete with critiques of IR theory, and its problematic nature, and problems in its application to societies outside the European system of states out of which it developed.[21] Moreover, contrary to the assumptions of universality of theory in many discussions of China, what is at issue in these critiques is not just one theory or another, but the status of theory itself. Ole Waever has put forward the interesting argument (following John Gunnell) that the predisposition to theory in United States political science was a consequence of the absence of a focus that led "generations from Charles E. Merriam to the present to seek 'the identity and authority of political science more in its method than its subject matter'" (Waever 1998, p. 713).[22] He has also suggested that practitioners of IR in Europe and the United Kingdom, who are much more sociological and historical in their approach, have never been receptive to the kind of abstract theorizing modeled on economics that has characterized mainstream US IR theory. The recognition of national differences from a more global perspective (including Africa and Asia) has led Stephen Chan to compare IR to the "Rashomon condition," after the movie directed by Akira Kurosawa in which each witness to a crime has a different story to tell about it. Chan writes that

> The Rashomon condition is the true condition which IR faces. It is not the post-war Western condition, with its modernist paradigm and its textual posturing, which spoke in the name of Enlightenment universality, and did so by means of an imperial practice of its own export, and extensive sense of what it excluded.

> (S. Chan 1993, p. 442)

Perhaps not very surprisingly, Marxist inspiration has been crucial in the critiques of IR theory that focus on its most fundamental assumption that states and their interactions may be isolated from the societies of which they are integral parts, or from the workings of an international political economy that provides their historically shifting structural context. This "reductionism" has led, in the words of John MacLean,

> to a failure of international relations to identify and explain its real object of enquiry, namely the form of social stratification and inequality, structured at the level of global relations, but mediated through the appearance of concrete separated units, historically developed.

The failure is ideological, MacLean, argues, because the distortion of the object of inquiry is what ideology is about after all (Maclean 1981, p. 113). "The statist discourse" created by the Treaty of Westphalia (1648), which is the inspiration for the study of modern IR, has been challenged by work that has proposed broader contexts for the understanding of territoriality (and, therefore, emergence of territorially defined notions of inside/outside, sovereignty and citizenship). John Ruggie and, more recently, Benno Teschke have questioned the assumptions underlying Westphalian notions of territoriality, the one on the basis of expanding notions of territoriality ("unbundling of territoriality"), the other by placing the emergence of the modern state within the perspective of changing property relations. More recently, Robbie Shilliam has expanded on Ruggie's arguments by introducing into the discussion of territoriality non-European perspectives (Ruggie 1993; Teschke 2003; Shilliam 2006). The statist argument has also been challenged by Robert Cox, who has emphasized the importance of social forces in international relations (Cox 1981). These critiques, inspired by Marxism, also show the impact on IR thinking of political and intellectual developments of the last three decades. Issues of transnationalism are very much in evidence in the discussions by Ruggie and Shilliam, whereas Cox's argument draws upon the evidence of the transnationalization of capital, and the new social movements that have arisen around the world in recent decades as a major force of politics. Ruggie, in his stress on epistemology and perception, also partakes of the postmodernist trends that have drawn attention to the importance of culture and language in the exercise of power in international relations.

In other words, far from being anomalous, IR in China may be viewed as an instance not of theoretical failure, but of one more addition to the "Rashomon condition" that represents not so much a fracturing of IR theory as a recognition of fractures that have been there all along, to which new ones are being added as modernity itself undergoes fragmentation in the process of its globalization. The contradictions of IR theory may be viewed as one more manifestation of the contradictions that characterize global modernity, or modernity globalized. The globalization of capitalism, ironically, has led not to the universalization of European modernity, which was its first historical product, but to the proliferation of claims on modernity in the form of "multiple" and "alternative" modernities. "Traditions," which a Eurocentric modernity once consigned to the proverbial "'dustbin of history," have enjoyed a resurrection in recent years, and now serve as the foundation for claims to alternative modernities. Along with these conflicting claims on modernity we witness demands for the inclusion of alternative epistemological traditions in the constitution of knowledge. The problem is whether these alternative traditions are to be incorporated into an existing system of knowledge, in which case the claim to universalism is still conditioned by its Eurocentric presuppositions, or whether the fundamental assumptions of knowledge are to be opened to questioning, which presents the predicament of fragmentation without end (Dirlik 2007, Chapter 3; see also Acharya and Buzan 2007, p. 26).[23] Compounding the problem is that traditions are themselves inventions of modernity, and sites of contention, so that they are subject to conflicting interpretations in accordance with different conceptions of the modern, and its relationship to the past. This is the case with "Chineseness" in IR, which not only is revealing of the problem of determining what constitutes a Chinese IR tradition, but is also caught up between remote imperial traditions, which need to be translated into the language of the present to be meaningful, and the more recent revolutionary tradition, equally subject to conflict and contention.

In the perspective of the developments that I have just outlined, it seems that Chinese IR theory should have the greatest affinity with the Marxist-inspired sociological and historical approaches I have just outlined. And in some ways they do, as in the case even of "liberal" IR practitioners such as Zhao and Ni, who insist nevertheless on the methodological primacy of historical materialism in the analysis of international relations. At the same time, however, these post-socialist recollections of Marxism are now placed in the service of an unwavering commitment to "globalization," understood as participation in a global market while keeping intact very modern notions of state and territorial sovereignty. Like the political policies of which it is in service, Chinese IR theory is torn between a revolutionary legacy, which contains within it an older historical legacy, and successful incorporation within a global capitalist economy that has been key to the country's newly acquired power and prestige. To speak of the failure of IR theory in China is to miss the point about its problems, if not to engage in ideological operations that privilege certain versions of IR over others. IR may be a new field in the PRC, but it is subject to the same ideological contradictions of global modernity as IR elsewhere – except that the contradictions in this case play out on a Chinese political and historical terrain that does indeed have its own characteristics, if not in the same sense conveyed by clichés about "Chinese characteristics."

Notes

1 I am grateful to Ana M. Candela and Robbie Shilliam for reading and commenting on this chapter.
2 Lapid (1996, p. 6) writes that "there is . . . little to gain and much to lose by mistaking the return for a 'revolutionary move' in IR scholarship." The statement is peculiar, considering that the author is quite aware of the momentous changes occurring in the world, and the necessity in IR theory of closer attention to history.
3 For other accounts that I draw upon in this discussion, see G. Chan (1998, 1999), Geeraerts and Jing (2001), and Yaqing (2007). I am grateful to Robbie Shilliam for bringing this last work to my attention.
4 Song is the Jean Monnet Professor for European Integration Studies at Renmin (People's) University (Renda) of China in Beijing. He was Director of the Centre for European Studies at Renda for 12 years, as well as Vice Chair and then the Associate Dean of the School of International Studies from 1988 to 2005.
5 Song (2001, p. 73); see also G. Chan (1999, p. 11). Interestingly, Song qualifies his statement by way of footnotes, noting not only that some senior scholars are more progressive than junior ones, but that "there can also be negative impacts as some younger scholars have become more conservative, more policy-oriented, and less academic and theory-oriented after being in higher academic or especially administrative positions." In other words, as they have become bureaucratized. See Song (2001, pp. 43, 44, 73ff.).
6 These differences apparently led to strong disagreements between Chinese and "Western" (mostly American) scholars in the first joint conference, held in 1987. The conference included "neo-realist: theorists such as Kenneth Waltz, Robert Gilpin, and Miles Kahler, as well as East Asia/China specialists such as Robert Scalapino, Allen Whiting, and Harry Harding.
7 Thus, Geeraerts and Jing (2001, p. 254), write that, "notwithstanding the tangible progress in the study of international politics, IR theory research was like a blank paper before the 1980s."
8 Although Jiang's "Three Represents" facilitated the admission into the Party of the "advanced" social groups of businessmen and intellectuals (along with a renewed commitment to "advanced forces of production"), ideological remolding, at least of the Party, is the unstated goal of the "Marxism project" (*Makesi zhuyi gongcheng*) launched under Hu-Wen's leadership. The project involves analyzing and interpreting classical Marxist texts (to some extent Lenin, but mainly Marx and Engels) from the perspective of contemporary socialism with Chinese characteristics, glossing key terms and concepts, and producing a series of theoretical works and textbooks. Hu's own concept of "the scientific outlook on development" (*kexue fazhan guan*) is the reference for the reinterpretation of Marxism. For further discussion, see Dirlik (2009).
9 The five principles formulated by then premier Zhou Enlai in 1953–1954 provided the basis for negotiations between the PRC and India over the issue of Tibet. They were (1) mutual respect for each other's territorial integrity and sovereignty, (2) mutual non-aggression, (3) mutual non-interference in each other's internal affairs, (4) equality and mutual benefit, and (5) peaceful co-existence.
10 The three worlds theory was developed by Mao Zedong, and acquired publicity with a speech Deng Xiaoping gave in 1974 in the United Nations. In contrast to the "three worlds" of modernization discourse, which are the capitalist, the socialist, and the

post-colonial third worlds, the three worlds theory of Chinese foreign relations in the 1970s was based on considerations of power, with the United States and the Soviet Union constituting the hegemonic First World, their allies constituting the Second World, and the non-aligned nations making up the Third World.

11 See the discussion in Yaqing (2007, pp. 17–19). Qin suggests that "traditional" ideas of *tianxia* and the "tribute system" may have some potential, but only if they are stripped of their assumptions of inequality – which means translated into modern terms, most importantly terms of "the nation," as these ideas, which included state-to-state relations, nevertheless did not conceive of states as nation-states. See the discussion below.

12 For a discussion of the conflicts over the use of *yi* in Qing treaties with Britain, see, Liu (2006). See also Candela (2007). I am grateful to Ms. Candela for sharing this paper with me.

13 This has found eloquent expression, most recently, in the movie *Hero*, directed by Zhang Yimou.

14 See, also, the essays collected in Dabringhaus and Ptak (1997), especially the essay by Wade.

15 See also Zhao and Ni (2007, pp. 250–3), for the passing of the *tianxia* paradigm with the globalization of Euro/American colonialism, as well as the transformation under pressures of globalization of notions of sovereignty that guided revolutionary policy under Mao.

16 The most comprehensive study to date is Svarverud (2007). See also the earlier work by Hsu (1960). Some Chinese scholars have claimed the existence of inter-state law in ancient China. See Hong (1965) and Chen (1967). These works freely blend law and ritual in their discussions, however, and it is not clear that the practices they describe had the status of "law," or any significance for understanding modern developments. Svarverud suggests that analogy with the Warring States period, which was not unusual in nineteenth-century Qing responses to the new "international" situation, may have facilitated the acceptance of international law (Svarverud 2007, pp. 98–100, 150–61). Svarverud study indicates that, by the end of the Qing, modern international law had come to serve as the core of the Chinese understanding of world order. It is also noteworthy that the notion of "public" (*gong*) was projected upon the global order beginning with translations of international law (*gongfa*) in the 1860s.

17 In his discussion of Kenneth Waltz's theories, Teschke (2003, p. 15) states in passing that "hierarchy eclipses the need for IR theory," which may be of some interest in speculating why there would be no IR theory in imperial China.

18 For a comprehensive discussion of Chinese struggles with globalization, see (Knight 2008).

19 Amitav Acharya and Barry Buzan (2007) suggest that "the hegemonic standing of Western IRT" offers the best explanation for the absence of '"non-Western IR theory'" with the possible exception of the PRC. The analysis here suggests that perhaps China is not an exception, except in the insistence on "Chinese characteristics." The hegemony of "Western IRT" itself needs to be explained, needless to say, not by its epistemological power, but as a theorization of an existing system of inter-state relations that has forced others into its arrangements and rules, so that it is only by going outside the system that an alternative to it may be imagined. Post-revolutionary China is too anxious to be admitted into the system to imagine such alternatives, and seeks whatever alternatives may be imagined in a past that may be rendered relevant to the present only by way of translation through a contemporary language.

20 See the discussion in Dirlik (2001), especially the appendix on "theory."

21 For a critique, by well-known practitioners, and bulwarks of the establishment, see Katzenstein *et al.* (n.d.). See also reflections on the difficulties of theory, and of its limitations in practice, by one of its foremost advocates, by (Waltz 1990).

22 The quotation within the quotation is from Gunnell.

23 The conflicts over modernity that are characteristic of global modernity have also
    been of crucial significance in the so-called "cultural turn" of the last two decades,
    corresponding to the conceptual emergence of "globalization." For a historical survey
    of culture in international relations see Reeves (2004). The issue, of course, is not just
    culture, but culture within changing contexts of power relations, which endows the
    present with its own characteristics. A critical perspective requires also that we speak
    not just of culture in international relations but also of the culture of international
    relations!

Part III
Beyond the nation-state

10 Alternative sources of cosmopolitanism

Nationalism, universalism and Créolité in Francophone Caribbean thought

Martin Munro and Robbie Shilliam

Introduction[1]

The recent construction of multilevel governance within and between states of the European Union has led to a plethora of commentary upon the ethical possibilities and practical pitfalls of a new 'post-national constellation' (Calhoun 2002; Diez and Whitman 2002; Zürn 2002).[2] For some celebrated commentators, such as Jürgen Habermas, the new European public sphere offers hope of a true world citizenship that can be extended outwards to progressively subsume within it the unilateralism and belligerency of the United States (Habermas 2006). Indeed, within international relations (IR) the very possibility of applying normative political theory to make sense of the anarchical international system of states has received a significant boost by the ongoing project of the European Union (Dobson 2006).[3] It is possible, some claim, that the cosmopolitan values of the European public sphere could come to inform an EU foreign policy. Specifically, the EU might exercise a transformative 'normative power' that eschews the poles of a realist proto-superpower and an idealist 'EUtopia' in order to substantively promote the conditions of possibility for world citizenship (Roscrance 1998; Dunne 2008; Manners 2008). Such views are not merely academic, but are evident amongst the wider European foreign policy intelligentsia.[4]

The liberal claims of a new normative power Europe rely heavily upon European-focused cosmopolitan thought. And within this tradition of thought there is a strong tendency to argue that a truly worldly orientation can be cultivated from an internal gaze upon European history. At worst, this leads to a definition of the 'political' proper that reads modern European politics back into Ancient Greece and at the same time allows for a cavalier claim that historically politics did not occur outside Europe (Žižek 1998). But more sophisticated is the argument that the European experience of Enlightenment/modernity has been of a unique quality that has prompted and required a critical introspection (Linklater 1998, p. 198–204; Habermas 2001, pp. 82–8; Delanty 2005; Beck 2006, pp. 2, 163, 166–7; Delanty 2006, p. 40; Garton Ash 2007; Habermas 2006, pp. 43–8).[5] Scholars argue that this introspection has necessarily led to the cultivation of a European 'self' that is disharmonious with itself, thus pluralized, thus cosmopolitan in orientation. For many, especially Habermas, the European project of cosmopolitanism is read as a contestation with its own production of nationalism and barbaric fascism. Echoes of this fundamentally contested history are observed in the present too; for example, the fallout of the Balkan Wars and the formal expansion of the EU exist in the same space in which there develops an increasingly pluralistic and multilevelled idea of citizenship. This even leads many to claim that the new European identity should not define itself in relation to an external 'other', because Europe's real defining other is its own previous self. Hence, scholars such as Gerard Delanty and Ulrich Beck claim that the new European cosmopolitanism arises out of the dissonance between the old straight-forwardly universalist cosmopolitanism and the worst excesses of introverted nationalism. Beck puts it like this:

> Cosmopolitanism which has taken up residence in reality is a vital theme of European civilization and European consciousness and beyond that of global experience. For in the cosmopolitan outlook, methodologically understood, there resides the latent potential to break out of the self-centered narcissism of the national outlook and the dull incomprehension with which it infects thought and action, and thereby enlighten human beings concerning the real, internal cosmopolitanization of their lifeworlds and institutions.
>
> (Beck 2006, p. 2)

There have been other renewals of cosmopolitanism within cultural studies and social theory that do not depend upon the fates of Europe. These investigations of – and prescriptions for – 'cosmopolitics' share with European scholars such as Beck a common desire to go beyond the universalist cosmopolitanism of European Enlightenment thought. In particular, the new cosmopolitics disavows the old triumphalist understanding of an elitist detached universality defined in opposition to ordinary locally bounded life. Instead, the new literature grounds cosmopolitics in the 'tenebrous moment of transition', that is to say within quotid-ian experiences that, defined by their concrete particularity, nevertheless have a transnational scale: the 'cosmos' and the 'politics' are thus inescapably plural and not singular and unified conditions (Robbins 1998; Cohen and Vertovec 2002; Hollinger 2002; Pollock *et al.* 2002; Banham 2007).[6] A key aim amongst these scholars, then, is to contextualize cosmopolitical projects: cosmopolitanism is *not* a view from nowhere, meaning it is not a particular locale masquerading as a detached space; rather, there has not been and is no privileged locale that in its particularity holds the essence of cosmopolitanism.

Crucially, some scholars have used this critique to disrupt the neat history of ideas from Zeno to Kant to Habermas in order to historically situate the European cosmopolitan tradition within practices of colonialism and imperialism (Pagden 2000; Mignolo 2002; Van Der Veer 2002). Standing at the heart of empire, after all, is a privileged position from which to judge what experiences are merely provincial. For example, Walter Mignolo posits a 'critical cosmopolitanism' that examines Enlightenment and modernity from a position of exteriority, that is, from the position of the 'to be included' colonized (Mignolo 2002, pp. 178–9). It is instructive to contrast Mignolo's definition of a critical cosmopolitanism with that of Delanty. Delanty claims that by focusing on the European experience a critical cosmopolitanism can be produced out of '. . . the internal transformation of social and cultural phenomena through self-problematization and pluralization' (Delanty 2006, p. 41). The difference in emphasis caused by the lens of examination is notable: Delanty looks inwards to Europe, from the inside of Europe, and somehow is rewarded with a cosmopolitan vista; Mignolo looks inside from the outside and in doing so breaks the assumption that all that is needed to cultivate a pluralisitc orientation to the world can be found within European history. At this point, it is apposite to remember Enrique Dussel's point, mentioned in Chapter 2, that thought from the periphery is more than simply derivative of the original centre, and that thought from the centre can never be critical of its own situated experienced if it presumes that there is nothing new to learn from the periphery.

To be clear, it should be noted that any attempt to cultivate a cosmopolitan outlook necessarily requires situating the 'self' within a wider context. What is not in question, then, is the necessity of self-referentialism per se. But for the purposes of this chapter, narcissism is used in a specific heuristic fashion to indicate a particular form of self-referentialism that, in the process of attributing meaning to the 'self', assumes that all that is important in and to the social world is already prefigured within the historical becoming of that discrete cultural self. An example of this narcissism would be to assume that, as a European, one's cultural filial links to European history act as a microcosm of global linkages, so that experiencing being European is all that is needed to experience being in the world. Indeed, one could go so far as to claim that the new European cosmopolitanism still consists of a particular masquerading as a universal. In other words, the narcissism of 'methodological nationalism', in Beck's terms, has been transposed to create a narcissism of methodological geo-cultural regionalism: from a critique of the European 'self' one cultivates the orientation to *then* find the world in the shape of European history.

And yet different worlds were always already complicating and unravelling the singular filial cultural links made necessary by the project of writing European history. However, these worlds were not simply – or even primarily – constructed through state-making, nation-building and the rights of man, but through colonialism, imperialism and slavery. It is telling that none of these later activities is included in the majority of European-focused cosmopolitan critiques as *foundations* of the barbaric side of European history. And that is because these later activities require something *other* than a reference to the European self, namely the enslaved and the colonized. This chapter explores Francophone Caribbean thought as a potentially alternative source of cosmopolitanism situated within these complicating worlds of colonialism and slavery. An examination of Francophone Caribbean thought puts into sharper comparative relief the danger of narcissism that, contra Beck's claim above, remains evident in much discussion of cosmopolitan Europe.

Francophone Caribbean thought can be considered as one of the richest, most diverse intellectual traditions in the New World. Its richness derives in large part from the starkly divergent historical and political experiences it reflects and explores. The islands of Martinique and Guadeloupe, along with French Guyana, remain fully fledged departments of the French Republic, and as such are some of the most developed territories in the region, while Haiti has been independent since 1804, and has, notoriously, the worst living and economic conditions in the hemisphere. Haiti and the French American departments therefore represent polar opposites of the Caribbean situation, caught as they are between 'the poles of impoverished isolation and chronic dependency' (Dash 1998, p. 134).

At this point, it is worthwhile returning to Mignolo's injunction to investigate the thought of those subjects historically situated on the exteriority of the (European) cosmos, because it is here that a non-narcissistic orientation becomes a *necessary* and not just *desirable* requisite for thinking politically. At the exteriority there is no easy, automatic or *prior* retreat into a narcissistic self-critique of ones positionality from within an already formed geo-cultural universe to which one is filially related. Alternatively, Caribbean thought examines integrations through slavery and colonialism into global racial hierarchies that have substantively and ideologically sought to deny any cultivation of the Caribbean 'self' as a modern political subject. Owing to this denial, the production of a modern Caribbean self became a process of Creolization that variously syncretized aspects of ideas and practices attributed to and deriving from African, European and later on Asian 'civilizations', all the while resonating with the forced absence of the region's indigenous peoples. In other words, occupying a subordinate position within global racial hierarchies, Francophone Caribbean intellectuals have historically been denied the space to cultivate a discrete Caribbean 'self' filially linked to an endogenously developed Caribbean culture. In such a situation, self-reflection on modern subjecthood is congenitally an act of reflecting upon a plurality of cultural selves. It is not that this plurality can afford to arise from out of the prior construction of national subjects possessing a singular filial link to a master culture.

The remainder of this chapter will trace and analyse how Francophone Caribbean thought has developed differentially across the islands, comparing Haitian lineages of thought with those found within Martinique and Guadeloupe. The investigation will also identify points of convergence and commonality, especially the way in which Francophone Caribbean thought, when taken as a whole, has been unable to straightforwardly embrace either national introversion or revolutionary universalism. This inhibition speaks, paradoxically, to the latent cosmopolitanism that is congenital to Francophone Caribbean thought, even if there has not always been a conscious intention to pass from the national political subject to the cosmopolitical subject, as has been the case in recent critical renewals of European cosmopolitanism. First, the universalistic discourse of the Haitian Revolution is discussed and the slow morphing of thought on the Haitian nation into a form of indigenism is assessed as the outcome of an inability to come to terms with the foundational ambiguity of Caribbean subject formation, as discussed above. Then, the alternative trajectory of thought in the French Antilles is explored, leading to the formation of a Créolité School that has attempted to embrace this founding ambiguity of constructing modern Caribbean subjects. The chapter will finish with some musings on how Francophone Caribbean thought complicates and unravels the world-historical narrative upon which European intellectuals have predicated their renewed cosmopolitan project.

Haiti, from revolution to indigenism

If Haiti's independence came almost two decades after that of the United States, the new Haitian state was in many crucial ways years ahead of the Americans. The first nation of the New World to be governed by former slaves, Haiti was instantly different, a startling exception in the broader colonized world, and a challenge to dominant ideas of European and white superiority. At the same time, the Haitian Revolution tapped into, appropriated and sought full, unreserved application of the revolutionary ideals of universal human rights that had swept across France in the late eighteenth century. The *Déclaration des droits de l'homme et du citoyen*, made in Paris on 26 August 1789, was at once the seminal event in the history of human rights and the document that initiated the Haitian Revolution. Although there had been other philosophical defences of human rights before 1789, the French declaration remains the most important because it was the first attempt to apply ideas of universal rights to an existing society (Nesbitt 2004, p. 19). As C.L.R. James puts it in *The Black Jacobins*:

> Phases of a revolution are not decided in parliaments, they are only registered there . . . [The slaves] had heard of the revolution and had construed it in their own image: the white slaves in France had risen, and killed their masters, and were now enjoying the fruits of the earth. It was gravely inaccurate in fact, but they had caught the spirit of the thing. Liberty, Equality, Fraternity.
>
> (James 1938, p. 63)

By seizing 'the spirit of the thing,' and translating its universalist discourse into the late eighteenth-century Caribbean, the slaves had made Saint-Domingue and the Caribbean in general one of the 'explosive borders of enlightened modernity' (Dash 2006, p. 10). The great political and philosophical achievement of the Saint-Domingue slaves lay in the way their actions exceeded those of the French Revolution, and globalized the ideals of revolutionary universalism. As Susan Buck-Morss argues: 'the black Jacobins of Saint Domingue surpassed the metropole in actively realizing the Enlightenment goal of human liberty, seeming to give proof that the French Revolution was not simply a European phenomenon, but world-historical in its implications'.[4] In effect, as Buck-Morss says, the events in Saint-Domingue were a 'trial by fire for the ideals of the French Enlightenment' (Buck-Morss 2000, pp. 835–6). The implications in terms of the communication, flow, and application of political ideals were also significant, as Dash points out:

> The Haitian Revolution can be seen as an emancipatory project within a globalized colonial world where ideas were now circulating freely and could take root in the most unexpected places. The liberatory possibilities of the

Enlightenment were not meant to be applied in Caribbean plantation society. Global interaction in a modernizing world meant, however, that the periphery could now become the site of a concrete, radical application of ideas from the centre, that a local European revolution could be 'world-historical in its implications.'

(Dash 2006, pp. 10–11)

The Haitian Revolution also exceeded events in France in that it was closer to a 'total' revolution, an unflinching, complete overturning of a despotic social order. It was in Saint-Domingue, not Paris, that revolutionary violence (on all sides) reached apogees of brutality, and that towns, plantations, and factories were literally, and repeatedly, reduced to ashes in the name of universal freedom. The slave leaders Jean-Jacques Dessalines and Henri Christophe willingly set their luxurious mansions alight to 'initiate the campaign of total war' that would lead finally to the declaration of independence on 1 January 1804 (Nesbitt 2004, p. 18). As Nesbitt says, nothing remained of the 'greatest overseas colony the world had known, and this fact of the total nature of the revolution serves as both its glory and its misery' (Nesbitt 2004, p. 18).

The Haitian Revolution effectively laid bare the universal truth of the *Déclaration des droits de l'homme et du citoyen* – that all humans were equal and should be free – and also revealed the limitations of the French Revolution, in its failure to abolish slavery. Events in Haiti exposed what Aimé Césaire would later call the 'false universalism' of the French Revolution, and of human rights discourse in general, which, as Césaire argues, often reduce and limit the rights of man to the rights of European man (Césaire 1981, p. 343). As Césaire indicates, it was Toussaint Louverture who made a concrete reality of the rights of man:

When Toussaint Louverture arrived, it was to take the Declaration of the Rights of Man at its word; it was to show that there is no pariah race; that there is no marginal country; that no one people can be excepted. It was to incarnate and particularize a principle: that is to say, to bring it to life. In history and in the domain of the rights of man, he was for the blacks the architect and the intercessor. [. . .] Toussaint Louverture's struggle was the struggle to transform the formal rights into real rights, the fight for the *recognition* of man and that is why he inscribed himself and the revolt of the black slaves of Saint-Domingue in the history of universal civilization.

(Césaire 1981, p. 29)

The strikingly modern aspirations of Toussaint, and of the revolution in general, were mirrored and extended in the immediate post-revolution era. Even if Haiti remains in the international popular imagination a pre-modern, Africanized enclave of the Caribbean, or, in Césaire's terms, the place where 'negritude stood up for the first time' (Césaire 1994, p. 23), post-revolutionary Haiti was never conceived of by its leaders as an isolated, culturally introverted nation but as a modern, socially progressive state. The revolution in effect envisaged a state that would resist 'atavistic longings for a racial past' and where 'the impulse was towards the future and not dwelling in mythical origins' (Dash 1998, p. 44). As Eugene Genovese rightly says, Haiti's revolution called for the 'Europeanization' of Haiti, just as it sought to compel Europeans to acknowledge the strikingly modern aspirations to freedom and democracy of colonial peoples. As such, Toussaint's revolution envisaged full 'participation in the mainstream of world history rather than away from it' (Genovese 1981, p. 92). Ironically perhaps, as the post-revolutionary period developed, and the United States became the major threat to Haitian independence, the island's intellectuals often aligned themselves culturally and socially with the former colonial power, and drew a contrast between the 'refinement and generosity' of France and the perceived vulgarity of the 'grasping and coarse' (Genovese 1981, p. 16).

At the same time, Haitian intellectuals in the nineteenth century often sought to 'rehabilitate' the nation in the Caribbean and the wider world. One of the fundamental aims of the new nation was to present itself as a progressive, *civilized* modern state. As such, Haitian culture – philosophy, anthropology, and especially literature – became a primary site for self-promotion and indeed rehabilitation in the eyes of a suspicious, hostile world. As the Haitian intellectual Anténor Firmin writes in the preface to his monumental 1885 rebuke to de Gobineau, the Haitian intellectual was charged not only with promoting Haiti, but with 'the rehabilitation of Africa'. Haiti was to Firmin the foremost example of what the 'black race' could achieve, and yet he lays bare a general Haitian anxiety when he asks if

> Haiti constitute[s] a sufficiently edifying example in favor of the race she is proud to represent among the civilized nations? What evidence does she offer that she possesses the qualities that are denied in African Blacks?
>
> (Firmin 2002, p. lvi)

Firmin's proof will lie, he says, in the many 'brilliant' works of his fellow Haitians, works of 'sophisticated logic and elegant science'.

A similar impulse to rehabilitate Haiti, and the 'black race' in general, informs the work of Firmin's contemporary Louis-Joseph Janvier, who also exemplifies the persistent strain of Francophilia that shaped much nineteenth-century Haitian culture and thought in his statement that 'French prose, Haitian coffee, and the philosophical doctrines of the French Revolution are the best stimulants of the Haitian brain' (cited in Dayan 1995, p. 7). The French-speaking Haitian peasants around whom Janvier constructed his fable of the nation were, as Joan Dayan says, 'proud, vital, earthy, and black', intimately connected to the land, which was itself the foundation of Haitian authenticity (Dayan 1995, p.7). Caught between European and African histories, the land became the site upon which Haitian culture, especially literature, *grounded* itself.

If the intellectuals sought to rehabilitate and 'ground' the Haitian people, Haiti's politicians seemed to thrive on chaos and disorder. By the end of the nineteenth century, a cycle of political and economic plunder had established itself, and between 1911 and 1915 a series of revolts saw six presidents take and leave office. Moreover, in the century that followed the revolution, colonial economic prosperity dramatically withered.[7] The causes of Haiti's economic and political crises were varied; external factors such as the collapse of the price of sugar in the nineteenth century and a post-colonial legacy of debt and international exclusion were significant. Internal factors were also important, as the author René Depestre indicates in his denunciation of the two centuries of the Haitian Republic:

> the nineteenth century in Haiti, as far as massacres, Papa Doc-style military satrapy, autocratic protectionism, corruption, State terrorism and systematic bleeding of national resources was just as bad as the [twentieth] century that is now ending in solitude and horror for most of the seven million people of Haiti.
>
> (Depestre 1998, pp. 71–2)

The Haitian intellectual Maximilien Laroche has persuasively argued that Haiti's problems lie in the 'militarization' of all aspects of post-independence Haitian life. Economically, he says, Haiti's leaders have acted like military generals. Because pillage and looting were 'acquired rights', the spoils of war, its leaders, on assuming leadership, have thought only of the 'booty to divide up'. In this sense, as Laroche points out, there is little difference between the Spanish conquistadors of 1492, the French colonials of the eighteenth century, and Haiti's political leaders since 1804. This common, largely uninterrupted history of plundering is, Laroche says, the 'double of official [Haitian] History, the phantom that haunts it' (Laroche 2005, pp. 7, 8, 10).

The American occupation: race and the new nationalism

After the lynching of President Vilbrun Guillaume Sam in July 1915, Admiral Caperton ordered his United States marines to occupy Haiti. The initial pretext for the occupation was the need to restore order, but the Americans were to stay for nineteen years; in effect, this was a new period of subjugation, a return to foreign rule. The rehabilitation that nineteenth–century intellectuals such as Janvier and Firmin had envisaged had come to nothing, and the stereotype of the politically incapable black nation had apparently been confirmed. There was little sustained overt resistance to the occupation until 1929, when a student strike at the School of Agriculture at Damiens sparked a series of sympathy strikes in Port-au-Prince.

The previous year, in a short article in the newspaper *Le Petit Impartial*, Georges J. Petit and Jacques Roumain had demanded 'Youth, where are you? For twelve years the white man has trampled like a master over the sacred soil that our phalanx of heroes watered with their blood.' Petit and Roumain attacked the indifference of Haiti's youth to the 'capitulations' of the 'servile and cynical' elite. The article ended with a rallying call to the youth – 'let's pull ourselves together! . . . We have set things in motion and we hope, after the difficult days of struggle, to strike up the anthem of deliverance!' – that began to be answered in the 1929 student strikes (Roumain 2003, p. 463). The rising nationalist movement forced a change in American policy in Haiti: the Forbes Commission of 1930 recommended that elections be held and that American troops be withdrawn. The strikes and the end of the occupation that followed in 1934 were to some extent attributable to the activities of the various literary, cultural and political movements that had slowly gestated in the 1920s. Georges Sylvain, for instance, formed the Union Patriotique, and through his newspaper *La Patrie* he articulated the growing anti-American indignation of the literate classes (Dash 1981, pp. 52–4). The occupation also transformed the role of the intellectual in Haiti; the introverted, highly literary debates of the pre-occupation *La Ronde* generation – Francophile, symbolist-inspired authors such as Edmond Laforest, Frédéric Marcelin and Etzer Vilaire – gave way to the more politically and historically engaged writings of figures such as Dominique Hippolyte, Frédéric Burr-Reynaud and Christian Werleigh.

Despite lingering Francophilia among the elite, there was also a growing dissatisfaction with cultural mimicry, and an increasing trend towards racial mysticism. The title of Stéphen Alexis's novel, *Le Nègre masqué* (1933), is indicative of a sentiment of repressed or hidden identity, and of the need for more 'authentic', indigenous models. At one point in the novel, Alexis's educated, urban protagonist, Roger Sinclair, lays bare the primitivist urge that was to underpin much subsequent indigenous thought: 'I have learnt too much Greek and Latin. If I was an isolated and naked negro in the jungle, I would be happy' (quoted in Dash 1981, p. 43). The idealization of the 'naked Negro' in Alexis's novel indicates a wider shift in Haitian thought, and a reordering of its spatio-cultural coordinates. As early as 1919, Jean Price-Mars's *La Vocation de l'élite* had evoked the concept of the 'national spirit' (*l'âme nationale*) and had warned of the dangers of 'fragmentation' if the Haitian people did not 'instinctively feel the need to create a national consciousness from the close solidarity of its various social strata' (quoted in Dash 1981, p. 67). The emphasis on 'instinct' and on essential differences between the races echoed the concerns of contemporary works of European ethnology, for example Lévy-Bruhl's *La Mentalité primitive*, which is widely quoted in Jean Price-Mars's *Ainsi parla l'oncle*, the seminal text of Haitian indigenism. Haitian indigenism also bore a discernible influence of European Dadaism and surrealism; emerging poet–activists like Normil Sylvain and Jacques Roumain translated the nihilistic anti-conformism they had encountered in Europe to Haiti, and used it as a mode of attack in their challenge to the Haitian elite.

The younger generation's stated disenchantment with European civilization and rationalist thought reoriented nationalist thinking towards Africa, which had previously been largely denigrated in Haitian writing as a place of cultural and social backwardness. The pre-indigenist rejection of Africa by Haitian intellectuals can be attributed to the paradoxical situation of post-independence Haiti: self-definition and international acceptance of the first black republic called for a negation of its 'blackness', and an image of the nation as a 'civilized', modern state, 'completely worthy, thanks to its elite, of taking its place in the concert of nations' (Hoffmann 1992, p. 134). The American occupation essentially laid bare the frailties and vanities of the elite's view of itself and of Haiti. The indignities of the occupation led to a radical re-evaluation of the elite's complacently held self-image, and specifically to a new identification with colonized Africa. As Hoffmann says: 'Treated now as underdeveloped natives, Haitians had to face the fact that their fight for independence and national dignity corresponded to that of their African brothers' (Hoffmann 1992, p. 144). The reorientation towards Africa was complemented by a turn inwards, a new interest in folklore and popular traditions. In the August 1927 edition of *La Revue indigène*, Normil Sylvain writes of Haiti's 'rich folklore,' its popular songs that are like 'tom-toms calling to dance from one hillside to another', of the 'beating, sensual rhythm of a meringue . . . that must become part of our poetry' (Metellus 1987, p. 184).

The influence of European ethnologists such as Lévy-Bruhl, as well as of French nationalist thinkers such as Charles Maurras and Maurice Barrès, who promoted the countryside as a site of primal cultural purity, and also of the Harlem Renaissance movement shapes and informs the most elaborate expression of Haitian indigenism, Jean Price-Mars's 1928 essay *Ainsi parla l'oncle*. Price-Mars's passionate censure of the Haitian elite caught the spirit of the younger Haitian radicals such as Brouard, Roumain and Émile Roumer. In particular, Price-Mars denounced the elite for its post-revolution adherence to Western civilization, its belief that it was its 'superior destiny' to shape its thinking by 'getting close to its former metropole, resembling it, identifying with it' (Price-Mars 1928, pp. 43–5). The elite's continued identification with France was derided as 'collective bovarysme', or 'the ability a society has to conceive of itself other than it really is', against which Price-Mars calls for the reclamation of Haiti's neglected indigenous culture. Haiti's writers were called upon to free themselves from the prejudices that limited them to cultural mimicry and to draw on the local and indigenous so that their works might give a sense of the 'singular aspects' of Haiti and the black race. The precarious straddling of the space between Europe and Africa was now seen as a source of insecurity, and a struggle ensued as to the authenticity of modern Haitian subjecthood.

Following the departure of the Americans, debates arose between Marxist and Africanist factions in the indigenist movement. The Marxists' tendency was to look outwards, to place Haiti, as Janvier and Firmin had hoped in the nineteenth century, in the vanguard of progressive nations. In September 1927, Jacques Roumain writes in *La Revue Indigène* of the importance of Haitian authors being aware of 'world literature', for in the twentieth century, he says, 'one is a citizen of the world' (Roumain 2003, p. 435). In contrast, the Africanist movement in post-occupation Haiti, and chiefly figures such as Brouard, Denis Lorimer and François Duvalier, tended to look inwards, and to further elaborate the theories of race and culture that had begun in the earlier investigations into 'the Haitian soul'.

Whereas the Haitian Marxists retained the loosely defined notions of race and cultural authenticity of indigenism, the Africanists tended to solidify and fix racial identity into a rigid, essentialized ideology. In the 1930s, as Africanism slowly mutated into the Griot movement, a distorted racial ideology became the vehicle for black, racially motivated politics looking to redress its sense of historical injustice and political isolation, which it blamed on the mulatto elite. The Griots' racial ideology implied a sliding scale of authenticity: the true Haitian soul was black, and the fairer the skin, the less Haitian one was. To the indigenists, the rediscovery of Africanity and popular culture had been a creative and open-ended act, but the Griots were strategically reductive, and systematically closed down the meanings associated with blackness and Haitian authenticity. Africanity and racial authenticity became the tenets of the political ideology of the rising black middle class, who saw in this ideology 'the rationale for a black cultural dictatorship' (Dash 1981, p. 101). The uncertainties and difficulties of post-occupation national reconstruction provided fertile conditions for the propagation of myths and mysticism. Complex questions and uneasy truths could be simplified and repressed by the fixed certainties that the Griots' Africanism offered. By remaining in the past in these crucial ways, the Griots neatly side-stepped the internal contradictions of colour and class politics in post-occupation Haiti, and effectively ensured that Haiti's future would be shaped by endless returns to those very same contradictions.

In contrast, the Marxist thought and poetry of this period – the mid to late 1930s and early 1940s – is more firmly connected with present and future time, and if the past is evoked it is used not reductively but to suggest a more creative vision of the present and future. Roumain's poetry exemplifies Haitian Marxism, in that it expresses a hybrid, loosely theorized set of ideas that retains the indigenists' interest in peasant beliefs and Africanity, but eschews the absolutism and mysticism of the Griots. Roumain tends also to demythologize questions of race and Africanity; peasant poverty and repression could be understood and addressed in terms of class rather than race, as for Roumain racial thinking in Haiti was nothing but 'the sentimental expression of the class struggle'. Roumain's solutions lay in 'freeing the Haitian masses from their mystical shackles', which could be achieved by 'progress in science, the continued development of human culture, a knowledge of the structure of the world' (quoted in Souffrant 1978, pp. 46–7).

On his return to Haiti from exile in 1927, Roumain almost immediately began to make an impression, taking part in the launch of two new reviews, *La Trouée: revue d'intérêt général* and, most significantly, *La Revue indigène: les Arts et la Vie*, journals that would call for a new role for Haitian writing, and also unwittingly help instigate a nationalistic thread of Haitian thought that would ultimately metamorphose grotesquely into Duvalier's *noiriste* totalitarianism. If Roumain had known how his call in the first issue of *La Trouée* for 'authenticity' in Haitian writing, how his demand that literature be 'the cry of a people', the expression of 'our ideas, our own Haitian ideas' (Roumain 2003, p. 433) would be adopted and adapted into an insular, reductionist ideology of black power, one wonders if he would have launched himself with such enthusiasm into the project of Haitian literary nationalism that became indigenism. And yet at the time, there seemed no other way forward for Roumain, who remained committed to the idea that literature must always be 'the servant of ideology' (Roumain 2003, xxxviii).

Négritude, Antillanité and Créolité in the French Caribbean

Although the histories of Haiti and its Francophone neighbours Martinique and Guadeloupe have much in common – the experience of plantation slavery and colonialism, class and colour divisions – they also demonstrate many fundamental differences. Most notably, Martinique, Guadeloupe and French Guyana have, since 1946, been fully fledged departments of the French Republic, and as such enjoy a higher standard of living than most other Caribbean islands, especially Haiti, notoriously the most impoverished nation in the Western hemisphere. But if, by the inter-war period, the Haitian intellectual tradition had started to veer towards an introverted indigenism, in the same period a different trajectory was being forged in the French departments.

In contrast to two hundred years of independent Haitian thought, the French departments had to wait until the 1930s to see the rise of its first wave of anti-colonial intellectuals. Before the 1930s, writing in Martinique largely consisted of minor works imitating French exoticist models of the nineteenth century. Antillean writers' imitation of the Romantics and Parnassians at once mimicked European form and also echoed Eurocentric views of the islands as places of exoticist escape. Such literary and cultural mimicry went largely unchallenged until the 1930s, when a new generation of young Antillean intellectuals emerged not in the islands, but in Paris. The initial products of this new sensibility were a series of student journals, the first of which, *Légitime défense* (1932), stridently denounced the assimilationism of the French Caribbean bourgeoisie and sought to reaffirm 'black' cultural values. Further journals followed, such as *La Revue du monde noir*, in which the founding fathers of negritude – Césaire, Damas and Senghor – proposed a wider, pan-African, diasporic framework, stressing similarities and commonalities of purpose across the colonized world.

It was to some extent ironic that the first expressions of Francophone anti-colonial sentiment were formulated in Paris, the metropole, and centre of colonial power. In another way, however, it is fitting and appropriate that Paris was the place where the ideas of negritude germinated. For, despite the narcissistic narratives of twentieth-century Europe, Paris in the 1920s and 1930s was a city in cultural ferment, as the anthropologist James Clifford explains:

> In the 1920s Paris was flooded with things *nègre*, an expansive category that included North American jazz, syncretic Brazilian rhythms, African, Oceanian, and Alaskan carvings, ritual 'poetry' from south of the Sahara and from the Australian outback, the literature of the Harlem Renaissance . . . The writings of the anthropologist–collector Leo Frobenius. . . . proposed East Africa as the cradle of civilization. Lucien Lévy-Bruhl's *La Mentalité primitive* . . . gave scholarly credence to a common image of black societies as 'mystical,' 'affective,' and 'prelogical.
>
> (Clifford 1989, p. 901)

In other words, Paris at the time was culturally and intellectually enthralled by all manifestations of the non-European, pre-modern 'other'. The surrealist movement was fascinated with the primitive in general, and with Africa in particular. In these societies, it was felt, resided remnants of a more 'authentic', 'essential' humanity, lost over the preceding centuries of industrial modernity in Europe.

Although Paris's interest in the primitive other was born out of specifically European preoccupations, there was much to attract Césaire and the nascent negritude movement to the French metropolitan scene. First, the Parisian revalorization of 'blackness', which was in essence a reversal or reconsideration of previous racist views of Africans as uncivilized and primordial, offered the negritude figures a reworked image of themselves that they could use to counter colonial imposition of degraded identities and inferiority complexes. For example, the work of the German ethnologist Leo Frobenius was a particular inspiration to negritude. Senghor talks of the profound effects of Frobenius's work on the negritude group, saying how he and his contemporaries were beginning to define 'black values', and of how these values nevertheless 'lacked vision in depth but also the basic philosophical explanation'. It was largely Frobenius who filled this void, who gave substance to what the young militants experienced essentially as urges and instincts, and who gave the term 'negritude' 'its most solid, and at the same time its most human significance' (Senghor 1973, p. viii). Although subsequent developments in ethnography have rendered much of Frobenius's work unviable, it was immensely influential on the negritude movement.

A further significant influence was the work of Sigmund Freud, in particular his idea of the 'collective unconscious'. Freud drew an analogy between the development of the individual and that of civilization: 'When . . . we look at the relation between the process of human civilization and the development or educative process of individual human beings', Freud says, 'we shall conclude without much hesitation that the two are very similar in nature, if not the very same process applied to different kinds of object' (Freud 1961, p. 141). This was important to negritude, and to Césaire in particular, as he felt that the Caribbean self had been subject to an extreme form of repression, and under the force of this had become in some ways 'neurotic'. Therefore, in looking to disalienate or 'cure' the Antillean, there would necessarily be a psychoanalytical component. Specifically, Césaire was interested in the collective unconscious which Freud describes as 'something past, vanished and overcome in the life of a people, which I venture to treat as equivalent to repressed material in the mental life of the individual' (Freud 1939, pp. 208–9). The idea of the collective unconscious offered Césaire the key to rediscovering the lost African-ness, the collective racial memory which might fill the existential and cultural void of colonial life for the alienated Antillean. If the collective unconscious was this common resource of images and symbols, then the question remained as to how to access it, to free these 'primordial images' and reacquaint the ruptured Antillean self with its ancient heritage. In fact, Césaire felt that poetry was the means which offered the most promising possibilities in reconnecting with the repressed elements of Caribbean identity. And, although he wrote important essays (notably, *Discours sur le colonialisme* and various articles in his influential journal *Tropiques*), and three very good plays, *Et les chiens se taisaient, Une Tempête* and *Une saison au Congo*, it is as a poet that he is best known.

Césaire's most influential poem was also his first published work: in 1939 the first edition of *Cahier d'un retour au pays natal* (*Notebook of a Return to My Native Land*) was published, and since then it has remained one of the most forceful and complex expressions of anti-colonial revolt. All of the influences that Césaire had absorbed in Paris fed into this long poem: there were touches of surrealist anti-rationalism, Frobenian valorization of Africanity and Freudian moments of rediscovery of the 'umbilical cord' between the Caribbean and Africa. Although it expresses a profound sense of disillusionment on returning to colonized Martinique, the poem evolves into a powerful, indignant rebuke of colonially imposed identities, as in the following passage:

> And this country shouted for centuries that we are brute beasts; that the puls-ing of humanity stops at the entrance of the slave–compound; that we are a walking manure a hideous forerunner of tender cane and silky cotton, and they used to brand us with red–hot irons and we used to sleep in our excre-ment and they would sell us in public and a yard of English cloth and salted Irish meat cost less than we did and this country was quiet, serene, saying that the spirit of God was in its acts.
>
> (Césaire 1995, p. 105)

After *Cahier d'un retour au pays natal*, Césaire produced five more collections of poems – *Les Armes miraculeuses* (1946), *Soleil cou coupé* (1948), *Corps perdu* (1950), *Ferrements* (1950) and *Moi, Laminaire* (1982) – as well as the essays and plays already mentioned. Importantly, though, he also had a remarkable political career. His most far-reaching and perhaps also controversial political act was to promote the 1946 departmentalization bill, which effectively made Martinique an integrated part of France, and which has perpetuated and strengthened the con-nections with the former colonial power. After 1945, when he was first elected as Fort-de-France's mayor, Césaire's political activities largely took precedence over his literary work and, as new generations of French Antillean authors have emerged, so his ideas have been increasingly challenged.

In considering the development of French Caribbean thought, each successive step does not mark a complete rupture with that which came before. Although certain ideas are rejected at each stage, there are also common preoccupations, and common areas of interests which link each stage with each other. The case of Frantz Fanon illustrates this play of commonality and difference well. Fanon shared with Césaire an interest in the psychological processes of colonialism, though his idea of a cure was less mystical and less poetic. In particular, *Peau noire, masques blancs* (1953) emphasizes the role of language in the colonial context. Language, to Fanon, was perhaps the most effective means of imposing colonial culture for, as he says: 'To speak is to be able to use a certain syntax, to possess the morphology of a certain language, but it involves above all assum-ing a culture, to bear the weight of a civilization' (Fanon 1952, p. 13). Also like Césaire, Fanon was interested in the inferiority complex that they felt was inher-ent to French Antillean experience. Unlike Césaire, however, Fanon did not see the solution to this inferiority complex in the recuperation of an Africanized collective unconscious. According to Fanon, the Martinican collective unconscious identified itself not with blackness or Africanity but with images of whiteness and Europeanness.

A contemporary of Fanon, Édouard Glissant has followed a quite different trajectory, and in his own way has forged a reputation as one of the region's most influential thinkers. Like Fanon, this novelist, poet, playwright and philosopher departs in his theoretical work from the essentialism of negritude, and rejects notions of absolute racial and cultural difference. Antillanité (Caribbeanness), a term coined by Glissant in his sprawling, dense collection of essays, *Le Discours antillais* (1981), is an attempt to redefine Caribbean culture in terms of its inherent qualities of relativity, contact, interdependence and hybridity.

Glissant shares with Césaire and Fanon a concern with history, with dealing with the consequences of the very particular traumas and disruptions of the Caribbean past. Unlike Césaire, however, and like Fanon, he dismisses the grand narratives of return to Africa, to a oneness of roots and identity. In *Le Discours antillais*, Glissant charts an alternative to the teleology of return. He starts by distinguishing between the situation of Caribbean peoples and others who have known exiles (the Jews, for example), but who have been able to transplant their own culture and language to the place of exile. In contrast to a people which 'maintains its original nature', Glissant sees in the Afro-Caribbean experience a history of deracination and of constant metamorphosis of identity (Glissant 1981, p. 14). As a counter to the myth of univocal identity, he proposes his theory of Relation, of a Caribbean culture and people which are in a constant process of Creolization. Relation proposes a situation of equality with, and respect for, the other as *different* from oneself. Importantly, Relation has no hierarchy and it is non-reductive, that is it does not try to impose a universal value system but respects the particular qualities of the community in question, in a movement away from imperialist 'generalization'. This is not to say that Relation involves a defence of cultures, but it allows a particularity only where this is outward looking and related to other cultures and values. Thus, Relation is more of an ongoing process than a fixed set of cultural relationships; it is fluid and unsystematic. Cultural diversity is a prime value of Relation; there is no centre any more, no periphery, only an unpredictable play of differences. To Glissant, the Caribbean is a prime location for Relation, which, he believes, is now becoming the condition of global society, as movements and plays between cultures multiply.

Glissant's Antillanité proposes Creole language as a linguistic manifestation or paradigm of Caribbean culture in general and of Relation in particular. Creole language to him, is 'variable', with no fixed form or essence. Moreover, as it arose out of the contact between different, fragmented language communities, it has no singular, organic origin but is instead 'organically linked to the worldwide experience of Relation. It is literally the result of links between different cultures and did not preexist these links. It is not a language of essence, it is a language of the Related' (Glissant 1981, p. 241). Creole language is also important to Glissant as it represents a prime example of what he calls detour. Detour is a strategy of resistance through indirection, through camouflaging, through remaining unknowable to the colonial other. To Glissant, Creole exemplifies detour as it 'was constituted around a strategy of trickery' (Glissant 1989, p. 21). This trickery, says Glissant, came about as a result of the imposition of French language on slaves, and functioned as an appropriation of French. Creole speakers used French in a derisive way, as if they were wreaking violence on the language itself. Creole continually works *not* to transcend the French language, but as a detour, a diversion or turning away, as transcendence would entail the definition of a Creole authenticity. It is ultimately this resistance to authenticity, to fixed notions of culture and identity which underpins Glissant's Antillanité, a multifaceted, deeply complex set of theories which have their (rhizomatic) roots in negritude but which cut across every generation, every movement in French Caribbean thought.

The Créolité movement owes much to Glissant's work, notably to his valorization of Creole language. This movement was effectively launched in 1989 with the publication of *Éloge de la créolité*, which later appeared in a bilingual edition with the English title of *In Praise of Creoleness*. The principal figures in this movement are the Martinicans Jean Bernabé, Patrick Chamoiseau and Raphaël Confiant, all of whom have also published novels and essays. Créolité shares with Glissant a belief in the importance of Creole language and culture. The opening paragraph of the prologue sets the tone for the book's strident and forceful proclamation of Creole identity:

> Neither Europeans, nor Africans, nor Asians, we proclaim ourselves Creoles. This will be for us an interior attitude – better a vigilance, or even better, a sort of mental envelope in the middle of which our world will be built in full consciousness of the outer world. These words we are communicating to you here do not stem from theory, nor do they stem from any learned principles. They are, rather, akin to testimony. They proceed from a sterile experience which we have known before committing ourselves to reactivate our creative potential, and to set in motion the expression of what we are. They are not merely addressed to writers, but to any person of ideas who conceives our space (the archipelago and its foothills of firm land, the continental immensities), in any discipline whatsoever, who is in the painful quest for a more fertile thought, for a more precise expression, for a truer art. May this positioning serve them as it serves us. Let it take part of the emergence, here and there, of verticalities which would maintain their Creole identity and elucidate it at the same time, opening for us the routes of the world and freedom.
>
> (Bernabé *et al.* 1989, p. 886)

Like Glissant, the Créolité group challenge the traditional, colonially inherited mimetic impulses in French Caribbean culture. Although they cited Glissant as an important influence, they pose a very direct challenge to Césaire and negritude. Although they recognize the importance of Césaire in revalorizing the African elements in Antillean culture and proclaim themselves 'forever the sons of Aimé

Césaire', they strongly criticize what they see as Césaire's disregard for Creole language. Because Césaire wrote only in French, they say, he neglected the island's 'authentic' language and the rich oral tradition.

The most forceful Créoliste challenge to Césaire has come from Raphaël Confiant in his 1993 polemical work *Aimé Césaire: une traversée paradoxale du siècle*. Confiant's argument is that there exists a clear discrepancy between the violence and anti-colonial revolt of Césaire the poet and the compromising, moderate actions of Césaire the politician. According to Confiant, Césaire discarded the revolutionary potential of Creole language and culture, while always privileging France and Frenchness and treating his fellow Martinicans as colonized subjects whose welfare was dependent on the generosity of the metropole. At every historical juncture, Césaire argued that independence was simply not an option for Martinique, and defended his concepts of assimilation and later of autonomy. All of this, argues Confiant, makes Césaire a highly ambivalent figure in the history of French Caribbean culture and society.

It is perhaps this figure of ambivalence and ambiguity that finally characterizes Francophone Caribbean thought. Some of the most incisive and complex conceptions of Caribbean history, society, culture and identity have emerged from these small islands that are still intimately connected to their former colonial power. One of Caribbean's most strident political poems, *Cahier d'un retour au pays natal*, was produced by a man who promoted departmentalization and reinforcement of ties with France in 1946. In another sense, there is little in this tradition of the romantic notion of revolutionary overcoming, the universalist discourse that David Scott critiques, and implicates in the post-colonial failures of Anglophone Caribbean nations (Scott 2004).

Conclusion

In Francophone Caribbean thought relations between races, nations and hemispheres have rarely been conceived of in terms of Manichean divisions. Instead, Francophone Caribbean intellectuals have engaged with, theorized and positioned themselves in relation to the inevitable interconnections and relationalism that have historically characterized the geo-cultural making of the Caribbean (just as they also are now seen to characterize the contemporary world). Paradoxically, however, many French Caribbean intellectuals are caught in a neocolonial political situation but they are also prophets of a world to come, a deracialized, related world that many other intellectual traditions are only just awakening to.

Through negotiating the legacy of slavery and colonialism, Francophone Caribbean thought has proceeded with a self-referentialism that was *from the start* unavoidably pluralistic and global in its context. In effect, French Caribbean intellectuals had to write ideals of Enlightenment and ideas of the modern self upon a *syncretic* medium, Europe/Africa/America (and, later, Asia). The twists and turns of revolutionary practices and outcomes engaged with in Haitian thought arise from negotiating the construction of a modern political self through this medium; but the anxiety to claim a singular filial culture evidenced in much Haitian thought clearly demonstrates (a) the influence of European ideals of homogeneous national identity and (b) that cosmopolitics in no way automatically develops out of this (or any other) colonial context. However, the creative acceptance of this medium – and its potential productivity – is evidenced most clearly by the Créolité group, which can be said to embody a cosmopolitical outlook, even if participants do not call this outlook directly by its Greek name.

Paradoxically, given the status of the small islands from which this group hails, the debates over Creole identity take place at the conceptual level of the post-national *even before/despite the attainment of national independence.* This issue of temporality and sequence is extremely important. The European narrative posits the generative sources of its cosmopolitan project in the dialectic of the emergence of the nation-state and the emergence of individual rights, that is to say, in the co-constitution of the singular collective self and the pluralistic individual self. In essence, the world-historical narrative of European cosmopolitanism assumes a sequence of empire to nation to cosmopolis that is woven together as the filial links of European culture. However, it could be argued that the far more intimate and close engagement with cosmopolitical plurality displayed in Francophone Caribbean thought is possible – necessary – precisely because this sequence does not hold in the colonial/slave-holding context. Does, then, this fundamental basis of plurality – Créolité – not complicate and unravel the (European) sequence that is assumed to hold universally but is, in fact, particular?

The tendency of IR literature to speak of post-national constellations and the normative power of cosmopolitical foreign policy overwhelmingly by reference to Europe is myopic. This is not to deny that interesting things might be happening to and within the EU. Nevertheless, to present these happenings as expressing, in its most advanced form, the global past and future significance of cosmopolitics is to have internalized the methodological regionalism evident in Beck *et al.* that, in fact, shares the narcissism of methodological nationalism. The point of this chapter has not been to substitute the Caribbean for Europe as the universal representative of cosmopolitical potential. Rather, the point has been to show that not all post-national ruminations and cosmopolitical projects start within or are derived from the contested cultivation of the European self. There are other intellectual traditions that have had to make far more foundational and urgent sense of the modern self through a cosmopolitical orientation. And there might, then, be other – perhaps deeper – sources of normative power running through the making of the modern world. Indeed, these traditions – and their ruminations of a post-national past and future – are arguably more apposite to the contexts in which most of the world's population considers the possibilities and pitfalls of contemporary political transformations.

Notes

1 Many thanks to Eşref Aksu for his careful and critical comments on cosmopolitanism.
2 The debate has been recently focused around Habermas (2001); see, for example, Wilde (2007), Borowiak (2008) and Kumar (2008).

3 Andrew Linklater is one of IR's most stalwart cosmopolitans. See, for example, Linklater (2002).
4 For example, Javier Solana, EU High Representative for the Common Foreign and Security Policy (2005) and Mark Leonard (2005), Executive Director of the think tank European Council on Foreign Relations.
5 For a critique of such narcissistic gazes upon European modern history see Bhambra (2007).
6 For an example of a cognate thought process in IR see Mandaville (2002).
7 For detailed accounts of the Haitian Revolution see James (1938), Césaire (1981) and Geggus (2001).

11 The internationalist nationalist

Pursuing an ethical modernity with Jawaharlal Nehru

Priya Chacko

His nationalism is equal to internationalism.

M.K. Gandhi (1999a, p. 94)

Introduction[1]

Jawaharlal Nehru had an enduring fascination with paradoxes. So it is fitting that the Mahatma Gandhi – whom Nehru once described as an 'extraordinary paradox' – would ground Nehru's anti-colonialism in the apparent paradox of internationalist nationalism. Nehru's political thought, however, has seldom been subjected to the penetrating and nuanced analysis that his mentor's writings have received (exceptions include Smith 1958; Chatterjee 1986; Lal 1990; Komf 1991; Seth 1992; Pantham 1998; Brown 200; Khilnani 2004; Majeed 2007). At first glance this seems inexplicable. Nehru wrote prolifically, was one of the most prominent of anti-colonial leaders, and as India's first prime minister and foreign minister he became a venerated world leader who played a key role in the United Nations (UN), conceived the notion of non-alignment, helped establish the Non-aligned Movement, and was among the first to propose the major non-proliferation regimes in existence today. Since his death in 1964, however, Nehru has often been reduced to caricature and has come under sustained attack from various quarters in the country he led, including from the Marxist, Hindu nationalist, Gandhian and neo-liberal perspectives.[2]

In the discipline of international relations (IR) there has long been a lack of deep, critical engagement with Nehru's political thought, which is reflective of the discipline's marginalization of non-Western thought in general (exceptions include Rana 1969, 1976; Acharya 2005). The lack of original theorizing in the discipline of IR in India and its intellectual dependence on Western frameworks have been linked to such disciplinary gatekeeping practices and, more generally, the epistemological dimension of Western power (Bajpai 2003; Mallavarapu 2005; Behera 2007). This is perhaps one of the reasons why there has been a tendency to reduce Nehru's international thought to simplistic frameworks of liberal internationalism and realism that do not do justice to the complexity of his ideas. Bharat Karnad, for instance, argues that Nehru's opposition to regional defence pacts such as the South-East Asia Treaty Organisation (SEATO) was not the result of deeply held moral convictions but reflected his 'hard realpolitik' desire for regional dominance and a belief that Pakistan's involvement in these pacts posed a threat to India (Karnad 2002a,b). Likewise, C. Raja Mohan, echoing an interpretation that was common among American analysts and politicians during the cold war, describes non-alignment in realist terms as 'a means to . . . maximize India's relative gains in the bipolar system' (Mohan 1992; see also Kissinger 1979). Mohan and Karnad's attempts to turn Nehru into a realist aim to present India as just another big country, as hard-headed and power driven as the best of them, while defending Nehru against critics of his foreign policy legacy who would paint him as a naive idealist. This interpretation of Nehru, however, requires a sustained disregard for his copious writings which display a consistent critique of the assumptions and outcomes of realist policies and assumptions. Moreover, they overlook the fact that the normative origins of his policies, such as non-alignment and the rejection of collective defence pacts, can be found in writings penned well before the beginning of the cold war or the creation of Pakistan.

More commonly, Nehru is labelled an idealist or a liberal internationalist and is often seen as a post-colonial leader who sought the extension of 'international society' to include India. A.P. Rana, for instance, traces the roots of non-alignment to Gandhi's influence on Nehru but nonetheless comes to the conclusion that Nehru lacked Gandhi's more transformational sensibility and eventually 'firmly linked his non-aligned policy to the maintenance of the structure of international society and continually manoeuvred towards this end' (Rana 1969, p. 311). Kanti Bajpai characterises Nehru's position as 'Westphalia plus nonalignment' because, while accepting basic Westphalian assumptions, Nehru challenged the idea that order and stability in the international system was dependent on great powers and instead argued that the non-aligned would be the most positive force in world politics (Bajpai 2003, p. 242). Yet, Bajpai does not elaborate on why Nehru arrived at this conclusion or question whether this should complicate the portrayal of him in conventional IR terms. Indeed, he insists on domesticating Nehru's seemingly more radical pronouncements into a Westphalian framework. For example, he is dismissive of Nehru's frequent comments on the inevitability of a 'world government' or 'world federation' suggesting that they should not be read literally because he 'was probably suggesting that states would increasingly collaborate in propagating international law and organisations' (Bajpai 2003, p. 240). As I will argue, however, this interpretation does not do justice to Nehru's intellectual vision, which was underpinned by a critique of the hierarchical nature of the emerging post-imperial world order and had as its ultimate goal a post-sovereign-state world community.

Gopal Krishna calls Nehru a 'pragmatic idealist' who tried, and failed, to 'promote the transformation of world order' by pursuing a foreign policy for India based on securing autonomy without power (Krishna 1984, pp. 272, 274, 285–6). Yet, as will be discussed, Nehru did not seek to rid international relations of power. Rather, like Gandhi, he sought to find ways of exercising power morally. Gandhi ultimately concluded that reason had its limitations and that, in some circumstances, moral questions could be answered only by moving beyond reason to the 'penetration of the heart' (quoted in Iyer 1973, p. 287). For Nehru, however, this was 'the pure religious attitude to life and its problems', and he was 'not fortunate enough to have this faith' (Nehru 1942, pp. 536, 538). Instead, as Sunil Khilnani – using a phrase reminiscent of Bertrand Russell – has argued, he spent much of his life trying to fashion a modern politics grounded in a 'reasoned morality' (Khilnani 2004, p. 28). A reasoned morality, according to Russell:

> does not defer blindly to authority, does not believe any precept because that precept is generally accepted, does not bow down before the wisdom of its ancestors; but reflects for itself on the ends of human life, and on the means for attaining those ends in its actual milieu.
>
> (Russell 1993, p. 325)

Russell was an early influence and long-standing acquaintance whose books made a significant impact on Nehru in the 1920s as he was becoming politically active. 'I think what is required in India most', he wrote in a letter to a friend in 1927, 'is a course of study of Bertrand Russell's books . . . Generosity of heart is a good thing but what is wanted is not an emotional outburst of generosity but coldly reasoned tolerance' (quoted in Gopal 1975, p. 98). In time, as we shall see, however, Nehru's reasoned morality would come to include insights from those, such as Gandhi and the Buddha, who went beyond a coldly reasoned tolerance.

The aim of this chapter is to show that Nehru's international thought should be understood in the context of his desire for an ethical project that is underpinned by a reasoned morality. His ethic of internationalism was the product of this project, which took shape in the context of the anti-colonial movement and drew on what Nehru would call a 'strange medley' of influences from Gandhi, Marxism, Buddhist philosophy and Rabindranath Tagore. Reading Nehru as a 'realist' or a 'liberal internationalist' does not take into account this genealogy and cannot explain his formulation of 'internationalist nationalism' which rejects the fundamental assumption of the equivalence of the 'nation' and the 'state' that underpins both 'realism' and 'liberalism'. This is why Nehru's more radical ideas, such as his long and consistent advocacy of a post-sovereign-state world order, are explained away as rhetoric that simply masked his true realpolitik intentions or watered down to the statist limitations of a liberal internationalist framework. In rejecting the conflation of the nation and the state, Nehru also problematized the distinction between an ordered domestic sphere and an anarchical international sphere and the assumptions about power and ethics that accompanies conventional renderings of world politics. For Nehru an ethical national project could flourish only within an internationalist, post-sovereign order and there was no question of deferring issues of ethics until a world community had been achieved or circumscribing ethics to a statist 'national interest'. Rather, there were ethical possibilities inherent in nationalism but, whereas a statist nationalism prioritised self-interest and could lead to exploitative relations, an internationalist nationalism was inherently concerned with ethical, non-exploitative relations with others.

Furthermore, reading Nehru as a realist or liberal internationalist does not take into account his disruption of the narrative of history based on a particular reading of the European experience – which proceeds from religious empires to Westphalian nation-states to a post-Westphalian order – that frames many discussions of ethics in IR theory. As we shall see, Nehru's narrative of world history, and the intellectual sources he draws on, problematizes this Eurocentric narrative that places the agency for ethical projects in IR with the West. In doing so, he anticipated contemporary debates about post-national and post-sovereign-state possibilities, pointed to the particularities of modern Western powers and their international systems and restored ethical agency to the non-West.

Nonetheless, although he thought it possible for India to cultivate an internationalist nationalism through an appropriately oriented foreign policy, Nehru's post-sovereign world order was, as mentioned above, a long-term goal to be worked towards through a temporary acceptance of existing state-dominated structures such as the UN. Nehru's normative project, therefore, is an act of what Shilliam, in Chapter 1, describes as 'translating modernity', for it is solely an act of neither resistance nor mimicry nor domination. Rather, it is a multifaceted process of knowledge production about modernity that reconfigures the meanings of modern concepts such as the 'nation' and the 'state' and, subsequently, reveals new avenues of thinking about the relationship between power and ethics in IR.

The chapter begins by tracing the origins of Nehru's ethic of internationalism and his rejection of 'narrow nationalism' in his pre-independence writings, primarily his three books, *Glimpses of World History*, *The Discovery of India* and *An Autobiography*, all three of which were written during periods of imprisonment by the British colonial authorities and are a mixture of autobiography, history and philosophy. Read together, these books make for a revealing account of Nehru's personal and intellectual development and are key to understanding his future politics in an independent India. *Glimpses of World History,* a collection of letters written to his daughter Indira between 1930 and 1933, was met with acclaim for its expansive and comparative exploration of 'world history' (Chamberlain 1942). The book is a clear departure from the dominant historiographical tradition of Nehru's time and succeeded in provincializing Europe long before it became fashionable to do so. Nehru's stated aim in *An Autobiography*, written between 1934 and 1935, was to 'attempt to trace . . . my own mental development' and was written in a 'mood of self-questioning' (Nehru 1942, p. vii). *Autobiography* contains a revealing and detailed account of the anti-colonial movement and his role in it and, although Nehru initially seems determined to construct firm dichotomies between tradition and modernity, masculinity and femininity, discipline and indiscipline, the autobiographical self that eventually emerges towards the end of the text is rooted in emotions, doubts, questions and cultural hybridity and is far from the tradition of autobiography that highlights a completed, autonomous and heroic self.[3] His self-questioning continues and is even more pronounced in *The Discovery of India*, which was written in 1944. Early in the book, Nehru puzzles over his 'philosophy of life', admitting that he did not know what it was. 'Some years earlier', he wrote, 'I would not have been so hesitant. There was a definiteness about my thinking and objectives then which has faded away since' (Nehru 2002, p. 25). The remainder of the book is as much a discovery of himself and his 'philosophy of life' as it is about a discovery of India. Indeed, the two are inseparable for Nehru constructs a self-questioning, plural and open-ended identity for both himself and India that is crucially dependent on an ethic of internationalism.

The chapter ends by considering Nehru's efforts to operationalize his internationalist ethic in the conduct of India's post-independence foreign policy. It is the apparent disjuncture between his pre-independence intellectual vision and the post-independence historical experience that is one of the sources of the wildly varying assessments of Nehru. Rather than accept the conventional explanations for this disjuncture – that Nehru was an idealist who eventually had to confront the realities of power or that he used idealistic rhetoric to paper over his true realpolitik intentions – I want to argue that Nehru's internationalist nationalism should be understood as a critique of liberal modernity's conceptions of nationalism and the state which, nonetheless, accepted both as necessary but transient features of the immediate post-colonial era. Nehru, I want to suggest, sought to create, both in his political writing and through his political practice, an alternative modernity underpinned by an ethic of internationalism. That he met with varying degrees of success had to do with the internal contradictions of his political project.

The next section focuses on the development of Nehru's anti-colonialism and lays out Nehru's criticisms of nationalism. Following this, I then proceed to examine Nehru's vision of an ethical modernity and the central role that an internationalist ethic and his critique of nationalism played in it. The last section examines Nehru's post-independence foreign policies, tracing their genealogy back to his 'ethical modernity' and reflecting on the inherent contradictions in this project which made this vision so difficult to achieve.

Against narrow nationalism

In his preface in *Autobiography* Nehru cautions the reader that the book, having been written 'during a particularly distressful period of my existence', may be occasionally lacking in restraint (Nehru 1942, p. vii). Yet, the book is scrupulously free of any sort of defensive nationalism or aggressive condemnation of his jailers. Instead, the pathologizing of 'narrow nationalism' and the normalizing of multiple attachments and miscegenous origins are features of all three of his books. Nehru wrote in *Glimpses* that one of his motivations for writing letters on history to Indira was to prevent himself from succumbing to a narrow nationalism. He warns Indira against being 'misled by the colours on the map or by national boundaries' for 'history is one connected whole and you cannot understand even the history of any one country if you do not know what has happened in other parts of the world' (Nehru 1996, p. 57). India's historical achievements are carefully situated within the context of India's interaction with various other cultures and peoples and in relation to the achievements of other societies. The rise of

Buddhism in India, for instance, is placed amongst 'a wave of thought going through the world, a wave of discontent with existing conditions and of hope and aspiration for something better' which produced Confucius and Lao-Tse in China, Zoroaster in Persia and Pythagoras in Greece (Nehru 2002, p. 35). Moreover, Nehru located what he considered the greatest moments of Indian history – the reign of the Mauryan emperor Ashoka and the Mughal emperor Akbar – during times of cultural mixing and conscious efforts to engage with the world (Nehru 1996, pp. 61–6, 305–11). In *Discovery* he would go even further, locating the source of India's deterioration in isolationism: 'the more she withdrew into her shell, intent on preserving herself, uncontaminated by external influences, the more she lost that inspiration and her life became increasingly a dull round of meaningless activities all centred in the dead past' (Nehru 2002, p. 209).

Not only did Nehru attempt to naturalize cultural and historical interlinkages, he also sought to normalize non-national forms of political organisation: '. . . there is a great deal of talk now-a-days of nationalism and patriotism – the love of one's country . . . This nationalism is quite a new thing in history' (Nehru 1996, p. 95). Rather, 'in the old days people often thought in terms of universal sovereigns and World-States. Long afterwards came nationalism and a new kind of imperialism, and between the two they have played sufficient havoc in this world' (Nehru 1996, p. 95). Touching on a theme to which he would repeatedly return in his writings, Nehru then noted that '[a]gain there is talk to-day of a World-State, not a great empire, or a universal sovereign, but a kind of World-Republic which would prevent exploitation of one nation or people or class by another' (Nehru 1996, pp. 95–6).

Nehru was an astute analyst of nationalism who anticipated aspects of the 'modernist' and neo-Marxist theories of nationalism which began emerging in the 1960s (Gellner 1964; Nairn 1977). Foreshadowing theories linking industrialization and nationalism, Nehru argued in *Glimpses* that nationalism was the product of the rise of industrial capitalism in Western Europe. This nationalism, in turn, gave rise to modern imperialism:

> [t]he capitalist organisation of industry and civilization led inevitably to this imperialism. Capitalism also led to an intensification of the feeling of nationalism . . . This nationalism was not merely a love of one's own country, but hatred of all others. From this glorification of one's own patch of land and contemptuous running down of others, trouble and friction between different countries were bound to result.
>
> (Nehru 1996, p. 399)

This was the case because industrial capitalism,

> bound together and separated; those living in one national unit came closer to each other, but they were cut off more and more from others living in a different national unit. While patriotism grew in one country, it was accompanied by dislike and distrust of the foreigner.
>
> (Nehru 1996, p. 402)

It was a visit to Europe in 1926–1927[4] and Nehru's participation as the Indian National Congress (INC) representative at the Congress of Oppressed Nationalities in Brussels that led to his adoption of a Marxist understanding of anti-imperialism as a global struggle linked to rejecting the acquisitiveness of capitalism and a narrow and intense nationalism. It was here that he made contact with, among others, anti-colonial leaders from Asia, Africa and Latin America and communists and trade union leaders from Europe. At the end of the conference, his 'outlook was wider and nationalism by itself seemed . . . a narrow and insufficient creed'. There had also developed a strong connection in Nehru's mind between social democracy and internationalism, on the one hand, and capitalism, imperialism and nationalism, on the other (Nehru 1942, p. 166).

The Brussels conference led to the establishment of the League against Imperialism and for National Independence, with Nehru appointed as honorary president (Nehru 1942, p. 163). The League Against Imperialism had been set up partly in reaction to the failure of the League of Nations to develop into an organization that addressed the issue of colonialism in any meaningful way. However, given the failures of the League of Nations, Nehru's expectations for the League against Imperialism, which foreshadowed his attitude towards the UN, were modest, for self-interested nationalism was still a major hindrance to the growth of internationalism. Nonetheless, working towards an internationalist ethic using the structures already in existence was still considered vital (quoted in Gopal 1975, p. 105).

Nehru's cosmopolitan upbringing and his culturally complex family background also played an important role in the development of his internationalist nationalism. He describes his upbringing in terms that display a lack of any hankering for a purity of origins. He writes that he was raised in a migrant family which, since its 'descent from Kashmir', had adapted easily to life in a Mughal court in Delhi and then, as the Mughal Empire declined, to life in British India. His father, an Anglophile educated in Persian, Arabic and English, took on the orthodoxies of the Kashmiri Brahmin community but was nonetheless 'of course, a nationalist in a vague sense of the word' (Gopal 1975, p. 5). His mother, on the other hand, is portrayed as a traditional Kashmiri Brahmin who tries but fails to interest him in traditional religious rites (Gopal 1975, p .8). He was educated by an English governess, an Irish-French/Belgian tutor, who introduced him to English literature, science and theosophy, and a Kashmiri Pandit tutor, who was employed to teach him Hindi and Sanskrit. He was aware, he writes, of the injustices of English rule but 'as much as I began to resent the presence and behaviour of the alien rulers, I had no feeling whatever . . . against individual Englishmen . . . In my heart I rather admired the English' (Gopal 1975, p. 6). The young Jawaharlal then went on to study at Harrow and Cambridge, where he developed an attraction to the so-called 'extremist' nationalist politics of Lokamanya Tilak[5] but still found himself contemplating a career in the Indian Civil Service to serve as a cog in the administrative apparatus of British India (Nehru 1942, pp. 24–5). Writing in the 'Epilogue' of *Autobiography* Nehru reflected on the impact of this composite identity in somewhat ambivalent terms that are crucial to understanding his pull towards internationalism as a part of a broader programme to construct an ethical modernity:

> I have become a queer mixture of East and West, out of place everywhere, at home nowhere. Perhaps my thoughts and approach to life are more akin to what is called Western than Eastern, but India clings to me . . . I cannot get rid of either that past inheritance or my recent acquisitions. They are both part of me, and, though they help me in both the East and the West, they also create in me a feeling of spiritual loneliness not only in public activities but in life itself. I am a stranger and alien in the West. I cannot be of it. But in my own country also, sometimes, I have an exile's feeling.
>
> (Nehru 1942, p. 596)

In *Discovery*, as we shall see, Nehru attempts to reconcile himself to the exile's 'feeling of spiritual loneliness by normalizing and celebrating cultural hybridity, both his and India's, while attempting a 'spiritualisation of politics' – where 'spiritualisation' referred to a reasoned morality rather than religion – something he first broached in *Autobiography* as a 'fine idea' which attracted him 'more and more' (Nehru 1942, p. 73).

The formative years of Nehru's intellectual development took place at a time when the horrors of the First World War had led a number of writers to turn to various types of post-nationalism and his reading materials during terms of imprisonment in the 1920s, 1930s and 1940s, which included works by Leonard Woolf, Harold Laski and H.G. Wells, indicate that Nehru was well aware of this tide of thought. More important, however, in shaping Nehru's ideas were other Indian anti-colonial figures, namely Gandhi and Rabindranath Tagore, both of whom paved the way in having 'a world outlook' but remaining 'wholly Indian' (Nehru 2002, p. 341). It is *Discovery* that most clearly displays the imprint of Gandhi and Tagore for it is in this book, written on the eve of India's independence, that Nehru is most preoccupied with fashioning India's future within the framework of an ethical modernity. Early on in the book he writes that 'events of the past few years in India, China, Europe, and all over the world have been confusing, upsetting and distressing'. The future had become 'vague and shadowy' and that had 'lost that clearness of outline which it once possessed' in his mind (Nehru 2002, p. 25). He had developed a 'growing distaste for politics' and his 'whole attitude to life seemed to undergo a transformation' (Nehru 2002, p. 25). Nehru then posed a series of questions, about human nature and ends and means, which he would go on to grapple with throughout the book in different ways.

An ethical modernity

'Some kind of ethical approach to life has a strong appeal for me', Nehru writes at the beginning of *Discovery*, adding, 'though it would be difficult for me to justify it logically' (Nehru 2002, p. 28). In his ensuing quest to discover an ethical approach that was underpinned by a reasoned morality, a number of different strands of thought captured his attention. Gandhi and Tagore, as mentioned, were important influences. 'Nationalism is a narrowing creed', Nehru wrote in *Discovery*, 'and nationalism in conflict with a dominating imperialism produces all manner of frustrations and complexes', but it was Gandhi and Tagore who 'forced the people in some measure out of their narrow grooves of thought and made them think of broader issues affecting humanity' (Nehru 2002, p. 340). Gandhi, a man of 'concentrated and ceaseless activity', contributed an ethical doctrine which emphasized the equivalence of ends and means and had shown how to apply this doctrine to large-scale public activity. Tagore, who was 'primarily a man of thought', had 'been India's internationalist par excellence, believing and working for international cooperation'. Yet, from Tagore he had learned that a commitment to universalism did not have to conflict with a commitment to a national community for 'with all his internationalism, his feet have always been planted firmly on India's soil and his mind has been saturated with the wisdom of the Upanishads' (Nehru 2002, p. 340).

Indeed, both Gandhi and Tagore had long been critical of unalloyed nationalism (see Nandy 2006). Tagore saw a healthy national spirit as vital for an internationalist ethic. He distinguished between the nation as a community and the nation as a mechanical organization of power and argued that it was the latter that underpinned modern nationalism while India had traditionally held to a concept of the nation as community. Modern nationalism, therefore, was explicitly anti-Indian in its denial of porous cultural boundaries, its negation of cultural and social hospitality and its organization of society according to an instrumental, bureaucratic rationality. Gandhi rarely mentioned the term 'nationalism' in his prolific writings, but when he did he was careful to distinguish it from a 'national spirit' that was inseparable from internationalism (Gandhi 1999b, p. 216). A nationalism based on selfishness and exploitation, for Gandhi, was the product of understanding truth as a cognitive notion which gives rise to the treatment of reality as something to be mastered and conquered.[6] This type of nationalism would, therefore, produce only an abstract and, therefore, potentially destructive internationalism. Gandhi's 'national spirit', on the other hand, was based on a notion of truth as resting on individual moral responsibility and this was essential for the creation of a non-abstract internationalism rooted in our practical relations with the world.

Although Gandhi had been a central character in *Autobiography*, Nehru's comments on him were ambivalent, often expressing bewilderment and sometimes harsh criticism. He disagreed with Gandhi's emphasis on individual-based change rather than society-wide structural change, his stance against industrialism, his outright dismissal of 'modern civilisation' and his criticisms of modern science and technology. Moreover, Gandhi's doctrine of non-violence had not been articulated in a manner scientific enough to be to Nehru's liking (Nehru 1942, pp. 73, 521, 538). Gandhi is less central a character in *Discovery* and, yet, his influence is palpable. Although Nehru still had many disagreements with Gandhi in 1944–1945 when *Discovery* was written, there is more hesitation in his discussions of science and industrialism and an even greater determination to fashion a different nationalism based on an internationalist ethic. Whereas in *Glimpses*, for instance, Nehru expressed concerns about bad applications of science, in *Discovery* it was science itself that was found to be at fault. Indeed, 'science does not tell us much . . . about the purpose of life' and scientific reasoning had to be complemented by 'intuition and other methods of sensing truth and reality' (Nehru 2002, pp. 26, 31). He worried that both science and industrialism, when divorced from morality and ethics, had the potential to produce a destructive and domineering nationalism (Nehru 2002, pp. 33, 554, 556).

Another long-standing influence on Nehru was Buddhist thought because it encouraged the deployment of rationality away from self-interest and towards the cultivation of a moral life by relying 'on reason and logic and experience' and using a method of 'psychological analysis' (Nehru 2002, p. 128). According to Nehru, by rejecting as illusory the concept of a permanent self, the Buddha came to the understanding that the 'essence of a thing is its immanent law of relation to other so-called things' (Nehru 2002, p. 129). Continuously seeking self-affirmation was, therefore, bound to result in frustration and anxiety. Given the knowledge of interdependence, however, Buddhist thought recognized that 'ethical relations have a definite value in our finite world. So in our lives and in our human relations we have to conform to ethics and live the good life'. To 'that life and to this phenomenal world we can and should apply reason and knowledge and experience' (Nehru 2002, p. 174). Thus, Buddhism provided a reasoned rationale for an ethic of interdependence. The 'ethical and social and practical idealism of Buddha', Nehru wrote, was grounded in an 'appeal to the nation but it was also more than the nation. It was a universal call for the good life and it recognized no barriers of class, caste or nation' (Nehru 2002, p. 176). Furthermore, Buddhism had universal appeal because although it was a 'child of Indian thought' and 'had its nationalist background', it was 'essentially international, a world religion, and as it developed and spread it became increasingly so' (Nehru 2002, p. 138).

This 'strange medley' of 'Buddha–Marx–Gandhi', as Nehru described it in his prison diary in 1935 – and to which we might add Tagore – underpinned his internationalist ethic (Nehru 1974, p. 367). With Marx he came to an understanding of a key problem – the exploitative and interlinked nature of certain forms of economic and political relations. In Buddhism, he found a deeper explanation for why this problem emerges and a rationale for an ethic of interdependence. In Tagore and Gandhi he found a way forward. Whereas Tagore provided an understanding of the nation as a community that is wholly consistent with internationalism, Gandhi taught the importance of grounding this internationalism in practical relations with the world. The implications of this internationalist ethic for an independent India is a consistent theme in *Discovery*, and early on in the book he argues that India 'for all her intense nationalistic fervour, has gone further than many nations in her acceptance of real internationalism and the co-ordination and even to some extent the subordination, of the independent nation-state to a world organization' (Nehru 2002, p. 53). In opting to offer support to Britain during the Second World War in exchange for acknowledgement of India's future freedom, the INC had shown that the 'national interest' did not equal narrow, nationalist self-interest and had instead taken an 'international view' which 'considered the war as something much more than a conflict between armed forces' (Nehru 2002, pp. 427–8). In this way the INC had brought the 'national interest' into line with an internationalist ethic. There were, of course, objectors to this policy in India, who argued that 'every enemy of Britain should be treated as a friend', and that 'idealism has no place in politics, which concerns itself with power and the opportune use of it' (Nehru 2002, p. 421). However, 'these objectors were overwhelmed by the mass sentiment the Congress had created and hardly ever gave public expression to their views' (Nehru 2002, p. 422).

The Congress's conditional offer to assist the British war effort was rejected, and Winston Churchill made clear in September 1941 that the Atlantic Charter[7] did not apply to India (Gopal 1975, p. 274). This led to the 'Quit India' Resolution of 8 August 1942, which was drafted by Nehru and demanded immediate recognition of India's independence but also outlined detailed and rather radical objectives for a future federation which would replace the system of sovereign nation-states:

> Such a world federation would ensure the freedom of its constituent nations, the prevention of aggression and exploitation by one nation over another, the protection of national minorities, the advancement of all backward areas and peoples, and the pooling of the world's resources for the common good of all. On the establishment of such a world federation, disarmament would be practicable in all countries, national armies, navies and air forces would no longer be necessary, and a world federal defence force would keep the world peace and prevent aggression.
>
> (Gandhi 1999c, p. 453)

Manu Bhagavan has argued that it as the 'Quit India' Resolution that most clearly set out Nehru's vision for the UN and that it was this vision that he and his sister, Vijaya Laxmi Pandit, who led the Indian delegation at the UN, attempted to make a reality in the post-independence period (Bhagavan 2008, pp. 8–9). In addition, Nehru's remarks in *Discovery* on his rejection of dominion status for India, which had been offered in place of full independence, were a precursor to his future rejection of exclusive regional alliances:

> It meant certainly a wider sphere of international cooperation, which was desirable, but it also meant at the same time lesser co-operation with countries outside that empire or commonwealth group. It thus became a limiting factor, and our ideas, full of the promise of the future, overstepped these boundaries and looked to a wider co-operation.
>
> (Nehru 2002, p. 421)

India's actions in the UN and its post-war stance against military alliances will be discussed in further detail in the next section. Here the pertinent point is that Nehru consistently and actively sought to entrench a vision of an independent India in a post-sovereign-state and post-regional framework.

Another nationalist issue that took on internationalist connotations in Nehru's writing was the growing demand for the partition of India, which other national-ists rejected on the grounds of India's essential unity. Given Nehru's emphasis on diversity and cultural inter-mixing, however, when he made claims about the essential unity of India, he often qualified them: 'Many of us are of the opinion that India is essentially a nation . . . But whether India is properly to be described as one nation or two or more really does not matter for the modern idea of nation-ality has been almost divorced from statehood' (Nehru 2002, pp. 530–1). Modern activities had outgrown national boundaries and 'as the world shrinks and its problems overlap' 'internationalization' was necessary (Nehru 2002, pp. 532–3). Only a large united India would be able to cope with the pressures of a world of internationalized activities for although 'India is big enough as a whole to give them scope for development', a partitioned India was not (Nehru 2002, pp. 532–3).

Here was the crux of Nehru's dilemma – his understanding of what it meant to be modern rested on notions of economic and technological progress that initially required 'a strong united state' (Nehru 2002, p. 535) if India was to participate in the world as an equal. This is not, however, an endorsement of Partha Chatterjee's influential reading of Nehru as representing nationalist thought 'at its moment of arrival' because it gives primacy to the economic sphere and, hence, places 'the idea of the national state at its very heart' (Chatterjee 1986, pp. 133, 227). Nehru's nationalist thought is far more ambivalent and ambiguous than Chatterjee allows for, as we saw earlier, Nehru was a critic of Western industrialism and Western modernity, which, he argued, were driven by the profit motive and a desire for power. Subsequently, his efforts to create a strong united nation-state would have to be undertaken in a framework of an alternative ethical modernity based on a 'spirit of renunciation' with which, he was convinced, India was already famil-iar (Nehru 2002, p. 559). This, then, was an attempt to replace the partnership between reason and capital that lies at the heart of the nation-state of Western modernity with one that joined reason with community and nationalism with internationalism in order to give rise to a post-sovereign-state world community (see Pantham 1998; Prakash 1999, Chapters 7 and 8).

Before we turn to the post-independence period, however, it is necessary to examine the revealing final sections of *Discovery*, which deal with the emerging post-war world order. In these sections Nehru critiqued the instrumental reason-ing that underpinned the prominent geo-political theories of his time, such as those of Nicholas Spykman and Walter Lippman, and the allusions to objectivity proffered by theories of realism in general (Nehru 2002, p. 539). Although a self-interest based on a reasoned morality 'should drive every nation to this wider co-operation in order to escape disaster in the future and build its own free life on the basis of others', the

> self-interest of the 'realist' is far too limited by past myths and dogmas, and regards ideas and social forms, suited to one age, as immutable and as unchanging parts of human nature and society, forgetting that there is nothing so changeable as human nature and society . . . war is considered a

biological necessity, empire and expansion as the prerogatives of a dynamic and progressive people, the profit motive as the central fact dominating human relations, and ethnocentrism, a belief in racial superiority, becomes an article of faith . . . Some of these ideas were common to the civilizations of east and west; many of them form the back-ground of modern Western civilization out of which fascism and nazism grew.

(Nehru 2002, pp. 540–1)

It is in this passage that Nehru makes his critique most explicit. He links Western modernity to an unreasoned amorality that produced a philosophy of history that gave rise to racism and imperialism, a society dominated by the concerns of capital rather than community and an erroneous theory of IR based on the idea of an unchanging and selfish human nature – a notion which, he claimed, 'takes refuge in irrationalism, superstition, and unreasonable and inequitable social prejudices and practices' (Nehru 2002, p. 30). The challenge for post-colonial India was clear – far from accepting the universal nature of the European experience Nehru sought a better, more ethical modernity, and IR was key to this project.

Towards a world community

One of the concluding passages of *Discovery* gives a good indication of the normative contours of Nehru's future foreign policies:

It was India's way in the past to welcome and absorb other cultures. That is much more necessary to-day, for we march to the *one world of to-morrow where national cultures will be intermingled with the international culture of the human race.* We shall therefore seek wisdom and knowledge and *friendship* and comradeship wherever we can find them, and *co-operate with others in common task*, but we *are no supplicants for others' favours and patronage.* Thus *we shall remain true Indians and Asiatics*, and become at the same time good *internationalists and world citizens.*

(Nehru 2002, p. 566, emphasis added)

Co-existence, non-alignment, rejection of collective defence pacts and active involvement in the UN: none of these policies was an ends in itself but rather they were a means towards achieving a world order in which nationalism would be subordinate to an internationalist ethic. Take for instance, Nehru's most famous foreign policy, non-alignment, the principle behind Nehru's opposition to membership in cold war blocs and collective defence pacts such as SEATO. In an essay discussing the lack of multilateral security organizations, such as the North Atlantic Treaty Organization, in Asia, Amitav Acharya argues that the absence is best explained by the emergence, through the post-war interaction of Asian states, of a norm against collective defence. He attributes 'the political ideas of actors like Nehru', such as the concept of non-alignment, with having 'infused and strengthened the legal norms of state sovereignty prevailing at the international level' (Acharya 2005, p .21). If this is indeed the case, however, I would suggest that it was not Nehru's intention, for, although he was committed to the principle of moral equality between nations, he was not wedded to a legalistic notion of absolute sovereignty. Indeed, his speeches on non-alignment and his opposition to defence pacts indicate that rather than being policies of disengagement he intended them to be a means of keeping alive a notion of security that did not depend on generating insecurity in others. In addition, Nehru aimed to promote an understanding of national autonomy that resisted interactions with individual countries and groups that were inherently unequal but still aimed for the subordination of state sovereignty to a higher world body in the interests of justice and cooperation. SEATO, Nehru said

> is inclined dangerously in the direction of spheres of influence to be exercised by powerful countries . . . it is the big and powerful countries that will decide matters and not the two or three weak and small Asian countries that may be allied to them.
>
> (Nehru 1961, p. 89)

While '[c]ountries in Asia as well as outside may have certain justifiable fears', the 'approach of this Treaty is wrong and may antagonize a great part of Asia. Are you going to have peace and security by creating more conflicts and antagonisms?' (Nehru 1961, p. 89). This, however, was not a rejection of supranational cooperation for 'I think the world is too small now for any few countries, including the Asian countries, to say that nobody else can interfere with an area and that that area is their sole concern' (Nehru 1961, p. 90).

Non-alignment was also a means of creating an environment in which dialogue with all parties, and therefore a move towards a post-sovereign world order, was possible. Conditioned to believe in the importance of dialogue during the anti-colonial movement and under Gandhi's influence, Nehru had come to 'realize that truth is many-sided and is not the monopoly of any group or nation' (Nehru 2002, p. 560). Hence, he justified non-alignment in the following terms: '. . . we should not align ourselves with power blocs' because '[w]e can be of far more service without doing so and I think there is just a possibility – and I shall not put it higher than that – that at a moment of crisis our peaceful and friendly efforts might make a difference and avert that crisis' (Nehru 1961, p. 47). It was not 'a question of our remaining isolated or cut off from the rest of the world . . . We wish to have the closest contacts, because we do from the beginning firmly believe in the world coming closer together and ultimately realizing the ideal of what is now being called One World' (Nehru 1961, pp. 47–8).

Nehru's alternative to military alliances in Asia was what he called the doctrine of Panchsheel, or Five Principles of Coexistence, which was first enunciated in an agreement with China in 1954 and consisted of (i) mutual respect for each other's territorial integrity and sovereignty, (ii) mutual non-aggression, (iii) mutual non-interference in each other's internal affairs, (iv) equality and mutual benefit and (v) peaceful co-existence (Nehru 1961, p. 99). According to Nehru, these five principles were 'the result of a long correspondence between the Government of India and the Government of China' and, therefore, the product of a dialogue rather than the inspiration of any individual leader. However, whereas the Chinese tended to refer to the agreement as the 'Five Principles', Nehru adopted a term derived from Sanskrit, Panchsheel, after he heard it used in Indonesia to refer to the basic principles of government: '. . . it struck me immediately that this was a suitable description of the five principles of international behaviour to which we had subscribed' (quoted in Fifield 1958, p. 505). This was particularly the case because the expression had 'been used from ancient times to describe the five moral precepts of Buddhism relating to personal behaviour' (Fifield 1958). He again explicitly linked his understanding of Panchsheel to Buddhist ethics in a speech in which he noted that the Emperor Ashoka, who adopted and adapted Buddhist practices after witnessing the horrors of a particularly bloody war, had set the precedent for adapting these moral precepts into the principles of government when he set forth five principles of Buddhist politics in his stone-carved edicts (Nehru 1961, pp. 101–2). Nehru's interpretation of Panchsheel as consistent with Buddhist philosophy implies that he did not mean it to be a doctrine aimed at strengthening state sovereignty. In Buddhist thought there is no conception of the isolated, unchanging self, and seeking self-affirmation leads only to more suffering and destruction. Thus, affirming one's own rights requires a willingness to give up those rights in order to affirm the rights of others (Unno 1988, p. 140). Applying a Buddhist-inspired ethic of interdependence to international relations, therefore, means that nation-states are also treated as social entities and that assertions of sovereign rights can contribute to a just world community of equals only when there is an understanding of an interdependent reality and responsibility to other nation-states. This is the context in which Nehru's enthusiasm for Panchsheel should be interpreted.

The agreement in which the Five Principles first appeared was one that implicitly recognized Chinese sovereignty in Tibet, although Nehru had initially criticized the Chinese invasion (Nehru 1961, pp. 302–3). Instead of confronting China, however, Nehru concluded that the invasion was a product of Chinese nationalism, which, in turn, was a reaction to imperialism (Nehru 1993, p. 475). His insistence on including the Five Principles in the trade agreement with China in addition to his push for UN recognition of the Chinese communist government were ways of creating an environment that would steer China away from a narrow nationalism, foster an ethic of interdependence and, thus, provide long-term protection for the Tibetans, who would be protected as a minority in China under a system of international law. The importance of inducing incremental changes in modes of thinking – what might today be called the 'diffusion of norms' – was something Nehru had learned during the anti-colonial movement (Nehru 2002, p. 560). In the post-independence period this belief underpinned the policy of Panchsheel and the 'fact that it will not be wholly acted upon here and there is really of little relevance' for '[y]ou make a law, and the law gradually influences the whole structure of life in a country . . . Even those who do not believe in it gradually come within its scope' (Nehru 1961, p. 100).

Not only was the UN a constant presence in Nehru's speeches on foreign policy, the Indian delegation at the UN was heavily involved in the establishment of the Human Rights Commission (HRC) and used the first session of the UN to raise the issue of South Africa's Asiatic Land Tenure and Indian Representation Act, a precursor to apartheid that effectively segregated the Indian community. India's resolution censuring South Africa won a two-thirds majority in the General Assembly and, according to Henri Laugier, the Assistant Secretary-General for Social Affairs, established a 'precedent of fundamental significance in the field of international action . . . that no violation of human rights should be covered up by the principle of national sovereignty' (quoted in Bhagavan 2008, p. 13).

Bhagavan has convincingly argued that Nehru saw in the HRC the first step towards developing the UN into a post-sovereign global body (Bhagavan 2008, p. 19). Indeed, this is made explicit in comments made by Nehru during this time (February 1947):

Today the Human Rights Commission is meeting in New York. Our representatives are there. The conception is that there are common individual rights which should be guaranteed all the world over.

. . . What is the UNO? It is developing into a world republic in which all States, independent States are represented and to which they may be answerable on occasions, for instance South Africa over the South Africa Indians' question, even though this was a domestic question because Indians are South African citizens.

(Nehru 1984, pp. 216–17)

The Indian representative to the HRC, Hansa Mehta, proposed an implementation framework that called for a special UN committee on human rights together with an international court to be given the power (to be applied by the General Assembly) to hear complaints by individuals, organizations and states. This was ultimately rejected by the HRC because of objections from various delegates that the proposal violated state sovereignty as it required the adoption of a covenant of human rights with the status of international law (Bhagavan 2008, p. 21). Mehta, nonetheless, continued to work on an international bill of human rights that would be actionable by international law, and in India she worked to embed the Universal Declaration of Human Rights as actionable rights into the Indian Constitution (Bhagavan 2008, pp. 24–5). As a speech to the UN General Assembly in 1956 titled 'Towards a World Community' makes clear, Nehru also had not given up on the promise of a post-sovereign-state world order:

In spite of the difficulties and the apparent conflicts, gradually the sense of a world community conferring together through its elected representatives is not only developing but seizing the minds of people all over the world . . . I hope that, gradually, each representative here, while obviously not forgetting the interests of his country, will begin to think that he is something more that the representative of his country, that he represents, in a small measure perhaps, the world community.

(Nehru 1961, p. 174)

There were, of course, times when Nehru himself could not live up to his own principles. Indeed, the contradictions inherent in a project that was driven by the simultaneous desire to create a united modern nation-state and an urge to overcome the ways in which modern nation-states were ontologically constituted and related to each other in the contemporary world would come to cause him immense moral anxiety and strain his vision of an ethical modernity. The lead-up to India's war with China in 1962, for instance, saw Nehru insisting on the inviolability of 'natural' and 'customary' borders, rhetoric typical of the modern-ist nation-state with its intolerance for the ambiguous boundaries of pre-colonial India (for instance, Government of India n.d., p. 55). Subsequently, the war pro-duced a growth in 'narrow nationalism' in both China and India. In India, Chinese shops and their owners were vandalized, a nationalist agitation with an explicitly Hindu tone emerged, Communist Party of India offices were attacked and Indian citizens of Chinese origin were interned or expelled (Zachariah 2004, p. 247).

In Kashmir, Nehru presided over the progressive whittling away of the state's constitutionally guaranteed autonomy. This contributed to a breakdown in his close relationship with Sheikh Mohammad Abdullah, the leader of the National Conference, the only mass-based political organization in Kashmir. Although Abdullah had initially favoured Kashmir's accession to India over Pakistan, by 1953 he started to publicly call for Kashmiri independence. This resulted in the dismissal of his government and his arrest and detention without trial, all of which occurred with Nehru's complicity. A remorseful Nehru – who once wrote a pseu-donymous self-critique denouncing his dictatorial potential[8] – wrote sympathetic letters to Abdullah in prison and helped care for his family. This did not, however, help to resolve the tension between ethical thought and instrumental action that characterized his entire political career.

Hannah Arendt once wrote of Lessing that he 'never felt at home in the world' but 'he always remained committed to it' (Arendt 1970, p. 5). Nehru, too, never entirely felt at home in the world, and after seventeen tumultuous years as prime minister of India the 'feeling of spiritual loneliness' he wrote about in his *Autobiography* was acute. In his last months, memories of Gandhi and the pre-independence past preoccupied him and he was troubled that he had not lived up to Gandhi's expectations (Nehru 1965, pp. vii–viii). Nevertheless, the last words he ever wrote – a verse from a poem by Robert Frost – indicate that, despite this, Nehru still felt compelled to remain committed to the world:

The woods are lovely, dark and deep.
But I have promises to keep,
And miles to go before I sleep,
And miles to go before I sleep.

(quoted in Gopal 1984, p. 267)

Conclusion

As a normative project which took form in the historical context of anti-colonial resistance and, later, in the politics of the post-colonial Indian state, Nehru's internationalist nationalism represented a novel contribution to IR which rejected the conflation of the nation and the state and, therefore, opened up a greater realm of possibility for ethics in world politics. Consequently, Nehru anticipated contemporary normative debates about nationalism and the nation-state but provincialized the Eurocentric narrative of history, which portrays only Europe as having the capacity to realize a post-Westphalian system that underpins many of these discussions. Drawing on a diversity of philosophical traditions Nehru negotiated the terrain between the exigencies of anti-colonial nationalism and an ethical awareness of the need for interdependence. Influenced by the Buddha, Gandhi, Marx and Tagore, he rejected the notion of essentialist and unchanging national identities, resisted a politics based on instrumental reasoning, rendered insular and univocal nationalist ideologies as dangerous and regressive and produced a critique of Western liberal modernity and its conceptions of both the nation and the state.

The result was not a post-national ethic for 'a real internationalism is not something in the air without roots or anchorage' (Nehru 2002, p. 565) – but a post-sovereign internationalist ethic which saw the national self as realizable only in its interdependence with others. In his role as a leading Indian nationalist and later as prime minister of India, Nehru sought, through both rhetoric and practice, to create the conditions necessary to think beyond the nation-state to a post-sovereign-state world order. In the interests of a more ethical modernity rooted in a reasoned morality, foreign policies such as non-alignment and Panchsheel were devised to produce incremental changes that would one day make possible a world community to which nation-states would be subordinate. The current international system may be far from Nehru's vision of a post-sovereign world community, but his efforts to bring about such a world community and the intellectual currents that underpinned his vision deserve to be recognized and engaged with far more extensively than they have, for the possibilities inherent in his ethical project remain potent and relevant.

Notes

1   Thanks to Robbie Shilliam and Sekhar Bandyopadhyay for their comments.
2   See Khilnani (2004) and Guha (2005) for discussions of why this may be.
3   For a discussion of this tradition of autobiography in the west see Evans (1999).
4   For his wife, Kamala, to have treatment for tuberculosis.
5   'Extremist' because this brand of nationalism rejected the 'moderate' nationalist leaders' faith in the benevolent intentions of the British and their political strategy of gradual constitutional change. Instead they advocated militant destabilization of the British colonial regime. As Nehru's father, Motilal, was a moderate, his newfound radicalism inevitably caused friction between father and son. See Nehru (1942, p. 24).
6   I draw here on Akeel Bilgrami's (2003) understanding of Gandhi's philosophy.
7   An agreement between Churchill and Franklin Roosevelt signed in July 1941 which

confirmed the right of colonized people to self-government and was upheld in the Declaration that established the UN.

8 'Anonymous article', *Modern Review*, November 1937, 546–7. Reprinted in Nehru (1965, pp. 498–501).

12 Radical anti-colonial thought, anti-colonial internationalism and the politics of human solidarities

Anthony Bogues

We demand for Black Africa autonomy and independence, so far and no further than it is possible in this One World for groups and peoples to rule themselves subject to inevitable world unity and federation.

Declaration to the Colonial Powers
(extract from Resolutions of Pan-African Congress, Manchester, 1945)

Introduction[1]

One conventional narrative about twentieth-century political decolonization recounts the creation of new nation-states and their integration into a world system of states characterized by territorial demarcations and nation-state sovereignty. The twentieth-century transformation of various European colonial territories into nation-states occurred within the context of an already existing territorial system of states that had historically emerged with the Westphalian peace of 1648. In European history the Peace of Westphalia had opened a period in which territorial nation-state sovereignty became the benchmark of state-to-state relationships.

In 1784, Immanuel Kant, preoccupied with the ways in which state conflicts could finally end, forcefully observed in the fifth thesis of his essay "Idea for Universal History with a Cosmopolitan Intent" that "The greatest problem for the human species, whose solution nature compels it to seek, is to achieve a universal *civil society* administered in accord with right" (Kant 1983, p. 33, emphasis in original). Of course, Kant did not include the colonial world within his matrix of universal civil society or his matrix of rights. The late African philosopher Emmanuel Eze has noted that Kant also produced a theory of race (Eze 1997). And Charles Mills has made the compelling case that we cannot ignore "the racial exclusions in Kant's (and other modern Western philosophers') moral and political theory . . . [and that] instead of pretending that Kant was arguing for equal respect [for] everybody, we should be asking how Kant's theory needs to be rethought" (Mills 2005, p. 95). This is not the place to take up Mills's challenge, therefore in this chapter I will offer neither another version nor interpretation of Kant's conceptions of the "right of hospitality" or of "cosmopolitan right." Rather, it seems to me that it may be more productive to probe two specific historical moments and by doing so illustrate some of the ways in which colonized and racialized subjects, excluded from systems of rights, worked out a set of conceptions about rights and internationalism based upon a notion of what I will call *human solidarities.*

However, I also invoke Kant here because his conception of "hospitality" is often deployed as an important argument in the construction of contemporary cosmopolitanism and rights which should accrue to those who are aliens, and generally to the category of person that is oftentimes called the "other" (see, for example, Benhabib 2004). This conception of *bestowed rights* formalized upon an "other" has a long history in Western thought and in part works its way through the Hegelian slave–master dialectic and a particular perspective on a politics of recognition. In the most recent past it has been the work of Charles Taylor which has generated debates within the field of political theory on this matter (Taylor and Gutmann 1992). However, the issue of recognition as one which is critical to politics has also been debated by those who have been historically considered as "other." From the perspective of the colonized and the slave, as Frantz Fanon points out, the dialectic of the politics of recognition needs to be viewed differently.

Fanon makes the point in *Black Skin White Masks* that the difficulty with the Hegelian dialectic of recognition is that the master wishes work from the slave and not recognition, whereas the slave wants to end his oppression (Fanon 1967, p. 218). In the master–slave dialectic, for the slave to be free he or she breaks out of a framework in which recognition seems to be more a cognitive act that does not adequately trouble relations of power. Indeed, I would argue that the politics of recognition, while seeking to create a world of human multiplicity, does so within the framework of a *logic of the same*. In such cases the politics of recognition can be embedded within asymmetrical relations of power. Second, if recognition occurs within the logic of the same then I would argue that Lévinas's "humanity of the human" and the "subjectivity of the subject" does not appear because the basis of recognition is, typically, not full equality. In other words, to grant recognition is itself an act of power that names, includes, or excludes. Its logic is one in which an "other," although different, is accommodated within normative frames of acceptance. Hannah Arendt had already noted in 1975 that we should be careful about embracing recognition. She cautions on the great temptation of recognition, "which, in no matter what form, can only recognize us *as* such and such, that is as something which we fundamentally are *not*" (cited in Markell 2003, p. 14).

We know that the politics of recognition is today an important liberal project and that it informs both ideas about democratic polity and is one of the terrains in which the current politics about immigration is being played out. We are also aware of the critiques of this dimension of the current liberal project in which recognition is perceived as the justice antidote to the injustice of misrecognition. Patchen Markell notes that "misrecognition . . . consists in the failure, whether out of malice or ignorance, to extend people the respect or esteem that is due to them . . ." (Markell 2003, p. 3). The real question, though, which one has to ask is: Do the roots of the lack of respect reside in lack of recognition or are they to be found in asymmetrical power relations? Robbie Shilliam argues in Chapter 2 that there is a sense that the radical alterity of non-European "others" is treated more as a threat than as an opportunity for understanding the European "self." It is a point that underscores the complexities of thinking about a politics primarily through questions of the other. The issue becomes a central one since, at the levels of intellectual history and political thought, when we examine the political ideas and praxis of some radical anti-colonial groups we see a different perspective on politics and on rights. It is a perspective in which the relationship between "other" as alien is leveled and replaced with a conception of the human. As such, the relationship between humans is constructed as one in which the self is never isolated, but participates in the making of a social world. This particular stance has enormous import for ways of understanding internationalism.

It is important, I think, for me to briefly describe what I mean by the term "human solidarities". When the voyages of Columbus opened a new phase in world history, one central problem which faced Western legal and religious thought was "Were the native Americans humans like the Spaniards, and what was the dividing line between this human population group, nature and animal life?" Central to Spanish and European conceptions at the time was Aristotle's view about various degrees of human and the idea that some were marked from birth to serve and others to rule. We know that for the Spanish colonial power the matter was finally resolved in the Las Casas–Sepulveda debate, in which the latter won the argument: the native American population was not rational and therefore human; they did not have Christian faith and private property; and therefore were not entitled to rights and their lands could be seized and be made Spanish possessions.

What is the point here? First, it is to note that this colonial encounter was integral to the inauguration of modernity. In this encounter there was the "discovery" of human difference, which was rapidly adapted and made hierarchical. In other words, at one of the moments that inaugurates modernity there was a concrete historical response to the encounter with a so-called "other." I wish to argue that this colonial encounter was generative, shaping Western preoccupations with the other, and has been one element of an overarching power.[2] Let us not forget that this power was, until the middle of the last century, the most formidable power on the planet. To make the point further, Hannah Arendt argues that "human distinctness is not the same as otherness" (Arendt 1958, p. 176). It is through a plurality of human ways of life that we express this distinctiveness. When we begin to conceptualize humans as others, rather than as distinctiveness, we open to door to making difference hierarchal. Second, the self is an embodied self; it is always a self within the world. And the world is a social one constructed through multiple relations. What this means is that when we encounter each other we do so both as part of a world but also as embodied beings with histories. What I am arguing here are two things: first, that difference recast as hierarchy haunts any discussion about self and other and, second, that one possible alternative is a conception of an other not as "other" but as *another*. In other words, two different logics operate. One reaches for separation and distance whereas the second logic of *another* reaches for embrace and touch, recognizing immediately the human in the form of another. It is this acknowledgment of another that I am calling "human solidarities."

During the early twentieth century the notion of human solidarity as a basis for rights emerged and was advocated by radical black diasporic intellectuals and activists. As a current within radical anti-colonial political thought, this notion was subsequently ignored by reformist anti-colonial nationalists in their drive to create nation-states. In making this reformist move, anti-colonialism narrowed the anti-colonial moment to primarily one of political equality. The idea of human solidarities emerged again during the late 1960s in a series of Tricontinental conferences held in Cuba, and was an integral dimension of what became known as the Bandung Moment and subsequently shaped the political thinking of the Non-aligned movement (NAM) in world politics. During the 1970s the conception was to appear again in the international dimensions of the political thought of Michael Manley and Julius Nyerere and their advocacy of the New International Economic Order and a politics of international equality. This notion of international equality extended the boundaries of liberal procedural equality because of its preoccupations with concerns of global justice.

In this chapter I trace the emergence of the idea of human solidarity in early twentieth century anti-colonial thought by examining the ideas of a black diasporic group that operated in London in the late 1930s, the International African Service Bureau (IASB). I will also briefly examine the Bandung Moment alongside a review of some elements of the political thought of Michael Manley and Julius Nyerere. In conducting these reviews I will in part be describing a genealogy of radical/reformist Third World thinking which highlights questions of the human, equality, and of social and distributive justice.

Early twentieth-century anti-colonial thought: the International African Service Bureau

There were many streams of early twentieth-century anti-colonial thought.[3] In 1937, London became the venue for a group of anti-colonial radicals including George Padmore, C.L.R. James, Amy Ashwood Garvey, Wallace Johnson, Jomo Kenyatta, and Ras Makonnen, who organized themselves into the International African Service Bureau (IASB).[4] Describing the work of the Bureau, Padmore noted that it was a "non-party organization . . . which owed no affiliation or allegiance to any political party, organization or group in Europe" (Padmore 1972, p. 125). The IASB quickly developed into a dynamic organization, becoming by 1938 one of the most active anti-colonial organizations in London, and for several months published the journal *The International African Opinion* (*IAO*). As a radical anti-colonial journal, the *IAO* editorial outlook was, of course, firmly rooted in anti-colonial politics. The journal demanded the ending of colonialism in Africa, the Caribbean, China, and India. Its pages focused on the different ways in which colonial powers practiced racial domination. The *IAO* reflected the outlook of the IASB as a black diasporic group whose gaze was firmly fixed always on the totality of the black world. The diasporic orientation of the IASB created the ground for both the group and journal to eschew any formal national allegiance. This fact allowed the politics of the IASB to escape the nation-state model of anti-colonial nationalism, thus making possible the emergence of an *anti-colonial internationalism* and the formulation of a position regarding rights based on a framework which Fanon would call, "a world of reciprocal recognitions" (Fanon 1967, p. 218). This world of "reciprocal recognitions" is what I wish to call human solidarities. I am suggesting that from the perspective of the ISAB a perspective rooted in a framework of common oppression made it possible for the group to develop a radical politics of human solidarity.

From the very first edition of the journal, the IASB made it clear that, although it was anti-colonial, preoccupied with both Africa and the African diaspora, its concerns were intimately linked to questions of internationalism. There were two aspects to the ISAB's internationalism. In the first instance the group paid close attention to all forms of political and social struggles around the globe. The first editorial of the journal proclaimed the group's support of the Spanish Revolution and for "the struggle of the workers everywhere against Fascism." It continued: "We unite ourselves not only in words but in action and shall strive to arouse in our people a consciousness of the *common destiny* of all the oppressed of whatever nationality or race. *International organization* of all forms of struggle is a necessity" (*International African Opinion* 1938, my emphasis). Clearly, for the IASB there was a "common destiny" for humanity. At this point one could perhaps claim that the idea of "common destiny" was shaped by the Marxism of two key individuals in the group, James and Padmore. However, one should recall that by 1938 Padmore had already broken from the Comintern, and although James was a Marxist others in the group were not. Thus, "common destiny" was not the communist telos. Rather, the IASB seems to have conceptualized a world in which colonial oppression was abolished and where all humans could live with secure democratic rights.

So in what political categories did the IASB express its ideas? For the IASB in the 1930s there were two social systems which dominated the world. One was imperial power and the other was "colonial fascism." Colonial fascism meant that conventional liberal rights were abrogated within the colonies. One example used in the *IAO* to develop this political category was the case of a Barbadian worker in the Caribbean sentenced for trying to organize workers, something which was legally possible in the colonial metropole. But there was another sense in which "colonial fascism" was used by the IASB. Hannah Arendt, in her seminal text on totalitarianism, makes it clear that colonialism was linked to and created the grounds for fascism. She writes: "Two new devices for political organization and rule over foreign peoples were discovered during the first decades of imperialism . . . race was discovered in South Africa and bureaucracy in Algeria, Egypt and India" (Arendt 1973, pp. 185–207). Arendt makes the point that these methods of rule then worked their way into the political repertoire of fascism.[5] Central to colonial rule was the establishment of foreign administrations, which required a new ordering of space, race, and the deployment of might/force as a right. It was this deployment of *might as right* which shaped colonial policy.

What the IASB did was to analyze the ways in which colonial power functioned and then to name its operation by linking it to the emergence of fascism in Europe. Consequently, any struggle against colonial power had to pay attention to the struggle against fascism. So, even though, in the view of the IASB, Africans were the "most oppressed and exploited," the journal made the point that "no cause was too big for us to embrace, no opinion too small for us to consider" (*International African Opinion* 1938). One clear indication of this kind of internationalism was the edition of the journal which called upon white workers to act in concert with all colonial subjects. The call proclaimed, "Workers of Britain: Though you have neglected us in the past, today this hour is our common crisis, we want you to know that we blacks bear you no ill will . . . Our freedom is a step towards your freedom . . ." (*International African Opinion* 1939). It would seem that here there are two things worth pointing out. The first is that the call addresses the historic racial relationships between black and white. Recognizing the character of this relationship the call makes a gesture toward reconciliation. However, it does so not out of any tactical necessity but rather on the ground that human freedom was a linked event in which the partial freedom of any one group was a limited freedom for all. The basis of this view was the idea of human solidarity.

The second dimension of the IASB anti-colonial internationalism resided in its preoccupations with the African diaspora. The history of colonial modernity was shaped by colonial conquest and the Atlantic slave trade. Stephanie Smallwood makes the point that that the transformation of "African captives into Atlantic commodities," displaced Africans from their original communities and turned "disappearance" into an absence which would make the slaves think about exile. She writes of the slaves' sense of their own disappearance from their communities this way: "Would the exiles be able to return home . . . would their deaths take place in isolation? Would their spirits wander aimlessly, unable to find their way home to the realm of the ancestors?" (Smallwood 2007, p. 60). The Atlantic slave trade created the African diaspora. Over time this diaspora constructed a complex set of political formations that challenged both racial and colonial power. With the late nineteenth-century colonial conquest of Africa, the relationship between Africa and its diaspora took on a different quality. The ex-slaves in the Americas could no longer think of themselves and their relationship to Africa without reference to colonialism. Consequently, over time the political idea emerged that African American freedom was linked to African political independence. The situation was similar in the Caribbean after the 1838 emancipation of slaves even though British colonial power continued.

At the beginning of the twentieth century the most significant manifestation of black diasporic politics was Marcus Garvey's Universal Negro Improvement Association (UNIA), formed in 1914. An international organization with chapters in thirty-eight American states and forty-one countries all over the world, the

UNIA developed an international political platform against colonial domination in Africa and the Caribbean and racial oppression in the United States.[6] At its peak the UNIA was one of the most important international political organizations of the period. By 1937, the organization was in decline, but its formidable presence had consolidated the political ground for black radicals to think about forms of black internationalism. It is within this context that we should understand the political perspective of the IASB and how it attempted to practice a politics which placed Africa, the United States, and the Caribbean into a complex relationship within a framework of a global politics of radical anti-colonial internationalism.

At the core of this relationship was something distinct from the ideas other currents in black diasporic politics had promulgated, particularly with reference to Africa. The IASB accepted that Afro-Caribbeans and African Americans were New World populations. What linked them to Africa was not their status of historic exile due to Atlantic slavery but the contemporary fact of their oppression, an oppression that was central to the global colonial system. Hence, in discussing colonialism and racism ,the *IAO* always made it clear that African freedom and the end of racial domination were linked first to the self-activities of Africans and black people and second to other struggles for freedom. All this was clear whether the journal was discussing fascism, the development of the colonial ideas of protectorates, or the various British commissions of the 1930s which investigated riots in some of the colonies.

There was, as well, another feature of the politics of the IASB which is noteworthy. Although standing squarely behind an anti-colonial politics of self-determination, not once in the several issues of the *IAO* did the group argue for the specific independence of any one colony. On the contrary, the journal in its news gathering printed all its stories about the colonial world under the general rubric "African World." It then separated these stories from news about African Americans, which went into columns titled "American Notes." These moves suggested that with reference to the colonial problem the politics of the IASB desired to place colonial issues within the frame of African problems while singling out African Americans for a different treatment.[7] The lack of any political call for the national independence of any single African or Caribbean colony was indicative of the IASB's political view that the anti-colonial struggle was an international one. From its analysis that colonialism was a global system of power, the political formulations of the IASB negated any gestures toward modular nationalism.

Partha Chatterjee divides anti-colonial nationalism into three different moments. In the third moment, "the moment of arrival," Chatterjee (1986, p. 51) argues that "nationalism is now a discourse of order, of the rational organization of power . . . conducted in a single, consistent unambiguous voice . . . glossing over all the earlier contradictions." Although capturing very well the trajectory of anti-colonial nationalism, what is missing from this exemplary account is the internationalist dimension of radical anti-colonial nationalism. This internationalist aspect, I would argue, was one way in which radical anti-colonial thought would distinguish itself from anti-colonial politics that simply mimicked nationalism. All this makes it impossible to describe anti-colonial nationalism as a homogeneous block of ideas. There was not one anti-colonial nationalism but several, each drawing from distinctive discursive and political contexts. In the case of the IASB it was clear that its anti-colonialism was a form of internationalism. This meant that the IASB overturned the Westphalia model of state relationships, a model of sovereignty that did not take into account the status of the colonial country and their populations.

As we have noted before, colonial empires created a global polity in many ways. The specific differences between different colonial powers, although important by themselves, were not in the view of the IASB pivotal to the world political system. With regards to rights, the IASB did not follow Marx's critique that rights were nothing more than bourgeois claims. Marx had suggested that from the French Revolution rights were about the separation of man from man, and that the rights of citizenship formalized this separation. In one sense Marx's critique has a ring of truth to it, in part because when citizenship is constituted as the sole repository of rights it excludes humans who are not citizens of a specific state from these rights. In this way citizenship, instead of being secondary to the human, trumps the human. The IASB critique of colonialism was based on the ways in which colonial power made *might right* – the ways in which colonial power negated rights and constructed human beings as "natives." Siba Grovogui has made the point that "from the 17th century onward, each hegemon and its inspired coalitions have prescribed standards of behavior for each region in conjunction with their power differentials" (Grovogui 2002, p. 323). Not only were citizenship rights negated within the colonies where might ruled but there was an expected set of behaviors from the so called "native." For the European the colony was a site of disorder and negativity; it produced great wealth but within the Western mind it was both spatially and figuratively out of bounds even when it was a "contact zone."

The politics of the IASB attempted to overturn this by constructing the colony not only as integral to the global nature of the colonial project, but by constructing the colony and the "native" as a human figure. Granted, this human was an oppressed subject and the argument can be made that the ISAB was simply substituting the colonial "native" for Marx's proletariat. But the central difference in the discursive core of racial and colonial power was the creation of populations which were classified as non-human.[8] Thus, the radical political act of constructing the "native" and the "black" into human figures had to be foundational to the politics of the IASB. Making solidarity the ground for radical anti-colonial politics was therefore more than a gesture of good radical politics – it was the ground for creating a new order based not on conventional political solidarity but on the search for *human solidarities*. This was a different political trajectory than the one proposed by many in the Marxist movement.

By the 1940s and 1950s James and Padmore in their different ways elaborated this view. For Padmore, as he moved into the direction of an explicit pan-Africanism, his internationalism became focused on the political independence of Africa. In 1945, he, along with Kwame Nkrumah and others, hosted the fifth Pan-African Congress in Manchester. This conference was a marker in the struggles for

Africa's political independence and represented some distinct shifts in Padmore's political thought. One of these shifts was his move to declare self-determination for all colonies within the framework of the nation-state as the "first step towards and the necessary prerequisite to, complete social, economic and political emancipation" (Langley 1979, p. 760). However, this shift seems to have been a tactical one, because once Ghana gained political independence in 1957, and he went to live there, both he and Nkrumah quickly began to organize a series of conferences with a larger agenda directed at the independence of other African colonies; the development of economic regional blocs; and the formal coordination of foreign policy for the newly independent states. All these policies were viewed in pragmatic terms as eventually leading to continental African political unity.

On the other hand, C.L.R. James visited the Unites States in 1938 and remained there for fifteen years. During this time he became a major independent Marxist theoretician developing a small Marxist current, the Johnson–Forrest Tendency. By the 1950s he had developed a complex array of political positions about American society and civilization, cultural and literary criticism, and of course international politics. At the core of these positions was James's belief in the capacity of ordinary people to operate a modern economy, to govern themselves, and to construct "the good life."[9] In his analysis of world politics, James argued that the national state had failed and was not viable. With regards to the "good life" he argued that the critical element was "the individual relationship to the society" (James 1973, p. 105). If Padmore had by 1950s become more preoccupied with the concrete elaboration of pan-Africanism, James had become focused on international revolution and was working through a Marxist theory of politics which attempted to shift the coordinates of Marxism.

We have discussed briefly some aspects of these two figures' political ideas and trajectories because it is important to grasp that anti-colonial politics was not homogeneous and can be grasped only through an understanding of specific moments. In the late 1930s, when radical black diasporic politics merged with anti-colonialism, there was a distinctive kind of anti-colonial internationalism. This moment did not last but left traces which were later picked up. The main difference which shaped the next moment of twentieth-century anti-colonial internationalism was the fact that individual colonies achieved their political independence. This independence was achieved within the international context of a growing cold war climate and a sentiment among many of the newly independent nations that, although they had achieved political independence, as nation-states they faced enormous obstacles to economic independence and development. It is within this context that the Bandung Conference emerged.

The second moment: Bandung and non-alignment

In post-colonial theory the Bandung Moment is viewed as the central moment in anti-colonialism. David Scott, in reflecting on the death of Michael Manley in 1997, notes that the event "signals the end of the historical form of the whole problem of anti-colonial sovereignty in the post-colonial world. This is an historical form of the nation-statehood project problematic [of] the nationalist movements for political independence . . ." (Scott 1998, p. 221). Although one could agree with Scott that anti-colonial sovereignty posed a series of historical problems about the nationalist movements and the nation-state, his formulation creates a smooth political surface for the anti-colonial movement and its political ideas. And, of course, it is of interest to note that Manley's own assessment was that the moment came to end in the 1980s with the apparent victory of neo-liberal politics and economics. However, my interest here is not to argue about endings or periodizations but rather to think about the ways in which the Bandung Moment posited a set of ideas about internationalism, and how these ideas worked their way through the political thought of Michael Manley and Julius Nyerere.

The Bandung Conference, held in April 1955,[10] was, writes Archie Singham, "an Asian–African conference – a turning point in modern world history . . . In an intense week of speeches and committee meetings, Third World leaders shared their similar problems [and talked] about maintaining their independence and opposing colonialism and neo-colonialism, specifically Western domination" (Singham and Hune 1986, p. 65). The conference proposed a new world order based upon fundamental respect for human rights, respect for sovereignty, the recognition of equality for all races, the principle of non-interference in the internal affairs of any nation, the settlement of international disputes by peaceful means, and respect for justice and international obligations. Beginning from the standpoint that the sovereignty achieved from colonial power created a space for a different international political order – one in which no state was oppressed by colonial domination – the Bandung Conference detailed a perspective of inter-state relations in which the newly independent states would not be under the political sway of major powers. Obviously, such a position not only opened the field of play in international relations (IR) but signaled a challenge to an era in which great powers could dictate the contours of global politics.

The Bandung Conference was a precursor to the Non-Aligned Movement (NAM). In 1961, a formal conference was held in Belgrade, which over the next fifteen years opened up a different space in IR. Between 1961 and 1979 the Non-Aligned Movement held six major meetings. At the fourth summit in Algiers two important developments occurred. The first was the centrality given to international economic questions along with open criticism of détente. The political declaration of the conference proclaimed:

> As long as colonial wars, apartheid, imperialist aggression, alien domination, foreign occupation, power politics, economic exploitation and plunder prevail, peace will be limited in principle and scope. In a world where side by side with a minority of rich countries there exists a majority of poor countries. It would be dangerous to accentuate this division by restricting peace to the prosperous areas of the world while the rest of mankind remained condemned to insecurity and the law of the strongest.
>
> (cited in Singham and Hune 1986, p. 127)

This political declaration did many things, but by linking peace to issues of economic justice on a global scale it critiqued the idea that matters of international relationships were composed primarily of diplomacy and politics. In the formulation of the declaration, political action and diplomacy were means to secure ends, and the most important end was that of transnational economic justice.

The second important strand of the NAM was the attention paid to anti-colonial and anti-apartheid struggles. In the 1970s there were two critical areas of anti-colonial struggles: the struggles in the Portuguese colonies of Africa – Angola, Mozambique and Gineau-Bissau, and Cape-Verde (see Chapter 4) – and the struggle against Ian Smith's regime in what was then called Rhodesia. These anti-colonial struggles had been caught up in the matrix of cold war politics and were viewed by the West as pawns in the games of "power politics" and "spheres of influence." Of course, the anti-apartheid struggle in South Africa over time became a singularly central issue in the international politics of the NAM. The fifth summit decided that the system of apartheid was organically linked to that of colonialism in Africa and that the major political struggle lay in ending colonialism and apartheid in the southern African region. The conference was persuaded on this point by African delegations in attendance, many of whom were at the time giving active support to these national liberation movements. By 1979, prior to the seventh conference in Havana, the bureau preparing the meeting held a summit in Maputo, the capital of a now independent Mozambique. At this meeting both the anti-colonial struggles and the anti-apartheid struggle were tied together in an analysis that argued that South Africa was the last bastion of Western power in Africa. This was a point made in the United States and the Caribbean by supporters of the African liberation movement from as early as 1973. The summit noted that apartheid was being given tacit political support by the governments of the United States, France, and Israel. By meeting in Maputo, the NAM concretely demonstrated solidarity with states in the southern African region. The summit meeting made the Patriotic Front of Zimbabwe a member of the movement and established a fund for the South West Africa People's Organization (SWAPO), which at the time was engaged in a struggle against the apartheid regime in South-West Africa (present-day Namibia).

These two actions – the turn toward issues of transnational economic justice and the different political analysis of the southern Africa region – would over the next two years become the centerpieces of non-aligned confrontation with the West. Central to this confrontation were two political figures, Michael Manley and Julius Nyerere.

Manley and Nyerere: the NIEO

Both Manley and Nyerere were shaped politically and intellectually by a variety of political ideas and currents. These included a current of left democratic socialism – a radical form of anti-colonialism in which regional economic cooperation was paramount and necessary to undergird economic independence. Both men's political thought included a deep commitment to equality as the premier political value. Michael Manley became the political leader of Jamaica in 1972, winning a general election under the political slogans "Power for the People" and "Betta mus Come." As the leader of the People's National Party (PNP) he belonged to a political movement formed in 1938 after the major workers rebellion in Jamaica; thereafter the party become the nationalist movement in the country and developed a brand of anti-colonial nationalism which has been called "Creole nationalism."[11] By the time Manley became political leader of the country, the island had been politically independent for a decade. Additionally, Manley came to office within the context of the emergence on the world stage of the Black Power Movement in the late 1960s and other social explosions that rocked many Western powers. As leader he faced the fact that political independence had not transformed the economic and social arrangements in the island. Reflecting on some of the major social features of Jamaica in 1972, when he became prime minister, Manley noted that he would spend the next eight years trying to develop some measure of "social justice for the people" (Manley 1982, p. 8).

Julius Nyerere led the struggle for Tanzanian political independence and was the founder-president of the Tanganyika African Nationalist Union (TANU). A staunch advocate of African regional integration, he gave fervent and consistent material and political support to the southern African liberation movements. A theoretician of African socialism, by the late 1960s Nyerere adumbrated a complex set of political ideas about African society, socialism in Africa, and alternative meanings of development in Africa.[12] Thus, by the time these the two political figures met, the ground had been created for major international collaboration around the issues of southern Africa and transnational economic justice.

The issue of international economic relations, which both faced, merits careful consideration. Manley writes that after 1972 he was increasingly aware of the "negative effect of the international economic system on Third World efforts at development." After a few years in office he became further convinced that "there was no viable future for Jamaica, indeed mankind, outside of a transformation of the old-world economic order" (Manley 1987, p. xii). For his part, Nyerere recognized the centrality of the structures of the world economy and the need for change. He had already argued that colonial power had produced three kinds of inequalities: "between the colonizer and the colonized; between races; and between the rich and the poor" (cited in Bogues 2003, p. 116). By 1970 he had also forcefully stated that the real threat to political independence was "the economic power of the big states [and] poverty which constitutes our greatest danger" (Nyerere 1974a, p. 71).

At the sixth summit of the NAM, Manley and Nyerere delivered a series of speeches designed to push the summit toward developing a concrete international plan of action for the movement. In his speech Manley detailed a plan that proposed south–south economic cooperation as a way for Third World economies to uncouple themselves from their former colonial masters while creating the basis for a general economic strategy essential to solve national unemployment and inflation. Pushed to think and debate economic issues, the conference adopted the general concept of the new international economic order (NIEO). The NIEO became the summary economic platform for Manley's and Nyerere's international political practice. Subsequently, it would lead to the formation of a South Commission, headed by Nyerere, in which detailed economic policies were developed.[13]

The NIEO was first developed by Third World countries working through the United Nations Conference on Trade and Development (UNCTAD). In 1974, it proposed a revision of the Bretton Woods system and in 1979, under pressure from Third World nations, the revision was adopted by the UN General Assembly. This adoption of the NIEO was to designed to accelerate its implementation and create a common platform from which the NAM would enter into economic negotiations with Western powers. Its adoption also showed that many Third World nations were frustrated with the workings of the UN and desired to develop alternative international fora. The proposed NIEO was founded on the following basic principles:

(a) Sovereign equality of States, self-determination of all peoples; (b) the broadest co-operation of all states members of the international community, based on equity, whereby the prevailing disparities in the world may be banished and prosperity secured by all; (c) full and effective participation on the basis of equality of all countries in solving of the world economic problems in the common interest of all countries, bearing in mind the necessity to ensure the accelerated development of all developing countries while devoting particular attention to the adoption of special measures in favour of the least developed, land-locked and island developing countries; (d) the right of all states, territories and peoples under foreign occupation, alien and colonial domination or *apartheid* to restitution and full compensation for the exploitation and depletion of, and damages to, the natural resources; (e) regulation and supervision of the activities of transnational corporations.

(NIEO 1979)

These founding principles of the NIEO were extrapolated from and rested upon two values: equality and justice. The former was the central political value of both Manley and Nyerere. Manley had made it clear from 1972 that although justice was a prime value in human society it could be only attained under the aegis of equality. In his book *The Politics of Change* he made the point that justice is defined as a "form of social organization consciously seeking to regulate the relations between all its members . . . taking into account the equal weight of members claim" (Manley 1990, p. 51). The taking into account of these claims in Manley's thought was predicated upon a commitment to equality and an egalitarian society. For Manley, equality was a value which required the dismantling of any "apparatus of privilege" (Manley 1990, p. 37). And because it was the central political value, it was the foundation of democratic politics. Nyerere evinced a similar position. In an extempore speech given in KiSwahili in 1972 he noted that, "all human beings are equal. This being so we have to accept that the exploitation, the humiliation, the suffering, of all men – wherever it takes place – means the exploitation, humiliation, and the suffering of mankind. All men are reduced by it" (Nyerere 1974b). The value of equality also animated Nyerere's definition of socialism. He declared in 1967 that:

> Socialism . . . is not simply a matter of methods of production. They are part of it but not all of it. The essence of socialism is the practical acceptance of human equality. That is to say, every man's equal right to a decent life before any individual has any surplus above his needs; his equal right to participate in Government; and his equal responsibility to work and contribute to the society to the limit of his ability.
>
> (Nyerere 1968, pp. 324–5)

Both political figures debated at various international forums and planned joint political work which challenged the West, with this value of equality always to the fore.[14] I would also suggest that, at the level of the global polity, the notion of equality did not simply refer to individual state sovereignty but was integrated into a view that sought to address historical injustices. The idea of compensation for colonial conquest and apartheid policies in the NIEO was triggered by an understanding that colonialism was a social, economic, and political system that had devastated lands and nations. This understanding rejected the cost–benefit model analysis of colonial domination, something which is still very current in commentary on Africa.

With regard to the southern African national liberation movements the driving values were also equality, the idea of the interdependence of free persons, and the practice of international politics in which solidarity was the highest principle. In 1967, Nyerere made it clear that, "we [meaning Tanzanians] shall never be really free and secure while some parts of our continent are still enslaved" (cited in Legum and Mmari 1995, p. 164). In practical terms this was a costly principle for both political figures and their nations. In the Tanzanian case, consistent support of the African National Congress and other movements, the creation of a safe haven for refugees, and turning the country into a base for the national liberation movements often resulted in drastic cuts in national budgets.[15] In the Jamaican case, Manley argued that Third World nations should not fall into the trap of "seeing Southern Africa as an isolated phenomenon." Instead, he argued, "we must insist upon the recognition of the global context" (Manley 1977). In 1975, Henry Kissinger asked that Manley not support or at least abstain from a UN General Assembly vote in support of Cuban troops in Angola. Manley notes in the fragments of an unpublished memoir that in January 1976, after full investigation of the matter, and after Jamaica's decision that Cuban troops were necessary to halt the military incursions into Angola of the then apartheid regime, US–Jamaican relations took a turn for the worst. He writes:

> Having advised Kissinger in advance with full explanations . . . [the expected from US] loan did not come through; but the number of operatives attached to the CIA's Kingston station was doubled by February. Simultaneously, a series

of vicious articles about Jamaica and its government began appearing in the *New York Times* By mid-1976 Jamaica had become the target of a text-book destabilization campaign.[16]

What should be clear from this is that the conception of equality for all humans at the level of global polity had consequences for those who struggled to give it practical expression. These consequences are often ignored in discussions and debates about internationalism.

Manley's and Nyerere's conception of equality differed from conventional Western political theory primarily in the following ways. Their conception of equality began from the ground of the procedural conventions of liberal equality but did not end there. The members of a society are equal before the law; they all have political equality; and they have equal access to the different aspects of the society, in particular education. But although liberal equality tends to limit itself to procedural matters and to what one may call basic access, the conception of Manley and Nyerere goes beyond these liberal boundaries.

Of course, there are many streams of liberalism, and of course there is a liberal cosmopolitanism, which makes a defense of individuals without recourse to natural rights. However, as I have argued elsewhere, this idea of cosmopolitanism carries an idea of the "other" that continues to be hierarchically defined and thus continues to be rooted in a subject–other relationship of power (see Bogues 2006). Although Manley's and Nyerere's notion of equality begins with the idea that humans are ends within themselves, they add other elements that make it a complex and substantive concept rather than simple and procedural. Their conception of equality is in the first instance intimately linked to an idea of social justice. So, although it is safe to say that justice is conventionally linked to equality (after all, Aristotle made the point that equality implied two things, one of which was the just), the difficulty, in liberal terms, appears when equality is linked to social justice and distributive justice.

Conclusion

To think about social and distributive justice is to operate at the levels of the social and economic. In other words, it is to broaden the conception of human beings as ends in themselves to include the entire fabric of human life. It is to pay attention to the question of conditions, to the *how* of equality and the conditions for its practices. It is not about the idea of "having," as some theorists have enunciated. Rather, it is about the history, of *how* "having" was constructed. I am not proposing here any idea of moral obligation or "morality in international affairs." Rather, I want to suggest that that we cannot begin to think seriously about international relations or a global polity without the considerations of colonial history.[17] Colonial empires were global entities. They structured the world for over 500 years, creating subjects, new spaces, new "natives," and international inequities. Grovogui reminds us that what is today considered as "Westphalian commonsense" is not just a "normative lack" when it is applied to Africa but that this common sense is held together by "historic power relations" (Grovogui 2002, p. 316).

To put the matter another way: even if we begin from the ground of formal equality because human beings are ends in themselves, the issue becomes "What are the blockages to an equality which is broad and complex?" From the perspective of Manley and Nyerere, the weight of colonial history and the structures of the world economy were huge blockages. Removing them meant developing an idea of equality which was broad enough to challenge the structures of the global economy. For Manley and Nyerere a framework of equality triggered a politics in which questions of justice and inequality required challenging the world order. Thus, they advocated in a moment of the post-colonial period an internationalism and equality of *transnational justice* . . . a justice which is distributive across spatial boundaries. For such a notion to be conceptually operational required a notion of equality based upon a conception of human solidarities across territorial borders.

In the end my argument is simply this: in the 1930s a group of black diasporic radicals developed a political platform which postulated ideas of rights and internationalism operating outside the boundaries of the nation-state. The platform of this group required them to think against the convention that rights are reposed in the logic of national citizenship. Rather, this group thought about rights within the logic of common oppression. In the 1970s, when the global context had changed, another current rooted in the anti-colonial experience emerged and attempted to argue globally that the issues of rights needed to be embedded within a broad notion of equality linked to social justice and economic equality on a global scale. These currents operated at different times, but both in their own ways challenged the West and perhaps opened different spaces for us to think about equality, rights, and internationalism. In both, the notion of the stranger, of the "other," was absent. At the level of the political this was possible because each of the two currents desired an international politics that fully supported, no matter what the consequences were, the ongoing struggles against colonialism and apartheid. All this today has been lost. I do not make a case for retrieval because no past can be fully retrieved – it can only be understood as a sign of possibility, something which may animate our present. In 1998 Nyerere was asked about the contribution of the anti-colonial movement to the history of the twentieth century. His response was this:

> There are two fundamental things that the anti-colonial liberation movement contributed to humanity. The first is simply that the suffering of a whole chunk of human beings through the actions of others was halted. The arrogance of one group of people in lording it over the human race . . . was challenged and discredited . . . that was a positive contribution made by the liberation struggle to all humanity.
>
> (Nyerere 1999)

All the elements of that contribution need to be figured in our thinking about the present.

Notes

1 My thanks go to Geri Augusto, whose critical eye made this a better chapter and to Robbie Shilliam and the readers of this volume for comments.

2 For a discussion of how colonialism shaped and still leaves traces in the contemporary world see Dussel (2008).

3 For a discussion of some of these streams see Dura (2004).

4 C.L.R. James was a Trinidadian political theorist, historian, and literary figure. He is best known as the author of *The Black Jacobins*. George Padmore was in the late 1920s and early 1930s the most important black communist affiliated with the work of the Communist International. He is known as one of the "fathers of African independence." Amy Ashwood Garvey was the first wife of Marcus Garvey and was central to the organizational development of the UNIA. She was an activist in her own right. Jomo Kenyatta became the first president of independent Kenya.

5 This has been confirmed by recent historical work on the question of genocide. See, for example, Dirk Moses and Stone (2007).

6 For discussion of the UNIA and the ideas of Garveyism see Martin (1976) and Lewis (1987). For a full documentary history of the UNIA see the remarkable numerous volumes of Robert Hill (1995).

7 Clear indications of this are the table of contents from the third edition of the journal: "African World, American Notes, Politics and the Negro, Negro Life and Letters." It is interesting that the journal, when it came to book reviews and literature, made no distinction between different geographical sites as it did in the reporting of political items.

8 Aime Césaire (2000, p. 42) had noted in 1956 that the drive of colonial power was what he called "thingification."

9 For a discussion of James political thought see Bogues (1997). For a summary in James's own writings of his political thought see James (1973).

10 For a description of the meeting itself and the various personalities see Wright (1956).

11 For a discussion on the political ideas of Creole nationalism in the PNP see Bogues (2002).

12 A partial listing of some of Nyerere writings would include Nyerere (1966, 1968, 1969).

13 The Commission published a report on the international economy as late as 1990.

14 Author's interview with Michael Manley, April 1995.

15 The idea that "refugees" were second class and should not be treated as citizens was anathema to Tanzania at the time. This is an important point to note.

16 Fragments of unpublished memoirs of Michael Manley in the author's possession.

Part IV

Reflections

13 Untimely reflections

Mustapha Kamal Pasha

One of the more stubborn features of Western international relations (IR) is its refusal to embrace its own peculiarity. This refusal, however, is not as simple it seems. On an initial reading, it allows a *particular* intellectual practice with *particular* imaginaries and rationalities to serve as a universal reference for *all* IR theoretical practices with alternative imaginaries and rationalities. The distinctiveness of difference emerges against the image of this universal reference. Negation of its own peculiarity creates a general narrative in which other particularities can be effectively subsumed or discarded. In this manner, a naturalized meta-narrative is also deployed to manage internal dissent. The latter is typically assumed as a form of domestic squabble ready for arbitration under established disciplinary rules. In extreme cases, however, naughty dissenters who refuse to be co-opted are given the option of exile to the borderlands of the discipline, stripped of effective power, but with the right of protest. For both domestic exile and erasure of 'foreign' elements, the boundaries are vigorously defended with strict enforcement mechanisms to determine what does or does not constitute IR. Epistemology and methodology provide the gatekeeping function to place questions of ontology or history on the margins. In other cases, a particular classification of the *international* becomes the determining factor to grant entry or rejection.

The refusal to acknowledge its self-particularity rests on historicism – stories of origins, tribulations and triumphs woven into a journey of ascent. Another name given to this journey is the civilizing process, a two-part affair involving internal pacification of barbarism and a more expansive, albeit unfinished, worldwide *mission civilisatrice*. The key to this process is the unfurling of modernity, originating in the West and, through its midwifery, extended elsewhere. That elsewhere – a non-place – is the non-West, separated in time and space from the West, never fully coming into its own to be anything except the West's shadow. Having authored its own past in which the time of modernity is readily dissolved into its own, the West can authorize the non-West as an outside, distant in time or place; it occupies another time–place (Fabian 1983). Paradoxically, however, it is only in reference to this non time–place that the West can realize its own distinctiveness. The refusal to acknowledge its own peculiarity speedily metamorphoses into cultural uniqueness, but a uniqueness contingent upon a coerced dialogue with the non-West. This ambivalent engagement *both* denies and acknowledges the non-West, concurrently repelled and necessitated by its existence.

Although Western exceptionalism rests on historicism, it also relies on histori- cal erasure, both of its own genealogy and genealogies of others. The non-West enters the fray only to confirm the legitimacy of its own death or marginaliza- tion and its attendant histories and imaginaries. Hence, the non-West can be present only as absence. Spectres of this absence, nonetheless, haunt IR as *the* congealed history of the non-West's erasure. Once the non-West reappears either to authenticate the legitimacy or universality of the West and its projects or as the consequence of Western munificence, it often takes the form of anthropologi- cal curiosity or nominal tolerance of difference without co-evalness. The terms of incorporation into history or *modern* time and space are not the fruition of negotiation, dialogue or exchange, but prefabricated. The universal reference is already available as Western modularity.

The knotted and complex legacy of erasure is difficult to unfasten. The greater the urge to recover the repressed past, the greater the risk of relativization. Recovery buttresses alterity, naturalizing Western IR *as* IR. Non-Western thought can attain presence only by conceding its alterity or by surrendering its distinc- tiveness. In either case, the non-West is not permitted to generate narratives of universality; its primary function is reduced to confirming or falsifying specula- tions in Western theory, as a limitless reservoir of data production to illuminate the validity of Western thought or as a living mirror of the (pre-modern) past.

Naturalization of Western IR *as* IR, however, is neither a wholesale product of hubris nor conceit nor neglect; it is embedded in the imbrications of theory in the world. It is also made opaque by the uneven character of a global cultural economy premised on established modalities of valorization, institutional power and habitus. As a particular form of cultural (and political) practice, IR theory helps shape the world, but is also shaped by it. Similarly, the horizon of alterna- tives is also conditioned.

This backdrop presents a useful source to better appreciate alternatives to assimilation or erasure sought by Robbie Shilliam and other contributors to this volume. Shunning the conventional strategy of compiling yet another anthology of alterity focused on representing different non-Western cultural zones with distinct styles of imagining IR, *Non-Western Thought* seeks to reconstruct the historical ledger of modernity, one that shifts intellectual scrutiny away from the West to the world, from exclusivity to inclusiveness, from Western self-subsist- ence to relationality, from imitation to hybridity, from subordination to autonomy. Recognizing the absence or under-representation of sustained engagement with non-Western thought in the canon on any of the major debates of our times, *Non-Western Thought* challenges the received current. Latent to this enterprise is a desire to offer the lineaments of a non-Western IR., but also a repudiation of standard mappings of the canon in which other geo-cultural sites can be merely represented (Acharya and Buzan 2007). The task here, it seems, is not additive but reconstructive.

On an apparently unconventional strategy, the addition of other sites and cul- tural zones would provide a more comprehensive, more representative, portrait of

IR in a globalizing setting (Tickner and Waever 2009). A larger cultural sample of an IR *conditioned* by its Western patrimony can be offered as a viable alternative. Conversely, the 'pre-theoretical' (Acharya and Buzan 2007, p. 427) can be given greater audibility. The sensitive task of recovering subaltern histories, multiple subjectivities and the mutual constitution of the West and non-West, however, would remain. *Non-Western Thought* seeks to address this vital problematic.

Throughout the various moments of this undertaking the contributors appear to deploy 'strategic essentialism' (Spivak 1993) to the category of the non-West, a self-conscious strategy to recognize the ambivalence, but also a political dimension, attached to this label. The 'non-West' is not an immutable, but disruptive, category; it refutes the self-subsistent character of Western IR, but, more crucially, it gives voice to silence. Buried in the hegemonic account of IR is the tortured history of erasure and silence of extra-European worlds. This silence allows Western IR to disown the 'entangled histories' of the production of global modernity. The 'savage' non-West is the other side of world history (Trouillot 1995; Blaney and Inayatullah 2010).

The context of rediscovery and excavation is provided both by the provincial character of Western IR, its unwillingness to examine non-Western political imaginaries and their historical construction, and by the objective positionality of subordination that renders alternative voices illegitimate or woefully inadequate (or 'pre-theoretical' as Acharya and Buzan suggest). A twin peril, in turn, accompanies acts of retrieval: the potential to exoticize the non-West or to grant it self-sufficiency (always assumed for Western IR) it may not entirely possess. Exoticization is another form of delegitimation afforded by Orientalist reductionism (Said 1994); the non-West can only appear mysterious and unusual, in possession of 'fixity' (Bhabha 1983) outside of time and history. The assumption of the non-West's apparent self-sufficiency rests on the fiction of its splendid isolation before contact with (Western) modernity. Exoticization empties non-Western thought of any meaningful content, imputing a non-Western rationality to it. This sheltered image consigns non-Western thought to the realm of sheer curiosity, to be interrogated by modernity but not allowed to interrogate modernity. A crucial aspect of the non-West's epistemological subordination is the production of two separate worlds in the non-West: the material and the spiritual. The West colonizes the former, but the latter remains largely untouched. Colonialism operates in the world of materiality, leaving the spiritual world unscathed (Chatterjee 1991). The non-West can seek its own salvation only in the realm of spirituality.

This twin peril of retrieval can be resisted, first by repudiating the notion of temporal distancing, but also by redrawing the cartography of origins. The assumption that non-Western thought is contemporaneous and entangled in the global history of modernity challenges the *reactive* nature of non-Western thought. There is, no doubt, a reactive aspect to engagements with the problematic of modernity, but that is equally true for the West. The challenge of modernity is universal, notwithstanding the idiom it elects in historical time. Similarly, the condition of modernity produces particular rationalities of engagement, including translation, hybridity or Creolization. The quest for pristine cultures untouched by modernity in the non-West can be abandoned in favour of recognition of greater heterodoxy and cross-contamination. The principal task of retrieval, above all, is an acknowledgement of the *specificity* of projects arising within alternative spaces and particularities these projects imbibe. This is possible only with an 'an *explicit* and *sustained* critical engagement with non-Western thought on modernity and its importance to the subject and theories of IR', one of the main aims of the volume.

Implicit in the promise of *Non-Western Thought* are the contours of several key spaces of enacting non-Western IR. These untimely reflections in this chapter – coming as a postscript to a wide-ranging project, but also at the supposed twilight of Third World consciousness – seek to extrapolate some of the principal vectors of an IR resistant to exoticization and other forms of alterity. Standing at the margins, these fragmentary notes do not provision a ready summary or review of the various contributions. The modest aim here is to synthesize and highlight key themes that can prolong the conversation on the possibility of a non-Western IR. The untimely nature of these reflections is also intensified by the awareness that, in globalizing times, it seems quite unfashionable to speak about the 'non-West', unless, of course, the term is used literally to designate geographical regions within an established cartography of Western IR (Acharya and Buzan 2007; Tickner and Waever 2009). Nonetheless, the compulsions of fashion or normalization must be resisted. One form of resistance is to recover the intellectual counterpart to a Bandung spirit buried under the dead weight of Eurocentrism. The themes considered in the remaining pages of this chapter may, perhaps, offer a sketch of the shape and salience of such resistance. To be certain, resistance connotes the active strategy of presenting a critical challenge not so much to Western IR, which it may, but to the recolonization of the non-West under the sign either of globalization or of the expansion of hegemonic theory to the periphery of the international system. The latter is reasonably discernible in building 'the IR tradition' in other geo-cultural sites in lieu of recognition of other imaginaries of the world order.

First, consideration of 'global modernity' as a heuristic to transcend the limits of Western IR presents more fruitful avenues. Implicitly, this pathway can also overcome the restrictions of the notion of 'alternative modernities', one that carries the traces of relativism. Central to 'global modernity' is the idea of co-constitution of modernity. Conjoining imperial and colonial histories avoids the self-justifying Westcentric narrative of the rise of the modern world or the 'expansion of international society', with the non-West perpetually reduced to the role of latecomer, bystander or consumer of modernity. The frame of 'global modernity' also disrupts the assumption of monadic development of different cultural zones. Specifically, the entanglement of imperial and colonial histories produces a world of immanence that implicates, albeit unevenly, the West and the non-West in the shaping of the world order. A critical implication of this strategy is to conjoin the storyline of *sovereignty* with that of *colonialism and imperialism* to provide a fuller picture of the international.

Western IR occludes colonial and imperial formations in place of Westphalian sovereignty as the vital core of IR theory. On this view, the *international* emerges within the endogenous confines of Europe, seeking worldwide expansion over time. Unstated in the account is the dialect of violence and order; processes of colonization and cultural erasure; or domination and resistance. *Non-Western Thought* heightens the necessity of re-inscribing the inextricable nexus between imperial and colonial history *in rethinking IR* and *rethinking about IR*. The ontological primacy of imperial domination/colonial subordination in the making of modern subjectivity cannot be overstated. Coloniality radically alters the way modern sovereignty is conceived. This strategy also helps account for the recognizable presence of non-Western actors in IR, but *not* non-Western thought. Non-Western subjects materialize as objects in IR; non-Western subjectivities can only remain invisible or mute. Coloniality offers a clue to understanding this paradox.

The condition of coloniality dislocates the seamless teleology of the rise of the West to which Western IR subscribes. It is also attentive to the 'construction of colonial/imperial epistemology' which produces the category of 'non-Western thought'. Coloniality furnishes the source to undo Western (or non-Western) exceptionalism. It allows the possibility to see the rise of European colonial empires as the 'inaugural moment' of modernity. The present global order is neither the fulfilment of (Kantian) providence nor 'the expansion of international society'. Rather, it emerges out of 'articulations of the *relationality* of entities' enabled by the colonial condition. Against the recognition of coloniality, the temporal divide between a 'modern' West and the 'pre-modern' rest succumbs to the force of diachronic equivalence. It equally dislodges the legitimacy of teleological models premised on the fictive disjuncture between modernity and colonialism. Diachronic equivalence allows recognition of multiple subjectivities without invoking notions of a 'time lag' (Ayoob 1995) between the West and the non-West. The latter assigns a perpetual place of marginality to the non-Western world.

Beneath the putative rise of the West lie processes of primitive accumulation, the slave trade and the construction of plantation systems in the Americas, development of world commerce under the aegis of European powers, and the 'darker side of the Renaissance' (Mignolo 1995). These processes yield the modern world and its projects. Coloniality aids the task of provincializing the 'Western experience of modernity'. Instead, the 'global' experience of modernity overrides the easy equation between the West and universality. To that end, the acknowledgement that 'the global' rather than European or Western context within which knowledge of modernity has been developed is essential. In that context, the 'local' encounter with universalizing discourses is fundamental to the production of a *distinctive* register of non-Western thought. The colonial enterprise rests often on an unreflexive deployment of force, but it is usually rationalized in claims of civilization, progress or humanity. Rival empires, in turn, have offered different pathways to fulfilling the civilizing mission. Colonization and self-colonization were inextricably connected; in the latter instance, non-Western societies measured themselves against a mobile European 'standard of civilization' and found themselves lacking. In turn, intellectuals in the colonial and post-colonial world have been alert to resisting the 'conflation between the materiality of modernization with modernity'. Distinction between the two tends to subvert the reducibility of human worth to material accoutrements, shifting the focus to the wider world of meaning-generating cosmologies that feed into life-worlds. This avenue does not privilege 'spirituality' over 'materiality', but allows better appreciation of the situatedness of life-worlds, their histories and aspirations.

A key precondition for a critical non-Western IR is recognition of the onto-logical primacy of 'global modernity' in any alternative (re)mapping. It has the important effect of placing the international as *the* condition for IR theory. It also provides the particular context for the instantiation of a distinctive non-Western IR. Unlike the Eurocentric Westphalian narrative of origins and the assumed flowering of IR within a geographically narcissistic post-Reformation Europe, non-Western IR is attentive to context produced by imperial and colonial relation-ality. In essence, the ontology of non-Western IR is neither the nation-state nor the Westphalian system, but the experience of coloniality and the formation of global modernity. The latter provides the ground for creative agency. Unsurprisingly, the supposed 'pre-theoretical', and markedly political, languages of its articulation resist normative and epistemological domestication. On this view, the question 'Why is there no non-Western IR?' exposes its essential import. The key point, nonetheless, is the intertwinement of non-Western IR with the West, the appre-ciation of relationality competing for a highly overdue scrutiny with monotonic regurgitations of the myth of Westphalia.

As *Non-Western Thought* shows, non-Western discourses bearing upon the international have been characteristically framed in the universal language of justice, equality and fairness, emphasizing the unavoidable legacy of the colonial past, including the formation and consolidation of a unified, but unequal, world. Implicit in these discourses, however, is recognition of cultural distinctiveness, of forms of life and the legitimacy of alternative life projects. Recognition of distinctiveness can help overcome hierarchical classificatory schemes. Different conceptions of humanity, solidarity or cosmopolitanism dislodge the self-certainty of hegemonic constructs. Western political theory takes solace in the supposi-tion that its products have universal validity. Remarkable in this assurance is the absence of a substantive recognition of the nexus between power and claims to universality. The hegemonic narrative tends to explain the rise of Western power in terms of the latter. This is the essence of imperial reason.

On closer scrutiny, the normative content in Western discourses conceals the *effects* of political struggles, including alternative stories of erasures, exclusions and silences. Western claims to universality are contested not because of their strangeness, but because of their disguise; they effectively seek to conceal the dynamics of the will to power (Nandy 1993). The terrain of global modernity allows non-Western discourses to give audibility to historical silence. Inescapably, for every universal claim originating in the province of Europe, there are rejoin-ders coming from the extra-European world. Yet, these rejoinders carry the awareness of *differential* power relations and subject positions. This is effectively demonstrated in virtually all the contributions to this volume. The world in which non-Western thought arises is not the world of its own choosing, but its protago-nists strive to make their own history, to reshape and transform this world. Hence, non-Western IR refutes the false dichotomy between normative commitments and understanding. This privileged dichotomy is possible in a world of hegemony, but also necessary for hegemonic IR to promote the fiction of its universality. Ethical neutrality disguises the political settlements already fully entrenched in knowledge systems. Above all, it conceals the underside of the so-called 'civilizing process'.

The enticement to read contemporary non-Western accounts of ethics through comparative political theory or philosophy, with an emphasis on 'functional equivalence', can also reproduce the hegemony of Western thought. This may not be readily apparent as it tends to stress cultural empathy. The search for familiarity often comes at the price of denying originality or creative agency to difference. In turn, alternative mappings of sovereignty, political order or obligation can be lifted out of their embedded cultural contexts to appear similar. The homogenizing effect latent in comparison overrides recognition of *difference as difference*. Comparisons cannot hide their extraordinary quality to patronize or to condescend. Similarly, a call for recognizing 'alternative' or 'multiple' modernities in lieu of a singular Western transcript fails to provincialize Europe or the West. Rather, the structuration of global modernity offers a more fruitful avenue of engagement. The former remains committed to Eurocentric assumptions on the character of modernity, including presuppositions concerning the nature of society, institutional structures, ideational practices and conduct. The appearance of like features in other geo-cultural settings rationalizes the image of 'alternative' or 'multiple' modernities. However, the original template of modernity remains the European West. Implicit in the quest for 'functional equivalence' is also the unacknowledged presence of a time lag to which the non-West must remain perpetually chained. The template of 'global modernity' presupposes co-constitution.

Non-Western discourses transmit distinctive vernaculars centred on questions of identity and recognition which makes them appear as discordant with the meta-narrative of Western IR. Yet, it is through these vernaculars that the nominal universality of Western Enlightenment – the source of inspiration and legitimacy for Western IR – is challenged. These vernaculars mark the existential reality of non-Western cultural zones. However, it is misleading to divorce either existence or idiom from the global modern, and therefore, the universal. The latter can be expressed only through vernaculars if it seeks to retain concreteness. At the core of non-Western thought lays dialogue, either muted or audible, with the universal promise of modernity. On this take, non-Western thought is intrinsically *modern*, whether bearing the idiom of authenticity, difference, hybridity or convergence. All expressions materialize their content in relation to the processes marking the global modern.

The international context of non-Western thought refutes the assumption of cultural narcissism. Despite the choice of idiom, non-Western thought emerges through chains of relationalities with the global modern. Specifically, in its interrogations of the world to which it belongs, it draws from a variety of metropolitan and peripheral sites. It also borrows from a multiplicity of pasts, avoiding the isomorphic linkage between a singular 'national essence' and common culture.

Indeed, contestations over different interpretations of the past resist the temptation to write *national* IRs, promising a more inclusive enterprise positioned against the limiting horizon of Western IR (Acharya and Buzan 2007; Tickner and Waever 2009). To retain its *international* character, therefore, non-Western IR must avoid submission to the desire to discover an exportable *national* imaginary in different geo-cultural sites. This sentiment does not, however, sanction a decontexualized, or even deterritorialized IR, but a caution against producing inventories of culturally narcissistic IRs. The terrain of the international cannot be abandoned, nor can the prospect of cultural synthesis.

Both translation and travel provide vehicles of cultural synthesis. Taken 'as a generative act of knowledge production', translation is not mere imitation, but an active strategy to transform. Travel, on the other hand, stresses a cosmopolitan tendency to embrace the world. Hence, one of the distinctive features of non-Western thought is its willingness to overcome cultural entrapment, an openness to borrow from multiple geo-cultural zones, and transform. For all its universal artifice, hegemonic IR can scarcely undo cultural narcissism. Its general failure to recognize difference is linked to this important facet.

Second, a more emancipatory IR requires an explicit acknowledgement of the limited and limiting field of Western subjectivity. Post-Westphalian IR takes the 'impersonalized, desacralized and individualized' subject as the ideal type of modern subjectivity. This image assumes the secularization of religion, counteracting the alternative hypothesis of secularism itself as a religious construct. The narrow frame of secularity evades the presence of religious currents within modernity, Western or non-Western. It also stresses the visible instantiations of religiosity above its latent presence in the formation and materialization of modern subjecthood. Finally, it presents a singular pathway for the realization of modern subjecthood. The colonial context mitigates against singularity, but especially against the removal of 'embodied, communal and sacral subjectivities' from social consciousness. Rather, struggles to resist the advance of the ideal–typical modern subject infuse the processes of the formation of emancipatory projects in the colonial world. Subjectivities that emerge in these struggles are not anti- or pre-modern, but *modern*, ensconced within global, *not* Western, modernity. To be certain, non-Western intellectuals face global modernity in multiple contexts under various guises. No a priori claims are available to comprehend the colonial encounter. Neither mimicry (barring its innovative deployment) nor repulsion presents an adequate image of this encounter. However, the imperial and colonial setting is inescapable. In virtually all historical instances examined in this volume, this context releases creative agency. Hence, what can make non-Western IR distinctive is the commonality underwriting global modernity as much as the proposal that 'non-Western thought is constitutive of global thought on modernity'. Western IR has elected to efface the relation non-West bears to IR, but it is also a spectre, as noted, that refuses to disappear.

A third space of enactment for non-Western IR is the recognition of violence and the brutal mobilization of military and political power throughout the colonial encounter, which is also the formative process of global modernity.

The cartography of the modern world is inexplicable without this recognition. Non-Western thought carries the burdens of a Manichean colonial world (Fanon 1968), engages with that world, and seeks to overcome its traumas. Notions of autonomy, political freedom and citizenship carry the weight of this living legacy. Subordination, inferiority and the desire for imitation are also a part of this bequest. At the heart of non-Western thought lie the struggle over sovereignty and different meanings attached to its historical inscription. The present world order appears to fulfil a singular (Westphalian) destiny. However, there are also competing notions and imaginaries of aligning territory and identity. Recognition of the historical forms shaping the spatial construction of the modern world can provide access to multiple notions of modern subjecthood.

The appreciation of multiple modern forms of sovereignty can ill-afford circumventing recognition of heterodox notions of sovereignty antecedent to the colonial encounter, but drastically shaped by it. Alternative notions of government, rule of law or democracy continue to provide inspiration for seeking post-Westphalian settlement either through the medium of religiously-textured 'national projects' or post-national constellations. The difficulties faced by Western IR in deciphering the subjective worlds of the non-West in part arise from its failure to appreciate the historical sources of alternative notions of political agency. Predictably, the gaze of Western modernity intercedes to offer comfort through temporal distancing or exoticization.

The spectre of the non-West in Western IR shares affinity with other spectres *within* the canon and its social world. The reigning logic of IR has resisted grasping 'its internal tensions' produced by the ontological, if ambivalent, presence of domestic others. These tensions are visible in multiple forms of entanglement between secularization and modernity, but especially pronounced in the undecidable presence of dissidence over the question of the making of modern subjecthood. They are equally discernible in debates over the character of the colonial enterprise and its domestication of 'natives' with particular reference to the confining choice of slavery or salvation. The Western canon, therefore, does not display linear progression; it is confounded by traces and memories of many inclusions and exclusions. These traces condition notions of sovereignty and power or citizenship and political obligation. Non-Western IR cannot escape interrogation of fault lines within the received canon. This is the fourth space of enactment. Non-Western IR can be meaningful only if it engages with the recessive parts of Western IR. The mixed genealogy of 'hegemonic' IR can expose its claim to universality.

The avoidance of a strictly 'internal gaze upon Western history', therefore, must be accompanied by recognition of other narratives within that history, those voices that have been suppressed. There are multiple 'Wests' (Nandy 1993) occluded in any homogenized account of hegemonic IR. Suppressed or silenced histories also provide a window to capture the effects of empire and colonialism on the metropolis, especially on subaltern metropolitans (Nandy 1988): those seeking alternatives to empire-making with different conceptions of humanity and political power and a more inclusive cosmopolitanism. In the latter instance, the storyline linking polis to cosmopolis involves a plurality of pathways, with different conceptions of selfhood.

The difficulties facing a critical, more autonomous, non-Western IR are considerable. Despite the non-West's integral historical presence in the shaping of the global modern, the post-colonial world emerges only within 'an already existing territorial system of states' linked to Westphalia. The 'modularity of the "nation-state" inhibits post-national imaginings of territory, subjectivity, and identity' (Walker 2010). Once an aspiration, 'national' sovereignty becomes a fetter on providing better worlds in a world of diversity, multiplicity and difference. Alternatively, the logic of globalization retains the 'national' container, while draining it of capacities to envisage or realize alternative societal projects that are unhinged from narrower notions of human happiness, individual liberty or community. Can non-Western IR concurrently overcome the strictures of hegemonic IR and also bypass the West?

There are no definitive answers offered to this question in *Non-Western Thought*, nor is there any attempt to present simple axioms to develop a self-subsistent non-Western IR. Part of the provocation is to avoid producing a mirror-image of hegemonic IR, now only from a different vantage point. The principal trajectory of a critical non-Western, it seem, lies in exploring the implications of a different ontology, one that also carries with it different substantive and methodological commitments. Once this trajectory is entertained, it can unfreeze IR from the fetters of self-referential Westcentrism. This aspiration is neither novel nor surprising; it *defines* post-colonial thought. However, within the protected walls of IR, this appears as a radical possibility. It is unlikely that hegemonic IR would ever be willing or able to grasp the full scope of this alternative.

Appendix

Working on non-Western perspectives in both theory and practice: an interview with Christopher LaMonica

The following is the transcript of an interview with Christopher LaMonica, a US scholar who has worked within both Western-supported international institutions and the IR discipline, in both civilian and military academies, *and* during this period he has developed an abiding concern for the exclusion of non-Western perspectives by those who are employed within all these globally oriented institutions. The interview can be read – intellectually and politically – as a revealing testimony of the various negotiations and strictures of a Western scholar working in the halls of Western institutional power while wishing to break with the colonial hermeneutic that outlaws the legitimacy of non-Western thought.

Question: Aside from teaching in Western universities – and unlike the majority of critical IR scholars – you have also worked for state and inter-state institutions that might be seen as neo-imperialist. Given these – I would imagine, contrasting – experiences, why is it that you think non-Western thought needs to be engaged with in IR?

One of the greatest frustrations that I had working for international organizations was the lack of concern for non-Western points of view. Working at the OECD, for example, there was little motivation or time for 'listening' to the concerns of non-member states. To the extent that OECD staff pay heed to the various local woes of the world, it is only through the narrow lens of modernization – specifically, the gathering of data that best fit their developmental models. What I soon discovered was that my colleagues, employed in the field of development, were generally *not* rewarded for developing an understanding of local concerns or political philosophies. The institutionalized disregard of local governance among 'donor states' in sub-Saharan Africa is a case in point. Following in the footsteps of the colonizer, a disproportionate amount of effort and resources is spent on dealing with central government bureaucrats. In other words, international practitioners are rewarded for establishing working relationships with those in power in state capitals and not for their knowledge of circumstances in vast countrysides, where many non-Western state citizens generally reside.

In response to critique, there will sometimes be a kind of 'listening' effort, of the kind the World Bank started in the 1990s, under the title of a *Participation Action Plan*. In that instance, a bank-wide Participatory Learning Development Group (PLDG) was established, with a starting budget of over US$4 million, whose main task was to mainstream local participation with bank projects. A world-wide effort to collect 'regional' participation action plans led to a 1996 *World Bank Participation Sourcebook* that, today, does little more than collect dust on bookshelves. The initiative was, in fact, completely disbanded when Wolfenson – an advocate of 'inclusion' – stepped down as president of the World Bank. Employees of the World Bank, critical of the lack of any real change in procedure, stated that 'the World Bank declared victory and moved on'. And so it has. It was at that time that I stepped out of the international development industry and into the classroom, first as a graduate student at the Harvard Kennedy School and later as a doctoral student at Boston University. I was angry about the lack of inclusion of local, non-Western, voices in international affairs and have made it my focus as a lecturer and researcher. In fact, my first academic project – a masters thesis at Harvard University – was an investigation of the aforementioned World Bank plan.

In IR scholarship, of course, the problems are very similar. There can be little doubt that the prevailing norm among international organizations seems to be that Western ideas are 'best' and non-Western ideas impractical, radical and/or scarcely worth consideration. Would it be an exaggeration to say that non-Western ideas are considered a kind of hindrance to the priorities of modernization? I think not. You would think that IR scholars would be more open to real engagement of ideas, so that we could learn from one another. Instead, what I have found is that a Western intellectual framework still dominates the discipline and that scholars generally do one of two things: join the traditional group, in one way or another, or engage in an entirely different dialogue. A recent example of this, for me, was at a conference of the South African Philosophical Society, during which there was a marked rift between 'African' philosophical discussions and the more traditional ones that made reference only to Western scholarship. In other words, neither 'side' was listening to the other. And this is what, I think, is needed in both practice and scholarship: to listen. True engagement is not only the right thing to do in principle; it is also a practical concern, as a great many philosophers from all over the world have long argued.

Question: There was an interesting move at the end of that reply. You highlight the basically imperialist nature of much IR scholarship in terms of not listening to non-Western voices. But then the example you give places to the fore a kind of mutual non-listening between partici- pants in the South African Philosophical Society. Why do you think that it is necessary to move the focus away from the uneven power dynamics of conversation to a position that places the participants of this conver- sation as equals?

There are many ways in which non-inclusion of voice can be presented and dis- cussed. Without doubt there is a Foucauldian problem in all dialogue, whether it be in international practice or scholarship. If there is a fault in any of these dialogues one could, and perhaps should, point to those who have heretofore held the preponderance of power. I guess my own hope is that scholars can start the process of inclusion of voice by, first, openly recognizing the glaring biases and agendas that have, up to now, dominated IR discourse. If scholars truly value 'free and open debate' of ideas, they should be much more open to inclusion of non-Western ideas; right now they seem to be more concerned with what they 'need to know' to have professional credibility.

A former colleague, who specialized in Indian philosophy, struggled for professional credibility his entire career. His subject was deemed peripheral, at best, to the 'important' debates taking place within his discipline, and he was therefore obliged to teach Western philosophy his whole life. Furthermore, he was denied promotion to professor as many of his publications – and he is incredibly prolific – were published in journals and books based in Asia. In the meantime, scholars from all over the world, who are aware of his remarkable work on analytical philosophy (in the Indian philosophical traditions), put together a *festschrift* – a remarkable honour and life achievement for any scholar. For now this former colleague is left feeling like a second-class citizen amongst his colleagues, who are all trained in, and teach, only Western philosophical ideas. At some point this kind of colonial behaviour that summarily marginalizes non-Western scholars and scholarship has got to stop.

One of the target audiences, therefore, has to be those who currently dominate IR scholarship, i.e. those who currently support and benefit from the Foucauldian problem I previously referred to. As we enter the twenty-first century there can be no denying these simple facts: (1) the discipline of IR remains dominated by Eurocentric 'classics' and (2) it is essentially a discourse amongst Western state citizens. The irony, of course, is that IR pretends to be a global discipline, when in fact the leading ideas and participants are engaged in a dialogue that has been, up to now, incredibly limited in scope. Scholars and scholarship can do better than this, and part of the responsibility has to fall squarely on the shoulders of those individuals and institutions who continue to dominate the scene.

Often, however, non-Westerners respond to the state of the discipline either by simply ignoring it or by creating another pride-driven dialogue, often with nationalistic or cultural overtones, that says: 'We're smarter than you.' Given the intransigence of the intellectual structure of IR, both of these responses make perfect sense. One way of thinking of the problem with Western scholarship is, as Martin Bernal has stated, 'European cultural arrogance'. Let us be clear: up to now, non-Western areas of the world have been referred to in a range of derogatory ways in what has become 'mainstream' scholarship, from 'wastelands' (in Adam Smith's *Wealth of Nations*) to direct assumptions of cultural, racial and other inferiorities. All of it reeks of arrogance and a very clear message: 'we're smarter than you'. But to respond in kind, to label entire cultures, geographic regions, a people, or even institutions, as 'pure foolishness' is similarly non-productive. Neither 'side' is right to deem the other wholly foolish, yet this is the shape that the global debate on IR is now taking.

Having worked in international organizations has made me realize that they are made up of very different people, with a wide range of ideas as to what can and should be done and how to view the world. Labelling whole peoples or organizations as 'neo-imperialist' or 'imperial', dare I say, can become part of the problem. Put simply, the growing diversity that one finds in all Western societies is reflected in the many organizations that they work in. It would be the same as labelling all US or British citizens, or all employees of Oxford University or Harvard University 'imperialist.' My point is that moving away from the 'us versus them' way of engaging in IR dialogue will require a whole new approach, one that integrates history, as scholars such as Bernal and Edward Said have done, to remind us of our common humanity. Although the primary burden can and perhaps should be the responsibility of those 'benefiting' from teaching within the discipline, all of us need to rethink the assumptions that were made in traditional scholarship, good and bad. So, to the extent that scholars emphasize the brilliance of 'their own' in response to the state of IR scholarship I would say that, while that makes sense, we – all of us – need to think of a better way to engage and to listen. For the moment it seems that too many are too quick to repeat the errors of the past: labelling 'others' as nothing more than fools.

The efforts to correct the problems of IR scholarship will have to be multi-dimensional and involve many. No one can expect to adequately address every aspect of the problem in one career or even one lifetime. But the promoters of any status quo in IR can certainly do better than what Baylis and Smith have done with their leading text *The Globalization of World Politics: An Introduction to International Relations* (Oxford University Press, 2008) – a confused title at best – which includes only 'experts' with entirely Eurocentric points of view, or the popular *Theories of International Relations* (Routledge, 2009) by Scott Burchill *et al.*, which mentions Africa *once,* on one page, and only in passing! The authors and publishers of those very books can correct those kinds of problems immediately or, at least, in their next editions. Admittedly, to date, this does not seem to be happening. Much of this, I have come to believe, has to do with institutional inertia. But I do think that there is a growing sensitivity to the problem and that the discipline will be required to change.

Amongst those who have already worked to break the status quo of scholarship, I applaud the efforts of post-colonial writers who address the many aspects of 'European cultural arrogance'. IR scholarship can be greatly enhanced by these approaches as, among other things, they question basic assumptions of IR with a particular sensitivity to non-Western points of view.

Along the way, we must remember that the discipline of IR is relatively young. Many start with the works of Carr and Morgenthau, who simply followed the already established 'intellectual framework' of Western civilization. In other words, traditional IR has continued first to mirror and refer to the classics of Ancient Greece, then to 'skip' the Dark Ages, and then to continue with the modern-age contributions of, say, Locke, Rousseau, Kant, and so on. At least for the moment, that is the target of my current effort: to integrate the arguments found in the classic philosophies of the 'other' in an effort to get a better sense of the flow of ideas from all Ancient worlds, not just that of the Ancient Greeks. Put simply, to isolate the historical experiences, cultures and ideas of the Ancient Greeks from the rest of the world is not only wrong, it has proven to be quite harmful. Yes, there are 'good' ideas that come from the Ancient Greeks – and we should celebrate all helpful ideas – but scholars of all disciplines need to recognize that (1) many of the arguments that, for the moment, are solely attributed to the Ancient Greeks can be found in the classics of other, non-Western, regions of the world and (2) as human beings, we share a common history, during which we have all learned from one another. The aforementioned story of Western civilization, which conveniently skips over one thousand years of human history and neglects to mention the 1452 fall of Constantinople, following which the Ancient Greek and Latin texts became European 'classics', would have us think otherwise. In other words, the history of human beings is presented as a history of non-equals that systematically dehumanizes the 'other', and it is that impulse that needs to be corrected.

Question: So we've moved from the imperialism of discourse, into concerns over – effectively – reverse Orientalism, and now we have arrived at the notion of common humanity. But hasn't humanity always been a category of exclusion as much as inclusion? I'm reminded of what I know is an author that you greatly admire – Frantz Fanon – and his reply to Sartre: how can you presume to know what universal subjecthood lies after the end of an oppression that you haven't experienced? Indeed, many scholars influenced by post-colonial studies have an aversion to claims of commonalities, and prefer to focus methodologically and ethically upon 'difference'.

All human beings experience, at various times in their lives, inclusion and exclusion. In his lifetime, Fanon must have experienced both. As a product of the French university system, he must have felt 'included' in many ways but also 'excluded' at the same time; certainly, as a practising psychologist in Algeria, he sympathized with those who felt permanently excluded because of their race, culture or creed. Fanon reminds us of the profound psychological damage – the sense of worthlessness and/or loss of hope – that can result from feeling permanently excluded. Mahmood Mamdani's work, which distinguishes between *citizen* and *subject*, is similarly important in this regard. Although colonial history is over, there can be no doubt that the institutional norms and practices of that period continue, as do the processes of inclusion and exclusion of which writers like Fanon and Mamdani speak. Why, then, do we have this tendency to include and exclude others?

As many psychologists and linguists have argued, human beings do have a strong tendency – perhaps need – to categorize 'reality', to break the things that surround us into understandable compartments. And this mental process of categorization, which is probably needed for human beings to feel more secure with what surrounds them, is undoubtedly applied to human beings as well as to objects. Noam Chomsky, for example, suggests that language is largely a result of this human need. Yet he also argues that language is an innate human ability that includes what he terms a 'universal grammar' that is hard-wired in all of us. So if a visitor from another planet were to listen to our languages, Chomsky argues, she/he/it would hear only variants of what is essentially one universal pattern of communication. This idea is not without controversy, and other thinkers, notably Isaiah Berlin, have argued that language is best thought of in terms of a kind of hierarchy, i.e. there are very simple ways of communication, such as hand gestures, and gradually more sophisticated or complex forms of language. The problem that I have with the latter approach to understanding differences in human communication is that it essentially ranks certain languages and, in turn, peoples and cultures; the conclusion that many draw from this is that certain peoples or cultures are more clever than others, etc.

So, given this, my reaction to your question is to say that there are essentially two ways to speak of 'humanity': (1) in terms of commonalities and universal experiences and (2) in terms of hierarchical rank. Although there are certainly benefits to saying one concept or argument is better than another, as we do in our debates within the social sciences, there are serious misgivings to the ranking of peoples. As Edward Said has amply argued, these kinds of approaches to 'understanding' others has led to nothing less than the *dehumanization* of the 'them' and, all too often in history, as the justification for conflict. Alas, it is a pattern that humanity has fallen into time and again, which could lead one to conclude that humanity is simply part of the problem. But Said also reminds us that, as a student of the Enlightenment, he does believe in the inherent worth of all human beings and that, of course, is his real message to all of us: that we can all back away from that human tendency of separation, of the categorization of peoples into good, bad and the other, to remember the essential fact that we are all human. The late Said has been an inspiration to many, which leads me to believe that humanity could also be part of the solution. One could also say that a 'solution' is required only if there is a 'problem'. So this is not exactly a chicken and egg issue: human beings do tend to revert to the same pattern of group/tribal behaviour, of isolating others, of the categorization of human beings and, in response, human beings do also have a tendency to seek 'solutions'.

Finally, I would add that there are others who, like Chomsky, seek to identify the existence of recurring patterns or structures among human beings. I am thinking notably of the late Levi-Strauss, who argued that these occurred in human art, ritual, myth and politics, among other areas of inquiry. But his resulting structural anthropology has not been without controversy. Are these patterns that have been created by human beings to better understand 'reality', and only after the fact? I guess that while these academic debates rage on, I have nevertheless found these arguments compelling and have sought scholars in other fields who have similarly attempted to identify universal patterns, e.g. Max Müller, Carl Jung and Joseph Campbell.

Question: With these thoughts in mind, I want to ask you about the pedagogical challenges of your current position, teaching members of

the US Coast Guard Academy. Working for an organization, the remit
of which is surely – in large part if not solely – to protect 'us' from
'them', how do you think that you might retain, or impart, this message
of a common humanity beyond US shores when you teach international
relations to its functionaries?

I can certainly understand how or why a US military academy could be thought of as an 'us' versus 'them' organization, but this would be an inappropriate interpretation. When the US military was first used on a broad scale, in the twentieth century, it wasn't portrayed as such; much like the US itself, the military was viewed as being on the 'right side' of things, defeating dictatorships, fascism and Nazism. But, as we all know, in its quest for 'democracy' the US backed questionable regimes, such as that of Pinochet and Mobutu, with seemingly little regard for political realities on the ground. 'Dissident' author Noam Chomsky has written extensively on US violation of international laws during this period, to include the bombing of Tripoli and the invasion of Grenada, and argued that these kinds of violations would set a dangerous precedent. The United States did, for an extended period of time, have a monopoly on traditional forms of military power – and probably still does – the problem is that other, non-traditional forms of power (chemical and biological weapons, suicide bombers, roadside attacks, the hijacking of passenger planes to be used as weapons, the hacking of computer software) are now being used and have proven difficult, if not impossible, to 'check'. Apparently, this inability to check these new forms of power was not entirely foreseen, and this has highlighted the 'arrogance' that pervaded the US use of power since the end of the Second World War. This is not to say that the aims of the United States, as a country, were always misguided. But the limitations as to what the United States (or any) military establishment can achieve has now become an important topic for discussion in the classroom, in policy circles, and in recent books such as *Blowback: The Costs and Consequences of American Empire,* by Chalmers Johnson. Another way of thinking of this change is to say that, in the twenty-first century, power has become much more democratized.

Military establishments, such as the US Coast Guard, are not monolithic, and they are not staffed only by ideological non-thinkers. In fact, I do think that there is a growing awareness, within the US government and amongst the American public, that a number of US-led military campaigns of recent note have clearly had shortcomings. Some of the critics who have come from within the US military now argue that part of the problem was that the military was thinking in 'old' ways, assuming that it still had a monopoly of power, and that 'victory' was the only proper conclusion to any conflict. General McCrystal has had a very different approach to the conflict in Afghanistan, for example, in that he has acknowledged the very real problem of having so many civilian casualties. Although he is fully aware of the fact that a more humanistic approach that takes into account the local concerns and needs of the Afghani people could well lead to more US casualties, he has nevertheless insisted on a complete re-evaluation of the US use of 'hard power' in that conflict – and rightly so in my view. Furthermore, critics outside the United States, to include both Western and non-Western contexts alike, should remember that there has always been a lot of critique within the United States itself over these matters. This is a crucially important point to remember, lest we fall prey to the 'us' versus 'them' mode of thinking about the US versus the 'rest'. Within the United States itself, within its governing institutions, its military establishments, its universities, amongst the general population, there is always room for discussion and critique. I see my own involvement in the US Coast Guard Academy as promoting exactly that . . . my employers are aware of this aim and, frankly, have encouraged me to promote the free and open debate of ideas in the classroom.

So, although the US Coast Guard's motto is *semper paratus,* which means 'always ready', its members are always thinking, that is, there is always room for critical discussion within its ranks. There is also an awareness that the global perception of the US military is very important, and it does not take too much critical thought to realize that its effectiveness, in the field, was likely impacted negatively by growing anti-American sentiment over the last decade. We heard some acknowledgement of this problem in the last presidential campaign. As a candidate, Hillary Clinton argued that the United States was 'better than this . . .' (in the final months of Bush's second term) and the current US president, Barack Obama, has stated very clearly that the United States cannot unilaterally achieve 'victory' over global terrorism. This is very different language from what we heard during the Bush administration, which was largely of an essentially unilateral 'victory' in Iraq and an American 'war on terror'. This shift, from unilateralism to multilateralism, is very important to keep in mind as it is a testament to what open critique can potentially lead to: policy change.

Therefore, as stated in the response to your first question, the United States cannot be labelled as being 'one' way, or consistently pursuing the same policies; it is a dynamic country that is made up of many different voices. Similarly, its policies are not uniformly centred on the use of 'hard power', or military might, to achieve its foreign policy objectives. And although there are undoubtedly those who do think ideologically about the world in terms of 'us' versus 'them', as might happen amongst citizens of virtually any country (free or otherwise), this is not the case for all. Our free democratic state approaches to global problems are not only motivated by capitalist or imperialist profit; they are multidimensional and represent a vast array of ideas and policies.

Nevertheless, let us assume, for the moment, that the United States (and all) bases of power were stuck in an 'us' versus 'them' mode of thinking. Furthermore, let us assume that you believe that is not a good thing. What kinds of tactics or strategies could you use to alter that state of circumstances? One is to remain outside of the halls of government power and to make others aware of that problem. In a sense, this is the important role that many scholars play and one of the reasons why they are often portrayed as 'liberal' (in the US sense of the word) or overly critical of the establishment: they tend to look critically at what they perceive as the abuse of power. Civil society groups of all kinds similarly act as important crit-ics and possible counterweights or 'checks' to political abuse in democratic state contexts. But another possibility is to join the ranks of those in political power, to attempt, as best one can, to steer matters in your own preferred direction. This is what all politicians do ,and it is a process that is central to free democratic governance. Barack Obama's efforts have already demonstrated an interest, and some success, at altering US government policy, that is, he is an example of what an individual can do to help promote policy change in a different/preferred direction. When Frederick Douglass was asked what others could do to help end slavery in the United States he simply stated: 'agitate, agitate, agitate'. W.E.B. DuBois spent his entire life using different approaches to promoting change: journalism, university teaching, academic writing and politics. I guess you can say that I view all of these methods as being valid. Like others in International Relations I have noticed that there is an almost complete disregard for non-Western perspectives. And so, like others before me, I will use any and all means at my disposal to 'agitate, agitate, agitate' until there is improvement on that score.

Question: Finally, what pedagogical strategies does successful agitation of this kind require? Having experienced the relative freedom of academia and the relative unfreedom of working for state and interstate institutions, what kind of knowledges, or orientations to knowledge formation and production, would you like to see your students take seriously?

Teaching at a US military academy, I have several objectives. The first is to remind cadets that they are being prepared for positions of leadership. And, as is the case for the United States as a world power, with leadership comes responsibility. In fact, I have emphasized this same message in all of my previous teaching at university. Upon graduation, university students everywhere become members of an elite group as, from a global perspective, only 1 per cent of the population has a BA or better. In Western democracies students often lose sight of this simple fact, as roughly 25 per cent of their fellow citizens have a university degree. But, even in their home contexts they have a distinct edge over most: with those university credentials, with those 'pieces of paper', others will tend to look to them for 'answers' and to take on positions of responsibility. Of course, the same is especially true for students from developing country contexts.

Second, although I do stress the importance of knowing the 'classic' arguments of political science and international relations, I do also try to remind students of the importance of critical thinking. The quest for 'knowledge' is, of course, an ongoing process but, particularly in this age of the internet, many seem to believe that the answers are to be found via a Google search – that someone else has already done the necessary research and careful investigations. This is a challenge that all social science lecturers now face, as many students believe in the overarching myth about university study, i.e. that (1) 'knowledge' is simply acquired over a period of study, (2) a university credential is then duly awarded and (3) students then move on with life. Nothing could be more wrong and, in short order, more boring! Largely as a result of this still pervasive myth, many students have become quite cynical about the merit of time in the classroom. What's the point of being there if, after all, 'knowledge' can be acquired via an internet search engine? I try to remind all students that learning is a lifelong quest and to help them appreciate the value of time at university. There is a wonderful joy, even 'romance', to this lifelong journey of learning, perhaps best captured in the term *aun apprendo*: I'm still learning – a term used by both Aldous Huxley and J. Krishnamurti.

Conversely, there is an inherent danger to claiming absolute knowledge about anything that is debated in the social sciences and to, essentially, tell others to 'shut up' in political fora. The British philosopher Isaiah Berlin spent his entire life reminding others of the dangers of claiming absolute knowledge or answers to philosophical questions, as that has, time and again, led to the promotion, through public policy, of 'rational' solutions to social woes. This, Berlin argued, was the well-trodden path of too many in history. In the twentieth century, he suggested, this kind of logic led to fascism and communism. Time and again, people fall into the trap of accepting the 'rational' solutions of 'leaders', undoubtedly owing to their great appeal: they make people feel certain, secure in themselves and in their future. It is a trap that conservatives and progressives alike, from all cultures, can fall into. Berlin's message, and that of Canadian thinker, John Ralston Saul, is that we should always remember that critical, yet essential 'other' concern of the Enlightenment: *reasonableness*. Saul interestingly suggests that some of us have walked away from the Enlightenment with the wrong message – that of 'rationality' and not of 'reasonableness' – and that, therefore, some of us were in his words 'Voltaire's bastards'. Scientific, rational approaches to understanding are, of course, powerful and have led to amazing accomplishments in the modern age. But we can never lose sight of reasonableness – a term that asks us to consider the impact of any policy on human beings.

This, of course, has particular relevance to the promotion of any 'ideology' including, to the surprise of some, liberalism. Liberalism in the classic sense, or 'freedom', is a wonderful thing, but its promotion in the world has led to many unintended consequences. Scholars such as Amy Chua (*World on Fire*) have reminded us of this, as have the many critics of the International Monetary Fund and World Bank's pursuit of 'structural reform' that has, time and again, harmed the weakest members of 'developing' societies. In short, students have to be reminded that 'facts' and certainty can occur only in the realm of the 'hard sciences' (chemistry, physics) and not in the social sciences. Even the late political realist Samuel Huntington was obliged to remind his former student, Francis Fukuyama, of his grave mistake when speaking of the 'End of History'. In Huntington's response, entitled 'The Errors of Endism', he tells Fukuyama that he has 'overemphasized the permanence of the moment'. And, on that score, Huntington was right. In fact, careful readers will notice that Fukuyama's book, which followed his successful 'End of History' article, was decidedly less certain in its claims. These, I would suggest, are all examples of 'successful agitation' within the social sciences – a process that starts with critical thinking and that can eventually have great relevance to 'practice'.

Third, and perhaps most controversial, I like to remind students of the 'parochially Western' nature of the social sciences, as they are still taught to this day. For the most part I have already addressed the issue in our discussion, but I will add here that this notion takes on special relevance when speaking to future military leaders. We need only consider the appeal of the aforementioned guru's article, then book, *The Clash of Civilizations*. The title of Huntington's article, of course, ended in a question mark; the book's title no longer had one. In other words, he made Fukuyama feel less certain about his ideas, yet seemed to become more certain about his own! Before Huntington's recent passing I heard him defend his 'clash of civilizations' thesis, to a largely critical audience, in one of Harvard's lecture theatres. As is the case in his writings, he emphasized the conflictual/tribal nature of all human beings and spoke in surprisingly 'postmodern' ways about the changing identities of human beings: whereas previous generations had, for millennia, closely identified with their geographic homeland, or their tribe, individuals were now including larger geographical spaces and cultures as part of their identity. In his book he cites the work of Donald Horowitz, who speaks of an Ibo, from Nigeria, being in London. Back home, he can be of several Ibo tribes; within Nigeria he would be an Ibo; outside Nigeria, he is a Nigerian; and in London he might be thought of as an African. All of us, Huntington argued, were adopting similar ranges of identities and, as the world's cultures were encountering one another, the broader identity was becoming more relevant to all. It is a compelling argument and has appealed to many.

I must say, it was hard not to be impressed with Huntington's ability to address the critical questions posed by his audience. Politics, Huntington suggested, has always been about conflict and if conflict was to be less state-to-state oriented, the next logical step was culture-to-culture. And this is where, I think, Huntington could well be wrong: the encounter of different cultures does not have to result in a 'clash', and, in fact, history has many examples of more peaceful encounters of peoples. Huntington's future is but one possibility, and one of the ways we can help to change that possible future is to teach our students about the dangers of 'labelling' whole cultures, or peoples, as being 'one way' or another. I recall here the comments I made at the start: it makes no sense to label all British, all Americans, all Westerners, all Muslims, or any group of people as being of one mind, one way. I cannot improve on the thoughtful commentary made by Edward Said to Huntington's aforementioned thesis in 'The Clash of Ignorance'. But I will say, as an American who now teaches at a US military academy, that there is a great range of opinion among Americans and even within the ranks of the US military. Again, to label any group of people as being one way or another is not only wrong, it is also the path towards *dehumanization* of 'others', says Said. His emphasis, of course, was on the plight of the weak, and one must applaud him for his life effort of reminding us of this recurring problem.

The 9/11 attacks remind us that this process of *dehumanization* can work in many different directions. The architects of 9/11 similarly oversimplified 'others' and demonstrated how that process of thinking can be similarly wrong and destructive. It is for this reason that I have always promoted the notion of similarities and patterns, as opposed to emphasizing only *difference* – still the reigning methodology of the social sciences. It is really amazing how everyone seems to ignore our common historical past, as *Homo sapiens sapiens* residing together in the north-eastern reaches of the African continent; some among us migrated in different directions, resided in different physical environments and developed different physical features. But we are all, still, human beings! The study of IR reminds us that we are now, after several tens of thousands of years of relative isolation from one another, meeting one another again and asks us: How are we doing?

Bibliography

Abedi, M. 1986. Ali Shariati: the Architect of the 1979 Islamic Revolution in Iran. *Iranian Studies*, 19(3–4), 229–234.

Abrahamian, E. 1982. Ali Shariati: Ideologue of the Iranian Revolution. *MERIP Reports*, 102, 24–28.

Abrahamian, E. 1989. *Radical Islam: The Iranian Mojahedin*. London: Taurus.

Abu Zahrah, M. 1957. *Al-Ahwal al-Shakhsiyyah, 3rd edn*. Cairo: al-Fikr.

Acharya, A. 2005. *Why Is There No NATO in Asia? The Normative Origins of Asian Multilateralism*. Cambridge, MA: Weatherhead Center for International Affairs.

Acharya, A. and Buzan, B. 2007. Why is there no Non-Western IR Theory?: Reflections on and from Asia: An Introduction. *International Relations of the Asia-Pacific*, 7(3), 1–26.

Aching, G. 2005. Against 'Library-Shelf Races': José Martí's Critique of Excessive Imitation. In L. Doyle and L. Winkiel, eds. *Geomodernisms – Race, Modernism, Modernity*. Bloomington: Indiana University Press, pp. 151–169.

Adesanmi, P. 2004. 'Nous les Colonisés': Reflections on the Territorial Integrity of Oppression. *Social Text*, 22(1), 36–58.

Agathangelou, A. and Ling, L. 2004. Power, Borders, Security, Wealth: Lessons of Violence and Desire from September 11. *International Studies Quarterly*, 48, 517–538.

Ahluwalia, P. 2005. Out of Africa: Post-structuralism's Colonial Roots. *Post-colonial Studies*, 8(2), 137–154.

Ahmad, M. 1962. The Classical Muslim State. *Islamic Studies*, 1(3), 83–104.

Ajami, F. 1992. *The Arab Predicament: Arab Political Thought and Practice since 1967*. Cambridge: Cambridge University Press.

Akbarzadeh, S. 2004. Calculating the Risk in Central Asia: The Case of Uzbekistan. In M. Vicziany, D. Wright-Neville and P. Lentini, eds. *Regional Security in the Asia Pacific*. Cheltenham: Edward Elgar Publishing, pp. 112–127.

Akhavi, S. 1983. The Ideology and Praxis of Shi'ism in the Iranian Revolution. *Comparative Studies in Society and History*, 25(2), 195–221.

Al-Banna, H. 1992. *Rasa'il al-Imam al-Shahid*. Cairo: al-Tawzi wa al-Nashr.

Al-Bardisi, M. 1985. *Usul al-Fiqh*. Cairo: al-Thaqafah.

Al-Khalidi, S. 1994. *Sayyid Qutb mina al-Milad ila al-Istishhad*. Damascus: al-Qalam.

Alker, H.R. and Beirsteker, T. 1984. The Dialectics of World Order: Notes for a Future Archeologist of International Savoir Faire. *International Studies Quarterly*, 28, 121–142.

Al-Kilani, M.Z. 1995. *A-Harakat al-Islamiyyah fi al-Urdun wa Filistin [Islamic Movements in Jordan and Palestine]*. Beirut: Mu'assasat al-Risalah.

Alonso, C. 1998. *The Burden of Modernity: The Rhetoric of Cultural Discourse in Spanish America*. Oxford: Oxford University Press.

Al-Mawardi, A.A. 1966. *Al-Ahkam al-Sultaniyyah*. Beirut: al-Fikr.

Almond, I. 2004. 'The Madness of Islam': Foucault's Occident and the Revolution in Iran. *Radical Philosophy*, 128, 12–22.

Al-Nawawi, M. 1993. Nizam al-Islam al-Siyasi. *Al-Ashar*, 66(6), 878–884.

Al-Quds al-Arabi, 2007. Al-Quds al-Arabi. Available at: www.alquds.co.uk:9000/afpticker/data/journal/moyenorient/071110152246.a6o4 xaq9.html.

Al-Qurtubi, A.A. 1985. *Al-Jami'li Ahkam al-Qur'an, 20 vols*. Beirut: Ihya' al-Turath.

Al-Zalabani, R. 1947. Al-Siyasah Dusturiyyah. *Al-Azhar*, 18(7), 130–136.

Al-Zawahiri, A., *Al-Hasad al-Murr*. Jordan: al-Bayariq.

Al-Zawahiri, A. 2002. *Knights Under the Prophet's Banner*. FBIS translated text.

de Andrade, M. 1973. *A Geração de Cabral: Palestra feita na Escola-Piloto, em 8 de Fevereiro de 1973*. Bissau: Instituto Amizade, PAIGC.

de Andrade, M. 1980. Biographical Notes. In *Amílcar Cabral. Unity and Struggle: Speeches and Writings*. London: Heinemann, pp. xvii–xxxv.

Anghie, A. 2005. *Imperialism, Sovereignty, and the Making of International Law*. Cambridge: Cambridge University Press.

Anon. 1986. *Kexue fazhan guan xuexi duben [Reader on the Scientific Outlook on Development]*. Beijing: Hongqi chuban she.

Archibugi, D. and Held, D. eds. 1995. *Cosmopolitan Democracy: An Agenda for a New World Order*. Cambridge: Polity Press.

Arendt, H. 1958. *The Human Condition*. Chicago: University of Chicago Press.

Arendt, H. 1970. *Men in Dark Times*. London: Cape.

Arendt, H. 1973. *The Origins of Totalitarianism*. New York: Harcourt Brace Jovanovich.

Arjomand, S. 1996. The Crisis of the Imamate and the Institution of Occultation in Twelver Shiism: A Sociohistorical Perspective. *International Journal of Middle East Studies*, 28(4), 491–515.

Asukai, M. 1978. Kōtoku Shūsui: His Socialism and Pacifism. In B. Nobuya and J.F. Howes, eds. *Pacifism in Japan: The Christian and Socialist Tradition*. Vancouver: University of British Columbia Press, pp. 123–141.

Aydin, C. 2007. *The Politics of Anti-Westernism in Asia: Visions of World Order in Pan-Islamic and Pan-Asian Thought*. New York: Columbia University Press.

Aysha, E. 2006. Foucault's Iran and Islamic Identity Politics: Beyond Civilizational Clashes, External and Internal. *International Studies Perspectives*, 7, 377–394.

Ayoob, M. 1995. *The Third World Security Predicament: State Making, Regional Order and the International System*. Boulder, CO: Lynne Rienner.

Bajpai, K. 2003. Indian Conceptions of Order and Justice: Nehruvian, Gandhian, Hindutva and Neo-liberal. In R. Foot, J.L. Gaddis and A. Hurrell, eds. *Order and Justice in International Relations*. New York: Oxford University Press, pp. 236–261.

Balibar, É. 1998. The Nation Form: History and Ideology. In É. Balibar and I. Wallerstein, eds. *Race, Nation, Class: Ambiguous Identities*. London: Verso, pp. 37–85.

Banham, G. 2007. Introduction: Cosmopolitics and Modernity. In D. Morgan and G. Banham, eds. *Cosmopolitics and the Emergence of a Future*. Basingstoke: Palgrave, pp. xii–xvii.

Barkawi, T. and Laffey, M. 2002. Retrieving the Imperial: Empire and International Relations. *Millennium: Journal of International Studies*, 31(1), 109–127.

Barradas, A. 2005. O Nascimento de um Líder: a descoberta do mundo e a afirmação da personalidade de Agostinho Neto. In A. Barradas, ed. *Agostinho Neto – Uma Vida Sem Tréguas 1922–1979*. Lisbon: Edição Alusiva.

Bassin, M. 1991. Russia Between Europe and Asia: The Ideological Construction of Geographical Space. *Slavic Review*, 50(1), 1–17.

Baucom, I. 2005. *Specters of the Atlantic: Finance Capital, Slavery, and the Philosophy of History*. Durham, NC: Duke University Press.

Bayat, A. 1990. Shariati and Marx: A Critique of an 'Islamic' Critique of Marxism. *Alif: Journal of Comparative Poetics*, 10, 19–41.

Beardsworth, R. 2005. The Future of Critical Philosophy and World Politics. *Millennium*, 34, 201–261.

Beasley, W. 1987. *Japanese Imperialism 1894–1945*. Oxford: Clarendon Press.

Beck, U. 2006. *Cosmopolitan Vision*. Cambridge: Polity Press.

Behera, N.C. 2007. Re-imagining IR in India. *International Relations of the Asia-Pacific*, 7, 341–368.

Behnke, A. 2004. Terrorizing the Political: 9/11 Within the Context of The Globalization of Violence. *Millennium*, 33(2), 279–312.

Behrooz, M. 1999. *Rebels with A Cause: The Failure of the Left in Iran*. London: I.B. Taurus.

Bell, D. and Chaibong, H. 2003. Introduction: The Contemporary Relevance of Confucianism. In D. Bell and H. Chaibong, eds. *Confucianism for the Modern World*. Cambridge: Cambridge University Press, pp. 1–28.

Bell, J. 1971. Contemporary Revolutionary Organizations. *International Organization*, 25(3), 503–518.

Benhabib, S. 2004. *The Rights of Others*, Cambridge: Cambridge University Press.

Benítez-Rojo, A. 1998. *La isla que se repite*. Hanover, NH: Ediciones del Norte.

Benjamin, W. 1985. Theses on the Philosophy of History. In H. Arendt, ed. *Illuminations*. New York: Schocken Books, pp. 253–264.

Berman, R. 1998. *Enlightenment or Empire: Colonial Discourse in German Culture*. Lincoln: University of Nebraska Press.

Bernabé, J., Chamoiseau, P. and Confiant, R. 1989. *Éloge de la créolité*. Paris: Gallimard.

Bernabé, J., Chamoiseau, P. and Confiant, R. 1990. In Praise of Creoleness. *Callaloo*, 13(4), 886–909.

Bernasconi, R. 2003. Will the Real Kant Please Stand Up: The Challenge of Enlightenment Racism to the Study of the History of Philosophy. *Radical Philosophy*, 117, 13–22.

Bernestein, R. 1991. *The New Constellation: The Ethical-Political Horizons of Modernity/ Postmodernity*. London: Polity Press.

Bhagavan, M. 2008. A New Hope: India, the United Nations and the Making of the Universal Declaration of Human Rights. *Modern Asian Studies*, 44(2), 311–347.

Bhabha, H.K. 1983. The Other Question. *Screen* 24(6): 18–36.

Bhambra, G.K. 2007. *Rethinking Modernity: Post-colonialism and the Sociological Imagination*. Basingstoke: Palgrave.

Bilgrami, A. 2003. Gandhi, the Philosopher. *Economic and Political Weekly*, 38(26), 4159–4165.

Bilgin, P. 2008. Thinking Past 'Western' IR? *Third World Quarterly*, 29(1), 5–23.

Biswas, S. 2007. Empire and Global Public Intellectuals: Reading Edward Said as an International Relations Theorist. *Millennium*, 36(1), 117–133.

Black, A. 2001. *The History of Islamic Political Thought From the Prophet to the Present*. New York: Routledge.

Blaney, D. and Inayatullah, N. 1994. Prelude to a *Conversation* of Cultures in International Society? Todorov and Nandy on the Possibility of Dialogue. *Alternatives*, 19(1), 23–51.

Blaney, D. and Inayatullah, N. 2002. Neo-Modernization? IR and the Inner Life of Modernization Theory. *European Journal of International Relations*, 8(1), 103–137.

Blaney, D. and Inayatullah, N. 2004. *International Relations and the Problem of Difference*. London: Routledge.

Blaney, D.L. and Inayatullah, N. 2010. *Savage Economics: Wealth, Poverty, and the Temporal Walls of Capitalism*. Basingstoke: Routledge.

Bogues, A. 1997. *Caliban's Freedom: The Early Political Thought of C.L.R. James*. London: Pluto.

Bogues, A. 2002. Nationalism and Jamaican Political Thought. In K. Monteith and G. Richards, eds. *Jamaica in Slavery and Freedom: History, Heritage and Culture*. Kingston: University of the West Indies Press, pp. 363–388.

Bogues, A. 2003. *Black Heretics, Black Prophets: Radical Political Intellectuals*. New York: Routledge.

Bogues, A. 2006. Imagination, Politics, and Utopia: Confronting the Present. *Boundary 2: An International Journal of Literature and Culture*, 33(3), 151–159.

Borowiak, C. 2008. Review Essay: Theorizing Europe and its Divisions. *Political Theory*, 36(1), 152–160.

Brassett, D. and Bulley, D. 2007. Ethics in World Politics: Cosmopolitanism and Beyond? *International Politics*, 44, 1–149.

Brown, C. 2006. *Moral Capital: Foundations of British Abolitionism*. Chapel Hill: University of North Carolina Press.

Brown, J. 2003. *Nehru: A Political Life*. London: Yale University Press.

Breuer, M. and Graetz, M. 1996. *German–Jewish History in Modern Times*, Vol. 1. New York: Columbia University Press.

Buck-Morss, S. 2000. Hegel and Haiti. *Critical Inquiry*, 26(4), 821–865.

Burgess, A. 1988. Foreword: On Drawing A Line. In A. Shariati, *Religion vs. Religion*. Albuquerque: Abjad, pp. 5–10.

Bull, H. 1984. The Revolt Against the West. In H. Bull and A. Watson eds. *The Expansion of International Society*. Oxford: Clarendon Press, pp. 217–228.

Buzan, B. 2006. Will the 'Global War on Terrorism' Be the New Cold War? *International Affairs*, 82(6), 1101–1118.

Cabral, A. 1969. *Revolution in Guinea: An African People's Struggle. Selected Texts by Amílcar Cabral*. London: Stage 1.

Cabral, A. 1973. Connecting the Struggles: an Informal Talk with Black Americans. In Africa Information Service, ed. *Return to the Source: Selected Speeches of Amilcar Cabral*. London: Monthly Review Press, pp. 75–92.

Cabral, A. 1980. *Unity and Struggle: Speeches and Writings*. London: Heinemann.

Cabrera, L. 2006. *Political Theory of Global Justice: A Cosmopolitan Case for the World State*. London: Routledge.

Caldarola, C. 1979. *Christianity: The Japanese Way*. Leiden: Brill.

Calhoun, C. 2002. Constitutional Patriotism and the Public Sphere: Interests, Identity and Solidarity in the Integration of Europe. In P. De Greiff and C. Cronin, eds. *Global Justice and Transnational Politics*. Cambridge, MA: MIT Press, pp. 275–312.

Callahan, W.A. 2001. China and the Globalisation of IR Theory: Discussion of 'Building International Relations Theory with Chinese Characteristics'. *Journal of Contemporary China*, 10, 75–88.

Calvert, J. 2000. The World is an Undutiful Boy! *Islam and Christian Muslim Relations*, 11(1), 90–91.

Campbell, D. 1999. The Deterritorialization of Responsibility: Lévinas, Derrida, and Ethics After the End of Philosophy. In D. Campbell and M. Shapiro, eds. *Moral Spaces: Rethinking Ethics and World Politics*. Minneapolis: University of Minnesota Press, pp. 29–56.

Campbell, H. 2006. Re-visiting the Theories and Practices of Amílcar Cabral in the Context of the Exhaustion of the Patriarchal Model of African Liberation. In J. Fobanjong and T. Ranuga, eds. *The Life, Thought, and Legacy of Cape Verde's Freedom Fighter Amílcar Cabral (1924–1973): Essays on his Liberation Philosophy*. New York: Edwin Mellen, pp. 79–102.

Canclini, G. 2005. *Hybrid Cultures: Strategies for Entering and Leaving Modernity*. Minneapolis: University of Minnesota Press.

Candela, A.M. 2007. Performing Citizenship: Overseas Laborers and Qing Nation Building. Paper presented at Asia–America–Pacific Research Cluster Graduate Student Conference, Santa Cruz, CA.

Carreira, I. 1996. *Pensamento Estratégico de Agostinho Neto: Contribuição Histórica*. Lisbon: Publicações Dom Quixote.

Carroll, C. and King, P. eds. 2003. *Ireland and Post-Colonial Theory*. Cork: Cork University Press.

Césaire, A. 1981. *Toussaint Louverture: La Révolution française et le problème colonial*. Paris: Présence Africaine.

Césaire, A. 1994. *La Poésie*. Paris: Seuil.

Césaire, A. 1995. *Notebook of a Return to My Native Land*. Newcastle upon Tyne: Bloodaxe.

Césaire, A. 2000. *Discourse on Colonialism*. New York: Monthly Review Press.

Chabal, P. 1983. *Amílcar Cabral: Revolutionary Leadership and People's War*. Cambridge: Cambridge University Press.

Chacko, P. 2008. *Decolonising International Relations: Indian Foreign Policy and the Politics of Post-colonial Identity*. DPhil. thesis, University of Adelaide.

Chakrabarty, D. 1992. Post-coloniality and the Artifice of History: Who Speaks for 'Indian' Pasts? *Representations*, 37, 1–26.

Chakrabarty, D. 2000. *Provincializing Europe: Post-colonial Thought and Historical Difference*. Princeton, NJ: Princeton University Press.

Chamberlain, J. 1942. Review of Glimpses of World History. *New York Times*, 13 June 1947.

Chan, G. 1998. Toward an International Relations Theory with Chinese Characteristics? *Issues and Studies*, 34(6), 1–28.

Chan, G. 1999. *Chinese Perspectives on International Relations: A Framework for Analysis*. London: Macmillan.

Chan, S. 1993. Cultural and Linguistic Reductionisms and a New Historical Sociology for International Relations. *Millennium*, 22(3), 423–442.

Chan, S. 1999. Chinese Perspectives on World Order. In T. Paul and J. Hall, eds. *International Order and the Future of World Politics*. Cambridge: Cambridge University Press, pp. 197–212.

Chan, S., Mandeville, P. and Bleaker, P. eds. 2001. *The Zen of International Relations: IR Theory from East to West*. Basingstoke: Palgrave.

Chatterjee, P. 1986. *Nationalist Thought and the Colonial World: A Derivative Discourse?* Delhi: Oxford University Press.

Chatterjee, P. 1991. Whose Imagined Community? *Millennium: Journal of International Studies*, 20(3): 521–525.

Chen, G. 1967. *Zhongguo guojifa suyuan [Sources of Inter-state Law in China]*. Taipei: Taiwan Commercial Press.

Chilcote, R. 1991. *Amílcar Cabral's Revolutionary Theory and Practice*. Boulder, CO: Lynne Rienner Publishers.

Chowdhry, G. and Nair, S. eds. 2004. *Power, Post-colonialism and International Relations*. London: Routledge.

Christie, I. 1989. *Samora Machel: A Biography*. London: Panaf.

Clifford, J. 1989. Negrophilia. In D. Hollier, ed. *A New History of French Literature*. Cambridge, MA: Harvard University Press, pp. 901–908.

Clifford, J. 1992. Travelling Cultures. In L. Grossberg, C. Nelson and P. Treichler, eds. *Cultural Studies*. London: Routledge, pp. 96–112.

Cohen, R. and Vertovec, S. 2002. Introduction: Conceiving Cosmopolitanism. In R. Cohen and S. Vertovec, eds. *Conceiving Cosmopolitanism: Theory, Context, and Practice*. Oxford: Oxford University Press, pp. 1–22.

Cone, J.H. 1970. *A Black Theology of Liberation*. Philadelphia: J.B. Lippincott.

Connell, R. 2007. *Southern Theory*. Cambridge: Polity Press.

Corwin, A.F. 1967. *Spain and the Abolition of Slavery in Cuba, 1817–1886*. Austin: University of Texas Press.

Costa Pinto, A. 2001. *O Fim do Império Português: A Cena Internacional, a Guerra Colonial, e a Descolonização, 1961–1975*. Lisbon: Livros Horizonte.

Cox, R.W. 1981. Social Forces, States and World Orders: Beyond International Relations Theory. *Millenium*, 10(2), 126–155.

Cox, R.W. 1995. Towards a Posthegemonic Conceputalization of World Order: Reflections on the Relevancy of Ibn Khaldun. In R. Cox and T. Sinclair, eds. *Approaches to World Order*. Cambridge: Cambridge University Press, pp. 144–173.

Crowley, J. 1974. A New Asian Order: Some Notes on Prewar Japanese Nationalism. In B. Silberman and H. Harootunian, eds. *Japan in Crisis: Essays on Taishō Democracy*. Princeton, NJ: Princeton University Press, pp. 270–298.

Cruz e Silva, T. 1998. The influence of the Swiss Mission on Eduardo Mondlane (1930–61). *Journal of Religion in Africa*, 28(2), 187–209.

Dabashi, H. 1984. Review: The Revolutions of Our Time: Religious Politics in Modernity. *Comparative Sociology*, 13(6), 673–676.

Dabashi, H. 2002. *Authority in Islam: From the Rise of Muhammad to the Establishment of the Umayyads*. New Brunswick: Transaction.

Dabashi, H. 2006. *Theology of Discontent: The Ideological Foundation of the Islamic Revolution in Iran*. New Brunswick: Transaction.

Dabringhaus, S. and Ptak, R. eds. 1997. *China and Her Neighbours: Borders, Visions of the Other, Foreign Policy 10th to 19th Century*. Wiesbaden: Harrassowitz Verlag.

Dallmayr, F. 1994. Western Thought and Indian Thought: Comments on Ramanujan. *Philosophy East and West*, 44(3), 527–542.

Dallmayr, F. 1996. *Beyond Orientalism: Essays on Cross-Cultural Encounter*. Albany: State University of New York Press.

Dallmayr, F. 1999. *Border Crossings: Towards a Comparative Political Theory*. Boulder, CO: Lexington Books.

Dallmayr, F. 2001. Conversation Across Boundaries: Political Theory and Global Diversity. *Millennium*, 30(2), 331–347.

Dallmayr, F. 2004. Beyond Monologue: For A Comparative Political Theory. *Perspectives on Politics*, 2(2), 249–257.

Darby, P. 1997. *At the Edge of International Relations: Post-colonialism. Gender and Dependency*. London: Pinter.

Dash, J. 1981. *Literature and Ideology in Haiti, 1915–1961*. Basingstoke: Macmillan.

Dash, J. 1998. *The Other America: Caribbean Literature in a New World Context*. London: University of Virginia Press.

Dash, J. 2006. Haïti Chimère: Revolutionary Universalism and its Caribbean Context. In M. Munro and E. Walcott-Hackshaw, eds. *Reinterpreting the Haitian Revolution and its Cultural Aftershocks*. Kingston: University of the West Indies Press, pp. 9–19.

Davies, A. 1998. *History of Linguistics, Vol. 4*. London: Longman.

Davis, D.B. 1975. *The Problem of Slavery in the Age of Revolution*. Ithaca, NY: Cornell University Press.

Davis, E. 1987. The Concept of Revival and the Study of Islam and Politics. In B. Stowasser, ed. *The Islamic Impulses*. Washington DC: Centre for Contemporary Arab Studies, pp. 37–58.

Davis, M. 1999. *Sylvia Pankhurst: A Life in Radical Politics*. Sterling, VA: Pluto Press.

Dayan, J. 1995. *Haiti, History, and the Gods*. Berkeley: University of California Press.

Defoort, C. 2001. Is There Such a Thing as Chinese Philosophy? Arguments of an Implicit Debate. *Philosophy East and West*, 51(3), 393–413.

Delanty, G. 2005. The Idea of a Cosmopolitan Europe: On the Cultural Significance of Europeanization. *International Review of Sociology*, 15(3), 405–421.

Delanty, G. 2006. The Cosmopolitan Imagination: Critical Cosmopolitanism and Social Theory. *British Journal of Sociology*, 57(1), 25–47.

Deng, Y. 1998. The Chinese Conception of National Interests in International Relations. *The China Quarterly*, 154, 308–329.

Depelchin, J. 1983. African anthropology and history in the light of the history of FRE-LIMO. *Contemporary Marxism*, 7, 69–88.

Depestre, R. 1998. *Ainsi parle le fleuve noir*. Grigny: Editions Paroles d'Aube.

Dicey, A. and Wade, E. 1941. Introduction to the Study of the Law of the Constitution. *Political Science Quarterly*, 56(1), 125–126.

Diez, T. and Steans, J. eds. 2005. A Useful Dialogue? Habermas and International Relations. *Review of International Studies*, 31(1), 127–209.

Diez, T. and Whitman, R. 2002. Analysing European Integration: Reflecting on the English School – Scenarios for an Encounter. *Journal of Common Market Studies*, 40(1), 43–67.

Dirk Moses, A. and Stone, D. 2007. *Colonialism and Genocide*. London: Routledge.

Dirlik, A. 1989. Postsocialism: Reflections on 'Socialism with Chinese Characteristics. In A. Dirlik and M. Meisner, eds. *Marxism and the Chinese Experience*. Armonk, NY: ME Sharpe, pp. 362–384.

Dirlik, A. 1997. *Third World Criticism in the Age of Global Capitalism*. New York: Westview Press.

Dirlik, A. 2001. *Theory, History, Culture: Cultural Identity and the Politics of Theory in Twentieth Century China*. Academia Sinica: Institute of Modern History.

Dirlik, A. 2007. *Global Modernity: Modernity in the Age of Global Capitalism*. Boulder, CO: Paradigm Publishers.

Dirlik, A. 2009. *Back to the Future: Contemporary China in the Perspective of Its Past, circa 1980*. Unpublished paper.

Dobson, L. 2006. Normative Theory and Europe. *International Affairs*, 82(3), 511–523.

Dohm, C. 1973. *Ueber die bürgerliche Verbesserung der Juden*. Hildesheim: Olms.

Dunch, R. 2002. Beyond Cultural Imperialism: Cultural Theory, Christian Missions, and Global Modernity. *History and Theory*, 41(3), 301–325.

Dunne, T. 2008. Good Citizen Europe. *International Affairs*, 84(1), 13–28.

Dura, P. 2004. *Decolonization: Perspectives From Then and Now*. London: Routledge.

Dussel, E.D. 1985. *Philosophy of Liberation*. New York: Orbis Books.

Dussel, E.D. 1993. Eurocentrism and Modernity: Introduction to the Frankfurt School. *Boundary 2: An International Journal of Literature and Culture*, 20(3), 65–76.

Dussel, E.D. 2001. La filosofía de la liberación, los subaltern studies y el pensamiento post-colonial norteamericano. In E. Dussel, ed. *Hacia una filosofía crítica*. Bilbao: Desclée de Brouwer.

Dussel, E.D. ed. 2008. *Coloniality at Large; Latin America and the Post Colonial Debates*. Durham, NC: Duke University Press.

Eagleton, T. 2003. *Figures of Discontent: Critical Essays on Fish, Spivak, Žižek and Others*. London: Verso.

Edwards, B.H. 2001. The 'Autonomy' of Black Radicalism. *Social Text*, 19(2), 1–13.

Elliot, G. 2006. *The Detour of Theory*. Leiden: Brill.

Esposito, J. 1986. Foreword. In *What Is to be Done: The Enlightened Thinkers and an Islamic Renaissance*. Houston: Institute for Research and Islamic Studies (IRIS), pp. ix–xii.

Esposito, J. and Voll, J. 1996. *Islam and Democracy*. Oxford: Oxford University Press.

Euben, R.L. 1997. Comparative Political Theory: An Islamic Fundamentalist Critique of Rationalism. *Journal of Politics*, 59(1), 28–55.

Euben, R.L. 2002. Contingent Borders, Syncretic Perspectives: Globalization, Political Theory and Islamizing Knowledge. *International Studies Review*, 4(1), 23–48.

Euben, R.L. 2004. Travelling Theorists and Translating Practices. In S.K. White and J.D. Moon, eds. *What Is Political Theory?* London: Sage Publications, pp. 145–173.

Evans, M. 1999. *Missing Persons: The Impossibility of Auto/biography*. London: Routledge.

Eze, E.C. 1997. The Color of Reason: The Idea of 'Race' in Kant's Anthropology. In C. Eze, ed. *Post-colonial African Philosophy: A Critical Reader*. Cambridge, MA: Blackwell Publishers, pp. 103–140.

Eze, E.C. 1997. *Post-colonial African Philosophy: A Critical Reader*. London: Blackwell Publishers.

Fabian, J. 1983. *Time and the Other: How Anthropology Makes its Object*. New York: Columbia University Press.

Fahmi, A.A. 1963. *Hadhihi Hayati*. Cairo: al-Hilal.

Fanon, F. 1952. *Peau noire, masques blancs*. Paris: Seuil.

Fanon, F. 1967. *Black Skin, White Masks*. New York: Grove Press.

Fanon, F. 1968. *The Wretched of the Earth*. New York: Grove Press.

Faraj, A.A. 1981. *Al-Faridah al-Gha'ibah*. Cairo.

Faure, B. 1995. The Kyoto School and Reverse Orientalism. In C. Wei-hsun Fu and H. Steven, eds. *Japan in Traditional and Postmodern Perspectives*. New York: State University of New York Press, pp. 245–281.

Fifield, R. 1958. The Five Principles of Peaceful Co-Existence. *American Journal of International Law*, 52(3), 504–510.

Firmin, A. 2002. *The Equality of the Human Races*, Champaign, IL: University of Illinois Press.

Fobanjong, J. 2006. The Regional Context of the Liberation Struggle in Lusophone Africa. In J. Fobanjong and T. Ranuga, eds. *The Life, Thought, and Legacy of Cape Verde's*

Freedom Fighter Amilcar Cabral (1924–1973): Essays on his Liberation Philosophy. New York: Edwin Mellen.

Fobanjong, J. and Ranuga, T. eds. 2006. *The Life, Thought, and Legacy of Cape Verde's Freedom Fighter Amilcar Cabral (1924–1973): Essays on his Liberation Philosophy.* New York: Edwin Mellen.

Fraginals, M. 2001. *El ingenio: complejo económico social cubano del azúcar.* Barcelona: Editorial Crítica.

Freud, S. 1939. *Moses and Monotheism*, London: Hogarth Press.

Freud, S. 1961. Civilization and its Discontents. In A. Freud, ed. *The Complete Psychological Works of Sigmund Freud.* Vol. XXXI . London: Vintage, pp. 64–145.

Friedrichs, J. 2001. The Meaning of New Medievalism. *European Journal of International Relations*, 7(4), 475–502.

Frost, M. 1996. *Ethics in International Relations: a Constitutive Theory.* Cambridge: Cambridge University Press.

Gadamer, H. 2004. *Truth and Method.* London: Continuum.

Gandhi, M. 1999a. Foreword to 'Nehru Your Neighbour', September 30, 1945. In *The Collected Works of Mahatma Gandhi.* New Delhi: Publications Division, Ministry of Information and Broadcasting, Government of India, pp. 94–95.

Gandhi, M. 1999b. Speech at public meeting, Tinnevelly, October 7, 1927. In *The Collected Works of Mahatma Gandhi.* New Delhi: Publications Division, Ministry of Information and Broadcasting, Government of India, pp. 216–220.

Gandhi, M. 1999c. Appendix V: Resolution Passed By All-India Congress Committee. In *The Collected Works of Mahatma Gandhi.* New Delhi: Publications Division, Ministry of Information and Broadcasting, Government of India, pp. 445–447.

Ganhão, F. 2001. Samora Machel: a lightning in the sky. In A. Sopa, ed. *Samora, Man of the People.* Maputo: Maguezo.

Garner, S. 2007. Atlantic Crossing: Whiteness as a Transatlantic Experience. *Atlantic Studies*, 4(1), 117–132.

Garraway, D. 2005. *The Libertine Colony: Creolization in the Early French Caribbean.* Durham, NC: Duke University Press.

Garton Ash, T. 2007. Europe's True Stories. *Prospect Magazine*, 131.

Geeraerts, G. and Jing, M. 2001. International Relations Theory in China. *Global Society*, 15(3), 251–276.

Geggus, D. ed. 2001. *The Impact of the Haitian Revolution in the Atlantic World.* Columbia: University of South Carolina Press.

Gellner, E. 1964. *Thought and Change.* London: Weidenfeld & Nicolson.

Genovese, E. 1981. *From Rebellion to Revolution: Afro-American Slave Revolts in the Making of the New World.* New York: Vintage.

Giddens, A. 1990. *The Consequences of Modernity.* Stanford: Stanford University Press.

Giesen, B. 1998. *Intellectual and German Nation: Collective Identity in An Axial Age.* Cambridge: Cambridge University Press.

Gilroy, P. 1993. *The Black Atlantic: Modernity and Double Consciousness.* Cambridge, MA.: Harvard University Press.

Glissant, É. 1981. *Le Discours antillais.* Paris: Seuil.

Glissant, É. 1989. *Caribbean Discourse: Selected Essays.* Charlottesville: University Press of Virginia.

Glissant, É. 1990. *Poétique de la relation.* Paris: Gallimard.

Gluck, C. 1985. *Japan's Modern Myths: Ideology in the Late Meiji Period.* Princeton, NJ: Princeton University Press.

Goetschel, W. 1999. Land of Truth – Enchanting Name! Kant's Journey at Home. In S. Friedrichsmeyer, S. Lennox and S. Zantop, eds. *The Imperialist Imagination: German Colonialism and Its Legacy*. Ann Arbor: University of Michigan Press, pp. 321–336.

Goetschel, W. 2004a. *Spinoza's Modernity: Mendelssohn, Lessing, and Heine*. Madison: University of Wisconsin Press.

Goetschel, W. 2004b. Heine's Critical Secularism. *Boundary 2: An International Journal of Literature and Culture*, 31(2), 149–171.

Goetschel, W. 2007. Mendelssohn and the State. *Modern Language Notes*, 122(3), 472–492.

Gong, G.W. 1984. *The Standard of 'Civilization' in International Society*. Oxford: Clarendon Press.

Gopal, S. 1975. *Jawaharlal Nehru: A Biography*, Vol. 1. London: Jonathan Cape.

Gopal, S. 1984. *Jawaharlal Nehru: A Biography*, Vol. 3. London: Jonathan Cape.

Government of India, n.d., (1954–1959) *Notes, Memoranda and Letters Exchanged and Agreements Signed Between the Governments of India and China: White Paper No. I*. New Delhi: Ministry of External Affairs.

Greason, D. 2005. Embracing Death: the Western Left and the Iranian Revolution. *Economy and Society*, 34(1), 105–140.

Grosfoguel, R. 2007. The Epistemic Decolonial Turn: Beyond Political-Economy Paradigms. *Cultural Studies*, 21(2–3), 211–223.

Grovogui, S.N. 2002. Regimes of Sovereignty: International Morality and the African Condition. *European Journal of International Relations*, 8(3), 315–338.

Grovogui, S.N. 2006a. Mind, Body and Gut! Elements of a Post-colonial Human Rights Discourse. In B. Gruffydd Jones, ed. *Decolonising International Relations*. Lanham, MD: Rowman & Littlefield Publishers, pp. 179–196.

Grovogui, S.N. 2006b. *Beyond Eurocentrism and Anarchy: Memories of International Order and Institutions*. Basingstoke: Palgrave Macmillan.

Gruffydd Jones, B. ed. 2006a. *Decolonizing International Relations*. London: Rowman & Littlefield Publishers.

Gruffydd Jones, B. 2006b. International Relations, Eurocentrism and Imperialism. In B. Gruffydd Jones, ed. *Decolonising International Relations*. Lanham, MD: Rowman & Littlefield Publishers, pp. 1–22.

Gruffyd Jones, B. 2008. 'Tell No Lies, Claim No Easy Victories': Possibilities and Contradictions of Emancipatory Struggles in the Current Neo-Colonial Condition. In A. Ayers, ed. *Gramsci, Political Economy and International Relations Theory: Modern Princes and Naked Emperors*. New York: Palgrave, pp. 209–228.

Guha, R. 2005. Verdicts on Nehru: Rise and Fall of a Reputation. *Economic and Political Weekly*, 40(19) 1958–1962.

Gurel, M.L. 1990. Hate. In *The World Book Encyclopaedia*. Volume 9. Chicago: World Book Inc., pp. 87–88.

Haas, R. 1999. *Intervention: The Use of American Military Force in the Post-Cold War*. Washington, DC: The Brookings Institution.

Habermas, J. 1994. Modernity: An Incomplete Project. In P. Waugh, ed. *Postmodernism: A Reader*. London: Routledge, pp. 160–170.

Habermas, J. 1998. A Genealogical Analysis of the Cognitive Content of Morality. In C. Cronin and P. De Greiff, eds. *The Inclusion of the Other: Studies in Political Theory*. Cambridge, MA: MIT Press, pp. 3–46.

Habermas, J. 2001. The Post-national Constellation and the Future of Democracy. In M.

Pensky, ed. *The Post-national Constellation: Political Essays*. Cambridge, MA: MIT Press, pp. 58–112.

Habermas, J. 2006. February 15, or What binds Europeans. In C. Cronin, ed. *The Divided West*. Cambridge: Polity Press, pp. 39–48.

Habermas, J. 2008. Notes on Post-Secular Society. *New Perspectives Quarterly*, 25(3), 17–29.

Hammudah, A. 1990. *Sayyid Qutb mina al-Qaryah Ila al-Mishnaqah*, Cairo: Sina Li al-Nashr.

Hanson, B. 1983. The 'Westoxification' of Iran: Depictions and Reflections on Behrangi, al-e Ahmad, and Shariati. *International Journal of Middle East Studies*, 15(1), 1–23.

Hashmi, S. 1998. Islamic Ethics in International Society. In D. Mapel and T. Nardin, eds. *International Society: Diverse Ethical Perspectives*. Princeton, NJ: Princeton University Press, pp. 215–236.

Haykal, M.H. 1976. *The Life of Muhammad*. Kuala Lumpur: Islamic Book Trust.

Hegel, G. 2004. *The Philosophy of History*. New York: Dover Publications.

Heidegger, M. 1996. *Being and Time*. Albany: State University of New York.

Heine, H. 1906. Pictures of Travel. In *The Works of Heinrich Heine*, Vol. 3. London: William Heinemann.

Heine, H. 2007. T. Pinkard, ed. *On the History of Religion and Philosophy in Germany and Other Writings*. Cambridge: Cambridge University Press.

Held, D. 2002. Globalization, Corporate Practice and Cosmopolitan Social Standards. *Contemporary Political Theory*, 1, 59–78.

Held, D. 2003. Cosmopolitanism: Globalization Tamed? *Review of International Studies*, 29(4), 465–480.

Herf, J. 1984. *Reactionary Modernism: Technology, Culture, and Politics in Weimar and the Third Reich*. New York: Cambridge University Press.

Hill, R. ed. 1995. *The Marcus Garvey and UNIA Papers*. Berkeley: University of California Press.

Hill, S. 1984. International Solidarity: Cabral's Legacy to the African-American Community. *Latin American Perspectives*, 11(2), 67–80.

Hilton, B. 2001. *The Age of Atonement: The Influence of Evangelicalism on Social and Economic Thought, 1785–1865*. Oxford: Oxford University Press.

Hochschild, D. 2006. *Bury the Chains: Prophets and Rebels in the Fight to Free an Empire's Slaves*. New York: Mariner.

Hodgson, M. 1993. *Rethinking World History: Essays on Europe, Islam, and World History*. Cambridge: Cambridge University Press.

Hoffmann, L. 1992. *Haïti: Lettres et l'être*. Toronto: Editions du GREF.

Hoffmann, S. 1987. An American Social Science: International Relations. In S. Hoffman, ed. *Janus and Minerva: Essays in Theory and Practice of International Relations*. Boulder, CO: Westview Press, pp. 3–24.

Hollinger, D. 2002. Not Universalists, Not Pluralists. The New Cosmopolitans Find Their Own Way. In S. Vertovec and R. Cohen, eds. *Conceiving Cosmopolitanism: Theory, Context, and Practice*. Oxford: Oxford University Press, pp. 227–239.

Hong, J. 1965. *Chunqiu guoji gongfa [Inter-state Law during the Spring Autumn Period]*. Taipei: Literature-History-Philosophy Publishers.

Hourani, A. 1983. *Arabic Thought in the Liberal Age 1798–1939*. Cambridge: Cambridge University Press.

Howitt, R. 2002. Scale and the Other: Lévinas and Geography. *Geoforum*, 33(3), 299–313.

Hsu, I. 1960. *China's Entry into the Family of Nations*. Cambridge MA: Harvard University Press.

Huang, X. 2007. The Invisible Hand: Modern Studies of International Relations in Japan, China, and Korea. *Journal of International Relations and Development*, 10, 168–203.

Huntington, S.P. 1996. *The Clash of Civilizations and the Remaking of World Order*. New York: Simon & Schuster.

Hurd, E.S. 2004. The Political Authority of Secularism in International Relations. *European Journal of International Relations*, 10(2), 235–262.

Hurrell, A. 1999. Power, Principles and Prudence: Protecting Human Rights in a Deeply Divided World. In T. Dunne and N. Wheeler, eds. *Human Rights in Global Politics*. Cambridge: Cambridge University Press, pp. 277–302.

Husayn, M. 1985. *Al-Islam wa al-Hadarah al-Gharbiyyah*, Beirut: Mu'assasat al-Risalah.

Huysmans, J. and Waever, O. eds. 2009. International Political Sociology Beyond European and North American Traditions of Social and Political Thought. *International Political Sociology*, 3(3), 327–350.

Ince, B. 1974. *Decolonization and Conflict in the United Nations: Guyana's Struggle for Independence*. Cambridge, MA: Schenkmam.

Ishemo, S. 2000. A Symbol that Cannot be Substituted: The Role of Mwalimu J K Nyerere in the Liberation of Southern Africa, 1955–90. *Review of African Political Economy*, 27(83), 85–94.

Iyer, R. ed. 1965. *The Glass Curtain Between Asia and Europe*. London: Oxford University Press.

Iyer, R. 1973. *The Moral and Political Thought of Mahatma Gandhi*. New York: Oxford University Press.

Jahn, B. 2000. *The Cultural Construction of International Relations: The Invention of the State of Nature*. Basingstoke: Macmillan.

James, C.L.R. 1938. *The Black Jacobins: Toussaint L'Ouverture and the San Domingo Revolution*. New York: The Dial Press.

James, C.L.R. 1973. *Modern Politics*. Detroit: Bewick.

Jameson, F. 2002. *A Singular Modernity: Essay on the Ontology of the Present*. London: Verso.

Jarvis, D. 2001. Beyond International Relations: Edward Said and the World. In M. Crawford, ed. *Still an American Social Science? Towards Diversity in International Thought*. New York: State University of New York Press, pp. 349–367.

Jawhar, S. 1977. *Al-Mawta Yatakallamun 2nd edn*. Cairo: al-Maktab al-Misri al-Hadith.

Johnston, A. 1995. *Cultural Realism: Strategic Culture and Grand Strategy in Chinese History*. Princeton, NJ: Princeton University Press.

Jones, C. 2002. If Not a Clash, Then What? Huntington, Nishida Kitarô and the Politics of Civilizations. *International Relations of the Asia-Pacific*, 2, 223–243.

Jones, C. 2003. Interman and the 'Inter' in International Relations: Watsuji Tetsurô and the Ethics of the Inbetween. *Global Society*, 17(2), 135–150.

Jones, L. 1992. Culture and Politics in the Weimar Republic. In G. Martel, ed. *Modern Germany Reconsidered*. London: Routledge.

Joseph, J. 2009. Governmentality of What? Populations, States and International Organisations. *Global Society*, 23(4), 413–427.

Jum'ah, A. and Siraj, M. 1999. *al-Muqaranat al-Tashri'iyyah: Tatbiq al-Qanun [al-Faransawi] al-Madani wa-alJjina'i 'ala Madhhab al-Imam Malik (Comparative Legislations: The Application of [the French] Civil and Criminal Law to the Law of Imam Malik). 2 vols*. Cairo: Dar al-Salam lial-tiba'ah wa al-Nashr.

Jung, H. ed. 2002. *Comparative Political Culture in the Age of Globalization: An Introductory Anthology*. Boulder, CO: Lexington Books.

Kant, I. 1983. *Perpetual Peace and Other Essays*. Indianapólis: Hackett Publishing Company.

Karnad, B. 2002a. *India First*. Available at: http://www.india-seminar.com/2002/519/519bharatkarnad.htm (accessed 1 December 2008).

Karnad, B. 2002b. *Nuclear Weapons and Indian Security: The Realist Foundations of Strategy*. New Delhi: Macmillan.

Katzenstein, P., Keohane, R.O. and Krasner, S.D. 1998. International Organization and the Study of World Politics. *International Organization*, 52(4), 645–685.

Kaviraj, S. 2005. On the Enchantment of the State. *Archives Europeennes de Sociologie*, 46(2), 263–296.

Keddie, N. 1981. *The Roots of Revolution: An Interpretive History of Modern Iran*. New Haven, CT: Yale University Press.

Keddie, N. 1983. *An Islamic Response to Imperialism: Political and Religious Writings of Sayyid Jamal al-Din al-Afghani*. Berkeley: University of California Press.

Keene, E. 2002. *Beyond the Anarchical Society: Grotius, Colonialism and Order in World Politics*. Cambridge: Cambridge University Press.

Kepel, G. 2002. *Jihad: The Trail of Political Islam*. Cambridge MA: Harvard University Press.

Khatab, S. 2001. Al-Hudayb's Influence on the Development of Islamist Movements in Egypt. *The Muslim World*, 91(3–4), 451–480.

Khatab, S. 2002. Citizenship Rights of Non-Muslims in the Islamic State of Hakimiyyah Espoused by Qutb. *Islam and Christian-Muslim Relations*, 13(2), 163–187.

Khazanov, A. 1986. *Agostinho Neto*. Moscow: Progress Publishers.

Khilnani, S. 2004. Nehru's Faith. *New Republic*, 230(19), 27–33.

Kim, J. 2007. The Temporality of Empire: The Imperial Cosmopolitanism of Miki Kiyoshi and Tanabe Hajime. In S. Saaler and J. Koschmann, eds. *Modern Japanese History*. London: Routledge, pp. 151–167.

Kissinger, H. 1979. *White House Years*. Boston: Little, Brown and Co.

Knei-Paz, B. 1978. *The Social and Political Thought of Leon Trotsky*. Oxford: Clarendon Press.

Knight, N. 2008. *Imagining Globalisation in China: Debates on Ideology, Politics and Culture*. London: Edward Elgar.

Komf, D. 1991. A Look at Nehru's World History from the Dark Side of Modernity. *Journal of World History*, 2(1), 47–63.

Konoe, F. 1918. Eibei Hon'i no Heiwa Shugi wo Haisu[Reject the Anglo-American-Centred Peace]. *Nihon oyobi Nihonjin*, 746, 23–26.

Krishna, G. 1984. India and the International Order: Retreat From Idealism. In H. Bull and A. Watson, eds. *The Expansion of International Society*. Oxford: Clarendon Press, pp. 269–288.

Krishna, D. 1988. Comparative Philosophy: What It Is and What It Ought to Be. In G. Larson and E. Deutsch, eds. *Interpreting Across Boundaries: New Essays in Comparative Philosophy*. Princeton: Princeton University Press, pp. 71–83.

Kumar, K. 2008. The Question of European Identity: Europe in the American Mirror. *European Journal of Social Theory*, 11(1), 87–105.

Kurzman, C. 2004. *The Unthinkable Revolution in Iran*. Cambridge, MA: Harvard University Press.

Lal, V. 1990. Nehru as a Writer. *Indian Literature*, 135, 20–46.

Langley, A. 1979. *Ideologies of Liberation in Black Africa (1856–1970)*. London: Rex Collings.

Lapid, Y. 1996. Culture's Ship: Returns and Departures in International Relations Theory. In Y. Lapid and F. Kratochwil, eds. *The Return of Culture and Identity in IR Theory*. Boulder, CO: Lynne Rienner Publishers, pp. 3–20.

Laranjeira, P. 1995. *A Negritude Africana de Língua Portuguesa*. Porto: Edições Afrontamento.

Laroche, M. 2005. The Founding Myths of the Haitian Nation. *Small Axe*, 19(2), 1–15.

Larrain, J. 2000. Oligarchic Modernity, 1810–1900. In *Identity and Modernity in Latin America*. Cambridge: Polity Press, pp. 70–91.

Larson, G. and Deutsch, E. eds. 1988. *Interpreting Across Boundaries: New Essays in Comparative Philosophy*. Princeton, NJ: Princeton University Press.

Ledwidge, M. 2007. *African-Americans and the Formation of the United Nations Organisation*. Centre for International Politics Working Paper Series No. 31.

Legum, C. and Mmari, G. 1995. *Mwalimu: The Influence of Nyerere*. Trenton, NJ: Africa World Press.

Lentini, P. 2004. The Shanghai Cooperation Organization and Central Asia. In M. Vicziany, D. Wright-Neville and P. Leninti, eds. *Regional Security in the Asia Pacific Region*. Cheltenham: Edgar Edward Publishing, pp. 128–148.

Leonard, M. 2005. Europe's Transformative Power. *CER Bulletin*, 40, February/March.

Lewis, B. 1993. *Islam and the West*. New York: Oxford University Press.

Lewis, B. 1998. *The Political Language of Islam*. Chicago: University of Chicago Press.

Lewis, B. 2002. *What Went Wrong?: The Clash Between Islam and Modernity in the Middle East*. London: Weidenfeld & Nicolson.

Lewis, R. 1987. *Marcus Garvey: Anti-Colonial Champion*. London: Karia Press.

Lévinas, E. 1969. *Totality and Infinity: An Essay on Exteriority*. Pittsburgh: Duquesne University Press.

Linklater, A. 1998. *The Transformation of Political Community: Ethical Foundations of the Post-Westphalian Era*. Columbia: University of South Carolina Press.

Linklater, A. 2001. Citizenship, Humanity and Cosmopolitan Harm Conventions. *International Political Science Review*, 22(3), 261–277.

Linklater, A. 2002. Cosmopolitan Political Communities in International Relations. *International Relations*, 16(1), 135–150.

Linklater, A. 2005. Dialogic Politics and the Civilising Process. *Review of International Studies*, 31(1), 141–154.

Liu, L. 2002. The Problem of Language in Cross-Cultural Studies. In H. Jung, ed. *Comparative Political Culture in the Age of Globalization: An Introductory Anthology*. Boulder, CO: Lexington Books, pp. 305–357.

Liu, L. 2006. *The Clash of Empires: The Invention of China in Modern World-Making*. Cambridge, MA: Harvard University Press.

Lu, C. 2005. Cosmopolitan Liberalism and the Faces of Injustice in International Relations. *Review of International Studies*, 31, 401–408.

Luhmann, N. 2002. W. Rasch, ed. *Theories of Distinction: Redescribing the Descriptions of Modernity*. Stanford: Stanford University Press.

Lynch, M. 2000. The Dialogue of Civilisations and International Public Spheres. *Millennium*, 29(2), 307–330.

McCall, L. 2005. The Complexity of Intersectionality. *Signs: Journal of Women in Culture and Society*, 30(3), 1771–1800.

McCulloch, J. 1983. *In the Twilight of Revolution: The Political Theory of Amílcar Cabral.* London: Routledge & Kegan Paul.

Machel, S. 1979. *Unidade Anti-imperialista é a Base do Não-alinhamento. Speech to Non-Aligned summit in Havanna, 4 September 1979.* Maputo: FRELIMO, Palavras de ordem.

Machel, S. 1980. *A vitória do povo do Zimbabwe é fruto da luta armada, da unidade e do internacionalismo.* Maputo: Partido FRELIMO.

Machel, S. 1982. The Coup d'Etat of April 25. A statement on April 27, 1974. In A. Bragança and I. Wallerstein, eds. *The African Liberation Reader: Documents of the National Liberation Movements.* Vol. 1: *The Anatomy of Colonialism.* London: Zed Press.

Maclean, J. 1981. Political Theory, International Theory, and Problems of Ideology. *Millennium,* 10(2), 102–125.

Majeed, J. 2007. *Autobiography, Travel and Post-national Identity: Gandhi, Nehru and Iqbal.* New York: Palgrave Macmillan.

Mallavarapu, S. 2005. Introduction. In K. Bajpai and S. Mallavarapu, eds. *International Relations in India: Bringing Theory Back Home.* New Delhi: Orient Longman, pp. 17–38.

Mandaville, P. 2002. Reading the State from Elsewhere: Towards an Anthropology of the Post-national. *Review of International Studies,* 28, 199–207.

Manley, M. 1977. Freedom, Justice, Majority Rule, Now! Address in Maputo, Mozambique.

Manley, M. 1982. *Jamaica: Struggle in the Periphery.* London: Writers and Readers Cooperative.

Manley, M. 1987. *Up the Down Escalator: Development and the International Economy – A Jamaican Case Study.* London: Andre Deutsch.

Manley, M. 1990. *The Politics of Change.* Washington, DC: Howard University Press.

Manners, I. 2008. The Normative Ethics of the European Union. *International Affairs,* 84(1), 45–60.

Markell, P. 2003. *Bound by Recognition,* Princeton, NJ: Princeton University Press.

Martin, T. 1976. *Race First: The Ideological and Organizational Struggles of Marcus Garvey and Universal Improvement Association.* Westport, CT: Greenwood Press.

Martinho, F. 1980. O Negro Americano e a América na Poesia de Agostinho Neto. *Literatura, Arte e Cultura,* 2(7), 164–174.

Marx, K. and Engels, F. 2005. The Communist Manifesto. In A. Hart, ed. *Manifesto: Three Classic Essays on How to Change the World.* Melbourne: Ocean Press.

Maruyama, M. 1998. *Chusei to Hangyaku [Loyalty and Resistance].* Tokyo: Chikuma.

Massignon, L. 1994. *Hallāj: Mystic and Martyr.* Princeton, NJ: Princeton University Press.

Mateus, D. 1999. *A Luta pela Independência.* Lisbon: Editorial Inquérito.

Matin, K. 2006. Uneven and Combined Development and Revolution of Backwardness: The Iranian Constitutional Revolution: 1906–11. In B. Dunn and H. Radice, eds. *100 Years of Permanent Revolution: Results and Prospects.* London: Pluto Press, pp. 119–132.

Matin, K. 2007. Uneven and Combined Development in World History: The International Relations of State-formation in Premodern Iran. *European Journal of International Relations,* 13(3), 419–447.

Matin, K. 2009. *The Refractory Transformation: The International Relations of the Iranian Revolution.* DPhil. thesis, University of Sussex.

Mawdudi, A.L., *Islamic Way of Life.* Kuwait: International Islamic Federation of Student Organizations.

Mazlish, B. 2004. *Civilization and Its Contents*. Stanford, CT: Stanford University Press.

Mazrui, A. 1964. The United Nations and some African Political Attitudes. *International Organization*, 18 (3), 499–520.

Mbembe, A. 2000. African Modes of Self-Writing. *Public Culture*, 14(1), 239–274.

Memmi, A. 1990. *The Colonizer and the Colonized*. London: Earthscan.

Mendelssohn, M. 1938. *Gesammelte Schriften: Jubiläumsausgabe*. Berlin: Akademie Verlag.

Mendelssohn, M. 1971. *Gesammelte Schriften: Jubiläumsausgabe*. Stuttgart: Frommann.

Mendelssohn, M. 2002. *Moses Mendelssohn: The First English Biography and Translations, Vol.* 2. London: Longman and Co.

Mendlovitz, S. 1975. Introduction. In S. Mendlovitz, ed. *On the Creation of a Just World Order*. Amsterdam: North-Holland Publishing Company, pp. vii–xviii.

Metellus, J. 1987. *Haïti, une nation pathétique*. Paris: Editions Denoël.

Mignolo, W. 1995. *The Darker Side of the Renaissance: Literacy, Territoriality, and Colonization*. Ann Arbor: University of Michigan Press.

Mignolo, W. 2000. *Local Histories/Global Designs: Coloniality, Subaltern Knowledges, and Border Thinking*. Princeton, NJ: Princeton University Press.

Mignolo, W. 2002. The Many Faces of Cosmo-polis: Border Thinking and Critical Cosmopolitanism. In C.A. Breckenridge, S. Pollock, H.K. Bhabhaand D. Chakrabarty, eds. *Cosmopolitanism*. London: Duke University Press, pp. 157–187.

Mill, J.S. 1929. *On Liberty*. London: Thinker's Library.

Miller, D. 2007. *National Responsibility and Global Justice*. New York: Oxford University Press.

Mills, C. 1999. *The Racial Contract*. Ithaca, NY: Cornell University Press.

Mills, C. 2005. Kant's Untermenschen. In A. Valls, ed. *Race and Racism in Modern Philosophy*. Ithaca, NY: Cornell University Press, pp. 169–193.

Mirsepaasi, A. 1994. The Crisis of Secular Politics and the Rise of Political Islam in Iran. *Social Text*, 38, 51–84.

Mirsepassi, A. 2000. *Intellectual Discourse and the Politics of Modernization: Negotiating Modernity in Iran*. Cambridge: Cambridge University Press.

Mitter, R. 2003. An Uneasy Engagement: Chinese Ideas of Global Order and Justice in Historical Perspective. In R. Foot, J.L. Gaddis and A. Hurrell, eds. *Order and Justice in International Relations*. New York: Oxford, pp. 207–235.

Miwa, K. 1990. Japanese Policies and Concepts for a Regional Order in Asia, 1938–40. In J. White, M. Umegaki and T. Havens, eds. *The Ambivalence of Nationalism: Modern Japan between East and West*. Lanham, MD: University Press of America, pp. 133–156.

Moaddel, M. 1992. Ideology as Episodic Discourse: The Case of the Iranian Revolution. *American Sociological Review*, 57(3), 353–379.

Moaddel, M. 1993. *Class, Politics and Ideology in the Iranian Revolution*. New York: Columbia University Press.

Mondlane, E. 1969. *The Struggle for Mozambique*. Harmondsworth: Penguin.

Mohan, C.R. 1992. Balancing Interests and Values: India's Struggle with Democracy Promotion. *The Washington Quarterly*, 30(3), 353–379.

del Monte, D. 2002. *Centón epistolario, Vol.* I. La Habana: Imágen Contemporánea.

Montesquieu, C. 1989. A. Cohler, B. Miller, and H. Stone, eds. *The Spirit of the Laws*. Cambridge: Cambridge University Press.

Morgenthau, H. 1960. *The Purpose of American Politics*. New York: Alfred A. Knopf.

Mudimbe, V. 1988. *The Invention of Africa – Gnosis, Philosophy and the Order of Knowledge*. London: James Curry.

Muhammad, A. 1931. Al-Shura wa al-Isti'bad. In R. Rida, ed. *Tarikh al-Ustath al-Imam Muhammad Abduh*. Cairo: al-Manar, pp. 210–213.

Mullins, M.R. 1998. *Christianity Made in Japan: A Study of Indigenous Movements*. Honolulu: University of Hawai'i Press.

Munslow, B. 1983. *Mozambique: the Revolution and its Origins*. London: Longman.

Munslow, B. ed. 1985. *Samora Machel: An African Revolutionary. Selected Speeches and Writings*. London: Zed Books.

Murray, D. 2002. *Odious Commerce: Britain, Spain and the Abolition of the Cuban Slave Trade*. Cambridge: Cambridge University Press.

Mwenda, A. 1985. *Amílcar Cabral and the Theory of the Revolutionary African Petty-Bourgeoisie*. PhD thesis, University of Leeds.

Nairn, T. 1977. *The Break-up of Britain*. London: New Left Books.

Nakano, R. 2006. Uncovering *Shokumin*: Yanaihara Tadao's Concept of Global Civil Society. *Social Science Japan Journal*, 9(2), 187–202.

Nakano, R. 2007. 'Pre-History' of International Relations in Japan: Yanaihara Tadao's Dual Perspective of Empire. *Millennium*, 35(2), 301–319.

Nandy, A. 1988. *The Intimate Enemy: Loss and Recovery of Self Under Colonialism*. New Delhi: Oxford University Press.

Nandy, A. 1993. From Outside the Imperium: Gandhi's Cultural Critique of the West. In *Traditions, Tyranny and Utopias: Essays in the Politics of Awareness*. New York: Oxford University Press, pp. 127–162.

Nandy, A. 2002. The Beautiful, Expanding Future of Poverty: Popular Economics as a Psychological Defense. *International Studies Review*, 4(2), 107–121.

Nandy, A. 2006. Nationalism, Genuine and Spurious: Mourning Two Early Post-Nationalist Strains. *Economic and Political Weekly*, 3500–3504.

Nardin, T. 1992. Ethical Traditions in International Affairs. In T. Nardin and D. Mapel, eds. *Traditions of International Ethics*. Cambridge: Cambridge University Press, pp. 1–22.

Nehru, J. 1942. *Jawaharlal Nehru: An Autobiography (With Musings on Recent Events in India)*. London: The Bodley Head.

Nehru, J. 1961. *India's Foreign Policy: Selected Speeches, September 1946–April 1961*. Delhi: Publications Division, Ministry of Information and Broadcasting, Government of India.

Nehru, J. 1965. *Nehru: The First Sixty Years*, Vol. 1. D. Norman, ed. London: Bodley Head.

Nehru, J. 1996. *Glimpses of World History: Being Further Letters to His Daughter Written in Prison, and Containing a Rambling Account of History for Young People*. New York: Jawaharlal Nehru Memorial Fund.

Nehru, J. 1974. *Selected Works of Jawaharlal Nehru*, Vol. 6, Series One. New Delhi: Orient Longman.

Nehru, J. 1984. *Selected Works of Jawaharlal Nehru*, Vol. 2, Series Two. New Delhi: Orient Longman.

Nehru, J. 1993. *Selected Works of Jawaharlal Nehru*, Vol. 15, Series Two. New Delhi: Orient Longman.

Nehru, J. 2002. *The Discovery of India*. New Delhi: Jawaharlal Nehru Memorial Fund.

Nesbitt, N. 2004. Troping Toussaint, Reading Revolution. *Research in African Literatures*, 35(2), 18–33.

Neto, A. 1974. *Quem é o inimigo? Qual é o nosso objectivo?* Lisbon: Edições Maria da Fonte.

Neto, A. 1982. Not an Isolated Struggle. From a Message by the President of MPLA, Broadcast on 6 June 1968 on the 'Voice of the Angolan Freedom-Fighter' on Radio

Tanzania. In A. Bragança and I. Wallerstein, eds. *The African Liberation Reader: Documents of the National Liberation Movements. Vol. 2: The National Liberation Movements.* London: Zed Press.

Neuman, S. 1998. *International Relations Theory and the Third World.* London: Palgrave.

Neumann, I. 1999. *Uses of the Other: 'The East' in European Identity Formation.* Minneapolis: Minnesota Press.

NIEO, 1979. Declaration of the Establishment of a New International Economic Order. In J. Ayo, ed. *Ideologies of Liberation in Black Africa, 1856–1970.* London: Rex Collings, pp. 814–835.

Northrop, F. ed. 1949. *Ideological Differences and World Order: Studies in the Philosophy and Science of the World's Cultures.* New Haven, CT: Yale University Press.

Nyerere, J. 1966. *Freedom and Unity.* London: Oxford University Press.

Nyerere, J. 1968. *Uhuru na Ujamaa: Freedom and Socialism. A Selection from Writings and Speeches.* London: Oxford University Press.

Nyerere, J. 1969. *Mapebariwa Venisi.* Dar-es-Salaam: Oxford University Press.

Nyerere, J. 1974a. All Men Are Equal. In *Man and Development.* London: Oxford University Press, pp. 106–110.

Nyerere, J. 1974b. Developing Tasks of Non-Alignment. In *Man and Development.* London: Oxford University Press, pp. 65–81.

Nyerere, J. 1999. Interview with Ikaweba Bunting. *New International Magazine*, 309 (Jan–Feb) http://www.newint.org/features/1999/01/01/anticolonialism/.

Odysseos, L. 2007. *The Subject of Coexistence: Otherness in International Relations.* Minneapolis: University of Minnesota Press.

Oguma, E. 1998. *Nihonjin no Kyōkai: Okinawa, Ainu, Taiwan, Chōsen, Shokuminchi Shihai kara Fukki Undō made [The Boundaries of the Japanese: Okinawa, Ainu, Taiwan, Korea, From the Colonial Control to the Movement for the Return].* Tokyo: Shin'yōsha.

O'Hagan, J. 2005. Beyond the Clash of Civilizations? *Australian Journal of International Affairs*, 59(3), 383–400.

Ong, G. 2004. Building an IR Theory with 'Japanese Characteristics': Nishida Kitaro and 'Emptyness'. *Millennium*, 33(1), 35–58.

Ortiz, F. 1963. *Contrapunteo cubano del tabaco y el azúcar [Cuban Counterpoint: Tobacco and Sugar].* Santa Clara: Universidad central de Las Villas, Dirección de publicaciones.

Osterhammel, J. 1992. CCP Foreign Policy as International History: Mapping the Field. In M. Hunt and J. Niu, eds. *Towards a History of Chinese Communist Foreign Relations, 1920s–1960s: Personalities and Interpretive Approaches.* Washington, DC: Woodrow Wilson International Center for Scholars, Asia Program, pp. 129–161.

Ōta, Y. 1977. *Uchimura Kanzō: Sono Sekaishugi to Nihonshugi wo Megutte [Uchimura Kanzō: On its Cosmopolitanism and Japanese Nationalism].* Tokyo: Kenkyūsha.

Padmore, G. 1972. *Pan-Africanism or Communism.* New York: Anchor Books.

Pagden, A. 1982. *The Fall of Natural Man: the American Indian and the Origins of Comparative Ethnology.* Cambridge: Cambridge University Press.

Pagden, A. 2000. Stoicism, Cosmopolitanism, and the Legacy of European Imperialism. *Constellations*, 7(1), 3–22.

Pagden, A. and Canny, N. 1989. Afterword: From Identity to Independence. In N. Canny and A. Pagden, eds. *Colonial Identity in the Atlantic World, 1500–1800.* Princeton: Princeton University Press, pp. 267–278.

Panikkar, R. 1988. What is Comparative Philosophy Comparing? In G. Larson and E.

Deutsch, eds. *Interpreting Across Boundaries: New Essays in Comparative Philosophy.* Princeton, NJ: Princeton University Press, pp. 116–136.

Pantham, T. 1998. Understanding Nehru's Political Ideology. In F. Dallmayr and G. Devy, eds. *Between Tradition and Modernity: India's Search for Identity: A Twentieth Century Anthology.* New Delhi: Sage, pp. 216–233.

Parel, A. and Keith, R. eds. 1992. *Comparative Political Philosophy – Studies Under the Upas Tree.* London: Sage.

Parkes, G. ed. 1987. *Heidegger and Asian Thought.* Honolulu: Hawaii Press.

Pasha, M. 1997. Ibn Khaldun and World Order. In S. Gill and J. Mittelman, eds. *Innovation and Transformation in International Studies.* Cambridge: Cambridge University Press, pp. 56–70.

Paul, L. 1999. 'Iranian Nation' and Iranian-Islamic Revolutionary Ideology. *Die Welt des Islams*, 39(2), 183–217.

Persaud, R. 1997. Frantz Fanon, Race and World Order. In S. Gill and J. Mittelman, eds. *Innovation and Transformation in International Studies.* Cambridge: Cambridge University Press, pp. 170–184.

Philpott, D. 2000. The Religious Roots of Modern International Relations. *World Politics*, 52(2), 206–245.

Piscatori, J. 2003. Order, Justice and Global Islam. In R. Foot, J.L. Gaddis, and A. Hurrell, eds. *Order and Justice in International Relations.* New York: Oxford University Press, pp. 262–286.

Pollock, S. 2002. Cosmopolitanisms. In C.A. Breckenridge, S. Pollock, H.K. Bhabha and D. Chakrabarty, eds. *Cosmopolitanism.* London: Duke University Press, pp. 1–14.

Povinelli, E. 1999. Settler Modernity and the Quest for an Indigenous Tradition. *Public Culture*, 11(1), 19–48.

Prakash, G. 1999. *Another Reason: Science and the Imagination of Modern India.* Princeton, NJ: Princeton University Press.

Prawer, S. 1985. *Heine's Jewish Comedy: A Study of his Portraits of Jews and Judaism.* Oxford: Oxford University Press.

Price-Mars, J. 1928. *Ainsi parla l'oncle.* Paris: Imprimerie de Compiègne.

Quijano, A. 2000. Coloniality of Power and Eurocentrism in Latin America. *International Sociology*, 15(2), 215–232.

Qutb, S. 1946. Madaris al-Sukht. *Al-Risalah*, 691(14 September), 1080–1082.

Qutb, S. 1950. Akhi Abbas. *Al-Risalh*, 887 (3 July 1950), 756–756.

Qutb, S. 1951. America al-Lati Ra'ayt'. *A-Resalah*, 957, 1245–1247.

Qutb, S. 1983. *Al-'Adalah, al-Adalah al-Ijtima'iyyah fi al-Islam.* Cairo: al-Shuruq.

Qutb, S. 1992. *Fi Zilal a-Qur'an.* Cairo: al-Shuruq.

Qutb, S. 1993a. *Nahwa Mujtam' Islami.* Cairo: al-Shuruq.

Qutb, S. 1993b. *Ma'alim fi al-Tariq.* Cairo: al-Shuruq.

Qutb, S. 1993c. *Al-Islam wa al-Ra'smaliyyah.* Cairo: al-Shuruq.

Qutb, S. 1993d. *Al-Salam al-'Alami wa al-Islam.* Cairo: al-Shuruq.

Qutb, S. 1993e. *al-Naqd al-Adabi.* Cairo: al-Shuruq.

Qutb, S. 2007. *Milestones.* New Delhi: Islamic Book Service.

Rafael, V. 1988. *Contracting Colonialism – Translation and Christian Conversion in Tagalog Society Under Early Spanish Rule.* London: Cornell University Press.

Rahman, F. 1970. Islamic Modernisms: Its Scope, Method and Alternatives. *International Journal of Middle East Studies*, 1(4), 317–333.

Rahman, F. 1982. *Islam and Modernity: Transformation of An Intellectual Tradition.* Chicago: University of Chicago Press.

Rahnema, A. 2000. *An Islamic Utopian: A Political Biography of Ali Shariati*. London: I.B. Taurus.

Rama, A. 1982. *Transculturación narrativa en América Latina*. Fundación Angel Rama.

Ramanujan, A. (1990) Is There an Indian Way of Thinking? An Informal Essay. In M. Marriot, ed. *India Through Hindu Categories*. London: Sage, pp. 41–58.

Rana, A. 1969. The Intellectual Dimensions of India's Nonalignment. *Journal of Asian Studies*, 28(2), 299–312.

Rana, A. 1976. *The Imperatives of Nonalignment: A Conceptual Study of India's Foreign Policy Strategy in the Nehru Period*. Delhi: Macmillan.

Raud, R. 2007. A Comparative Analysis of Challenge Discourses: 'Overcoming Modernity' and the 'Asian Value' Debate. In R. Raud, ed. *Japan and Asian Modernities*. London: Kegan Paul, pp. 167–182.

Reeves, J. 2004. *Culture and International Relations: Narratives, Natives and Tourists*. London: Routledge.

Ribeiro, S. 1983. *A questão da unidade no pensamento de Amílcar Cabral*. Lisbon: Tricontinental Editora.

Robbins, B. 1998. Introduction. In P. Cheah and B. Robbins, eds. *Cosmopolitics: Thinking and Feeling Beyond the Nation*. Minneapolis: University of Minnesota Press, pp. 1–19.

Rojas, R. 1998. *La isla sin fin: contribución a la crítica del nacionalismo cubano*. Miami: Ediciones Universal.

Roscrance, R. 1998. The European Union: A New Type of International Actor. In J. Zielonka, ed. *Paradoxes of European Foreign Policy*. Hague: Kluwer Law International, pp. 15–23.

Rosenberg, J. 2006. Why is There No International Historical Sociology? *European Journal of International Relations*, 12, 307–340.

Rosenberg, J. 2007. International Relations – The 'Higher Bullshit': A Reply to the Globalization Theory Debate. *International Politics*, 44, 450–482.

Rossabi, M. ed. 1983. *China Among Equals: The Middle Kingdom and Its Neighbours, 10th to 14th Centuries*. Berkeley: University of California Press.

Roumain, J. 2003. *Œuvres completes*. L. Hoffmann, ed. Madrid: Collection Archivos.

Roy, O. 1994. *The Failure of Political Islam*. Cambridge, MA: Harvard University Press.

Roy, O. 2004. *Globalised Islam: The Search for A New Ummah*. London: Hurst & Company.

Rubin, B. 2002. *The Tragedy of the Middle East*. Cambridge: Cambridge University Press.

Ruggie, J.G. 1993. Territoriality and Beyond: Problematizing Modernity in International Relations. *International Organization*, 47(1), 139–174.

Rundell, J. 1987. *Origins of Modernity: The Origins of Modern Social Theory from Kant to Hegel to Marx*. Cambridge: Polity Press.

Russell, B. 1993. Mechanical Morals and the Moral of Machinery. In K. Blackwell, A. Brink, N. Griffin, R.A. Rempel and J.G. Slater, eds. *The Collected Papers of Bertrand Russell*. Vol. 1. London: George Allen and Unwin, pp. 324–328.

Sachedina, A. 1983. Ali Shariati: Ideologue of the Iranian Revolution. In J. Esposito, ed. *Voices of Resurgent Islam*. Oxford: Oxford University Press, pp. 191–214.

Saco, J., 1935a. Carta de un patriota, o sea clamor de los cubanos. In J. Saco, ed. *Ideario Reformista*. Madrid/La Habana: Publicaciones de la Secretaría de Educación.

Saco, J., 1935b. Paralelo entre la isla de Cuba y algunas colonias inglesas. In J. Saco, ed. *Ideario Reformista*. Madrid/La Habana: Publicaciones de la Secretaría de Educación.

Said, E.W. 1984. *The World, the Text and the Critic*. London: Routledge.

Said, E.W. 1994 (1978). *Orientalism*. London: Vintage.

Sajed, A. 2011. The Post Always Rings Twice? The Algerian War, Poststructuralism and the Postcolonial in IR Theory. *Review of International Studies* (forthcoming).

Sakai, N. 1989. Modernity and Its Critique. In M. Miyoshi and H. Harootunian, eds. *Postmodernism and Japan.* Durham, NC: Duke University Press, pp. 93–122.

Sakai, T. 2007. *Kindai Nihon no Kokusai Chitsujoron [The Political Discourse of International Order in Modern Japan].* Tokyo: Iwanami.

Samarah, I. 1991. *Mafum al-Adalah al-Ijtima'iyyah fi al-Fikr al-Islami al-Mu'asir.* Beirut: al-Nahdah al-Islamiyyah.

San Juan, E. 2002. Post-colonialism and the Problematic of Uneven Development. In C. Bartolovich and N. Lazarus, eds. *Marxism, Modernity and Post-colonial Studies.* Cambridge: Cambridge University Press, pp. 221–239.

Sartre, J. 2001. Preface to *The Wretched of the Earth.* In *Colonialism and Neocolonialism.* London: Routledge, pp. 136–155.

Sayer, D. 1991. *Capitalism and Modernity: An Excursus on Marx and Weber.* London: Routledge.

Schacht, J. and Bosworth, C. 1960. *The Legacy of Islam 2nd edn.* Oxford: Oxford University Press.

Scott, D. 1998. *Refashioning Futures: Criticism after Post-coloniality.* Princeton, NJ: Princeton University Press.

Scott, D. 2004. *Conscripts of Modernity: The Tragedy of Colonial Enlightenment.* Durham, NC: Duke University Press.

Senghor, L. 1973. The Lessons of Leo Frobenius. In *Leo Frobenius 1873–1974, An Anthology.* Wiesbaden: Franz Steiner Verlag, pp. vii–xiii.

Seth, S. 1992. Nationalism, National Identity and 'History': Nehru's Search for India. *Thesis Eleven,* 32(37), 37–54.

Shani, G. 2007. Provincialising Critical Theory: Islam, Sikhism and International Relations. *Cambridge Review of International Affairs,* 20(2), 417–433.

Shapcott, R. 2001. *Justice, Community and Dialogue in International Relations.* Cambridge: Cambridge University Press.

Shariati, A. 1968. *Islamology [Islamshinasi].* Mashhad: Chap-i Tus.

Shariati, A. 1970. *Kavir [Desert].* Mashhahd: Chap-i Tus.

Shariati, A. 1971. *Alavid Shi'ism and Safavid Shi'ism.* Tehran: Hosseyniyyeh'i Ershad Press.

Shariati, A. 1972. *Red Shi'ism vs. Black Shi'ism.* The Union of Islamic Associations of Iranian Students in Europe.

Shariati, A. ed. 1977a. *Man and Islam.* Solon, OH: The Union of Islamic Student Associations in Europe, America and Canada.

Shariati, A. 1977b. *Mission of a Free Thinker.* Available at http://www.evans-experientialism.freewebspace.com/shariat.htm.

Shariati, A. 1977c. *Religion versus Religion.* Tehran: Safir.

Shariati, A. 1977d. *The Mission of the Intellectual for Building Society.* Available at http://www.drshariati.org/show.asp?ID=117.

Shariati, A. 1979a. *On the Sociology of Islam: Lectures by Ali Shriati.* Berkeley, CA: Mizan Press.

Shariati, A. 1979b. *Economic Root of Renaissance.* Mashhad: Hejrat.

Shariati, A. 1979c. *Intizar.* Tehran: s.n.

Shariati, A. 1980a. *Reflections of A Concerned Muslim: On the Plight of Oppressed Peoples.* Houston: Free Islamic Literatures.

Shariati, A. 1980b. *Marxism and Other Western Fallacies: An Islamic Critique*. Berkeley, CA: Mizan Press.

Shariati, A. 1986. *What Is to Be Done: The Enlightened Thinkers and An Islamic Renaissance*. Houston: IRIS.

Shariati, A., n.d. *Civilization and Modernization*. Available at www.shariati.com/machine. html (accessed 13 January 2008).

Shilliam, R. 2006a. What about Marcus Garvey? Race and the Transformation of Sovereignty Debate. *Review of International Studies*, 32(3), 379–400.

Shilliam, R. 2006b. Marx's Path to Capital: the International Dimension of an Intellectual Journey. *History of Political Thought*, 27(2), 349–375.

Shilliam, R. 2009. *German Thought and International Relations: The Rise and Fall of a Liberal Project*. Basingstoke: Palgrave Macmillan.

Shilliam, R. 2010. Modernity and Modernization. In R. Denemark, ed. *The International Studies Encyclopedia*, Vol. 8. Oxford: Wiley-Blackwell, pp. 5214–5232.

Shore, H. 1983. Resistance and Revolution in the life of Eduardo Mondlane. In E. Mondlane, *The Struggle for Mozambique*. London: Zed Press, pp. xiii–xxxi.

Singham, A. and Hune, S. 1986. *Non-Alignment in an Age of Alignments*. London: Zed Books.

Smallwood, S. 2007. *Saltwater Slavery: A Middle Passage from Africa to the American Diaspora*. Cambridge, MA: Harvard University Press.

Smith, D. 1958. *Nehru and Democracy: The Political Thought of an Asian Democrat*. Bombay: Orient Longman.

Smith, L.T. 1999. *Decolonizing Methodologies: Research and Indigenous Peoples*. London: Zed Books.

Smith, S. 2000. The Discipline of International Relations: Still An American Social Science? *British Journal of Politics and International Relations*, 2(3), 374–402.

Snodgrass, J. 2003. *Presenting Japanese Buddhism to the West: Orientalism, Occidentalism, and the Columbian Exposition*. Chapel Hill: University of North Carolina Press.

Solana, J. 2005. *Give Europe More Weight in the World: The Three Reasons for Europe*. NRC Handelsblad, 17 May. http://www.consilium.eurpoa.eu/ueDocs/csm_Data/docs/pressdata/en/articles/84861.pdf

Somerville, K. 1986. *Angola: Politics, Economics and Society*. London: Frances Pinter.

Song, X. 2001. Building International Relations Theory with Chinese Characteristics. *Journal of Contemporary China*, 10(26), 61–74.

Sopa, A. ed. 2001. *Samora, Man of the People*. Maputo: Maguezo.

Soroush, A. 2000. Tolerance and Governance: A Discourse on Religion and Democracy. In M. Sadri and A. Sadri, eds. *Reason, Freedom and Democracy in Islam: Essential Writings of 'Abdolkarim Soroush*. Oxford: Oxford University Press, pp. 156–170.

Souffrant, C. 1978. *Une Négritude socialiste*. Paris: L'Harmattan.

Spinoza, B. 2000. *Political Treatise*. Indianapolis: Hackett.

Spivak, G.C. 1988. Can the Subaltern Speak? In C. Nelson and L. Grossberg, eds. *Marxism and the Interpretation of Culture*. Basingstoke: Macmillan, pp. 271–313.

Spivak, G.C. 1993. An Interview with Gayatri Chakravorty Spivak [by Sara Danius and Stefan Jonsson]. *boundary* 2, 20(2): 24–50.

Strong, C. 1963. *Modern Political Constitution*. London: Sidgwick and Jackson.

Sud, U. 1983. *Decolonization to World Order: International Organizations and the Emerging Pattern of Global Interdependence*. New Delhi: National.

Sugirtharajah, R. 2001. *The Bible and the Third World: Precolonial, Colonial and Postcolonial Encounters*. Cambridge: Cambridge University Press.

Sulayman, A. 1987. *Towards an Islamic Theory of International Relations: New Directions for Islamic Methodology and Thought.* Herndon, VA: International Institute for Islamic Thought.

Sutch, P. 2006. *Ethics, Justice and International Relations: Constructing an International Community.* London: Routledge.

Svarverud, R. 2007. *International Law as World Order in Late Imperial China: Translation, Reception and Discourse, 1847–1911.* Leiden: Brill.

Tabata, S. 1959. *Katō Hiroyuki. [Katō Hiroyuki]* Tokyo: Yoshikawa Kōbunkan.

Tamimi, A. 2003. *Democratic Synergies.* Leicester: University of Leicester Press.

Tanaka, S. 1993. *Japan's Orient: Rendering Pasts into History.* Berkeley: University of California Press.

Taylor, C. and Gutmann, A. 1992. *Multiculturalism and the 'Politics of Recognition'.* Princeton, NJ: Princeton University Press.

Teschke, B. 2003. *The Myth of 1648: Class, Geopolitics and the Making of Modern International Relations.* London: Verso.

Tibi, B. 1986. Islam and Modern European Ideologies. *International Journal of Middle East Studies*, 18, 15–29.

Tibi, B. 1998. *The Challenge of Fundamentalism: Political Islam and the New Word Order.* Berkeley: University of California Press.

Tickner, A. 2003. Seeing IR Differently: Notes from the Third World. *Millennium*, 32(2), 295–324.

Tickner, A. and Waever, O. eds. 2009. *International Relations Scholarship Around the World (Worlding Beyond the West).* London: Routledge.

Torres, A. 1977. *O Neo-Realismo Literário Português.* Lisbon: Moraes.

Trigo, S. ed. 1989. *A Voz Igual: Ensaios Sobre Agostinho Neto.* Oporto: Fundação Eng. António de Almeida.

Trotsky, L. 1985. *The History of the Russian Revolution.* London: Pluto Press.

Trouillot, Michel-Rolph. 1995. *Silencing the Past: Power and Production of History*: Boston: Beacon Press.

Uchimura, K. 1892. Japan's Future as Conceived by a Japanese. *Uchimura Kanzō Zenshū*, 1, 243–254.

Uchimura, K. 1894a. Japan and the Japanese. *Uchimura Kanzō Zenshū*, 3, 169–297.

Uchimura, K. 1894b. Justification for the Korean War. *Uchimura Kanzō Zenshū*, 3, 38–48.

Uchimura, K. 1897. A Retrospect. *Uchimura Kanzō Zenshū*, 5, 191–196.

Uchimura, K. 1920. Japanese Christianity. *Uchimura Kanzō Zenshū*, 25, 191–196.

Unno, T. 1988. Personal Rights and Contemporary Buddhism. In L. Rouner, ed. *Human Rights and the World's Religions.* Notre Dame: Notre Dame Press, pp. 129–147.

Van Der Veer, P. 2002. Colonial Cosmopolitanism. In R. Cohen and S. Vertovec, eds. *Conceiving Cosmopolitanism: Theory, Context, and Practice.* Oxford: Oxford University Press, pp. 165–179.

Vieira, S. 1988. *Vectors of Foreign Policy of the Mozambique Liberation Front (1962–1975): A Contribution to the Study of the Foreign Policy of the People's Republic of Mozambique.* Maputo: Universidade Eduardo Mondlane.

Vincent, R. 1982. Race in International Relations. *International Affairs*, 58(4), 658–670.

Waever, O. 1998. The Sociology of a Not So International Discipline: American and European Developments in International Relations. *International Organization*, 52(4), 687–727.

Walker, R.B.J. ed. 2006. Special Section: Theorizing the Liberty-Security Relation: Sovereignty, Liberalism and Exceptionalism. *Security Dialogue*, 37(1), 7–82.

Walker, R.B.J. 2010. *After the Globe, Before the World*. New York: Routledge.

Walsh, C. 2007. Shifting the Geopolitics of Critical Knowledge: Decolonial Thought and Cultural Studies 'Others' in the Andes. *Cultural Studies*, 21(2–3), 224–239.

Waltz, K.N. 1990. Realist Thought and Neorealist Theory. *Journal of International Affairs*, 44(1), 21–37.

Watson, A. 1992. *The Evolution of International Society: A Comparative Historical Analysis*. London: Routledge.

Watt, M. 1961. *Islam and the Integration of Society*, Evanston: Northeastern University Press.

Weiner, M. 1994. *Race and Migration in Imperial Japan*. London: Routledge.

Weiss, L. 1980. *The Principles of State and Government in Islam*. Gibraltar: al Andalus.

Wilde, L. 2007. Europe and the 'Re-regulation of World Society': A Critique of Habermas. *Capital and Class*, 93, 47–66.

Williams, D. 2000. In Defence of the Kyoto School: Reflections on Philosophy, the Pacific War and the Making of a Post-White World. *Japan Forum*, 12(2), 143–156.

Wright, R. 1956. *The Colour Curtain*. Jackson: Banner Books.

Wyn Jones, R. 2001. Introduction: Locating Critical International Relations Theory. In R. Wyn Jones, ed. *Critical Theory and World Politics*. Boulder, CO: Lynne Rienner Publishers, pp. 1–19.

Wynter, S. 2003. Unsettling the Coloniality of Being/Power/Truth/Freedom: Towards the Human, After Man, Its Overrepresentation – An Argument. *CR: The New Centennial Review*, 3(3), 257–337.

Yanaihara, T. 1926. Chōsen tōchi no Hōshin [The Direction of Rule in Korea]. *Yanaihara Tadao Zenshū*, 1, 725–744.

Yanaihara, T. 1929. Sekai Keizai Hatten Katei to Shite no Shokuminshi [The History of Migrations as the Process of Developing a World Economy]. *Yanaihara Tadao Zenshū*, 4, 141–169.

Yanaihara, T. 1937a. Shina Mondai no Shozai [Locating the China Question]. *Yanaihara Tadao Zenshū*, 4, 326–340.

Yanaihara, T. 1937b. Shokumin Seisaku yori Mitaru Inin Tōchi Seido [The Mandate System in Relation to Colonial Policy]. *Yanaihara Tadao Zenshū*, 4, 170–195.

Yanaihara, T. 1937c. Tairiku Seisaku no Saikentō [Re-Examination of the Policy towards the Continent]. *Yanaihara Tadao Zenshū*, 5, 94–105.

Yaqing, Q. 2007. Why is there no Chinese International Relations Theory? *International Relations of the Asia-Pacific*, 7(3), 313–340.

Yeh, M. 1998. International Theory and the Transnational Critic: China in the Age of Multiculturalism. *Boundary 2: An International Journal of Literature and Culture*, 25(3), 193–222.

Young, R. 2002. *Post-colonialism: An Historical Introduction*. Oxford: Blackwell.

Yuan, H. ed. 2007. *Houshehui zhuyi [Postsocialism]*. Beijing: Zhongyang bianyi chubanshe.

Zabih, S. 1986. *The Left in Contemporary Iran: Ideology, Organisation and the Soviet Connection*. London: Croom Helm.

Zachariah, B. 2004. *Nehru*. London: Routledge.

Zhang, Y. 2001. System, Empire and State in Chinese International Relations. *Review of International Studies*, 27, 43–63.

Zhao, K. and Ni, S. 2007. *Zhongguo guoji guanxi lilun yanjiu [Examination of Chinese International Relations Theory]*. Shanghai: Fudan University Press.

Zielonka, J. 2006. *Europe as Empire: the Nature of the Enlarged European Union*. Oxford: Oxford University Press.

Zimmerman, J.C. 2004. Sayyid Qutb's Influence on the 11 September Attacks. *Terrorism and Political Violence*, 16(2), 224–226.

Žižek, S. 1998. A Leftist Plea for 'Eurocentrism'. *Critical Inquiry*, 24(4), 988–1009.

Zürn, M. 2002. Political Systems in the Post-national Constellation: Societal Denationalization and Multilevel Governance. In V. Rittberger, ed. *Global Governance and the United Nations System*. Tokyo: United Nations University Press, pp. 48–87.

Index

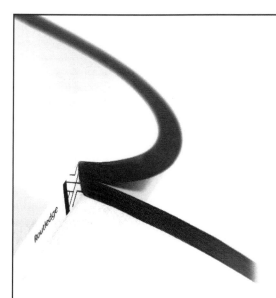